Film Review
2008-2009

Quentin Tarantino mixes a heady cocktail in *Death Proof*.

Film Review

2008-2009

Michael Darvell and **Mansel Stimpson**

FOUNDING FATHER:
F. MAURICE SPEED 1911-1998

Reynolds & Hearn Ltd
London

To Peter Ritchie, for practically everything – MD

*To Alex Buchan, for his invaluable help in preparing
my contributions for this annual – MS*

Acknowledgements

The Editors would like to thank the following, without whose help this book
might not have appeared: Carol Allen, Clive Baxter, Alex Buchan, James
Cameron-Wilson, Jeremy Clarke, Peri Godbold, Marcus Hearn, Tony Hillman,
Marshall Julius, Penny Lucas, Carolynn Reynolds, Richard Reynolds, Jonathan
Rigby, George Savvides and Derek Winnert.

In Memoriam pictures: The Tony Hillman Collection
All other pictures © their respective distributors

First published in 2008 by
Reynolds & Hearn Ltd
61a Priory Road
Kew Gardens
Richmond
Surrey
TW9 3DH

© Michael Darvell and Mansel Stimpson 2008

A CIP catalogue record for this book is
available from the British Library.

ISBN 1 978 1 905287 79 6

Designed by Peri Godbold.

Printed and bound in Great Britain
by MPG Books Ltd, Bodmin, Cornwall.

Contents

Introduction

L ast year there were around 400 films released in the UK over the period covered by this book; this year it is more than 450. More and more titles are released every week, but are the films getting any better? I am afraid that the answer is no, because in this context more generally means less. We wonder why or how many of the 450 plus films get made. What audience did their makers think they were chasing? Was it just for the DVD release which comes ever sooner hot on the heels of a theatrical release? It used to be predicted that the future of cinemas was just as preview houses for the inevitable release onto video. However, now that the cost of going to the pictures is becoming dearer than buying the DVD, is this supposition still valid? Cinemagoing is such a dispiriting experience nowadays that exhibitors ought to find a better way of attracting audiences to see their films.

These are some of the topics dealt with in this volume of *Film Review*.

Critical loss

During the year in question it has become increasingly clear that distributors couldn't care less whether or not they screen their films for the critics before they open them to the general public. Would they rather spend money on publicity they can control, ie paid advertising, or risk getting a whole load of bad reviews from the press? It seems that they are tending to veer

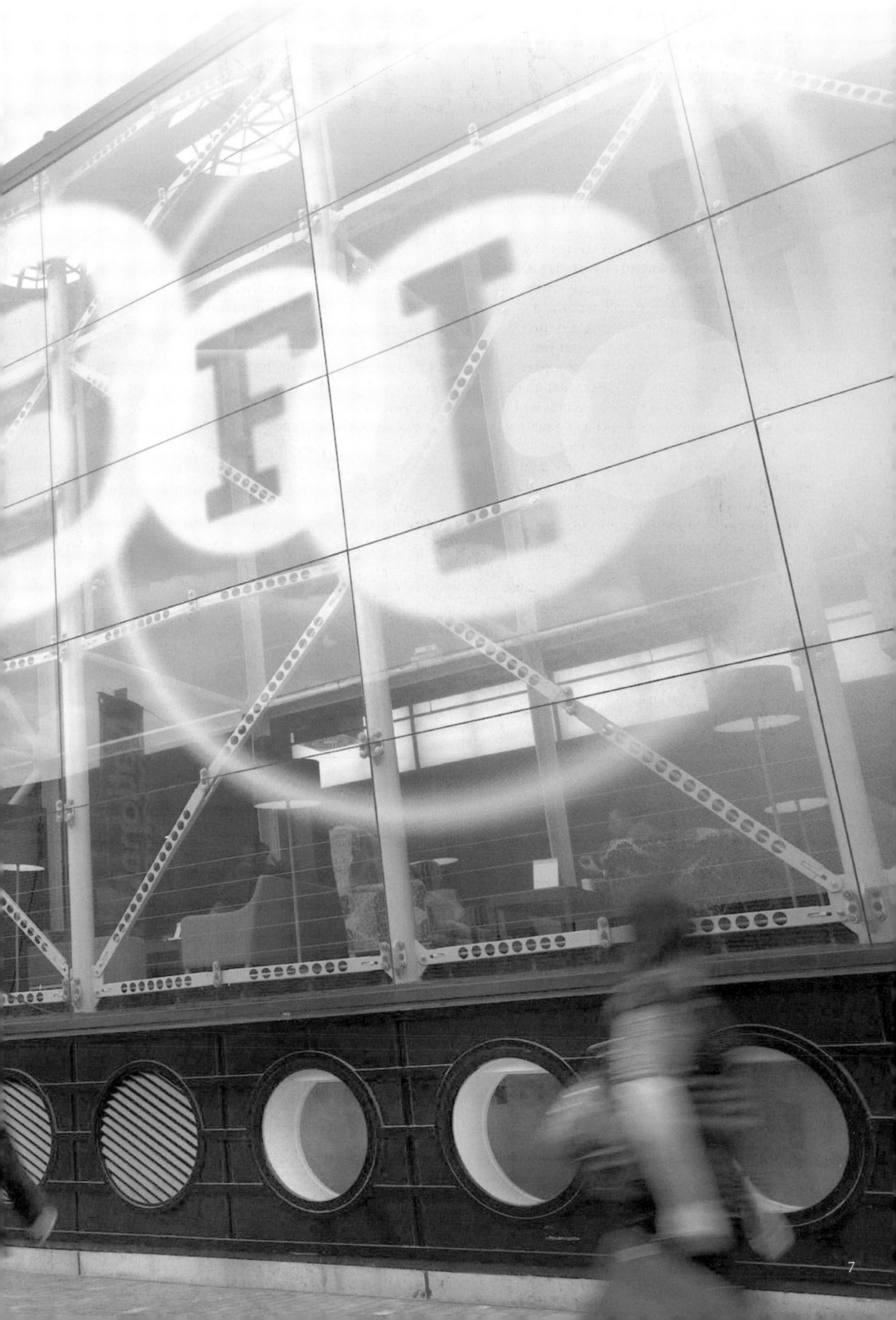

towards the former. They obviously know when they have a piece of schlock on their hands and, if it's aimed at an audience of 16 to 25 year olds, why would they bother screening it for an older audience of ageing, white, male, Anglo-Saxon reviewers? It probably does make sense, which is presumably why there was no press show for *Harold and Kumar Escape from Guantanamo Bay*. It's not as if the first Harold and Kumar opus, *…Get the Munchies* (aka *…Go to White Castle*) was completely slated; in fact many reviewers found it a refreshing, albeit intermittently gross, comedy. You might therefore think that it was worth showing the sequel at least to the UK film critics, but no… *Harold and Kumar Escape from Guantanamo Bay* opened blind and in London lasted a week or two at the most.

Now, was this a short run for the film because nobody had reviewed it, or was it because word had got around that it truly was terrible? Either way, it will probably clean up at Blockbuster where I suspect nobody reads reviews anyway. The Film Section of the Critics' Circle queried this action with the distributor who claimed they were experimenting by not press showing the film. It was odd that the Film Distributors' Association, an organisation that monitors film openings and arranges national press screenings, did not seem unduly bothered about this. With often a dozen or more films opening in any one week, obviously some national newspapers don't have enough space to review everything, but now there are so many more outlets for film reviews and features with a multiplicity of newer film magazines and general interest magazines also reviewing films, not to mention all the movie websites and blogs, it is quite easy to get a wide range of different views of a film very quickly. But then, if the FDA doesn't want to know, why should we worry?

Although there are many more outlets for film and other critics to air their views, there is a worrying trend, starting in the US, of critics being given their marching orders. It appears that many newspapers feel they can live without a specific film critic and instead rely on general feature writers to cover the cinema. Of course, all-purpose journalists do not necessarily have any knowledge of, or indeed interest in, the cinema, which is often considered something that anybody can write about. The attitude is, well, after all, we all go to the pictures, don't we, so how hard can it be to write about them? It is a worrying development and one that, we hope, will not spread to the UK, if it hasn't already.

On the rise

If we do ever run out of film critics, it's good to know that cinema in the UK is still flourishing. According to the 2008 *Statistical Yearbook* published by the UK Film Council, UK cinema admissions and the box office share of UK films are both on the increase. UK cinema admissions in 2007 were up by four per cent and the jump in the box office share of UK films has increased from 19 per cent in 2006 to 29 per cent in 2007. The Council finds these figures particularly encouraging considering all the alternative ways of viewing films now readily available. Despite piracy and copyright theft, increased sales and hire of films on DVD, an upturn in the viewing of films on television and the general rise in admission prices, the cinema still seems to be where audiences prefer to see their films. The collective experience is no doubt the reason for this, plus the fact that new technologies are attracting more audiences with advances in digital projection and the 3D format.

On the telly

In the UK in 2007 the total audience for film on television was 3.1 billion, 19 times larger than the cinema audience and three times larger than the estimated audience for film on DVD and video. It was *Shrek 2* that held top place for a film screening on television in 2007 with 9.4 million viewers, closely followed by *The Queen* and *Harry Potter and the Prisoner of Azkaban*. Films arrive on DVD and/or satellite television so soon now that it's a wonder that anybody bothers to go to the cinema any more, apart from those who wish to enjoy the social aspect of filmgoing. The UK theatrical audience is formed mainly of under 25s, although the over-45 age group has increased its visits over the last decade and it accounted for some 19 per cent of UK cinema visits (31 million) in 2007.

On the upgrade

Staying with the UK Film Council, Lottery funds have been made available by the Council to some 56 independent cinemas across the UK to help upgrade facilities and enhance the cinemagoing experience for audiences, including building refurbishment, lighting and seating, as well as new projection, sound and digital equipment and improved access for people with sensory impairment by introducing audio description and subtitling kits. The total available was £475,000 which has been divided into sums ranging from £510 to £35,000. Among those cinemas to receive these grants are the Cine Lumière in London, the Curzon Manchester, the Everyman Hampstead, the Glasgow Film Theatre, the Lynton Cinema, the Parkway Barnsley, the Phoenix East Finchley, the Swell Cinema Whitby and the Tyneside Cinema Newcastle.

New ways

Apart from investing in British films and

cinemas, the UK Film Council is also helping British cinema in other ways. This year it announced that it is to help 12 small independent British film companies to embrace new business growth opportunities through digital distribution. Over an 18 month period they are teaming them with specialist partners to help them develop content, marketing and digital distribution potential of their films to audiences around the world in new ways. Among the companies chosen are BreakThru Films Ltd, a UK-based production company which promotes live orchestral screenings; Film Export UK, a trade association for companies with international film sales and distribution operations in the UK; Hollywood Classics, which markets and distributes the theatrical rights of classic films; Luxonline which is devoted to British films and video artists; Metrodome Distribution Ltd, a well-established UK independent, all rights distributor; Mosaic Films, specialists in high quality documentaries, and Revolver Entertainment, another independent UK rights distributor.

They're off!

You have to be quick to catch some films at the cinema today. Blink and they're gone for good. A case in point was *The Oxford Murders* which opened in London in April 2008 but vanished soon afterwards, only to turn up on DVD less than six months later. Little seems to have been done by the distributors or their PR company to promote the film which sounded intriguing at the time and had a respectable cast including British cult actor John Hurt, busy US film actor Elijah Wood and Lenor Watling from *Paris, je t'aime*. Perhaps some films are predestined to do better on DVD and, if you think so, then give *The Oxford Murders* a look. It's out now from Contender Home Entertainment.

75 not out

This year the British Film Institute is 75. The anniversary has been celebrated with a month of special programming, events, debates and surprises at BFI Southbank, the artistic venue formerly known as the National Film Theatre, plus other events around the UK and online, DVDs, regional partnerships and touring programmes. Central to the celebrations was 'The Time Machine', a season of films examining cinema's relationship with time, with extended runs of Powell & Pressburger's *A Matter of Life and Death*, Terrence Malick's *Badlands* and Eric Rohmer's latest, *The Romance of Astrea and Celadon*. The films of Clint Eastwood and Chaplin and the British Silent Film Festival are all part of the 75th

John Hurt in *The Oxford Murders*.

anniversary celebrations. As the GPO Film Unit is also celebrating its 75th anniversary this year, there are nationwide screenings of some of the best short films from the Unit which have been restored by the BFI National Archive and the British Postal Museum & Archive. *Addressing the Nation* is the first of three double-disc DVDs to be released of highlights from the GPO Film Unit's output. Worth a view.

Showing online

British Film Magazine is a new online publication covering all aspects of British movie making with ten sites devoted to such topics as new films, filmmaking, on location, indie acts, shorts, training and other news. It was founded by and edited by Terence Doyle. The site is free to consult and you can find it at http://britishfilmmagazine.com where, as they say, you will find the British film world... on one site. It's been a good year after all.

Michael Darvell

Despite ending on an up-beat note, Michael's introduction has some harsh things to say about the state of cinema today, and it is hard to disagree with him. Indeed, I have myself commented on the drawbacks that have resulted from the ever higher number of film releases in the UK, that being one of the threads in my article *So What's New?* which appears in these pages.

Nevertheless, something exists to counter even the most justified criticisms of the industry and that is the life-long love of cinema which surely dwells within most of those who read this annual. For those who share this passion the phrase 'film enthusiast' is the only fitting description, and that enthusiasm cannot be destroyed by passing displeasures – be they bad films, tiresome audiences or the smell of popcorn.

Whether or not this will still be the case as the 21st century proceeds may be more of an open question. Love of filmgoing in the past has indeed been born of the delight of visiting

A scene from the GPO Film Unit's *6.30 Collection*.

a cinema and not as a result of viewing films at home on television or on DVDs. Almost every adult film lover has childhood memories linked to the feeling of sitting within an audience and being carried away by magical images on a big screen. Experience that at an early age and it's in the blood. If certain present trends continue – increases in cinema prices that make home viewing so much more tempting, the quick disappearance of many titles so that the more adventurous viewer is driven to seek out titles on DVD because they were never screened locally in the first place – then we may have a younger generation for whom viewing films is something undertaken in the home most of the time. One wonders if the same opportunities to fall under the spell of movies are to be found in those conditions.

But, whatever questions one asks oneself about film viewing in 2008, the fact remains that, as Michael's introduction points out, the figures for cinema admissions are on the increase, being higher in 2007 than in 2006. Even if the number of visits is fewer than it once was when there were more cinemas, a handful of memorable occasions may be enough to ignite that enthusiasm known to regular cinemagoers. Furthermore, even if we older viewers tend to complain that current films and current stars compare poorly with those of the past, the fact is that amid the dross (which has always existed, even if memory tends to expunge it) there remain great films to be found, great performances to be applauded and great experiences to be had. For some they will be discovered among the arthouse films, while others will find their excitements in the sphere of blockbusters and movies with special effects so astounding that they go beyond anything that could have been imagined in the past. If some are drawn to cinema by the stars (Johnny Depp still at number one), others will be beguiled by the imagination of a director (since *Pan's Labyrinth* the name of Guillermo del Toro helps any film with which he is involved or which he endorses). What appeals most varies from person to person, but all true lovers of cinema recognise that passion as something deep within themselves: for all of us it's something that is part of the person we are and once imbedded in us it's there to stay.

Mansel Stimpson

The films of Clint Eastwood were part of the BFI's 75th anniversary celebrations.

Top 20 UK Box-Office Hits

Daniel Radcliffe in the year's most successful film, *Harry Potter and the Order of the Phoenix.*

1 August 2007 – 31 August 2008

1. *Harry Potter and the Order of the Phoenix*
2. *Pirates of the Caribbean: At World's End*
3. *Indiana Jones and the Kingdom of the Crystal Skull*
4. *The Simpsons Movie*
5. *Shrek the Third*
6. *Spider-Man 3*
7. *Mamma Mia!*
8. *The Golden Compass*
9. *Sex and the City*
10. *I Am Legend*
11. *The Dark Knight*
12. *Ratatouille*
13. *Transformers*
14. *Hancock*
15. *The Bourne Ultimatum*
16. *Iron Man*
17. *Enchanted*
18. *Kung Fu Panda*
19. *Stardust*
20. *Die Hard 4.0*

Top 10 Box-Office Stars

Star of the Year: *Johnny Depp*

2. **Will Smith**
3. **Matt Damon**
4. **Harrison Ford**
5. **Bruce Willis**
6. **George Clooney**
7. **Keira Knightley**
8. **Simon Pegg**
9. **John Travolta**
10. **Cameron Diaz**

At the time of going to press, the four top-grossing films of 2008 in the UK were *Indiana Jones*, *Sex and the City*, *Iron Man* and *Sweeney Todd*. Nothing odd about that, you may think – except that in the States *Sweeney Todd* came 49th in the year's box-office. Considering that none other than Johnny Depp was dishing out the bloodshed – and that the film cost a pretty $50 million – this was considered a major commercial disappointment. It didn't help that Warner Bros' marketing pretended it wasn't a musical and that the film's Gothic sensibility was perhaps better appreciated by British tastes. And we love Johnny Depp. For the third consecutive year, Mr Depp has snatched the number one slot on this list, making him something of a hardy perennial. Meanwhile, Will Smith was snapping at his heels, *Hancock* being the ninth highest grossing film of 2008 (at the time of going to press...) and *I Am Legend* coming in eighth on our 2007-2008 tabulation. Runners-up include James McAvoy, Nicolas Cage, Brad Pitt and Sacha Baron Cohen.

Johnny Depp as the demon barber of Fleet Street in *Sweeney Todd*.

James Cameron-Wilson, July 2008

Releases

of the Year

This section contains details of all the films released in the UK between 1 July 2007 and 30 June 2008, the period covered by all the reference features in this volume.

The film reviews are followed by the main credits for the film, beginning with names of the leading actors, then the Director, Producer(s), Screenplay Writer, Cinematographer, Production Designer or Art Director, Editor, Soundtrack Composer and Costume Designer.

For technical credits the normal abbreviations operate and are as follows: Dir – for Director; Pro – for Producer; Ph – for Cinematographer; Pro Des – for Production Designer; Art Dir – for Art Director; M – for Composer; and Cos – for Costume Designer. The production companies involved are listed with the final name in the list being the distributor. The credits end with the film's running time, the country or countries of origin, the year of production, the UK release date and the British Board of Film Classification's certificate.

Reviewers: Carol Allen (CA); Clive Baxter (CB); James Cameron-Wilson (JC-W); Jeremy Clarke (JC); Michael Darvell (MHD); Marshall Julius (MJ); Penny Lucas (PL); George Savvides (GS); Mansel Stimpson (MS); and Derek Winnert (DW).

Star ratings

★★★★★   **Exceptional**
★★★★   **Very Good**
★★★   **Good**
★★   **Mediocre**
★   **Insulting**

The Accidental Husband ★

Dr Emma Lloyd is a popular New York radio DJ whose wedding plans to Richard are ruined when she finds out that she is unknowingly already married to someone else. This is a totally misjudged and unfunny romantic comedy with a sleepwalking performance from Colin Firth and a desperate one from Uma Thurman who tries hard to keep her dignity. Poor Uma! GS

▷ Uma Thurman, Colin Firth, Jeffrey Dean Morgan, Sam Shepard, Lindsay Sloane, Isabella Rossellini, Keir Dullea.
▷ Dir Griffin Dunne, Pro Thurman, Jason Blum, Jennifer Todd, Suzanne Todd and Bob Yari, Screenplay Mimi Hare, Clare Naylor and Bonnie Sitkowitz, Ph William Rexer II, Pro Des Mark Ricker, Ed Suzy Elmiger, M Andrea Guerra, Costumes David C Robinson.

Blumhouse Productions/Team Todd/Yari Film Group-Momentum Pictures.
91 mins. USA. 2008. Rel: 29 Feb 2008. Cert 12A.

Across the Universe ★★★

Julie Taymor, who staged The Lion King on Broadway, now gives us a film musical using Dick Clement and Ian La Frenais as writers. They provide a story about an English boy from Liverpool travelling to America in the 1960s. Consciously carrying echoes of the life of John Lennon it utilises music by the Beatles in new arrangements. A great deal of it is truly filmic in its choreography and highly engaging, but then it expands fatally into psychedelic effects and poor judgment. It's the more irritating because at least a third of it is brilliant. MS

▷ Evan Rachel Wood, Jim Sturgess, Joe Anderson, Dana Fuchs, Eddie Izzard, Bono.
▷ Dir Julie Taymor, Pro Suzanne Todd, Jennifer Todd and Matthew Gross, Screenplay Dick Clement and Ian La Frenais from a story by them and Taymor, Ph Bruno Delbonnel, Pro Des Mark Friedberg, Ed Françoise Bonnot, M (Original Score) Elliot Goldenthal, Costumes Albert Wolsky.

Matthew Gross/Team Todd/Revolution Studios-Sony Pictures Releasing.
133 mins. USA. 2007. Rel: 28 Sept 2007. Cert 12A.

Adulthood ★★★★

Continuing the tale told in Kidulthood (2006) by revisiting the characters six years later, this again plays as a tough but concerned drama with an eye on younger audiences. Central this time is the

Adulthood:
Noel Clarke and Scarlett Alice Johnson confront life in London today.

threat of vengeance hanging over the reformed youngster who had brought about a death by assault and who is now released from prison. The film's writer Noel Clarke again plays this role but unexpectedly and resourcefully also takes over the direction. MS

❭ Noel Clarke, Adam Deacon, Scarlett Alice Johnson, Femi Oyeniran.
❭ *Dir* and *Screenplay* Noel Clarke, *Pro* Damian Jones and George Isaac, *Ph* Brian Tufano, *Pro Des* Murray McKeown, *Ed* Tom Hemmings, *M* Chad Hobson, *Costumes* Andy Blake.
UK Film Council/Pathé/Limelight/A Cipher Films/DJ Films production etc-Pathé Distribution.
99 mins. UK. 2008. Rel: 20 June 2008. Cert 15.

Ahlaam (Dreams) ★★★

Filmed in Baghdad in 2003 after the fall of Saddam Hussein, this heartfelt drama exploring the continuing tragedy of Iraq as experienced by those living there has to be admired – and not only because it was made at great personal risk to all concerned. Yet, however admirable the intentions, the stories featured lack the depth of characterisation that would render depressing material cathartic. Sometimes clumsy, always deeply sincere, the film provides a numbing experience. MS

A frenzied competitor in Air Guitar Nation.

❭ Aseel Adil, Basher Al-Majidi, Mohamed Hashim, Talib Al-Furati.
❭ *Dir*, *Screenplay* and *Ph* Mohamed Al-Daradji, *Pro* Atia and Mohamed Al-Daradji, *Pro Des* Hasan Falih, *Ed* Ghassan Abdallah and Ian Watson, *M* Naseer Shamma, *Costumes* Luay Fadhil and Ali Mohammed Dishar.

Iraq Al-Rafidain/Human Film-ICA Films.
111 mins. Iraq/UK. 2005. Rel: 2 Nov 2007. Cert 15.

Air Guitar Nation ★★★★

The notion of people in organised competitions emulating a performance to guitar tracks but without an instrument – the supposed guitar is just air – sounded to me like an April Fools' Day joke. But it's for real, and there's even a world championship event in Finland. Alexandra Lipsitz's film follows the competitors with great good humour, the personalities are engaging and it's unexpectedly heart-warming. The film offers more fun than I ever would have guessed. MS

❭ With Kriston Rucker, Cedric Devitt, C-Diddy, Björn Türoque, Krye Tuff.
❭ *Dir* Alexandra Lipsitz, *Pro* Dan Cutforth, Jane Lipsitz and Anna Barber, *Ph* Anthony Sacco, *Ed* Conor O'Neill, *M* Dan 'Björn Türoque' Crane.

A Magical Elves production-Contender Entertainment Group.
82 mins. USA. 2006. Rel: 9 Nov 2007. Cert 15.

The Air I Breathe ★★½

Look at the cast list and be amazed: how could so many decent actors agree to appear in this banal blend of four tales illustrating, according to the film's creator Jieho Lee, the key human emotions. Having characters called Happiness, Sorrow, Pleasure and Love should have set off danger signals and, although it's fast moving, the plotting grows increasingly ridiculous. The cast may help, but it's self-evidently rubbish. MS

▶ Kevin Bacon, Brendan Fraser, Julie Delpy, Andy Garcia, Sarah Michelle Gellar, Emile Hirsch, Forest Whitaker.
▶ Dir Jieho Lee, Pro Paul Schiff, Emilio Diez Barroso and Darlene Caamaño Loquet, Written by Lee and Bob DeRosa, Ph Walt Lloyd, Pro Des Bernardo Trujillo, Ed Robert Hoffman, M Marcelo Zarvos, Costumes Michele Michel.

NALA Films/Paul Schiff production-Pathé Distribution.
95 mins. USA. 2007. Rel: 16 May 2008. Cert 15.

Aliens vs Predator: Requiem ★★½

A significant improvement over the first *Alien/Predator* hybrid – hardly a tall order – this second horror/sci fi/action adventure sees the crossover franchise hitting Smalltown USA, home to multiple teenage victims and every cliché in the book. Directed by special effects wizards Greg and Colin Strause, this is a watchable but largely unexceptional time waster, sporadically exciting with some decent visuals but increasingly mundane and ultimately quite tiresome. MJ

▶ Steven Pasquale, Reiko Aylesworth, John Ortiz, Johnny Lewis, Ariel Gade, Kristen Hager.
▶ Dir Colin Strange and Greg Strause, Pro John Davis, Steven Giler and Walter Hill, Screenplay Shane Salerno based on 'Alien' characters by Dan O'Bannon and Ronald Shusett, and 'Predator' characters by John and Jim Thomas, Ph Daniel C Pearl, Pro Des Andrew Neskoromny, Ed Dan Zimmerman, M Brian Tyler, Costumes Angus Strathie.

Twentieth Century Fox Film Corporation/Brandywine Productions/Davis Entertainment/Dune Entertainment-20th Century Fox.
102 mins. USA. 2007. Rel: 18 Jan 2008. Cert 15.

All the Boys Love Mandy Lane ★½

Beautiful and untouched Mandy Lane against

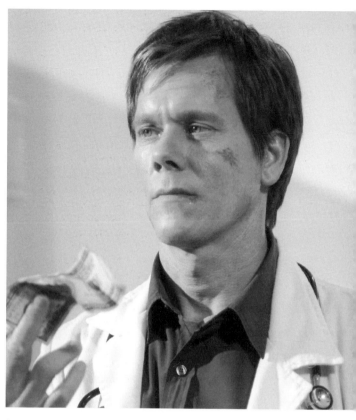

Kevin Bacon has a tough time in *The Air That I Breathe*.

her better judgement agrees to spend a weekend with some school friends at a remote ranch in Texas. Soon the countdown begins with horrific murders. This average slasher horror is not really scary – I only jumped once at a scene with a snake in the river – but it is very malicious and extremely nasty with an unexpected twist which leaves a bad taste in the mouth. GS

▶ Amber Heard, Anson Mount, Whitney Able, Michael Welch, Edwin Hodge, Melissa Price.
▶ Dir Jonathan Levine, Pro Chad Feehan, Felipe Marino and Joe Neurater, Screenplay Jacob Forman, Ph Darren Genet, Pro Des Thomas S Hammock, Ed Josh Noyes, M Mark Schulz, Costumes Michelle Lynette Bush.
Occupant Films/Productions-Optimum Releasing.
90 mins. USA. 2006. Rel: 15 Feb 2008. Cert 18.

Alvin and the Chipmunks ★★

It's sad to see Jason Lee, who's so brilliant in *My Name Is Earl* on TV, clearly struggling, despite giving his best shot as budding singer-songwriter Dave who adopts three mischievous singing chipmunks. Courtesy reasonable CGI, Alvin (voice of Justin Long), Simon (Matthew Gray Gubler) and Theodore (Jesse McCartney) soon become unexpected musical stars in this pleasant enough children's musical comedy with sufficient likeable nonsense to keep the young 'uns happy, though maybe not enough for their grown-ups. A bizarre $217 million

smash in the US, so *Alvin 2* can't be far off. Contains no material likely to offend or harm, unless you can't stand the Chipmunks' version of 'Funky Town'! DW

▶ Jason Lee, David Cross, Cameron Richardson, Jane Lynch and the voices of Jason Long, Matthew Gray Gubler, Jesse McCartney.
▶ *Dir* Tim Hill, *Pro* Ross Bagdasarian Jr and Janice Karman, *Screenplay* Jon Vitti, Will McRobb and Chris Viscardi, based on a story by Vitti and characters by Bagdasarian, *Ph* Peter Lyons Collister, *Pro Des* Richard Holland, *Ed* Peter E Berger, *M* Christopher Lennertz, *Costumes* Alexander Welker.

Bagdasarian Productions/ Fox 2000 Pictures/Regency Enterprises-20th Century Fox.
92 mins. USA. 2007. Rel: 21 Dec 2007. Cert U.

American Gangster ★★★★

Ridley Scott's best work since *Gladiator*, this is a splendidly staged tale of the rise and fall of a black drug dealer in New York that starts in 1968. Denzel Washington is the man, Russell Crowe his nemesis and older filmgoers will welcome the chance to see Ruby Dee again. Less melodramatic than *The Departed* and not without deliberate echoes of *The Godfather* films, this is not deep stuff but, based on real-life events, it's a highly competent entertainment. MS

▶ Denzel Washington, Russell Crowe, Chiwetel Ejiofor, Cuba Gooding Jr, Josh Brolin, Ted Levine,

Ruby Dee,. Lymari Nadal, Armand Assante.
▶ *Dir* Ridley Scott, *Pro* Brian Grazer and Scott, *Screenplay* Steven Zaillian based on Mark Jacobson's article *The Return of Superfly*, *Ph* Harris Savides, *Pro Des* Arthur Max, *Ed* Pietro Scalia, *M* Marc Streitenfeld, *Costumes* Janty Yates.

Universal Pictures/Imagine Entertainment/Relativity Media/Scott Free Productions-Universal Pictures International UK & Eire.
157 mins. USA. 2007. Rel: 16 Nov 2007. Cert 18.

And When Did You Last See Your Father? ★★★½

Blake Morrison's memoir about his troubled relationship with his father has been well adapted by David Nicholls of *Starter for Ten*. It boasts lovely performances from Jim Broadbent as dad, from Matthew Beard and Colin Firth portraying Blake in adolescence and adulthood respectively and from Juliet Stevenson never better as mother. But there's a fly in the ointment: Anand Tucker's mannered direction leading to an unnecessarily sentimental close. MS

▶ Jim Broadbent, Colin Firth, Juliet Stevenson, Gina McKee, Sarah Lancashire, Elaine Cassidy, Matthew Beard.
▶ *Dir* Anand Tucker, *Pro* Elizabeth Karlsen and Stephen Woolley, *Screenplay* David Nicholls based on Blake Morrison's book, *Ph* Howard Atherton, *Pro Des* Alice Normington, *Ed* Trevor Waite, *M* Barrington Pheloung, *Costumes* Caroline Harris.

Film4, UK Film Council, EM Media/Intandem/A Number 9 Films production etc-Buena Vista International (UK).
92 mins. UK/Ireland. 2007. Rel: 5 Oct 2007. Cert 12A.

Anna M ★★½

Great performance, shame about the film. Isabelle Carré is terrific as a woman so obsessed by a married doctor (Gilbert Melki) that she persuades herself that he is in love with her. Subsequently when he tactfully disillusions her, she starts to stalk him ever more threateningly as her love turns to hate. What begins believably turns into the most improbable tosh well before the end. Not French cinema's finest hour. MS

▶ Isabelle Carré, Gilbert Melki, Anne Consigny, Geneviève Mnich, Gaëlle Bona.
▶ Dir and Screenplay Michel Spinosa, Pro Patrick Sobelman, Ph Alain Duplantier, Art Dir Thierry François Ed Chantal Hymans, Costumes Nathalie Raoul.

Ex Nihilo/Rhône-Alpes Cinéma/Canal+/CinéCinéma etc-Metrodome Distribution Ltd.
107 mins. France. 2007. Rel: 16 Nov 2007. Cert 15.

Annie Leibovitz: Life Through a Lens ★★★½

What timing! The Queen walks out in a huff during a photo shoot with Annie Leibovitz (or, as it turns out, doesn't)) and now we have a documentary about the work and life of this photographer made by her sister. The film avoids pushing issues in both areas and could be more informative (two shooting sessions are linked to Sofia Coppola's Marie Antoinette but no details are provided). Pleasant enough, but not the definitive portrait it might have been. MS

▶ With Annie Leibovitz, Anna Wintour, Bette Midler, Tina Brown, Yoko Ono.
▶ Dir, Pro and Screenplay Barbara Leibovitz, Ph Eddie Marritz, Jaime Hellman, Ian Vollmer and Annie Leibovitz, Ed Kristen Huntley and Jed Parker, M Gaili Schoen.

Thirteen/WNET New York/Adirondack Pictures/Ranoah Productions-ICA Films.
90 mins. USA. 2006. Rel: 15 Feb 2008. No cert.

La Antena ★★★½

There's imagination to spare in this Argentinian film. Shot in black and white without spoken dialogue, it combines a homage to silent cinema (Fritz Lang in particular) with a futuristic drama about the control of the masses that is indebted to Orwell. Initially it hits you between the eyes but the last third rather falls away. Nevertheless it's still a film to seek out. MS

▶ Valeria Bertuccelli, Alejandro Urdapilleta, Julieta Cardinali, Rafael Ferro, Sol Moreno, Florencia Raggi, Ricardo Merkin, Jonathan Sandor.
▶ Dir and Screenplay Esteban Sapir, Pro Federico

Jim Broadbent and Juliet Stevenson at their best in And When Did You Last See Your Father?

Rotstein, *Ph* Cristian Cottet, *Art Dir* Daniel Gimelberg, *Ed* Pablo Barbieri Carrera, *M* Leo Sujatovich, *Costumes* Andrea Mattio.

ladobleA Productores-Dogwoof Pictures.
90 mins. Argentina/Netherlands. 2007. Rel: 16 May 2008. Cert PG.

Arctic Tale ★★★

This engaging documentary from National Geographic follows the stories of two new-born creatures in the icy kingdom of the North Pole. Nanu is a polar bear cub whereas Seela is a walrus pup and both are born in a hostile environment where survival is becoming increasingly more difficult because of global warming. Queen Latifah's narration and some of the sound effects are manipulative, aiming for sentiment rather that reality. GS

▶ Narrated by Queen Latifah.
▶ *Dir* Adam Ravetch and Sarah Robertson, *Pro* Adam Leipzig, *Narration* Linda Woolverton, Mose Richards and Kristin Gore, *Ph* Ravetch, *Ed* Beth Spiegel, *M* Jody Talbot.

Polar bears face the challenges of a changing climate in *Arctic Tale*.

Visionbox Pictures/National Geographic Films/ Starbucks Entertainment-Paramount Pictures.
96 mins. USA. 2007. Rel: 8 Feb 2008. Cert U.

As You Like It ★★★★

Kenneth Branagh's underestimated treatment of the Shakespeare play that includes 'The Seven Ages of Man' speech is engaging despite its rather irrelevant 19th-century Japanese setting. It's not the most poetic of interpretations, but the pleasing cast (Kevin Kline a fine Jaques) go for clarity of meaning and for a tone that beguilingly encourages audiences to identify with the ever pertinent comments on the behaviour of those in love. Not without faults, this nevertheless makes for an enjoyable piece. MS

▶ Bryce Dallas Howard, Romola Garai, Brian Blessed, Adrian Lester, Alfred Molina, Kevin Kline, David Oyelowo, Richard Briers, Janet McTeer, Jade Jefferies.
▶ *Dir* Kenneth Branagh, *Pro* Branagh, Judy Hofflund and Simon Moseley, *Based on* Shakespeare's play as adapted by Branagh, *Ph* Roger Lanser, *Pro Des* Tim Harvey, *Ed* Neil Farrell, *M* Patrick Doyle, *Costumes* Susannah Buxton.

HBO/BBC Films/Shakespeare Film Company-Lionsgate UK.
127 mins. USA/UK. 2006. Rel: 21 Sept 2007. Cert 12A.

The Assassination of Jesse James by the Coward Robert Ford ★★★½

Less a western than a psychological study with strikingly poetic images, this take on the last years of Jesse James and on the life of his killer is well directed. It's also slow-paced, over-literary, not fully focused or easy to follow but decidedly beautiful. Buy into it and you get rewards despite the questionable elements. Brad

Pitt (James) and Casey Affleck (Ford) both do well. MS

▶ Brad Pitt, Casey Affleck, Sam Shepard, Mary-Louise Parker, Paul Schneider.
▶ *Dir* Andrew Dominik, *Pro* Brad Pitt, Dede Gardner, Ridley Scott and others, *Screenplay* Dominik from Ron Hansen's novel, *Ph* Roger Deakins, *Art Dir* Troy Sizemore, *Ed* Dylan Tichenor and Curtiss Clayton, *M* Nick Cave and Warren Ellis, *Costumes* Patricia Norris.

Warner Bros Pictures/Virtual Studios/Scott Free/Plan B Entertainment-Warner Bros Distributors (UK).
160 mins. USA/Canada. 2007. Rel: 30 Nov 2007. Cert 15.

The Assembly ★★★★

Feng Xiaogang's magnificent anti-war epic follows one man's struggle to survive the terrible years of the Chinese Civil War and his subsequent quest to bring honour to his forty-six companions who sacrificed their lives on a sniper mission. The film boasts superb production values with stunning 'Scope cinematography and a powerful leading performance from Zhang Hanyu as Captain Guzidi. (Original title: *Ji Lie Hao*) GS

▶ Chao Deng, Heng Fu, Jun Hu, Phil Jones, Fan Liao, Naiwen Li, Yan Tang.
▶ *Dir* Feng Xiaogang, *Pro* Feng, John Chong,

Guan Yadi and Zhongjun Wang, *Screenplay* Heng Liu , *Ph* Yue Lu, *Pro Des* Zhang Chung, Zhao Jing and Zheng Xiao Feng, *Ed* Liu Miao Miao, *M* Wang Liguang, *Costumes* Zhao Hai.

China Film Company Co-Production Corporation/Huayi Brothers/MK Pictures etc-Metrodome Distribution.
124 mins. China/Hong Kong. 2007. Rel: 7 Mar 2008. Cert 15.

Asterix at the Olympic Games
★★★

This new instalment based on the cartoon strip series boasts superb production values and a wonderful performance from Alain Delon as Caesar who deliciously sends up his image. His foster son Brutus lusts after the Greek princess Irina whose heart belongs to a young Gaul but whose hand is to be given to the winner of the Olympic Games. It is enjoyable but overlong with endless chariot races particularly towards the end. (Original title: *Asterix aux jeux olympiques*) GS

▶ Gérard Depardieu, Clovis Cornillac, Benoît Poelvoorde, Alain Delon, José Garcia, Jean-Pierre Cassel.
▶ *Dir* Frédéric Forestier and Thomas Langmann, *Pro* Langmann, *Screenplay* Langmann, Olivier Dazat, Alexandre Charlot and Franck Magnier, from the comic books by René Goscinny and

Clovis Cornillac and Gérard Depardieu in *Asterix at the Olympic Games.*

Supporting players Juno Temple and Benedict Cumberbatch in the hit *Atonement*.

Albert Uderzo, *Ph* Thierry Arbogast, *Pro Des* Aline Bonetto, *Ed* Yannick Kergoat and Vincent Tabaillon, *M* Frédéric Talgorn, *Costumes* Madeleine Fontaine.

Pathé Renn Productions/La Petite Reine/Canal + etc-Pathé Distribution.
116 mins. France/Germany/Spain/Italy/Belgium. 2008. Rel: 1 Feb 2008. Cert PG.

Atonement ★★★½

No need for anyone to atone given the popular success of this adaptation of Ian McEwan's novel, although the piece is uneven. Brilliantly edited by Paul Tothill, the opening section of this tale of an ill-fated love across class divisions is set in 1935 and it's compelling despite plot contrivances. The middle sequences portray the Second World War era yet overall are more diffuse and less interesting. Fortunately a modern day coda rivets attention with Vanessa Redgrave at her finest in a cameo as memorable as that by Judi Dench in *Shakespeare in Love*. MS

▶ James McAvoy, Keira Knightley, Romola Garai, Saorise Ronan, Vanessa Redgrave, Brenda Blethyn, Benedict Cumberbatch, Harriet Walter, Gina McKee.
▶ *Dir* Joe Wright, *Pro* Tim Bevan, Eric Fellner and Paul Webster, *Screenplay* Christopher Hampton

from Ian McEwan's novel, *Ph* Seamus McGarvey, *Pro Des* Sarah Greenwood, *Ed* Paul Tothill, *M* Dario Marianelli, *Costumes* Jacqueline Durran.

Universal Pictures/StudioCanal/Relativity Media/ Working Title etc-Universal Pictures International UK & Eire.
123 mins. USA/UK/France. 2007. Rel: 7 Sept 2007. Cert 15.

August Rush ★½

This is an unashamedly sentimental film with a preposterous and laughable plot. August (Freddie Highmore), a young orphan, runs away from his orphanage to the streets of New York hoping to find his parents – his Irish guitarist father (Jonathan Rhys Meyers) who had a one-night stand with his mother, a promising cellist (Keri Russell). The acting is not bad apart from Robin Williams who plays a ridiculous OTT modern day Fagin in Kirsten Sheridan's overlong and predictable film. GS

▶ Freddie Highmore, Keri Russell, Jonathan Rhys Meyers, Terrence Howard, Robin Williams, Jama Simone Nash.
▶ *Dir* Kirsten Sheridan, *Pro* Richard Barton Lewis, *Screenplay* Nick Castle, James V Hart, based on a story by Paul Castro and Nick Castle, *Ph* John Mathieson, *Pro Des* Michael Shaw, *Ed* William

Steinkamp, *M* Mark Mancina, *Costumes* Frank
L Fleming.
CJ Entertainment/Odyssey Entertainment/Southpaw
Entertainment-Warner Bros.
114 mins. USA. 2007. Rel: 23 Nov 2007. Cert PG.

Awake ★★★

Multi-millionaire Clay (Hayden Christensen)
has everything in life but good health and is in
need of a heart transplant. Soon after his secret
marriage to Sam (Jessica Alba) his cardiologist
Harper (Terrence Howard) finds him a matching
donor and Clay goes ahead with the operation
despite the objections of his mother Lilith (Lena
Olin). It is an unusual subject for a thriller
– watching open heart surgery when the patient
is actually awake is hardly entertainment
and definitely not for the squeamish – but
surprisingly it works with an unexpected twist
and an excellent performance from Olin who
elevates the film to another dimension. GS

‣ Hayden Christensen, Jessica Alba, Terrence
Howard, Lena Olin, Sam Robards
‣ *Dir and Screenplay* Joby Harold, *Pro* Jason Kliot,
Fisher Stevens, John Penotti and Joana Vicente, *Ph*
Russell Carpenter, *Pro Des* Dina Goldman, *Ed* Craig
McKay, *M* Samuel Sim, *Costumes* Cynthia Flynt.

GreeneStreet Films/The Weinstein Company/Open
City Films-Icon Film Distribution.

84 mins. USA. 2007. Rel: 4 Apr 2008. Cert 15.

Azur & Asmar:
The Princes' Quest ★★★★

Another animated fable from Michel Ocelot who
gave us the exquisite *Kirikou and the Sorceress*.
Here he tells of two childhood friends who,
coming from quite different backgrounds,
become adult rivals in a bid to rescue the Djinn
Fairy from captivity. Initially the dubbing
distracts, but once the film moves to Tunisia
everything settles and Ocelot's wisdom and
humanity shine through in a film that grows ever
more beautiful with images influenced by Persian
miniatures and Renaissance paintings. MS

‣ With the voices of Steven Kyman, Nigel
Pilkington, Nigel Lambert, Imogen Bailey.
‣ *Dir* and *Screenplay* Michel Ocelot with George
Roubicek, *Pro* Christophe Rossignon, *Art Dir* Anne
Lise Lourdelet-Koehler, *Ed* Michèle Péju, *M* Gabriel
Yared, *Animation* Mac Guff Ligne etc.

Nord-Ouest Production/Mac Guff Ligne/Studio O/
France 3 Cinéma etc/Soda Pictures.
99 mins. France/Belgium/Spain/Italy. 2006.
Rel: 8 Feb 2008. Cert U.

Back to Normandy ★★★

This documentary comes from Nicolas Philibert

Hayden
Christensen
in *Awake*.

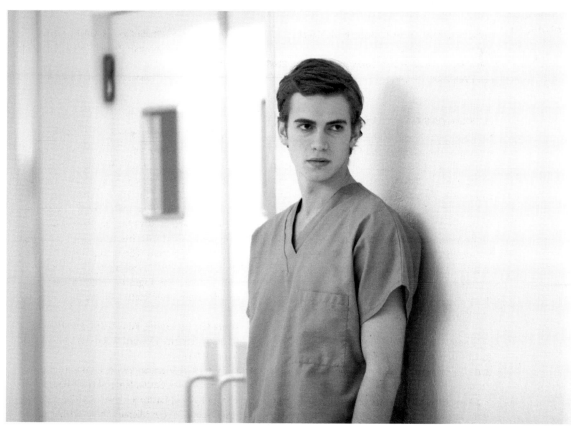

who had such a success with *Etre et Avoir* (2002). Here he revisits the rural community where in 1975 he was involved in René Allio's film *I, Pierre Rivière…* which used locals as actors. Clips from that film are included and interviews with the players are blended with scenes of country life. There's a touching conclusion, but the piece comes across as insubstantial and more appropriate to being seen as a DVD extra to Allio's movie. MS

▶ With Annick Bisson, Charles Lihou, Claude Hébert, Joseph Leportier.
▶ *Dir* and *Ed* Nicolas Philibert, *Pro* Serge Lalou and Gilles Sandoz, *Ph* Katell Dijan, *M* André Veil.

Les Film d'Ici/Maïa Films/ARTE France Cinéma etc-Tartan Films.
113 mins. France. 2006. Rel: 18 Jan 2008. Cert 15.

The Baker ★½

Damian Lewis is a charismatic performer who is usually good value for money but here he is totally wasted. He plays Milo, an assassin who, after failing to fulfil a contract runs away to a remote Welsh village where the locals mistake him for the new baker. The idea is not bad but Gareth Lewis' lame script coupled with weak direction is a muddled mess. His actors try hard but fail to make sense of their stereotypical characters. GS

▶ Damien Lewis, Kate Ashfield, Nikolaj Coster-Waldau, Michael Gambon, Annette Badland, Dyfan Dwyfor.
▶ *Dir and Screenplay* Gareth Lewis, *Pro* Damien

Lewis, Daniel Shepherd, Adrian Sturges and Justin Williams, *Ph* Sean Bobbitt, *Pro Des* Jennifer Kernke, *Ed* Alan Strachan, *M* Alex Wurman, *Costumes* Pam Downe.

Grandville Pictures/Picture Farm-2 Entertain.
86 mins. UK. 2007. Rel: 29 Feb 2008. Cert 12A.

Balls of Fury ★★★

The balls of the title are of the ping pong variety, the film itself a cross between *Enter the Dragon* and every sports movie you've ever seen. A deeply wacky adventure that scores more comedy hits than misses, *Balls of Fury* follows the exploits of a down-and-out former ping pong prodigy (chunky Dan Fogler) who's enlisted to bring down a table tennis-obsessed crime lord, played to the hilt by Christopher Walken. MJ

▶ Dan Fogler, Christopher Walken, Maggie Q, Terry Crews, Aisha Tyler, Thomas Lennon, Robert Patrick, Jason Scott Lee.
▶ *Dir* Robert Ben Garant, *Pro* Gary Barber, Roger Birnbaum, Jonathan Glickman and Thomas Lennon *Screenplay* Lennon and Garant, *Ph* Thomas E Ackerman, *Pro Des* Jeff Knipp, *Ed* John Refoua, *M* Randy Edelman, *Costumes* Maryann Bozek.

Rogue Pictures/Intrepid Pictures/Spyglass Entertainment-Universal Pictures.
90 mins. USA. 2007. Rel: 26 Dec 2007. Cert 12A.

The Band's Visit ★★★★

This Israeli film, a tragicomedy that echoes the 1960s films made in Czechoslovakia by Milos

Ronit Elkabetz and Sasson Gabai learn to live together in *Bikur Ha-Tizmoret* [*The Band's Visit*].

Jason Statham in
The Bank Job.

Forman, features an Egyptian band losing their way when in Israel to perform. Shared humanity is the theme and the colour photography is admirably crisp and clean. The screenplay, however, needs to go deeper to investigate the characters fully. Nevertheless, aided by ideally cast players in the two leading roles, the film wonderfully captures the sadness of essentially lonely lives. MS

▷ Sasson Gabai, Ronit Elkabetz, Saleh Bakri, Khalifa Natour, Rubi Moscovich.
▷ *Dir* and *Screenplay* Eran Kolirin, *Pro* Eilon Ratzkovsky, Ehud Bleiberg and others, *Ph* Shai Goldman, *Art Dir* Eitan Levi, *Ed* Arik Lahav Leibovitz, *M* Habib Shehadeh Hanna, *Costumes* Doron Ashkenazi.

July August Productions/Bleiberg Entertainment/ Sophie Dulac Productions etc-Sony Pictures Releasing. 87 mins. Israel/USA/France. 2007. Rel: 9 Nov 2007. Cert 12A.

The Bank Job ★★★★

Compromising pictures of a royal personage need to be retrieved from a bank deposit box, so the authorities set up their own heist with real villains who loot the deposit boxes of cash and jewels as well as the photographs. Jason Statham plays the lead villain commissioned to head the robbery which is based on real events.

Dick Clement and Ian La Frenais' screenplay is a model of good plotting and the whole show as directed by Roger Donaldson makes for very satisfying entertainment, a timely and enjoyable throwback to the heyday of the British crime caper of the 1950s and '60s. MHD

▷ Jason Statham, Saffron Burrows, Stephen Campbell Moore, Daniel Mays, James Faulkner, Peter Bowles, David Suchet, Keeley Hawes, Craig Fairbrass, Sharon Maughan.
▷ *Dir* Roger Donaldson, *Pro* Steve Chasman and Charles Roven, *Screenplay* Dick Clement and Ian La Frenais, *Ph* Michael Coulter, *Pro Des* Gavin Bocquet, *Ed* John Gilbert, *M* J Peter Robinson, *Costumes* Odile Dicks-Mireaux.

Arclight Films/Mosaic Media Group/Relativity Media/ Skyline (Baker Street)/Omnilab-Lionsgate. 111 mins. UK. 2008. Rel: 28 Feb 2008. Cert 15.

The Banquet ★★★★

Fast moving with a strong visual impact, this Chinese melodrama prompts comparison with *The Curse of the Yellow Flower* (2006) although it's less inclined to kitsch and more brutal. In fact it's a martial arts movie set in the 10th century, one which deliberately echoes Shakespeare's *Hamlet*. Such a weird mix may well limit its appeal but it's handled with great aplomb. MS

Jack Black as, er, Robocop in *Be Kind Rewind*.

invites us to understand if not to condone. This is a deeply humane film. MS

▸ Elliot Ruiz, Falah Flayeh, Yasmine Hanani, Andrew McLaren, Aya Abbas.
▸ *Dir* and *Pro* Nick Broomfield, *Screenplay* Broomfield, Marc Hoeferlin and Anna Telford, *Ph* Mark Wolf, *Pro Des* David Bryan, *Ed* Ash Jenkins and Stuart Gazzard, *M* Nick Laird-Clowes, *Costumes* Rosie Hackett.

Film4/Hanway Films-Contender Entertainment Group. 97 mins. UK. 2007. Rel: 1 Feb 2008. Cert 15.

Be Kind Rewind ★

Jack Black enters the eccentric world of Michel Gondry to play a man who, having become magnetised (don't ask), wipes all the tapes in a video store already threatened with closure. To keep the business going, famous titles lost are replaced by abysmal abbreviated amateur remakes but the customers who take them out love them. I found it utterly silly, as did some others, but the film has its admirers. Clearly a matter of taste. MS

▸ Jack Black, Mos Def, Danny Glover, Mia Farrow, Melonie Diaz.
▸ *Dir* and *Screenplay* Michel Gondry, *Pro* Georges Bermann, Gondry and Julie Fong, *Ph* Ellen Kuras, *Pro Des* Dan Leigh, *Ed* Jeff Buchanan, *M* Jean-Michel Bernard, *Costumes* Rahel Afiley and Kishu Chand.

Focus Features International/Partizan Films-Pathé Distribution. 100 mins. USA/France/UK. 2007. Rel: 22 Feb 2008. Cert 12A.

Beaufort ★★★

For Israelis this adaptation of Ron Leshem's novel may speak in personal terms, but for others it's likely to be an honest but ultimately wearying portrayal of the madness of war. Beaufort is the fortress in the Lebanon demolished by explosives when the Israeli soldiers stationed there moved out in 2000 after eighteen years. This film features its final days. Worthy indeed, but recent films from Eastwood, Broomfield and Bouchareb have all had something more individual to say about war. MS

▸ Oshri Cohen, Itay Tiran, Eli Eltonyo, Ohad Knoller, Arthur Faradjev.
▸ *Dir* Joseph Cedar, *Pro* David Mandil and David Silber, *Screenplay* Ron Leshem and Cedar from Lesham's novel, *Ph* Ofer Inov, *Pro Des* Miguel Merkin, *Ed* Zohar M. Sela, *M* Ishai Adar, *Costumes* Maya More.

United King Films/A Metro Communication, Movie

▸ Ziyi Zhang, Ge You, Daniel Wu, Zhou Xun, Ma Jingwu, Huang Xiaoming.
▸ *Dir* Feng Xiaogang, *Pro* Wang Zhongjun and John Chong, *Screenplay* Sheng Heyu and Qiu Gangian, *Ph* Zhang Li, *Pro Des* and *Costumes* Tim Yip, *Ed* Liu Miaomiao, *M* Tan Dun.

Huayi Brothers Pictures Co. Ltd/Media Asia Films Ltd etc-Metrodome Distribution. 131 mins. People's Republic of China/Hong Kong. 2006. Rel: 11 April 2008. Cert 15.

Battle for Haditha ★★★★½

The last shot of all may seem misjudged stylistically, but this take on Iraq, based on a tragic real-life incident in November 2005, is a triumph for Nick Broomfield, more usually associated with documentaries. Terrible reprisals by American marines on civilians who might possibly have aided two terrorist bombers are central to a narrative played by non-professionals with total conviction. What happened may be inexcusable, but the tragedy is the greater because in Renoir's phrase everybody has their reasons and Broomfield

Plus production etc-Trinity Filmed Entertainment.
131 mins. Israel. 2007. Rel: 28 March 2008. Cert 15.

Bee Movie ★★★★

A DreamWorks /PDI animated feature finally
fulfils the promise of *Antz* and *Shrek*. Screenwriter
Jerry Seinfeld voices Barry, a bee who refuses
to participate in honey production and instead
opts for dangerous group flights into the outside
world where he meets New York florist Vanessa
(voice: Renée Zellweger) and decides to sue
humans for stealing his species' honey. The script
is terrific, the overall level of invention high and
you'll be hooked throughout. JC

▶ Voices of Jerry Seinfeld, Renée Zellweger,
Matthew Broderick, John Goodman, Chris Rock,
Kathy Bates, Larry King, Ray Liotta, Sting, Oprah
Winfrey, Rip Torn.
▶ *Dir* Steve Hickner and Simon J Smith, *Pro* Jerry
Seinfeld and Christina Steinberg, *Screenplay*
Seinfeld, Spike Feresten, Barry Marder and Andy
Robin, *Pro Des* Alex McDowell, *Ed* Nick Fletcher,
M Rupert Gregson-Williams, *Costumes* Jane Poole.

DreamWorks Animation/Columbus 81 Productions/
DreamWorks SKG/Pacific Data Images-Paramount
Pictures.
90 mins. USA. 2007. Rel: 14 Dec 2007. Cert U.

Before the Devil Knows You're Dead ★★★★

An alert octogenarian, director Sidney Lumet
doesn't show his age in this astute crime thriller
built around a robbery. It's also an engrossing
family drama and a pessimistic comment on a
world in which human decency is losing out to
pressures inherent in a society that fails to value
it. With terrific performances all round, not least
from our own Albert Finney, this piece deserved
to do better than it did at the box-office. MS

▶ Philip Seymour Hoffman, Ethan Hawke, Marisa
Tomei, Albert Finney, Michael Shannon, Rosemary
Harris, Brían O'Byrne.
▶ *Dir* Sidney Lumet, *Pro* Michael Cerenzie,
Brian Linse, Paul Parmar and William S Gilmore,
Screenplay Kelly Masterson, *Ph* Ron Fortunato,
Pro Des Christopher Nowak, *Ed* Tom Swartwout,
M Carter Burwell, *Costumes* Tina Nigro.

Capitol Films & Funky Buddha Group present a Unity
Productions/Linsefilm Ltd. Production-Entertainment
Film Distributors Ltd.
117 mins. UK/USA. 2007. Rel: 11 Jan 2008. Cert 15.

Beowulf ★½

As technically remarkable as it is super dull,
this ancient tale of muscle-bound good versus
supernatural evil comes from *Roger Rabbit*
director Robert Zemeckis and stars the motion-
captured voice talents of Ray Winstone,
Anthony Hopkins and a scantily clad, computer
generated Angelina Jolie. Even on mighty IMAX
screens in gimmicky 3D the movie leaves a
lot to be desired, a humourless, slow-moving
affair that's too rude for kids and too boring for
adults. MJ

▶ Ray Winstone, Robin Wright Penn, Anthony
Hopkins, Greg Ellis, Charlotte Salt, Julene Renee,
John Malkovich, Crispin Glover, Angelina Jolie,
Dominic Keating.
▶ *Dir* Robet Zemeckis, *Pro* Steve Bing, Jack
Rapke, Steve Starkey and Zemeckis, *Screenplay*
Neil Gaiman and Roger Avary, based on the
anonymous epic poem, *Ph* Robert Presley, *Pro
Des* Doug Chiang, *Ed* Jeremiah O'Driscoll, *M* Alan
Silvestri, *Costumes* Gabriella Pescucci.

ImageMovers/Shangri-La Entertainment-Warner Bros.
113 mins. USA. 2007. Rel: 16 Nov 2007. Cert 12A.

Black and White ★★

Professor Mathur and his activist wife provide
shelter for Numair, a young boy who introduces
himself as a victim of the riots in Gujarat. He is
in fact an Afghanistan trained suicide bomber
on a mission to blow up the Red Fort in fifteen
days. This ambitious Bollywood epic boasts
strong production values but ultimately is
misconceived, overlong and predictable. It starts
well but it soon sinks into melodrama. GS

▶ Anil Kapoor, Anurag Sinha, Shefali Chhaya,
Akash Khurana, Aditi Sharma, Habib Tanvir.
▶ *Dir* Subhash Ghai, *Pro* Subhash Ghai, Raju
Farooqui, Rahul Puri and Mukta Ghai, *Screenplay*
Subhash Ghai, Sachin Bhowmick and Akash
Khurana, *Ph* Somak Mukherjee, *Pro Des* Leela
Chanda, *Ed* Subhash Ghai and Amitabh Shukla,
M Sukhwinder Singh.

Mukta Arts Ltd/Mukta Searchlight Films-Eros
International.
India. 2008. Rel: 7 Mar 2008. Cert 12A.

Black Sheep ★★★★

Henry, who has an irrational fear of sheep,
returns to the farm of his childhood unaware
that brother Angus is genetically modifying
the flock.When an unwitting environmentalist
releases a mutation which bites, mayhem
ensues. This New Zealand offering delivers
suitably menacing, man-eating sheep, *American
Werewolf in London* type transformation
sequences and just the right amount of gore. A

Maeve Dermody realises that the threatening crocodiles are the real thing in *Black Water*.

rare horror comedy that compromises neither genre, it constantly holds the attention. Shallow, but nonetheless hugely enjoyable. JC

▶ Matthew Chamberlain, Eli Kent, Nick Fenton, Sam Clarke, Glenis Levestam, Nahan Meister.
▶ *Dir & Screenplay* Jonathan King, *Pro* Philippa Campbell, *Ph* Richard Bluck, *Pro Des* Kim Sinclair, *Ed* Chris Plummer, *M* Victoria Kelly, *Costumes* Pauline Bowkett.

Livestock Films/New Zealand Film Commission-Icon Film Distribution.
87 mins. New Zealand. 2006. Rel: 12 Oct 2007. Cert 15.

Black Water ★★★★

In Australia a real-life incident saw two teenagers menaced by a crocodile after it had killed a friend of theirs during a river trip. This modest but effective film offers a fiction suggested by that event and invites its audience to identify with the characters on screen. The filmmakers avoid the gore of modern horror films and reject special effects (the crocodiles seen are real). The plot is not exactly novel but the treatment is intelligent. MS

▶ Diana Glenn, Maeve Dermody, Andy Rodoreda, Ben Oxenbould, Fiona Press.

▶ *Dir* and *Screenplay* Andrew Traucki and David Nerlich, *Pro* Michael Robertson, Traucki and Nerlich, *Ph* John Biggins, *Pro Des* Aaron Crothers, *Ed* Rodrigo Balart, *M* Rafael May, *Costumes* Justine Seymour.

Australian Film Commission/TFD Territorial Film Developments Ltd (London)/Underdog Pty Ltd-The Works UK Distribution Ltd.
89 mins. Australia/UK. 2007. Rel: 22 Feb 2008. Cert 15.

Blade Runner: The Final Cut ★★

Ridley Scott continues to flog his dead horse of a sci fi thriller with a minutely altered fourth version aimed at gullible fans with more cash than critical facility. Harrison Ford hits the trail of four renegade androids in a film that has been so wildly overrated by so many for so long, it's easy to forget that beyond the flashy production design and groundbreaking special effects, it's muddled, pretentious and dull. Enough already. MJ

▶ Harrison Ford, Rutger Hauer, Sean Young, M Emmet Walsh, Daryl Hannah.
▶ *Dir* Ridley Scott, *Pro* Michael Deeley, *Screenplay* Hampton Fancher and David Peoples, based on Philip K Dick's novel *Do Androids Dream of Electric*

Sheep?, *Ph* Jordan Cronenweth, *Pro Des* Laurence
G Paull, *Ed* Les Healey and Marsha Nakashima,
M Vangelis, *Costumes* Michael Kaplan and Charles
Knode.

Blade Runner Partnership/The Ladd Company/Run
Run Shaw/Shaw Brothers-Warner Bros.
117 mins. USA/Singapore. 1982. Rel: 23 Nov 2007.
Cert 15.

Blame It On Fidel! ★★½

Some people love this film by Julie Gavras,
daughter of the man who made *Z* in 1968. Nina
Kervel is undoubtedly splendid as the nine year
old central to the story. The girl is living in Paris
with her bourgeois parents who, this being the
1970s, take up left-wing causes. Significantly
some reviewers call it a comedy and some
a drama and I found that the two elements
cancelled each other out. (Original title: *La faute
à Fidel!*) MS

❧ Nina Kervel, Julie Depardieu, Stefano Accorsi,
Benjamin Feuillet.
❧ *Dir* and *Screenplay* Julie Gavras based on
Domitilla Calamai's novel *Tutta colpa di Fidel*, *Pro*
Sylvie Pialat, *Ph* Nathalie Durand, *Art Dir* Laurent
Deroo, *Ed* Pauline Dairau, *M* Armand Amar,
Costumes Annie Thiellement.

Gaumont/Les Films du Worso/B Movies/France 3
Cinéma etc-ICA Films.
98 mins. France/Italy. 2006. Rel: 19 Oct 2007. Cert 12A.

The Book of Revelation ★★★★

Daniel, a successful Melbourne dancer,
disappears without trace immediately before
an important performance. Twelve days later
he returns but he is too embarrassed to talk
about his ordeal. He had been abducted by three
women, was chained naked on the floor and
had been continuously sexually abused. Tom
Long is excellent as Daniel, giving a powerful
and raw performance in Ana Kokkinos' gripping
and highly erotic film. Greta Scacchi is also
effective as the Dance Company's director
who tries to help Daniel heal his psychological
wounds and re-examine his life. GS

❧ Colin Friels, Greta Scacchi, Tom Long, Deborah
Mailman, Zoe Coyle, Nadine Garner.
❧ *Dir* Ana Kokkinos, *Pro* Al Clark, *Screenplay*
Kokkinos and Andrew Bovell from the novel by
Rupert Thomson, *Ph* Tristan Milani, *Pro Des* Paul
Heath, *Ed* Martin Connor, *M* Cezary Skubiszewski,
Costumes Anna Borghesi.

Film Finance/Wild Heart Zizani-ContentFilm
International.
119 mins. Australia. 2008. Rel: 28 Mar 2008. Cert 18.

Born & Bred ★★★½

The Argentinian filmmaker Pablo Trapero, he
of *El Bonnerense and Familia Rodente*, certainly
doesn't repeat himself. This time his story
moves from Buenos Aires to the stark expanses
of Patagonia. There a married man begins a
new existence by taking work at a small remote
airport. This follows a car-crash and he seems
guilt-ridden although the film keeps the audience
guessing as to just how fatal the crash had been.
Some distant parallels with Nanni Moretti's *The
Son's Room* (2001) underline how much more
rewarding it is to feel involved rather than
viewing everything from a distance as here. MS

Guillermo Pfening
finds that life
can be harsh in
Born & Bred.

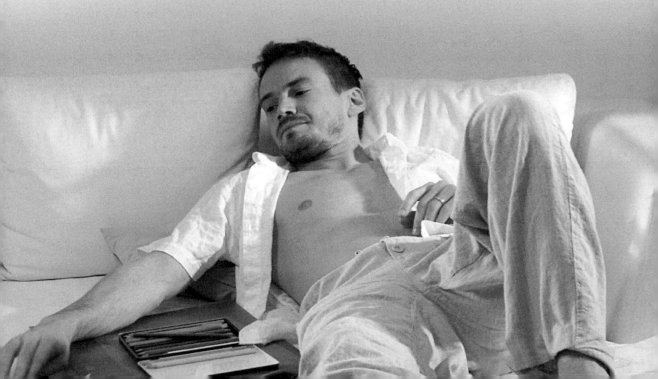

Alan Smyth in *Botched*.

Nadine Labaki, the director and leading lady of *Caramel*. She plays a member of a dancing troupe who is touring around Lebanon in an old autobus. Aractingi's attractive film boasts strong production values and likeable performances. He makes great use of the stunning locations and is clearly influenced by Bollywood with much singing and dancing. It is worth discovering despite the predictable ending. GS

▶ Rodney El Haddad, Nadine Labaki, Mounir Malaeb, Rana Alamuddin, Nada Abou Farhat, Omar Rajeh.
▶ *Dir, Pro and Screenplay* Philippe Aractingi, *Ph* Gary Turnbull, *Pro Des* Cynthia Zahar, *Ed* Dana K Trometer, *M* Ali El Khabib, Martin Russell and Simon Emmerson, *Costumes* Milia Maroun.

Fantascope Production-Zelig Films.
142 mins. Lebanon. 2005. Rel: 23 May 2008. Cert 15.

Botched ★

After a failed heist Ritchie (Stephen Dorff) is made to take the rap and is sent to Moscow in order to steal an antique cross. Things go from bad to worse when his accomplices kill a woman during the robbery and are forced to take hostages. Kit Ryan's muddled film with ridiculously over the top performances and unconvincing Russian accents to match can't make up its mind whether it's an action thriller or a horror but it definitely lives up to its title. GS

▶ Alan Smyth, Stephen Dorff, Sean Pertwee, Jamie Foreman, Russell Smith, Jaime Murray.
▶ *Dir* Kit Ryan, *Pro* Allan Balladur, Steve Richards, Thomas Fischer, Terence Ryan and Ken Tuohy, *Screenplay* Derek Boyle, Raymond and Eamon Friel, *Ph* Bryan Loftus, *Pro Des* Jon Bunker, *Ed* Jeremy Gibbs, *M* Tom Green, *Costumes* Erika Ő kvist.

Arcade Films/Barraboy Films/Madigan Film Productions etc-Optimum Releasing.
91 mins. USA/Germany/Ireland/UK. 2007.
Rel: 18 Apr 2008. Cert 15.

The Bourne Ultimatum ★★★★

Worlds better than the first two instalments, Paul Greengrass's *The Bourne Ultimatum* sees amnesiac superspy Matt Damon restoring his marbles while gunning for a fresh batch of bad guys. Exciting and suspenseful with lots of great London location work and a quality supporting cast including Paddy Considine, David Strathairn and Joan Allen, it's a sharply directed excuse for mayhem with no end of blasting, pounding and chasing to keep your heart racing. MJ

▶ Guillermo Pfening, Federico Esquerro, Martina Gusman, Tomás Lipán.
▶ *Dir* Pablo Trapero, *Pro* Trapero and Douglas Cummins, *Screenplay* Trapero and Mario Rulloni from Trapero's idea, *Ph* Guillermo Nieto, *Art Dir* Pablo Maestre, *Ed* Ezequiel Borovinsky and Trapero, *M* Palo Pandolfo, Luis Chomicz and Las Voces Blancas, *Costumes* Marisa Urruti.

Matanza Cine/Axiom Films/Sintra etc-Axiom Films Ltd.
99 mins. Argentina/UK/Italy. 2006. Rel: 24 Aug 2007.
Cert 15.

The Boss of It All ★

Unexpectedly and, alas, unsuccessfully, Lars von Trier tries his hand at comedy. The concept is promising: with a deal in sight an employer hires an actor to impersonate the company boss he has always pretended to have in order to avoid taking overt responsibility. Unfortunately, allowing the 'boss' to attend to business matters and not priming him on what he needs to know, destroys all credibility. Without it the piece is not so much humorous as just plain silly. MS

▶ Jens Albinus, Peter Gantzler, Fridrik Thór Fridriksson, Iben Hjejle, Sofie Gråbøl
▶ *Dir* and *Screenplay* Lars von Trier, *Pro* Meta Louise Foldager, Signe Jensen and Vibeke Windeløv, *Ph* 'Automavision', *Ed* Molly Marlene Stensgard, *Costumes* Manon Rasmussen.

Zentropa Entertainments21 ApS/Memfis Film International AB/Slot Machine Sarl/Lucky Red Sri etc-Diffusion Pictures Ltd.
99 mins. Denmark/Sweden/France/Italy/Germany.
2006. Rel: 29 Feb 2008. Cert 15.

Bosta [The Bus] ★★★½

This is a little charmer from Lebanon made a couple of years ago by Philippe Aractingi, the director of *Under the Bombs* and starring

➤ Matt Damon, Julia Stiles, David Strathairn, Scott Glenn, Paddy Considine, Albert Finney, Joan Allen.
➤ *Dir* Paul Greengrass, *Pro* Patrick Crowley and Frank Marshall, *Screenplay* Tony Gilroy, Scott Z Burns and George Nolfi, based on Robert Ludlum's novel, *Ph* Oliver Wood, *Pro Des* Peter Wenham, *Ed* Christopher Rouse, *M* John Powell, *Costumes* Shay Cunliffe.

Universal Pictures/Motion Picture Beta Produktionsgesellschaft/The Kennedy/ Marshall Company/Ludlum Entertainment-Universal Pictures.
115 mins. USA/Germany. 2007. Rel: 17 Aug 2007. Cert 12A.

Bratz: The Movie ★

Based on the popular fashion dolls, this dreadful teen comedy is one of the worst films of its year. Nathalia Ramos, Janel Parrish, Logan Browning and Skyler Shaye do their weary best as 'Best Friends Forever' Yasmin, Jade, Sasha and Cloe, who fight back when the school principal's bossy daughter tries to split them up into separate social cliques. It wants to be *Mean Girls*, but it hasn't got the style or witty script, while Jon Voight has his most rotten role ever as Principal Dimly. Paula Abdul found she was fired as the movie's executive producer, fashion designer and dance choreographer via an e-mail on her Blackberry during an episode of her reality TV series *Hey, Paula*. DW

➤ Logan Browning, Janet Parrish, Nathalia Ramos, Skyler Shay, Chelsea Staub, Jon Voight, Emily Everhard.
➤ *Dir* Sean McNamara, *Pro* Avi Arad, Isaac Larian and Steven Paul, *Screenplay* Susan Estelle Jansen, based on the story by Adam De La Pena and David Eilenberg, *Ph* Christian Sebaldt, *Pro Des* Rusty Smith, *Ed* Jeff Canavan, *M* John Coda, *Costumes* Bernadene Morgan.

Avi Arad & Associates/Crystal Sky Pictures/MGA Entertainment-Momentum Pictures.
110 mins. USA. 2007. Rel: 18 Aug 2007. Cert PG.

The Brave One ★★★½

New York; today. Erica Bain has it all: a top job as a radio host, a fiancé she adores and a future to look forward to. Then out of nowhere a brutal attack leaves her badly wounded and her fiancé dead. Her life in ruins, Erica decides to take the law into her own hands… Essentially *Death Wish* with a feminist twist, *The Brave One* is a morally dubious vigilante thriller. But it is extraordinarily gripping and extremely well made, while Terrence Howard and Jodie Foster – as hunter and hunted – humanise their roles with expertise. JC-W

➤ Jodie Foster, Terrence Howard, Nicky Katt, Naveen Andrews, Mary Steenburgen.
➤ *Dir* Neil Jordan, *Pro* Susan Downey and Joel Silver, *Screenplay* Roderick Taylor, Bruce A Taylor and Cynthia Mort, *Ph* Philippe Rousselot, *Pro Des* Kristi Zea, *Ed* Tony Lawson, *M* Dario Marianelli, *Costumes* Catherine Thomas.

Redemption Pictures/Silver Pictures/ Village Roadshow Pictures/ WV Films III-Warner Bros.
122 mins. USA/Australia. 2007. Rel: 28 Sep 2007. Cert 18.

Breach ★★★

It's the same old story: a film based on fact which incorporates characters and events fictionalised for dramatic purposes. As a reflection of CIA methods, this tale of an agent in training (Ryan Phillippe) required to check out secretly a senior man (Chris Cooper) suspected of being a double agent could have been gripping. There's novelty too in the emphasis on the Catholic beliefs of both men and Cooper is especially good. However, the facts (or more probably the inventions) are too often clichéd and unconvincing. The promise of the first half is not maintained. MS

Matt Damon in *The Bourne Ultimamtum*.

Brick Lane: Tannishtha Chatterjee adjusts to life in London.

▶ Chris Cooper, Ryan Phillippe, Laura Linney, Dennis Haysbert, Caroline Dhavernas.
▶ *Dir* Billy Ray, *Pro* Bobby Newmyer, Scott Strauss and Scott Kroopf, *Screenplay* Adam Mazer. William Rotko and Ray from the story by Mazer and Rotko, *Ph* Tak Fujimoto, *Pro Des* Wynn Thomas, *Ed* Jeffrey Ford, *M* Mychael Danna, *Costumes* Luis Sequeira.

Universal Pictures/SKE/Outlaw/Intermedia/Sidney Kummel Entertainment-20th Century Fox International (UK).
110 mins. USA 2006. Rel: 31 Aug 2007. Cert 12A.

Brick Lane ★★★½

This sympathetic adaptation of Monica Ali's popular novel concentrates on London's East End in 2001. Not without echoes of *Brief Encounter*, a married woman (here someone who had been married off in Bangladesh aged 17) falls for another man. He's younger and far more politicised than her traditionalist husband. The 'Scope format reduces intimacy and the flashbacks are over-romanticised but there's much that appeals, not least the acting by Tannishtha Chatterjee as the heroine and by Satish Kaushik as the husband. MS

▶ Tannishtha Chatterjee, Satish Kaushik, Christopher Simpson, Naeema Begum.

▶ *Dir* Sarah Gavron, *Pro* Alison Owen and Christopher Collins, *Screenplay* Abi Morgan and Laura Jones from the novel by Monica Ali, *Ph* Robbie Ryan, *Pro Des* Simon Elliott, *Ed* Melanie Oliver, *M* Jocelyn Pook, *Costumes* Michael O'Connor.

Film4/Ingeniouis Film Partners/UK Film Council/ Ruby Films etc-Optimum Releasing.
102 mins. UK. 2007. Rel: 16 Nov 2007. Cert 15.

The Brothers Solomon ★★

Two dumb brothers (Will Arnett and Will Forte), who have been brought up in isolation in the Arctic, try to carry out their father's dying wish to be a grandfather. What to do? Well, find somebody to have their baby, and where's that then? On the internet, of course. They try with would-be hilarious results, if only the situation and screenplay (by Forte) were better. Pretty average comedy for those times when you couldn't care less. CB

▶ Will Arnett, Will Forte, Chi McBride, Kristen Wiig, Lee Majors, Michael Ormsby, Bruce Green.
▶ *Dir* Bob Odenkirk, *Pro* Matt Berenson and Tom Werner, *Screenplay* Will Forte, *Ph* Tim Suhrstedt, *Pro Des* John Paino, *Ed* Tracey Wadmore-Smth, *M* John Swihart, *Costumes* Melina Root.

Carsey-Werner Company/Revolution Studios-Sony Pictures Releasing.
93 mins. USA. 2007. Rel: 2 Nov 2007. Cert 15.

The Bucket List ★★½

There's the undeniable pleasure here of watching the work of two fine actors, Jack Nicholson and Morgan Freeman. The concept, however, is a dud since the film tries to be a feelgood movie about two men dying of cancer. The hospital scenes can't conceal the depressing side of the story, despite the humour, while the bucket list – a shared rota of things to do before they die – yields scenes of utter absurdity plus a dollop of sentimentality. Memo to Jack and Morgan: making this film should not have been on your bucket list because you're too good for it. MS

▶ Jack Nicholson, Morgan Freeman, Sean Hayes, Beverly Todd, Rowena King.
▶ *Dir* Rob Reiner, *Pro* Craig Zadan, Neil Meron, Alan Greisman and Reiner, *Screenplay* Justin Zackham, *Ph* John Schwartzman, *Pro Des* Bill Brzeski, *Ed* Robert Leighton, *M* Marc Shaiman, *Costumes* Molly Maginnis.

Warner Bros Pictures/Two Ton Films-Warner Bros Distributors (UK).
97 mins. USA. 2007. Rel: 15 Feb 2008 Cert 12A.

Bug ★

William Friedkin, no less, saw Tracy Letts' play and hired him to rewrite it as a film. It sounds like a horror outing, but the genre here is instead filmed theatre. Damaged goods Ashley Judd and deranged beau Michael Shannon talk about, get bitten by and observe bugs under a microscope, but the camera never sees the insects – violating the basic Show Don't Tell rule of filmmaking. A great stage play maybe, but it's lousy cinema. JC

▶ Ashley Judd, Michael Shannon, Harry Connick Jr, Lynn Collins, Brian F O'Byrne.
▶ *Dir* William Friedkin, *Pro* Kimberley C Anderson, Michael Burns, Gary Huckaby, Malcolm Petal, Andrea S Schardt and Holly Wiersma, *Screenplay* Tracy Letts, based on his own play, *Ph* Michael Grady, *Pro Des* Franco Carbone, *Ed* Darrin Navarro, *M* Bryan Tyler, *Costumes* Peggy Schnitzer.

Holly Wiersma Productions/Lionsgate Films/Lift Production/Inferno Distribution-Lionsgate.
102 mins. USA. 2006. Rel: 9 Nov 2007. Cert 18.

Bunny Chow ★★½

This uninspired improvised comedy from South Africa may be a matter of taste but its trite story-line – friends including a would-be comic journey to a rock festival – is matched by feeble dialogue. It's certainly a macho male movie and for some it may seem uproarious, especially if viewed at home on DVD with plenty of cans of beer to hand. MS

▶ David Kibuuka, Kim Engelbrecht, Kagiso Lediga, Joey Rasdien, Keren Neumann.
▶ *Dir* John Barker, *Pro* Kagiso Lediga, Isaac Kaminsky and Leanne Callanan, *Screenplay* Barker and David Kibuuka from a story by them and by Joey Rasdien and Salah Sabiti, *Ph* Zeno Petersen, *Ed* Saki Bergh, *M* Joel Assaizky.

MTV Films Europe & Dog Pack, dv8 films etc-Dogwoof Pictures.
92 mins. South Africa/Sweden. 2006. Rel: 21 March 2008. Cert 12A.

Buy It Now ★★★½

New York newcomer Antonio G Campos has created for critics a unique problem of assessment. *Buy It Now* was originally a brilliant short film but is now yoked to a boring video diary covering the same material with the same actors. The subject is a 16 year old girl's attempt to sell her virginity on eBay to the highest bidder. In the award-winning segment the unease and pathos of the resulting encounter are most subtly conveyed. The dud piece at least makes for a fascinating contrast in approach, while together this offering provides ideal material for discussion in classes where filmmaking is taught. MS

▶ Chelsea Logan, Chris McCann, Rosemarie DeWitt, Tiffany Yaraghi.
▶ *Dir*, *Pro*, *Ed* and *Sceenplay* Antonio G. Campos, *Ph* T Sean Durkin.

Borderline Films/Young Indies-Dogwoof Pictures.
62 mins. USA. 2004. Rel: 20 July 2007. Cert 15.

California Dreamin' (Endless) ★★★

Within this massively over-long Romanian feature, there's a fine film trying to get out. It tells of an engaging rogue of a station master who in 1999 holds up a train headed for Kosovo with American marines on board while awaiting proper papers of transit. Echoing the Czech films of Milos Forman, Ealing comedy (*Passport to Pimlico*) and even Will Hay's *Oh, Mr Porter!*, it tops the lot with a serious attack on American policy abroad. Had the director Cristian Nemescu not died in a car crash, he might have edited it drastically and, sadly, at least an hour needs to go. MS

There's trouble ahead for Emilia Fox and Sean Biggerstaff in *Cashback*.

➤ Armand Assante, Razvan Vasilescu, Jamie Elman, Maria Dinulescu, Alex Margineanu, Ion Sapdaru.
➤ *Dir* Cristian Nemescu, *Pro* Andret Boncea, *Screenplay* Nemescu and Tudor Voican with Catherine Linstrum, *Ph* Liviu Marghidan, *Pro Des* Ioana Corciova, *Ed* Catalin Cristutiu, *Costumes* Ana Ioneci.

MediaPro Pictures/Centrului National al Cinematografiei-Artificial Eye.
154 mins. Romania. 2007. Rel: 30 May. 2008. Cert 15.

Captain Eager and the Mark of Voth ★

This is a strange sort of sub-Flash Gordon spoof that is remarkable only for its thorough ineptitude. Obviously shot on a low budget (or no budget at all) it tries to send up 1950s comic heroes such as Dan Dare with no humour to speak of and absolutely no imagination whatsoever. How Tamsin Greig wandered into this one is beyond belief and what it was doing at the ICA is totally mystifying. MHD

➤ Alexander Andrew, Lindsay Carr, Steve Clark, Tamsin Greig, James Vaughan, Russell Grant.
➤ *Dir and Screenplay* Simon Davison, *Pro* Rebecca Bazzard, *Ph* Martin Hill, *Pro Des* Damien Creagh, *M* Simon Davison, *Costumes* Michelle Barret.

Imperious Films-ICA.
95 mins. UK. 2008. Rel: 18 Apr 2008. Cert PG

Caramel ★★

One sympathises with Nadine Labaki's wish to make a contemporary film set in her native

Beirut that is not linked to war and violence. Unfortunately, despite good intentions, her mix of tales centred on a beauty salon emerges as soap opera at best, the characters lack depth and the tone pitched between comedy and drama is precarious. Well meant but vacuous. MS

➤ Nadine Labaki, Yasmine Al Masri, Joanna Moukarzel, Gisèle Aouad, Adel Karam.
➤ *Dir* Nadine Labaki, *Pro* Anne-Dominique Toussaint, *Screenplay* Labaki, Jihad Hojeily and Rodney Al Haddad, *Ph* Yves Sehnaoui, *Art Dir* Cynthia Zahar, *Ed* Laure Gardette, *M* Khaled Mouzanar, *Costumes* Caroline Labaki.

Les Films des Tournelles/Les Films de Beyrouth/Roissy Films/Sunnyland/Arte France Cinéma co-production etc-Momentum Pictures.
96 mins. France/Lebanon. 2007. Rel: 16 May 2008. Cert PG.

Cashback ★★½

Credit the adventurous director (Sean Ellis) but not the inept writer (also Sean Ellis). Extended from a short film, this take on teenage boys and their problems over girls and dull jobs is all over the place. There's a subplot about being able to stop time and a sub-subplot about football. Sean Biggerstaff is an engaging, good-looking hero, but Ellis might be better advised not to write his own films in future. MS

➤ Sean Biggerstaff, Emilia Fox, Shaun Evans, Michelle Ryan, Stuart Goodwin.
➤ *Dir* and *Screenplay* Sean Ellis, *Pro* Ellis and Lene Bausager, *Ph* Angus Hudson, *Pro Des* Morgan

Kennedy, *Ed* Scott Thomas and Carlos Domeque, *M* Guy Farley, *Costumes* Vicki Russell.

Left Turn Films in association with Daphne Guinness etc-The Works UK Distribution Ltd.
102 mins. UK. 2005. Rel: 9 May 2008. Cert 15.

Cassandra's Dream ★★½

Woody Allen's latest London film is, like *Match Point*, something of a thriller but this one is more of a moral drama as two brothers (Ewan McGregor and Colin Farrell) have to decide how far they are prepared to go for money desperately needed. Sidney Lumet pulled off this kind of piece brilliantly in *Before the Devil Knows You're Dead* (qv) but comparisons underline the sheer unlikelihood of Allen's plotting and he has a cloth ear for English speech. The two lead actors are good but it's sad to see a once great filmmaker floundering. MS

▶ Ewan McGregor, Colin Farrell, Hayley Atwell, Sally Hawkins, Tom Wilkinson, Phil Davis, Clare Higgins.
▶ *Dir* and *Screenplay* Woody Allen, *Pro* Letty Aronson, Stephen Tenenbaum and Gareth Wiley, *Ph* Vilmos Zsigmond, *Pro Des* Maria Djurkovic, *Ed* Alisa Lepselter, *M* Philip Glass, *Costumes* Jill Taylor.

Wild Bunch/An Iberville production etc-Optimum Releasing.
108 mins. UK/France. 2007. Rel: 23 May 2008. Cert 12A.

Change of Address ★★½

With occasional dialogue exchanges that could come from a *Carry On* comedy, this rom-com scuppers France's reputation for sexual sophistication. Described as a *fantasie amoureuse*, this is really an undistinguished tale of a young man, two girls and a stranger who may or may not deprive the youngster of the girl he has chosen. Passably acted though it is, the players can't make the behaviour of the characters seem other than silly. Very routine fare. MS

▶ Fanny Valette, Frédérique Bel, Emmanuel Mouret, Dany Brillant, Ariane Ascaride.
▶ *Dir* and *Screenplay* Emmanuel Mouret, *Pro* Frédéric Niedermayer, *Ph* Laurent Desmet, *Art Dir* David Faivre, *Ed* Martial Salomon, *M* Franck Sforza.

Moby Dick Films/Sofica Soficinéma/K-Films Amérique etc-Cinefile World.
85 mins. France/Canada. 2006. Rel: 30 May 2008. Cert 12A.

Les Chansons d'Amour ★★½

Paris is the place, relationships the theme but Christophe Honoré's musical (thirteen songs) is but a pale echo of Jacques Demy's 1964 masterpiece *The Umbrellas of Cherbourg*. From that film it borrows a three-part structure labelled *The Departure*, *The Absence* and *The Return* respectively. Alex Beaupain's numbers here are not a patch on Michel Legrand's score and we are never drawn in emotionally. However, Grégoire Leprince-Rinquet does well as a young gay man visiting Paris. MS

▶ Louis Garrel, Ludivine Sagnier, Chiara Mastroianni, Clotilde Hesme, Grégoire Leprince-Rinquet, Brigitte Roüan.

Louis Garrel and Clotilde Hesme make beautiful music in *Les Chansons d'Amour*.

▶ *Dir* and *Screenplay* Christophe Honoré, *Pro* Paulo Branco, *Ph* Rémy Chevrin, *Art Dir* Samuel Deshors, *Ed* Chantal Hymans, *M* Alex Beaupain, *Costumes* Pierre Canitrot.

Alma Films/Flach films etc-Artificial Eye Film Company. 96 mins. France. 2007. Rel: 14 Dec 2007. Cert 15.

Charlie Bartlett ★★½

The story of a young rich rebel (the talented but miscast Anton Yelchin) who wins the favour of his peers by dealing drugs, this film switches uneasily between comedy and drama and lacks both a clear viewpoint and at key moments credibility. There's good work from Hope Davis (mother) and Robert Downey Jr (school principal). But it's nowhere near as good as the much underrated 2005 film *The Chumscrubber*. MS

▶ Anton Yelchin, Hope Davis, Robert Downey Jr, Kat Dennings.
▶ *Dir* Jon Poll, *Pro* David Permut, Barron Kidd, Jay Roach and Sidney Kimmel, *Screenplay* Gustin Nash, *Ph* Paul Sarossy, *Pro Des* Tamara Deverell, *Ed* Alan Baumgarten, *M* Christophe Beck, *Costumes* Luis Sequeira.

Metro-Goldwyn-Mayer Pictures/Sidney Kimmel Entertainment/An Everyman Pictures, Texon Entertainment. Permut Presentations production etc-Verve Pictures. 96 mins. USA. 2007. Rel: 16 May 2008. Cert 15.

Charlie Wilson's War ★★★½

Charlie Wilson is a Member of the US House of Representatives, acting for the 2nd congressional district in Texas. He is also a whisky-quaffing, skirt-chasing hedonist who isn't above a bit of opportunistic adultery. Then he hears about the Russian invasion of Afghanistan and decides to pull some well-oiled strings to defuse the Cold War. Based on the book of the same name by CBS journalist George Crile, Mike Nichols' film is nothing short of extraordinary. Well-written and often very funny, it never ceases to beguile, although it's too much of a caricature to be taken seriously. However, Philip Seymour Hoffman is sublime. JC-W

▶ Tom Hanks, Amy Adams, Julia Roberts, Philip Seymour Hoffman, Emily Blunt, Ken Stott, Om Puri, Ned Beatty.
▶ *Dir* Mike Nichols, *Pro* Tom Hanks and Gary Goetzman, *Screenplay* Aaron Sorkin from the book by George Crile, *Ph* Stephen Goldblatt, *Pro Des* Victor Kempster, *Ed* John Bloom and Antonia Van Drimmelen, *M* James Newton Howard, *Costumes* Albert Wolsky.
Universal Pictures/Good Time Charlie Productions/

Playtone/Relativity Media/Participant Productions-Universal Pictures. 102 mins. USA. 2007. Rel: 11 Jan 2008. Cert 15.

Chemical Wedding ★½

With quantum physics hailed as the new alchemy, a Cambridge University techie converts black magic ceremonies into a series of digital equations. The result is that stuttering classics lecturer Dr Haddo (Simon Callow) is reincarnated into an evil form of the late occultist Aleister Crowley. An audacious attempt to meld fact and science with the milieu of Dennis Wheatley, *Chemical Wedding* blunders into high camp. Simon Callow enjoys himself enormously – at the expense of any shred of suspense or credibility. JC-W

▶ Simon Callow, Kal Weber, Lucy Cudden, Jud Charlton, Paul McDowell, John Shrapnel.
▶ *Dir* Julian Doyle, *Pro* Malcolm Kohll, Benjamin Timlett and Justin Peyton, *Screenplay* Doyle and Bruce Dickinson, *Ph* Brian Herlihy, *Pro Des* Mark Tanner, *Ed* Bill Jones, *M* André Jacquemin, *Costumes* Tabitha Doyle.

Focus Films/Bill and Ben Productions/Entertainment Motion Pictures-Warner Bros. 106 mins. USA. 2008. Rel: 30 May 2008. Cert 18.

Children of Glory ★★½

This Hungarian film portrays the ill-fated Hungarian Uprising of 1956 and its suppression by the Soviet Army. Such material calls for a director of the calibre of a Louis Malle or an Andrzej Wajda but gets Krisztina Goda whose previous film was *Just Sex and Nothing Else* and a script in which Joe Eszterhas had a hand. Technically adept, the piece is sadly superficial and cliché-ridden and never comes close to doing justice to its subject. MS

▶ Iván Fenyö, Kata Dobó, Sándor Csányi, Károly Gesztesi, Viktória Szávai.
▶ *Dir* Krisztina Goda, *Pro* Andrew G. Vajna, *Screenplay* Joe Eszterhas from his story with Éva Gárdos, Géza Bereményi and Réka Divinyi, *Ph* Buda Gulyás and János Vecsernyés, *Pro Des* János Szabolcs, *Ed* Gárdos and Annamária Komlóssy, *M* Nick Glennie-Smith, *Costumes* Beatrix Aruna Pásztor.

A BIBS Kft (Budapest)/Flashback Kft (Budapest)/Film and General Productions Ltd (London) co-production etc-Lionsgate UK. 120 mins. Hungary/UK. 2006. Rel: 14 March 2008. Cert 15.

Chromophobia ★★½

Weird, overlong study of a family falling apart,

with Damian Lewis married to bored housewife (Scott Thomas) who is losing her marbles, with a son who has a gay godfather (Fiennes) and who may need a shrink, a father (Holm) who gets his jollies from a prostitute (Cruz), whose social worker (Ifans) is on her case. Throw in an investigative journalist (Chaplin) on the make and you still have a very unsatisfactory film. London looks good but it's not enough to save the film from all the psychobabble. File under 'Tosh'. MHD

▷ Ben Chaplin, Penelope Cruz, Ralph Fiennes, Ian Holm, Rhys Ifans, Damian Lewis, Kristin Scott Thomas, Harriet Walter, Anthony Higgins.
▷ *Dir & Screenplay* Martha Fiennes, *Pro* Tarak Ben Ammar and Ron Rotholz, *Ph* George Tiffin, *Pro Des* Tony Burrough, *Ed* Tracy Granger, *M* Magnus Fiennes, *Costumes* Michele Clapton.

Isle of Man Film Commission/Quinta Communications/ Rotholz Pictures-Momentum Pictures.
136 mins. UK/France/USA. 2005. Rel: 14 Dec 2007. Cert 15.

The Chronicles of Narnia: Prince Caspian ★★★½

No concessions are made to those who missed the first instalment as we plunge into this resumption of the tale as the Pevensie children return to Narnia. Their task is to save that world from the ruling Telmarines led by the evil Miraz usurper of his nephew Prince Caspian. Andrew Adamson directs with gusto, merging all the elements with confidence but it is too long and the Christian parallels dealing with questions of faith lose their potency when the equivalent of the Second Coming saves the day. But, even allowing for weaknesses, the film delivers the goods as spectacle that effortlessly encompasses both talking animals and mass battle scenes. MS

▷ Ben Barnes, Georgie Henley, Skandar Keynes, William Moseley, Anna Popplewell, Peter Dinklage, Warwick Davis, Sergio Castellitto, Tilda Swinton, Liam Neeson.
▷ *Dir* Andrew Adamson, *Pro* Mark Johnson, Adamson and Philip Steuer, *Screenplay* Adamson, Christopher Markus and Stephen McFeely based on C S Lewis's book, *Ph* Karl Walter Lindenlaub, *Pro Des* Roger Ford, *Ed* Sim Evan-Jones, *M* Harry Gregson-Williams, *Costumes* Isis Mussenden, *Special Effects Supervisor* Gerd Feuchter.

Walt Disney Pictures/Walden Media/A Mark Johnson/Silverbell Films production etc-Buena Vista International (UK).
144 mins. USA. 2008. Rel: 26 June 2008. Cert PG.

Ben Barnes (centre) fights the good fight in *The Chronicles of Narnia: Prince Caspian.*

Michael Stahl-David, Lizzy Caplan and Jessica Lucas in *Cloverfield*.

Closing the Ring ★★★★

This is a love story, the narrative being one that covers events during the Second World War and also in the 1990s. At its centre are to be found the death of an American airman near Belfast in 1943 and the lifelong grief of the girl who had loved him. Popular romantic drama rarely wins critical plaudits and this example goes to extremes in tying up the story. Nevertheless, it works – not just because of fine performances (ranging from veteran Shirley MacLaine to newcomer Martin McCann) but on account of the total belief in this work communicated by its director Richard Attenborough. MS

▶ Shirley MacLaine, Christopher Plummer, Pete Postlethwaite, Martin McCann, Brenda Fricker, Mischa Barton.
▶ *Dir* Richard Attenborough, *Pro* Jo Gilbert and Attenborough, *Screenplay* Peter Woodward, *Ph* Roger Pratt, *Pro Des* Tom McCullagh, *Ed* Lesley Walker, *M* Jeff Danna, *Costumes* Hazel Webb-Crozier.

UK Film Council/Northern Ireland Film and Television Film Commission/Motion Picture Distribution LP/Jo Gilbert/ContentFilm/CTR Films/Prospero Pictures/Scion Films etc-The Works UK Distribution Ltd. 118 mins. UK/Canada. 2006. Rel: 28 Dec 2007. Cert 12A.

Cloverfield ★★★★

Matt Reeves' monster movie is an impressive response to the tragedy of 9/11. Just as the original *Godzilla* film was a reflection of the US bombing of Japan, so too is the giant beast in *Cloverfield* a parallel disaster that brings Manhattan to its knees. Shot in a pseudo-documentary style, with first person point of view, hand-held camera, it really captures the fear of the population having to deal with the unknown in the form of a behemoth with the ability to destroy everything in its wake. Using an unknown cast adds to the heightened reality of the film which at times is a truly scary experience. MHD

▶ Lizzy Caplan, Jessica Lucas, T J Miller, Michael Stahl-David, Mike Vogel, Odette Yustman.
▶ *Dir* Matt Reeves, *Pro* JJ Abrams and Bryan Burk, *Screenplay* Drew Goddard, *Ph* Michael Bonvillain, *Pro Des* Martin Whist, *Ed* Kevin Stitt, *M* various soundtracks, *Costumes* Ellen Mirojnick.

Paramount Pictures/Bad Robot-Paramount Pictures. 85 mins. USA. 2008. Rel: 1 Feb 2008. Cert 15.

Clubland ★★

Brenda Blethyn plays an English stand-up comic living in Australia, separated from her husband and possessive of her elder son. She is weighed down by a younger child who is brain damaged and is trying desperately to keep her career going. You can understand Blethyn (who is fine) being drawn to such a central role, but the

film swings wildly between comedy and drama. Worst of all there's a volte-face ending that tries to persuade us that this mother from hell could be lovable after all! MS

▶ Brenda Blethyn, Khan Chittenden, Emma Booth, Richard Wilson, Frankie J Holden.
▶ *Dir* Cherie Nowlan, *Pro* Rosemary Blight, *Screenplay* Keith Thompson, *Ph* Mark Wareham, *Pro Des* Neil Hanson, *Ed* Scott Gray, *M* Martin Armiger, *Costumes* Emily Seresin.

Warner Independent Pictures/Film Finance Corporation Australia/RB Films production etc-Warner Bros Distributors (UK).
105 mins. Australia. 2006. Rel: 21 Sept 2007. Cert 15.

Cocaine Cowboys ★★★½

This documentary is visually better suited to the small screen than to the cinema, but it tells the fascinating story of how Miami prospered as a centre for drug dealers. As rivals slug it out using bullets rather than fists, it's not a pretty affair. But if the cocaine wars of the early 1980s frightened tourists away, the criminal presence transformed the city's economy. A disturbing, intriguing true history. MS

▶ With Jon Roberts, Mickey Munday, Jorge 'Rivi' Ayala, Al Sunshine.
▶ *Dir* Billy Corben, *Pro* Alfred Spellman and Corben, *Ph* Armando Salas, *Ed* Corben and David Cypkin, *M* Jan Hammer and Eric Ransom.

Rakontur-Slingshot.
118 mins. USA. 2005. Rel: 23 Nov 2007. Cert 18.

Code Name: The Cleaner ★★

An incredibly broad, brain-in-neutral spy comedy starring Cedric the Entertainer as Jake, who, after waking up with memory loss, a gash on the head and a dead FBI agent in his hotel room, has to go on the run and becomes convinced he's an undercover agent. With a silly script that feels like the actors are making up their own dialogue as they go along and slapdash direction and pacing, it all depends on how much you like Cedric. Luckily, he is quite charming and entertaining, as his name implies – raising some decent laughs even in a daft romp like this. Lucy Liu is lost as Jake's girlfriend but Nicollette Sheridan is worse off as the femme fatale: she was nominated for a Razzie as worst supporting actress. DW

▶ Cedric the Entertainer, Lucy Liu, Nicollette Sheridan, Mark Dacascos, Callum Keith Rennie.
▶ *Dir* Les Mayfield, *Pro* Cedric the Entertainer, Brett Ratner, Jay Stern and Eric Rhone, *Screenplay* Robert

Adetuyi and George Gallo, *Ph* David Franco, *Pro Des* Douglas Higgins, *Ed* Michael Matzdorff, *M* George S Clinton, *Costumes* Jenny Gullet.

New Line Cinema/Bird and Bear Entertainment/Cleaner Films/Film Engine/Rat Entertainment-Verve Pictures.
84 mins. USA. 2007. Rel: 7 Dec 2007. Cert PG.

A Comedy of Power ★★★★

Don't be misled by the English translation of the title *L'Ivresse du pouvoir*: this is not a comedy and nor is it characteristic of its director, Claude Chabrol. It's a drama close to real-life events about the efforts of a French judge played by Isabelle Huppert to tackle fraud and misuse of funds by big corporations. It's able without being memorable, save for its central performance which is one of Huppert's best. MS

▶ Isabelle Huppert, Thomas Chabrol, François Berléand, Patrick Bruel.
▶ *Dir* Claude Chabrol, *Pro* Patrick Godeau, *Screenplay* Odile Barski and Chabrol, *Ph* Eduardo Serra, *Art Dir* Françoise Benoît-Fresco, *Ed* Monique Fardoulis, *M* Matthieu Chabrol, *Costumes* Mic Cheminal.

Alicéleo/France 2 Cinéma/Ajoz Films/Integral Film etc-ICA Films.
110 mins. France/Germany. 2005. Rel: 14 Dec 2007. Cert PG.

A Complete History of My Sexual Failures ★★★½

Here's a novel documentary: filmmaker Chris Waitt looks up the women once part of his life to contemplate where he went wrong. You can't help wondering how much of the footage has been rigged and the film is a bit shapeless, but Chris is no show-off and his problems will find young audiences caught between laughter and sympathetic identification. What's more the appeal could well be for males and females alike. MS

▶ With Chris Waitt, Martyn Waitt, Hilary Waitt, Vicky, Janet, Julia, Charlie.
▶ *Dir* Chris Waitt, *Pro* Mary Burke, Henry Trotter, Robin Gutch and Mark Herbert, *Ph* Steven Mochrie, *Ed* Chris Dickens and Mark Atkins.

A Warp X production for Film4, UK Film Council, EM Media and Screen Yorkshire etc-Optimum Releasing.
93 mins. UK. 2007. Rel: 27 June 2008. Cert 18.

Control ★★★½

Much more than a pop music film, this study of the sadly short life of Ian Curtis, lead singer

The outstanding Sam Riley with Alexandra Maria Lara in *Control*.

of Joy Division, is at heart a sensitive study of troubled relationships. Atmospherically photographed in black and white, it echoes 1960s features such as *A Kind of Loving* (1962) and has a tragic, romantic triangle at its centre. At two hours plus it comes to seem overlong, but it's superbly played by Samantha Morton (domesticated wife), Alexandra Maria Lara (foreign mistress) and Sam Riley. The latter as Ian Curtis is a newcomer who is beyond question outstanding. MS

▶ Sam Riley, Samantha Morton, Alexandra Maria Lara, Toby Kebbell, Joe Anderson.
▶ *Dir* Anton Corbijn, *Pro* Orian Williams, Corbijn and Todd Eckert, *Screenplay* Matt Greenhalgh based on Deborah Curtis's book *Touching From a Distance*, *Ph* Martin Ruhe, *Pro Des* Chris Roope, *Ed* Andrew Hulme, *M Score* New Order, *Costume* Julian Day.

A Northsee Ltd production in association with EM Media, Warner Music UK Ltd, IFF/CINV and Three Dogs and a Pony etc-Momentum Pictures. 122 mins. UK/Japan/Australia. 2007. Rel: 5 Oct 2007. Cert 15.

Copying Beethoven ★★★

Ed Harris is Beethoven! In fact this adept actor makes that far more convincing than you might expect and Agnieszka Holland directs decently. However, to pretend (there's no truth in it at all) that Beethoven had a female copyist, a would-be composer who helped him to improve his own compositions, is a pointless fiction. Musically, though, the extracts heard are adventurously offbeat even if the big set piece is a Reader's Digest version of the Choral Symphony! MS

▶ Ed Harris, Diane Krüger, Matthew Goode, Joe Anderson, Phyllida Law.
▶ *Dir* Agnieszka Holland, *Pro* Sidney Kimmel, Michael Taylor, Stephen J. Rivele and Christopher Wilkinson, *Screenplay* Rivele and Wilkinson, *Ph* Ashley Rowe, *Pro Des* Caroline Amies, *Ed* Alex Mackie, *M* Antonie Lazakiewicz and Beethoven *Costumes* Jany Temime.

A Copying Beethoven Ltd (UK), Eurofilm Stúdió, KFT (Hungary) co-production etc-Verve Pictures. 104 mins. Germany/UK/Hungary/USA. 2005. Rel: 17 Aug 2007. Cert 12A.

The Cottage ★★★★

Absurdly underestimated by many critics, this rollercoaster of a movie confirms the cinematic flair of Paul Andrew Williams first evidenced in *London to Brighton*. Set in the English countryside, it starts with a botched kidnapping and segues into a fully-fledged horror film featuring a maniac killer. The balance between tongue-in-cheek humour and genuine shocks, splendidly caught in Laura Rossi's music score,

echoes that classic, *An American Werewolf in London* (1981). MS

▶ Andy Serkis, Reece Shearsmith, Steven O'Donnell, Jennifer Ellison, Dave Legeno.
▶ *Dir* and *Screenplay* Paul Andrew Williams, *Pro* Ken Marshall and Martin Pope, *Ph* Christopher Ross, *Pro Des* Crispian Sallis, *Ed* Tom Hemmings, *M* Laura Rossi, *Costumes* Marianne Agertoft.

Isle of Man, UK Film Council and Screen Yorkshire present a Steel Mill Pictures production-Pathé Distribution.
92 mins. UK. 2008. Rel: 14 March 2008. Cert 18.

The Counterfeiters ★★★½

It's World War II again, but the story, a true one, told in this film from Germany is fresh. The central figure is a Jewish forger who, brought to a concentration camp, is given special treatment. He is required to forge pound notes and dollars for Nazi use – an arrangement that may preserve the lives of himself and his colleagues but would also be helpful to their oppressors. It's well acted and intriguing but let down by the director's fondness for frequent unnecessarily obtrusive camera movements. (Original title: *Die Fälscher*) MS

▶ Karl Markovics, August Diehl, Devid Striesow, Martin Brambach, Veit Stübner.

▶ *Dir* and *Screenplay* Stefan Ruzowitzky based on the book *The Devil's Workshop* by Adolf Burger, *Pro* Josef Aichholzer, Nina Bohlmann and Babette Schröder, *Ph* Benedict Neuenfels, *Pro Des* Isidor Wimmer, *Ed* Britta Nahler, *M* Marius Ruhland, *Costumes* Nicole Fischnaller.

An Aichholzer film and magnolia Filmproduktion etc-Metrodome Distribution Ltd.
99 mins. Germany/Austria/France. 2006. Rel: 12 Oct 2007. Cert 15.

Couscous ★★★½

This story of an extensive Franco-Arab family living in the French port of Sète comes to concentrate on a plan to open a harbour restaurant where couscous features on the menu. Echoing the Pagnol trilogy of the 1930s and more recent films by Robert Guédiguian, there's a lot to like here and even more that wins our sympathy. However, it's all too easy to become bemused by the large cast of characters and it's another overlong film that drags towards the close, despite being quite excellent in patches. (Original title: *La graine et le mulet*) MS

▶ Habib Boufares, Hafsia Herzi, Marzouk Bouraoucea, Faridah Benkhetache.
▶ *Dir* Abdellatif Kechiche, *Pro* Claude Berri, *Screenplay* Kechiche with Ghalya Lacroix, *Ph* Lubomir Bakchev, *Pro Des* Benoît Barouh,

The Cottage: grisly times for Reece Shearsmith, Jennifer Ellison and Andy Serkis.

Ed Camille Toubkis and Lacroix, *Costumes* Maria Beloso Hall.

Claude Berri presents a Hirsch/Pathé Renn Production, France 2 Cinéma co-production /Canal+/CinéCinéma etc-Artificial Eye Film Company.
154 mins. France. 2007. Rel: 20 June 2008. Cert 15.

A Crude Awakening: The Oil Crash ★★★★

Michael Moore isn't involved in this one: in fact it's a decidedly serious-minded, scholarly documentary and a good one. This history of our need for oil looks back with memorable historical footage, investigates the present in which the need for oil is now so vital that it has become a magnet for war and points to an alarming future. It comes across as a level-headed, necessary warning. MS

▶ With Wade Adams, Robert E Ebel, Terry Lyn Karl, Fadhil Chalabi.
▶ *Dir*, *Pro* and *Screenplay* Basil Gelpe and Ray McCormack, *Ph* Frank Messmer, *Art Dir* and *Graphics* Melinda Gelpe and Mich Hertig, *Ed* Georgia Wyss.

LAVA Productions AG, Switzerland-Dogwoof Pictures.
83 mins. Switzerland. 2006. Rel: 9 Nov 2007. Cert PG.

Daddy Day Camp ★★

Cuba Gooding Jr and Paul Rae step into the shoes of Eddie Murphy and Jeff Garlin as harassed child carers Charlie Hinton and Phil Ryerson, who this time take over a floundering children's summer camp in competition with the upscale resort nearby. This tedious sequel to the 2003 family comedy *Daddy Day Care* is full of dreadful jokes of the silliest slapstick kind and it strains its stars' appeal beyond breaking point. It deservedly won the Razzie Award for worst prequel or sequel of its year. DW

▶ Cuba Gooding Jr, Richard Gant, Lochlyn Munro, Tamala Jones, Paul Rae, Spencer Bridges, Brian Doyle-Murray.
▶ *Dir* Fred Savage, *Pro* John Davis, William Sherak and Jason Shuman, *Screenplay* Geoff Rodkey, J David Stern and David N Weiss, from a story by Rodkey, Joel Cohen and Alec Sokolow, *Ph* Geno Salvatori, *Pro Des* Eric Weiler, *Ed* Michel Aller, *M* James Dooley, *Costumes* Carolyn Leone-Smith.

Blue Star Pictures/Davis Entertainment/Revolution Studios/Tri-Star Pictures-Sony Pictures Releasing.
89 mins. USA. 2007. Rel: 19 Oct 2007. Cert PG.

Dangerous Parking ★★

As committed and cutting edge as Darren Aronofsky's *Requiem for a Dream* but much inferior, Peter Howitt's tale of an obnoxious alcohol-dependent filmmaker diagnosed with cancer arouses neither sympathy not amusement but hopes for both. Much of it is unconvincing, but it never holds back and could become a cult movie with some audiences. MS

▶ Peter Howitt, Saffron Burrows, Sean Pertwee, Rachael Stirling, Alice Evans.
▶ *Dir* and *Screenlay* Peter Howitt based on Stuart Browne's novel, *Pro* Howitt and Richard Johns, *Ph* Zoran Veljkovic, *Pro Des* Lisa Hall, *Ed* David Barrett, *M* Andre Barreau, *Costumes* Angela Billows, *Animation* Jellyfish Pictures.

Corniche Films/A Velvet Octopus presentation/A Flaming Pie Films production etc-Delanic Films.
110 mins. UK. 2007. Rel: 23 May 2008. Cert 18.

Dan in Real Life ★★★★

Beguiling is the word for this underrated rom-com which is superbly cast. Steve Carell is the widower attending a family reunion on Rhode Island and trying to ignore the fact that on first sight he has fallen for the woman (Juliette Binoche) who is then discovered to be his brother's new girlfriend. Although occasionally too artificial, this portrait of family life is unexpectedly persuasive for a rom-com and Binoche, rarely seen in comedy, is a radiant delight. MS

▶ Steve Carell, Juliette Binoche, Dane Cook, Dianne Wiest, John Mahoney.
▶ *Dir* Peter Hedges, *Pro* Jon Shestack and Brad Epstein, *Screenplay* Pierce Gardner and Hedges, *Ph* Larry Sher, *Pro Des* Sarah Knowles, *Ed* Sarah Flack, *M* Sondre Lerche, *Costumes* Alix Friedberg.

Touchstone Pictures/Focus Features-Icon Film Distribution.
99 mins. USA. 2007. Rel: 11 Jan 2008. Cert PG.

Daratt (Dry Season) ★★★½

Set in Chad, this is a drama about a young man expected to avenge the death of his father in the civil war. He traces the man responsible, a kindly baker, and, coming to know his man, starts to question how appropriate his mission is. Technically accomplished and undoubtedly a sincere example of humanist cinema, it never achieves the consistent tension and involvement attained in 1986 by the thematically similar Iranian film *The Mission*. Nevertheless, it is very sympathetic. MS

▶ Ali Bacha Barkaï, Youssouf Djaoro, Aziza Hisseine, Khayar Oumar Défallah.

▸ *Dir* and *Screenplay* Mahamat-Saleh Haroun, *Pro* Abderrahmane Sissako and Haroun, *Ph* Abraham Haile Biru, *Ed* Marie-Hélène Dozo, *M* Wasis Diop.

Chinguitty Films and Goï-Goï Productions/Arte France Cinéma/Entre Chien et Loup/New Crowned Hope Festival Vienna 2006/Araneo Belgium etc-Soda Pictures.
95 mins. France/Chad/Belgium/Austria/UK. 2006. Rel: 27 July 2007. Cert PG.

The Darjeeling Limited ★★★

Shot with affection in India, Wes Anderson's latest is a laid-back comedy about three siblings on a train trip. Their journey eventually becomes an opportunity to reunite with their mother who has entered a convent in India. It is not without serious scenes but the story line veers in mood and never really leads anywhere. Nice moments, nice photography, but there's not really enough here – not even when seen as on its release here with its prequel short *Hotel Chevalier*. MS

▸ Owen Wilson, Adrien Brody, Jason Schwartzman, Anjelica Huston, Amara Karan, Irrfan Khan, Camilla Rutherford, Barbet Schroeder, Bill Murray.
▸ *Dir* Wes Anderson, *Pro* Anderson, Scott Rudin, Roman Coppola and Lydia Dean Pilcher, *Screenplay* Anderson, Coppola and Jason Schwartzman, *Ph* Robert Yeoman, *Pro Des* Mark Friedberg, *Ed*

Andrew Weisblum, *M* Satyajit Ray, Ravi Shankar etc *Costumes* Milena Canonero.

Fox Searchlight Pictures/Collage/An American Empirical picture etc-20th Century Fox International (UK).
104 mins. USA. 2007. Rel: 23 Nov 2007. Cert 15.

The Dark is Rising ★★★

A nice 14-year-old American kid called Will Stanton (Alexander Ludwig) comes to rural England and learns he is 'special' – the last of a group of immortal warriors dedicated to fighting forces of The Dark. Then, with the aid of some helpful, eccentric locals – Miss Greythorne (Frances Conroy), Merriman (Ian McShane), Dawson (James Cosmo) and Old George (Jim Piddock), all guardians of The Light – Will has to battle a scary pursuing horseman called The Rider (Christopher Eccleston) to gain six signs and stave off some kind of apocalypse. With plenty of action, effects and flashy images, this is a slick and entertaining fantasy adventure that will please its teen audience, even if it betrays the spirit of Susan Cooper's original novel. (Original title: *The Seeker: The Dark is Rising*) DW

▸ Alexander Ludwig, Christopher Eccleston, Ian McShane, Frances Conroy, James Cosmo, Jim Piddock, Amelia Warner, Gregory Smith.

Dan in Real Life: Steve Carell and Juliette Binoche make a perfect team.

> *Dir* David L Cunninghham, *Pro* Marc E Platt, *Screenplay* John Hodge, based on Susan Cooper's novel *The Dark is Rising*, *Ph* Joel Ransom, *Pro Des* David Lee, *Ed* Geoffrey Rowland and Eric A Sears, *M* Christophe Beck, *Costumes* Vin Burnham.

20th Century Fox Film Corporation/Marc Platt Productions/Walden Media-20th Century Fox.
94 mins. USA. 2007. Rel: 19 Oct 2007. Cert 12A.

Day Watch ★★½

Timur Bekmambetov's sequel to his stylish cult thriller *Night Watch* is based on the novel by Sergei Lukyanenko and takes place in the Russian underworld of contemporary Moscow where good and evil forces are fighting for supremacy. This visually striking vampire film has superb production values but it is difficult to get involved with the over-complicated plot or to empathise with its unsympathetic characters. However, it boasts the best use of subtitles I have ever seen. (Original title: *Dnevnoy Dozor*) GS

> Konstantin Khabensky, Mariya Poroshina, Vladimir Menshov, Galina Tyunina, Viktor Verzhbitsky.
> *Dir* Timor Bekmambetov, *Pro* Konstantin Ernst and Anatoly Maksimov, *Screenplay* Bekmambetov, from Sergei Lukyanenko and Vladimir Vasiliev's novel *Dnevnoy Dozor* and a scenario by Alexander Talal, *Ph* Sergei Trofimov, *Pro Des* Valery Viktorov, *Ed* Dmitri Kiselev, *M* Yuri Poteyenko, *Costumes* Varvara Avdyushko.

Bazelevs Production/Channel One Russia/TABBAK-20th Century Fox.
132 mins. USA. 2006. Rel: 5 Oct 2007. Cert 15.

Dead Silence ★★

This is a disappointing film from James Wan, director of the surprise hit *Saw* a couple of years ago. It tells the story of Jamie (Ryan Kwanten) who, having lost his wife in a gruesome murder involving a ventriloquist's dummy, begins a journey back to his home town in order to solve the mystery. The film starts well with a likeable performance from Kwanten but it soon becomes very predictable and lacking in tension and suspense. GS

> Ryan Kwanten, Amber Valletta, Bob Gunton, Laura Regan, Judith Roberts.
> *Dir* James Wan, *Pro* Mark Burg, Gregg Hoffman and Oren Koules, *Screenplay* Wan and Leigh Whannell from their own story, *Ph* John R Leonetti, *Pro Des* Julie Berghoff, *Ed* Michael N Knue, *M* Charlie Clouser, *Costumes* Denise Cronenberg.

Universal Pictures/Evolution Entertainment/Twisted Pictures-Universal Pictures.
91 mins. USA. 2007. Rel: 6 Jul 2007. Cert 15.

Death at a Funeral ★★★½

A British farce with an American director: Frank Oz handles with skill the uneven script by the young British writer Dean Craig who has added black comedy and gay elements to the traditional farce of a family occasion being disrupted . The lavatorial humour is dire but otherwise the comedy set during a patriarch's funeral works well. Oz realises the need for comedy to be played with a straight face. In a good cast Peter Egan is particularly adept. MS

> Matthew Macfadyen, Rupert Graves, Keeley Hawes, Jane Asher, Ewen Bremner, Peter Dinklage, Andy Nyman, Alan Tudyk, Peter Egan, Peter Vaughan.
> *Dir* Frank Oz, *Pro* Sidney Kimmel, Share Stallings, Larry Malkin and Diana Phillips, *Screenplay* Dean Craig, *Ph* Oliver Curtis, *Pro Des* Michael Howells, *Ed* Beverley Mills, *M* Murray Gold, *Costumes* Natalie Ward.

Sidney Kimmel Entertainment/A Parabolic Pictures/Stable Way Entertainment production etc-Verve Pictures.
90 mins. Germany/USA/UK. 2007. Rel: 2 Nov 2007. Cert 15.

Death Note ★★★★

This is an exciting Japanese thriller based on a magazine serial about a student who finds a Death Note Book dropped on Earth by the Death God. He starts to eliminate all the criminals by simply writing their names in it and a cat and mouse chase begins in order to catch the mysterious 'Kira', widely assumed to be responsible. The investigation is led by the student's police inspector father and 'L', a genius mind. It's a gripping and clever film with nail-biting action that's very much worth seeing before the inevitable Hollywood remake. (Original title: *Desu Nôto*) GS

> Tatsuya Fujiwara, Ken'ichi Matsuyama, Asako Seto, Erika Toda, Shunji Fujimura.
> *Dir* Shusuke Kaneko, *Pro* Toyoharu Fukuda, Takahiro Kobashi and Takahiro Sata, *Screenplay* Tetsuya Oishi from the comic by Tsugumi Oba and Takeshi Obata, *Ph* Hiroshi Takase, *Pro Des* Hajime Oikawa, *Ed* Yousuke Yafune, *M* Kenji Kawai.

Death Note Film Partners/Nippon TV Network Corporation/Warner Bros.
126 mins. Japan. 2008. Rel: 25 Apr 2008. Cert 12A.

Death Proof ★★★★

Originally released in the US as part of *Grindhouse*, a pastiche double-bill of 1970s style exploitation pix, complete with spoof trailers and beat-up prints, *Death Proof* and its partner (Robert Rodriguez's *Planet Terror*, qv) were released separately in the UK in expanded versions of the originals. Tarantino's road movie sees stuntman Kurt Russell stalking women in his souped-up killer stuntmobile until the girls turn the tables on him in a very funny but grisly crash and smash movie that has you cheering them on. Impressive performances by Russell and all the girls. MHD

▶ Kurt Russell, Zoe Bell, Rosario Dawson, Vanessa Ferlito, Sydney Tamiia Poitier, Tracie Thoms, Rose McGowan, Mary Elizabeth Winstead.
▶ *Dir, Screenplay and Ph* Quentin Tarantino, *Pro* Elizabeth Avellán, Eric Steinberg, Robert Rodriguez and Tarantino, *Pro Des* Steve Joyner, *Ed* Sally Menke, *M* Various, *Costumes* Nina Proctor.

The Weinstein Company/Dimension Films/ Rodriguez International Pictures/Troublemakers Studios-Momentum Pictures.
114 mins. USA. 2007. Rel: 21 Sep 2007. Cert 18.

Death Sentence ★½

A loving husband and father of two boys, risk assessor Nicholas Hume (Bacon) lives the traditional – i.e. mythological – American dream. Then his son Brendan is murdered in an 'initiation killing' by a gang of thugs. Frustrated by the red tape impeding his sense of justice, Hume decides to take the law into his own hands... Four weeks before Neil Jordan's *The Brave One* opened in British cinemas, James Wan – director of *Saw* – gave us his own take on the vendetta thriller. The result is not only camp and morally reprehensible, but fails as exploitation by dressing up the carnage in stylistic pretension. JC-W

▶ Kevin Bacon, Garrett Hedlund, Kelly Preston, Aisha Tyler, Jordan Garrett, John Goodman, Leigh Whannell.
▶ *Dir* James Wan, *Pro* Ashok Amitraj, Howard Baldwin, Karen Elise Baldwin. *Screenplay* Ian Mackenzie Jeffers, from the novel by Brian Garfield, *Ph* John R Leonetti, *Pro Des* Julie Berghoff, *Ed* Michael N Knue, *M* Charlie Clouser, *Costumes* Kristin M Burke.

Hyde Park Films/Baldwin Entertainment Group/ Brasshat Films/Dune Entertainment-20th Century Fox.
106 mins. USA. 2007. Rel: 31 Aug 2007. Cert 18.

December Boys ★★

In the Australian Outback, four orphan teenagers come to realise that they may never find a family to call their own. Walled up at

During the filming of *Death Proof* Quentin Tarantino spoofs his reputation as a foot fetishist, with a little help from Kurt Russell.

Ryan Reynolds and Elizabeth Banks in *Definitely, Maybe*.

a Catholic orphanage, the boys have only a summer seaside trip to look forward to, an outing that none of them will ever forget… Adapted from the novel by Michael Noonan, *December Boys* is a doe-eyed dip into nostalgia. Unfortunately, it's crippled by banality and overly conventional direction, which no amount of pretty images can salvage. JC-W

▶ Daniel Radcliffe, Lee Cormie, Christian Byers, James Fraser, Jack Thompson, Teresa Palmer, Sullivan Stapleton, Victoria Hill.
▶ *Dir* Rod Hardy, *Pro* Richard Becker, *Screenplay* Marc Rosenberg, based on the novel by Michael Noonan, *Ph* David Connell, *Pro Des* Leslie Binns, *Ed* Dany Cooper, *M* Carlo Giacco, *Costumes* Marriott Kerr.

Australian Film Finance Corporation/Becker Group/ MBZ Film & Media GmbH/South Australian Film/ Village Roadshow Pictures-Warner Bros. 105 mins. USA. 2007. Rel: 14 Sep 2007. Cert 12A.

Deception ★

New York; today. Jonathan McQuarry (Ewan McGregor) is a nerdy, retiring audit manager who lives to work. He then meets the high-flying Wyatt Bose (Hugh Jackman), who introduces him to the possibilities of regular, commitment-free carnal gratification. The title is a giveaway. This is an elusive, formulaic, derivative and very silly thriller that has

already been done a hundred times better. The unflattering close-ups really don't help. JC-W

▶ Hugh Jackman, Ewan McGregor, Michelle Williams, Natasha Henstridge, Charlotte Rampling, Lisa Gay Hamilton, Maggie Q, Danny Burstein.
▶ *Dir* Marcel Langenegger, *Pro* Arnold Rifkin, Christopher Eberts, Hugh Jackman etc, *Screenplay* Mark Bombeck, *Ph* Dante Spinotti, *Pro Des* Patrizia von Brandenstein, *Ed* Douglas Krise and Christian Wagner, *M* Ramin Djawadi, *Costumes* Sue Gandy.

Rifkin-Eberts/Seed Productions/Media Rights Capital-Entertainment Film Distributors. 108 mins. USA. 2008. Rel: 25 Apr 2008. Cert 15.

Definitely, Maybe ★★★½

It would be easy to dismiss this as just another rom-com. In fact it's more than that. William (Ryan Reynolds) is a man awaiting a divorce. He is separated from his wife but has custody of his daughter Maya (Abigail Breslin) who is curious about how his parents met. The film provides a flashback to the three women in William's life (played by Isla Fisher, Elizabeth Banks and Rachel Weisz) and the upshot is that we eventually get to find out who he actually married. A refreshing take on a familiar situation is aided by good performances all round, particularly from the scene-stealing Miss Breslin. MHD

▶ Ryan Reynolds, Isla Fisher, Abigail Breslin, Elizabeth Banks, Kevin Kline, Derek Luke, Rachel Weisz, Fiona Lane.
▶ *Dir and Screenplay* Adam Brooks, *Pro* Tim Bevan and Eric Fellner, *Ph* Florian Ballhaus, *Pro Des* Stephanie Carroll, *Ed* Peter Teschner, *M* Clint Mansell, *Costumes* Gary Jones.

Universal Pictures/Working Title Films/Studio Canal-Universal Pictures.
112 mins. USA. 2008. Rel: 8 Feb 2008. Cert 12A.

The Devil Came on Horseback ★★★★

This documentary about genocide in Darfur does its job. It's sometimes rather rough and would be perfectly suited to television. However, what matters is that Brian Steidle, first revealing what he discovered as an observer and then tracing his subsequent attempts to get something done, brings to our attention facts that need highlighting. MS

▶ With Brian Steidle, John Danforth, Luis Moreno-Ocampo, Élie Wiesel.
▶ *Dir* and *Screenplay* Annie Sundberg and Ricki Stern, *Pro* Sundberg, Stern, Gretchen Wallace etc, *Ph* Jerry Risius, Phil Cox, Sundberg etc, *Ed* Joey Grossfield, *M* Paul Brill.

Break Thru Films/BBC/Global Grassroots/Three Generations-Dogwoof Pictures.

87 mins. USA/UK/Denmark. 2006. Rel: 11 April 2008. No cert.

Diary of the Dead ★★

Horror legend George A Romero returns to his low-budget roots with a fifth *Dead* picture, shot in the thrifty but annoying handicam style of *The Blair Witch Project*. A cast of talentless unknowns witnesses the beginning of the zombie holocaust, opting to video their increasingly gory misfortunes. Camp and amateurish, this looks like the work of a wannabe, not a master. MJ

▶ Joshua Close, Scott Wentworth, Michelle Morgan, Joe Dinicol, Amy Lalonde and the voices of Stephen King, Simon Pegg, Quentin Tarantino, Guillermo del Toro, George A Romero and Wes Craven.
▶ *Dir and Screenplay* George A Romero, *Pro* Artur Spigel, Ara Katz, Peter Grunwald and Sam Englebardt, *Ph* Adam Swica, *Pro Des* Rupert Lazarus, *Ed* Michael Doherty, *M* Norman Orenstein, *Costumes* Alex Kavanagh.

Artfire Films/Romero-Grunwald Productions-Optimum Releasing.
95 mins. USA. 2007. Rel: 7 Mar 2008. Cert 18.

Die Hard 4.0 ★★★½

Fiftysomething Bruce Willis proves he still has what it takes to play the hero game in

Romero's zombies come back for more in *Diary of the Dead*.

old-school actioner *Die Hard 4.0*, a thriller from *Underworld* director Len Wiseman that sees the wrong time/wrong place detective matching wits with a regrettably bland internet-based terrorist played by Timothy Olyphant. Though no classic, it's much more exciting and considerably more fun than the last *Die Hard* picture, released more than a decade earlier. Yippee ki yay indeed. (aka *Live Free or Die Hard* in the USA). MJ

▶ Bruce Willis, Timothy Olyphant, Justin Long, Maggie Q, Cliff Curtis, Kevin Smith.
▶ *Dir* Len Wiseman, *Pro* Michael Fottrell, *Screenplay* Mark Bomback, from a story by Bomback and David Marconi, *Ph* Simon Duggan, *Pro Des* Patrick Tatopolos, *Ed* Nicolas De Toth, *M* Marco Beltrami, *Costumes* Denise Wingate.

20th Century Film Corporation/Cheyenne Enterprises/Dune Entertainment/Ingenious Film Partners-20th Century Fox.
130 mins. USA. 2007. Rel: 4 Apr 2007. Cert 15.

Disturbia ★★★½

Kyle (Shia LaBeouf) feels responsible for his father's death after a dreadful car accident so, when his teacher brings up the subject in class, Kyle attacks and punches him. For punishment he is put under court-ordered house arrest for three months and having nothing else to do he starts spying on his neighbours with his binoculars. The story has familiar overtones (the parallel with *Rear Window* is intentional) and the result is a tense thriller with an excellent performance from LaBeouf. GS

▶ Shia LaBeouf, Sarah Roemer, Carrie-Anne Moss, David Morse, Aaron Yoo, Matt Craven.
▶ *Dir* D J Caruso, *Pro* Jackie Marcus, Joe Medjuck and E Bennett Walsh, *Screenplay* Christopher Landon and Carl Ellsworth, from a story by Landon, *Ph* Rogier Stoffers, *Pro Des* Tom Southwell, *Ed* Jim Page, *M* Geoff Zanelli, *Costumes* Marie-Sylvie Deveau.

DreamWorks SKG presents a Cold Spring Pictures production in association with the Montecito Picture Company-Paramount Pictures.
105 mins. USA. 2007. Rel: 14 Sep 2007. Cert 15.

The Diving Bell and the Butterfly ★★★★★

Jean-Dominique Bauby, former editor of *Elle* magazine, suffered a stroke which left him fully aware but paralysed with only the ability to move his head slightly and blink his left eyelid. Amazingly he managed to 'dictate' his autobiography just by blinking and using a special alphabet system. Julian Schnabel's film is exceedingly impressive and highly moving in its unflinching look at how one man overcame insuperable problems. Seen often from Bauby's own point of view, it details succinctly the loneliness of the stroke victim. Mathieu Amalric gives an amazingly selfless performance as Bauby in an almost impossible role. (Original title: *Le scaphandre et le papillon*) MHD

▶ Mathieu Amalric, Emmanuelle Seigner, Marie-Josée Croze, Anne Consigny, Max Von Sydow, Jean-Pierre Cassel, Patrick Chesnais.
▶ *Dir* Julian Schnabel, *Pro* Kathleen Kennedy and Jon Kilik, *Screenplay* Ronald Harwood, from the book by Jean-Dominique Bauby, *Ph* Janusz Kaminski, *Pro Des* Michel Eric and Laurent Ott, *Ed* Juliette Welfling, *M* Paul Cantelon, *Costumes* Olivier Bériot.

Pathé Renn Productions/The Kennedy-Marshall Company/Canal + etc-Pathé.
112 mins. France/USA. 2007. Rel: 8 Feb 2008. Cert 12A.

Don't Touch the Axe ★★★

Intriguingly the dramatic momentum in this adaptation of a Balzac story comes from the inter-titles thereby proving that a veteran, Jacques Rivette, can come up with something new. The storytelling is otherwise stately and distanced, making it difficult to become sufficiently involved in the tragic tale of two lovers never destined to fulfil their desires. Jeanne Balibar is fine but Guillaume Depardieu is no substitute for dad. MS

▶ Jeanne Balibar, Guillaume Depardieu, Anne Cantineau, Bulle Ogier, Michel Piccoli, Julie Judd, Mathias Jung.
▶ *Dir* Jacques Rivette, *Pro* Martine Marignac, Maurice Tinchant, Ermanno Olmi and others, *Screenplay* Pascal Bonitzer and Christine Laurent from Balzac's *La Duchesse de Langeais*, *Ph* William Lubtchansky, *Art Dir* Manu de Chauvigny, *Ed* Nicole Lubtchansky, *M* Pierre Allio, *Costumes* Maïra Ramedhan-Levi.

Pierre Grise Productions/Cinemaundici/Arte France Cinéma etc-Artificial Eye Film Company.
138 mins. France/Italy. 2006. Rel: 28 Dec 2007. Cert PG.

Doomsday ★★

Neil Marshall's disappointing post-apocalyptic film takes place in Scotland in 2008 after a killer virus almost wipes out the whole country. The few survivors are blocked in by a huge wall. In the year 2033 the British government wants to find a cure for the virus which has now spread

Mathieu Amalric and Marie-Josée Croze in *Le Scaphandre et le papillon* [*The Diving Bell and the Butterfly*].

Craig Conway and Rhona Mitra in *Doomsday*.

to London, so a group is assigned to enter the 'hot zone'. Well crafted but very similar to other recent and far superior films about a deadly virus. GS

❧ Caryn Peterson, Adeola Ariyo, Emma Cleasby, Vernon Willemse, Malcolm McDowell, Adrian Lester.
❧ *Dir and Screenplay* Neil Marshall, *Pro* Benedict Carver and Steven Paul, *Ph* Sam McCurdy, *Pro Des* Simon Bowles, *Ed* Marshall and Andrew MacRitchie, *M* Tyler Bates, *Costumes* John Norster.

Moonlighting Films/Crystal Sky Pictures/Intrepid Pictures/Rogue Pictures-Universal.
113 mins. UK/USA/South Africa. 2008. Rel: 9 May 2008. Cert 18.

Drawing Restraint 9 ★★★★

Matthew Barney's experimental film is set on the Nisshin Maru whaling ship in Japan where hot petroleum jelly is pumped into a mould on deck. The long voyage begins and the mass of petroleum cools while a western couple (played by Barney and Björk, his real life partner who also composed the atmospheric score) are finding love below

Dr Seuss' Horton Hears a Who!

deck. Barney is an ambitious visual artist, best known for the *Cremaster* cycle; his striking new film is an innovative piece of art and, although it requires patience, it is an hypnotic and mesmerising experience. GS

❧ Shigeru Akahori, Naomi Araki, Björk, Genishi Hakozaki, Matthew Barney.
❧ *Dir, Pro, Screenplay and Costumes* Matthew Barney, *Ph* Peter Strietmann, *Pro Des* Matthew D Ryle, *Ed* Luis Alvarez y Alvarez, Christopher Seguine, Barney and Strietmann , *M* Björk.

Restraint LLC-Celluloid Dreams
135 mins. USA/Japan. 2005. Rel: 28 Sep 2007. No cert.

Dr Seuss' Horton Hears a Who! ★★★★

Jungle elephant Horton (voice: Jim Carrey) hears a voice on a small speck of dust and, believing that "a person's a person, no matter how small", endeavours to protect it despite others' ridicule of him. The diminutive Whoville (with its Mayor voiced by Steve Carell) gets as much screen time as Horton's world. *Ice Age* animators, Blue Sky Studios, produce a riot of additional, colourful detail to stretch Dr Seuss' 1954 book to feature length. Surprisingly enjoyable. JC

❧ Voices of Jim Carrey, Steve Carell, Carol Burnett, Will Arnett, Seth Rogen, Dan Fogler, Charles Osgood.
❧ *Dir* Jimmy Hayward and Steve Martino, *Pro* Bob Gordon, *Screenplay* Ken Daurio and Cinco Paul from the book by Dr Seuss, *Pro Des* Thomas Cardone, *Ed* Tim Nordquist, *M* John Powell.

Blue Sky Studios/20th Century Fox Animation-20th Century Fox.
88 mins. USA. 2008. Rel: 21 Mar 2008. Cert U.

Drillbit Taylor ★★★

Three high school kids place an ad in *Soldier of Fortune* magazine, seeking a bodyguard to protect them from the school bully. The best candidate and the cheapest is the homeless Drillbit Taylor who jumps at the chance to train them mentally and physically in how to beat their hated enemy. Owen Wilson is perfectly cast and is in really good form in this very likeable but occasionally uneven comedy. GS

‣ Owen Wilson, Nate Hartley, Troy Gentile, Ian Roberts, Lisa Ann Walter, Adam Baldwin.
‣ *Dir* Steven Brill, *Pro* Judd Apatow, Susan Arnold and Donna Roth, *Screenplay* Kristofor Brown and Seth Rogen, from the story by Brown, Rogen and Edmond Dantes, *Ph* Fred Murphy, *Pro Des* Jackson De Govia, *Ed* Brady Heck and Thomas J Nordberg, *M* Christophe Beck, *Costumes* Karen Patch.

Paramount Pictures/Apatow Productions-Paramount Pictures.
109 mins. USA. 2008. Rel: 28 Mar 2008. Cert 12A.

Eagle vs Shark ★★½

Set in and around Wellington, this comedy from New Zealand is quirkily personal but ill-judged. There's a condescending tone here towards the unsophisticated young couple at the centre who may or may not make it to a happy ending. Additionally there's a failure to extend effectively to certain dramatic elements within the comedy. Furthermore, just when you think you may be undervaluing the good bits, the film concludes with some tiresomely whimsical animated footage. Different, yes; satisfying, no. MS

‣ Loren Horsley, Jermaine Clement, Brian Sergent, Joel Tobeck, Rachel House.
‣ *Dir* and *Screenplay* Taika Waititi from a story by Loren Horsley and Waititi, *Pro* Ainsley Gardiner and Cliff Curtis, *Ph* Adam Clark, *Pro Des* Joe Bleakley, *Ed* Jonno Woodford-Robinson, *M* The Phoenix Foundation, *Costumes* Amanda Neale, *Stop Motion Animation* Francis Salole and Guy Capper, *Special Effects/Animation* Another Planet Ltd.

Whenua Films/New Zealand Film Commission/Unison Films etc-Optimum Releasing.
87 mins. New Zealand/USA. 2006. Rel: 17 Aug 2007. Cert 15.

Owen Wilson in top form in *Drillbit Taylor*.

Earth ★★★★★

A marvellous example of total professionalism in every department, this documentary well narrated by Patrick Stewart draws on the BBC's

Planet Earth but don't let that deter you from seeing this. Ably shaped as we go through the year moving from the Arctic to the Antarctic with emotionally charged highlights perfectly placed, this work shows once again that, however good nature footage may look on television, seeing it in the cinema on the big screen is another experience altogether. Wonderful. MS

➤ With Patrick Stewart (narrator).
➤ *Dir* Alastair Fothergill and Mark Linfield, *Pro* Alix Tidmarsh and Sophokles Tasoulis, *Narration written by* Leslie Megahey, Fothergill and Linfield, *Ph* Various, *Ed* Martin Elsbury, *M* George Fenton.

Greenlight Media/BBC Worldwide/BBC Natural History Unit etc-Lionsgate UK.
99 mins. UK/Germany. 2007. Rel: 16 Nov 2007 Cert PG.

Eastern Promises ★★★

Technically adroit and well acted but overly violent, David Cronenberg's latest reunites him with the excellent Viggo Mortensen. Unfortunately Steve Knight's tale of Russian gangsters in London is routine stuff compared to the material that made this film's predecessor, *A History of Violence*, so intriguing. Professionally done though it is, this is essentially no more than multiplex fodder. MS

➤ Viggo Mortensen, Naomi Watts, Vincent Cassel, Armin Mueller-Stahl, Sinéad Cusack, Jerzy Skolimowski.
➤ *Dir* David Cronenberg, *Pro* Paul Webster and Robert Lantos, *Screenplay* Steve Knight, *Ph* Peter Suschitzky, *Pro Des* Carol Spier, *Ed* Ronald Sanders, *M* Howard Shore, *Costumes* Denise Cronenberg.

Focus Features/BBC Films/Astral Media/Corus Entertainment/Téléfilm Canada/ Kudos Pictures/ Serendipity Point Films/Scion Films etc-Pathé Distribution.
101 mins. UK/Canada/USA. 2007. Rel: 26 Oct 2007. Cert 18.

Ecoute le temps ★★★½

Emilie Dequenne from *Rosetta* (1998) effortlessly carries this film on her shoulders. The young actress is superb as a recording technician investigating the murder of her mother through sounds from the past picked up on her recording equipment. The rural setting recalls Chabrol's classic *Le Boucher* (1973) but by using semi-supernatural notions (in part perhaps for symbolic effect) writer/director Alanté Kavaïté ends up with an oddity only partly successful. Interesting, though. MS

➤ Emilie Dequenne, Mathieu Demy, Ludmila Mikaël, Jacques Spiesser.
➤ *Dir* and *Screenplay* Alanté Kavaïté, *Pro* Antoine Simkine, *Ph* Dominique Colin, *Pro Des* François Emmanuelli, *Ed* Agnès Mouchel, *Costumes* Charlotte Betaillole, *Visual Effects* Mac Guff Ligne.

Les Films d'Antoine/Centre national de la cinématographie etc-Dogwoof Pictures.
87 mins. France. 2005. Rel: 17 Aug 2007. Cert 12A.

The Edge of Heaven ★★★★½

Two families: two generations: two countries. This new feature from Fatih Akin turns aside from the confrontational style of his *Head-On* (2004) to offer a complex yet clear narrative partly set in Germany and partly in Turkey. It shows life as governed by fate and by interconnections and it ultimately encourages audiences to mull over what they have seen. Akin has referred to it as a piece about death being linked to a new birth, but I see it as an involving drama that centres on the need for reconciliation between individuals. Brilliant acting too, especially from Tuncel Kurtiz and Hanna Schygulla. MS

➤ Baki Davrak, Tuncel Kurtiz, Nursel Köse, Hanna Schygulla, Nurgül Yesilcay.
➤ *Dir* and Screenplay Fatih Akin, *Pro* Andreas Thiel, Klaus Maeck and Akin, *Ph* Rainer Klausmann, *Pro Des* Tamo Kunz and Sírma Bradley, *Ed* Andrew Bird, *M* Shantel, *Costumes* Katrin Aschendorf.

A Corazón International Anka Film production/Dorje Film/NDR-Artificial Eye Film Company.
121 mins. Germany/Turkey/Italy. 2007. Rel: 22 Feb 2008. Cert 15.

The Edge of Love ★★★½

Boasting four successful performances in the leading roles, this drama set in London during the Second World War looks at the intertwined lives of the poet Dylan Thomas (Matthew Rhys), his wife Caitlin (Sienna Miller), his soul mate and childhood friend Vera (Keira Knightley) and Vera's husband (Cillian Murphy). It's persuasive without offering any precise focus or viewpoint but John Maybury's direction is characteristically self-conscious. Not wholly successful but certainly interesting. MS

➤ Keira Knightley, Sienna Miller, Matthew Rhys, Cillian Murphy, Paul Brooke.
➤ *Dir* John Maybury, *Pro* Sarah Radclyffe and Rebekah Gilbertson, *Screenplay* Sharman Macdonald from Gilbertson's idea from books, *Ph* Jonathan Freeman, *Pro Des* Alan MacDonald, *Ed* Emma E Hickox, *M* Angelo Badalamenti,

Keira Knightley
and Matthew
Rhys near the
abyss in *The Edge
of Love.*

Costumes April Ferry.
**Capitol Films/BBC Films/Wales Creative IP Fund/
Prescience Film Partners 2/A Rainy Day Films
production etc-Lionsgate UK.**
111 mins.UK. 2007. Rel: 20 June 2008. Cert 15.

Edmond ★★★½

For once David Mamet opts out as director of
a filmed version of one of his plays. Instead
it's Stuart Gordon whose direction makes it
feel cinematic despite the theatrical tone of
the dialogue. He enables William H Macy in
the title role to shine once more. This faithful
rendering of the play shows Edmond's downfall
as he rebels against office work and marriage
and is subsequently horrified to discover just
how commercialised is the world of bought sex.
Edmond ends up by killing. There's a bizarre
hint of redemption at the close but it only
underlines the obscurity of the work's theme. MS

▶ William H Macy, Julia Stiles, Mena Suvari, Joe
Mantegna, Rebecca Pidgeon.
▶ *Dir* Stuart Gordon, *Pro* Chris Hanley, Molly
Hassell, Gordon etc, *Screenplay* David Mamet
based on his play, *Ph* Denis Maloney, *Pro Des* Alan
E. Muraoka, *Ed* Andy Horvitch, *M* Bobby Johnston,
Costumes Carol Cutshall.

**First Independent Pictures/ a Muse production/Tartan
films/Code Entertainment etc-Tartan films.**
82 mins. USA/UK. 2005. Rel: 6 July 2007. Cert 18.

The 11th Hour ★★★

Lacking both the personal impact that Al
Gore brought to *An Inconvenient Truth* and the
unshowy conviction of *A Crude Awakening*, this
latest documentary dealing with environmental
issues will nevertheless be welcomed by those
who can't get enough about these matters. Even
so, it's unnecessarily dominated by music and

its ultimate optimism may be pie in the sky. *Who Killed the Electric Car?* (2006) was far more downbeat but also more persuasive. MS

▶ With Leonardo DiCaprio, Stephen Hawking, Mikhail Gorbachev.
▶ *Dir* and *Screenplay* Leila Conners Petersen and Nadia Conners, *Pro* Leonardo DiCaprio, Petersen, Chuck Castleberry and Brian Gerber, *Ph* Peter Youngblood Hills, Andrew Rowlands and Brian Knappenberger, *Pro Des* Nadia Conners, *Ed* Pietro Scalia and Luis Álvarez y Álvarez, *M* Jean-Pascal Beintus and Eric Avery.

Warner Independent Pictures/An Appian Way/Green Hour/Tree Media Group production-Warner Bros Distributors (UK).
92 mins. USA. 2007. Rel: 14 March 2008. Cert PG.

Elizabeth: The Golden Age
★★★

Ten years on, the excellent Cate Blanchett stars in this sequel to Shekhar Kapur's *Elizabeth* resuming her titular role. But this time she can't really compensate for a treatment that begins as a promising but rushed historical drama, continues as an unduly romanticised period piece and then slides into melodrama as Clive Owen's Walter Raleigh comes to resemble Errol Flynn. Samantha Morton's cameo as Mary Queen of Scots is well judged. Both actresses deserved a better script. MS

▶ Cate Blanchett, Geoffrey Rush, Clive Owen, Abbie Cornish, Samantha Morton, Rhys Ifans, Jordi Mollà, Tom Hollander, David Threlfall, Eddie Redmayne.
▶ *Dir* Shekhar Kapur, *Pro* Tim Bevan, Eric Fellner and Jonathan Cavendish, *Screenplay* William Nicholson and Michael Hirst, *Ph* Remi Adefarasin, *Pro Des* Guy Hendrix Dyas, *Ed* Jill Bilcock, *M* Craig Armstrong and AR Rahman, *Costumes* Alexandra Byrne.

Universal Pictures/StudioCanal/MP Zeta Productions/ A Working Title production-Universal Pictures International UK & Eire.
115 mins. USA/Germany/UK/France. 2007. Rel: 2 Nov 2007 Cert 12A.

Enchanted ★★★

New York; today. A cynical divorcee and divorce lawyer (Dempsey) finds himself in the middle of a musical. And it turns out that the crazy woman (Adams) he has rescued is from a real fairyland far, far away. Considering the mischievous material, it's a shame that the film doesn't take it further; but, hey, this is a Disney pastiche on all things Disney. The saving grace

is Amy Adams, who is Julie Andrews incarnate. And the Oscar-nominated songs by Alan Menken and Stephen Schwartz are quite cute. JC-W

▶ Julie Andrews, Timothy Spall, Amy Adams, Patrick Dempsey, James Marsden, Susan Sarandon.
▶ *Dir* Kevin Lima, *Pro* Barry Josephson and Barry Sonnenfeld, *Screenplay* Bill Kelly, *Ph* Don Burgess, *Pro Des* Stuart Wurzel, *Ed* Gregory Perler and Stephen A Rotter, *M* Alan Menken, *Costumes* Mona May.

Walt Disney Pictures/Andalasia Productions/Josephson Entertainment/Right Coast Productions-Buena Vista International.
107 mins. USA. 2007. Rel: 14 Dec 2007. Cert PG.

The Escapist ★★

Rupert Wyatt's film thrusts us into a closed male society, that of a prison where brutality, violence and buggery flourish. The ever reliable Brian Cox is a lifer anxious to escape for one last sight of his dying daughter, but the film opts to pump adrenalin instead of making us feel for the characters. Strictly for lovers of macho action (who may well wish to increase my star rating), it has a totally misjudged finale when a predictable plot twist plays out unexpectedly in Charing Cross Underground station! MS

▶ Brian Cox, Damian Lewis, Steven Mackintosh, Dominic Cooper, Joseph Fiennes.
▶ *Dir* Rupert Wyatt, *Pro* Adrian Sturges and Alan Moloney, *Screenplay* Wyatt and Daniel Hardy, *Ph* Philipp Blaubach, *Pro Des* Jim Furlong, *Ed* Joe Walker, *M* Benjamin Wallfisch, *Costumes* Maeve Paterson.

UK Film Council/Irish Film Board present a Parallel Films/Picture Farm production etc-Vertigo Films.
102 mins. UK/Ireland. 2007. Rel: 20 June 2008. Cert 15.

Evan Almighty ★★½

A can-do, buttoned-up Congressman, Evan Baxter (Carell) is determined "to change the world." However, he didn't expect God to step in and lend a helping hand. Neither did he anticipate becoming a modern incarnation of Noah. A silly sequel to *Bruce Almighty*, this became known as the most expensive comedy ever made. But it's a one-gag film, which no amount of incontinent critters and in-jokes can resurrect. And the pratfall count is way too high. JC-W

▶ Steve Carell, Morgan Freeman, Lauren Graham, Jimmy Bennett, John Goodman, Harve Presnell, Wanda Sykes.

▶ *Dir* Tom Shadyac, *Pro* Gary Barber, Roger Birnbaum, Michael Bostick, Neal H Moritz and Shadyac, *Screenplay* Steve Oedekerk, based on a story by Oedekerk, Joel Cohen and Alec Sokolow, *Ph* Ian Baker, *Pro Des* Linda DeScenna, *Ed* Scott Hill, *M* John Debney, *Costumes* Judy L Ruskin.

Universal Pictures and Spyglass Entertainment in association with Relativity Media/ Shady Acres Entertainment/Barber/Birnbaum/Original Film-Universal Pictures.
95 mins. USA. 2007. Rel: 3 Aug 2007. Cert PG.

Evening ★★½

Great cast, feeble movie. It's a version of Susan Minot's novel that offers an American family saga set both in the present and in the 1950s. Failing to develop potentially interesting material, the screenplay features most of the clichés of romantic fiction but without relish. Nor does it help that Patrick Wilson is disastrously miscast as a man who turns heads (bring back Rock Hudson in his Douglas Sirk heyday). However, Vanessa Redgrave and Meryl Streep give performances of quality. MS

▶ Claire Danes, Vanessa Redgrave, Toni Collette, Patrick Wilson, Hugh Dancy, Natasha Richardson, Mamie Gummer, Eileen Atkins, Meryl Streep, Glenn Close.
▶ *Dir* Lajos Koltai, *Pro* Jeffrey Sharp, *Screenplay* Susan Minot and Michael Cunningham based on Minot's novel, *Ph* Gyula Pados, *Pro Des* Caroline Hanania, *Ed* Allyson C. Johnson, *M* Jan AP Kaczmarek, *Costumes* Ann Roth and Michelle Matland.

Focus Feature/A Hart Sharp Entertainment production etc-Icon Film Distribution.
117 mins. Germany/USA. 2007. Rel: 21 Sept 2007. Cert 12A.

Ex-Drummer ★★★½

Dries, a well known writer, is approached by three punk rockers looking for a drummer for their group called The Feminists. Fascinated by these characters he agrees despite the fact that he has never played the drums before. Belgian Koen Mortier makes an impressive debut with his extremely violent and shocking first feature based on the cult novel by Herman Brusselmans. He tries hard to offend everybody and manages mostly to succeed which he does with an abundance of mischievously dark humour and style. GS

▶ Dries Van Hegen, Norman Baert, Gunter Lamoot, Sam Louwyck, François Beukelaers.
▶ *Dir and Screenplay* Koen Mortier, from the

Dries Van Hegen in *Ex-Drummer*.

novel by Herman Brusselmans, *Pro* Mortier and Eurydice Gysel, *Ph* Glynn Speeckaert, *Pro Des* Geet Paredis, *Ed* Manu Van Hove, *M* Arno, Flip Kowlier, Millionaire and Guy Van Nueten, *Costumes* Catherine Marchand.

CCCP/Czar/Mercurio Cinematografica/Quad Productions-Tartan Films.
90 mins. Belgium. 2007. Rel: 9 Nov 2007. Cert 18.

The Extras ★★★

No, it's not Ricky Gervais! This is a modest Polish film about movie extras that threads together various mini-stories. It's not that novel – think *The Extra Day* (1956) – although here it's a team of Chinese filmmakers choosing to work in Poland. This is a lightweight piece not far removed from soap opera, a foreign film not aimed at a sophisticated audience that may well please those drawn to it. MS

▶ Kinga Preis, Bartosz Opania, Anna Romantowska, Malgorzata Buczkowska.
▶ *Dir* Michal Kwiecinski, *Pro* Kwiecinski and Katarzyna Fukacz-Cebula, *Screenplay* Jaroslaw Sokól, *Ph* Arek Tomiak, *Art Dir* Arkadiusz Kosmider, *Ed* Rafal Listopad, *M* Michal Lorenc, *Costumes* Pawel Grabarczyk etc.

Akson Studio/TVP Telewizja Polska/Canal+ etc-Dogwoof Pictures.
119 mins. Poland. 2006. Rel: 19 Oct 2007. Cert 12A.

The Eye ★½

Retread of the Chinese film *Gin gwai* (2002) about a girl who has an eye operation to make her see again. However, she comes to see more

Behind you!
Jessica Alba in
The Eye.

than she bargained for. Not only can she see what she has missed since the age of five when she lost her sight, but now she is also seeing dead bodies all over the place. Lacking the real horror of the Chinese original, this US remake just marks time and, as far as shocks go, it probably wouldn't even frighten your granny. PL

▶ Jessica Alba, Alessandro Nivola, Parker Posey, Rade Serbedzija, Fernanada Romero, Rachel Ticotin.
▶ *Dir* David Moreau and Xavier Palud, *Pro* Don Granger and Paula Wagner, *Screenplay* Sebastian Gutierrez, based on the 2002 screenplay *Gin gwai* by Jo Jo Yuet-Chun Hui, Oxide Pang and Danny Pang, *Ph* Jeffrey Jur, *Pro Des* James Spencer, *Ed* Patrick Lussier, *M* Marco Beltrami, *Costumes* Michael Dennison.

C/W Productions/Paramount Vantage-Lionsgate. 98 mins. USA. 2008. Rel: 24 Apr 2008. Cert 15.

Fade to Black ★★★

With strong echoes of Steven Soderbergh's underrated *The Good German* (2006), this is a fiction set in the post-war 'forties and linked to the cinema of the period. Here it's a tale of murder and corruption in Rome when Orson Welles (Danny Huston) was there filming *Black Magic* and seeking finance for his *Othello*. It lacks real flair but it's passable entertainment and the final comment from Huston's Welles as to the truth or otherwise of the tale is the film's best line. MS

▶ Danny Huston, Diego Luna, Paz Vega.

Christopher Walken, Anna Galiena.
▶ *Dir* and *Screenplay* Oliver Parker based on Davide Ferrario's novel, *Pro* Barnaby Thompson, Jonathan Olsberg and Massimo Pacilio, *Ph* John de Borman, *Pro Des* Luciana Arrighi, *Ed* Guy Bensley, *M* Charlie Mole, *Costumes* Louise Stjernsward.

Ealing Studios/Odyssey Entertainment/Thema Productions/Endgame Entertainment/Isle of Man Film/Fragile Films, Dakota Films etc-Lionsgate UK. 104 mins. UK/Italy/Serbia/Luxembourg/USA. 2006. Rel: 7 March 2008. Cert 15.

Feast of Love ★★★★

Tasty performances are on the menu for this lovely little romantic drama feast, with Morgan Freeman as an academic in Portland, Oregon, observing love stories played out by his friends and neighbours. Greg Kinnear takes the other main acting honours as an amiable café owner who jumps from the frying pan into the fire when his wife (Selma Blair) leaves him for another woman and he takes up with a two-timing estate agent (Radha Mitchell). The story involving Kinnear's employees Alexa Davalos and Billy Burke, who find solace together from their damaged childhoods, is a shade less involving but still good enough. The 75-year-old director Robert Benton handles it all with great flair and sensitivity – and couldn't you just listen to Freeman's wistful, wise voice-overs for eternity? DW

▶ Morgan Freeman, Greg Kinnear, Radha Mitchell, Billy Burke, Alexis Davalos, Jane Alexander, Fred Ward.

▶ *Dir* Robert Benton, *Pro* Gary Lucchesi, Tom Rosenberg and Richard S Wright, *Screenplay* Allison Burnett from the novel by Charles Baxter, *Ph* Kramer Morgenthau, *Pro Des* Missy Stewart, *Ed* Andrew Mondshein, *M* Stephen Trask, *Costumes* Renee Ehrlich Kalfus.

GreeneStreet Films/Lakeshore Entertainment/ Revelations Entertainment-Entertainment Film Distributors.
101 mins. USA. 2007. Rel: 5 Oct 2007. Cert 15.

Female Agents ★★★

This well-paced war-time drama about female resistance fighters in France in 1944 is ably presented but it brings exaggerated drama to a story which is passed off as closer to the truth than it is. The contrived melodrama that results is reminiscent of the style adopted in *Black Book* (2006) and those who admired that film can safely increase the rating shown above. (Original title: *Les femmes de l'ombre*) MS

▶ Sophie Marceau, Julie Depardieu, Marie Gillain, Déborah François, Moritz Bleibtrau, Maya Sansa, Vincent Rottiers, Julien Boisselier.
▶ *Dir* Jean-Paul Salomé, *Pro* Eric Névé, *Screenplay* Salomé and Laurent Vachaud, *Ph* Pascal Ridao, *Pro Des* Françoise Dupertuis, *Ed* Marie-Pierre Renaud, *M* Bruno Coulais, *Costumes* Pierre-Jean Larroque.

La Chauve-Souris/Restons Groupés Productions/TF1 International/TF1 Films Production etc-Revolver Entertainment.
117 mins. France. 2007. Rel: 27 June 2008. Cert 15.

A Few Days in September ★★

In trying to evoke *The Third Man* (1949), writer/director Santiago Amigoréna only shows his ineptitude. He has a good cast but no idea of how to find an approach that will yield a cohesive tone. Set in Paris and Venice, this is a spy drama linked to the events of 9/11. In that context some Hitchcockian fun, including an eccentric villain (John Turturro) who discusses his killings with his psychiatrist, just seems out of place. But in any case pretentious dialogue and an absurd stylised climax confirm what we have recognised all along: this is a disaster. (Original title: *Quelques jours en septembre*) MS

▶ Juliette Binoche, John Turturro, Sara Forestier, Tom Riley, Nick Nolte.
▶ *Dir* and *Screenplay* Santiago Amigoréna, *Pro* Paulo Branco, *Ph* Christophe Beaucarne, *Pro Des* Emmanuelle Duplay, *Ed* Sarah Turoche, *M* Laurent Martin, *Costumes* Isabelle Baudry.

Gemini Films/Les Films du rat/France2 Cinéma,

Production Group etc-Transmedia Pictures.
116 mins. France/Italy. 2006. Rel: 14 Sept 2007. Cert 15.

Firehouse Dog ★★★

A dog named Rex is a huge Hollywood star but when an aerial stunt for a commercial goes wrong he is presumed dead. However, he ends up in a small town in the company of 12-year-old Shane, whose father is the captain of the city's fire station. Hutcherson gives another mature performance as the rebellious boy who with the help of his new friend saves the day on a number of occasions. The opening is far too silly but ultimately the film is quite entertaining despite being over long and having too many false endings. GS

▶ Josh Hutcherson, Bruce Greenwood, Bill Nunn, Scotch Ellis Loring, Mayte Garcia, Teddy Sears, Steven Culp.
▶ *Dir* Todd Holland, *Pro* Michael Colleary, Michael J Maschio, Mike Werb, *Screenplay* Colleary, Werb and Claire-Dee Lim, *Ph* Victor Hammer, *Pro Des* Tamara Deverell, *Ed* Scott J Wallace, *M* Jeff Cardoni, *Costumes* Judith R Gellman.

CORE Digital Pictures/Regency Enterprises/New Regency Pictures-20th Century Fox.
111 mins. USA/Canada. 2007. Rel: 20 Jul 2007. Cert PG.

First Sunday ★

Durell (Ice Cube) and LeeJohn (Tracy Morgan), who are best friends and petty criminals, decide to rob their neighbourhood church in order to pay off some pressing debts. But they find out that someone has already beaten them to the money and resort to take the church's followers hostage, from whom they then learn a lesson or two. It's not a bad idea but it's badly directed

Chi McBride in *First Sunday*.

and the actors are encouraged to overact a totally unfunny script. GS

▶ Ice Cube, Katt Williams, Tracy Morgan, Loretta Devine, Michael Beach, Regina Hall, PJ Byrne.
▶ *Dir and Screenplay* David E Talbert, *Pro* Talbert, Matt Alvarez, Ice Cube, David McIlvain and Tim Story, *Ph* Alan Caso, *Pro Des* Dina Lipton, *Ed* Jeffrey Wolf, *M* Stanley Clarke, *Costumes* Gersha Phillips.

Cube Vision/Firm Films/The Story Company-Sony Pictures Releasing.
96 mins. USA. 2008. Rel: 28 Mar 2008. Cert PG.

Flanders ★★★★½

There's a marvellous sense of cinema in this latest piece from controversial French auteur Bruno Dumont. As a study of rural types called up to go to war and of the girls they leave behind, this movie offers an unsparing portrait of male insensitivity and of animalistic sex failing to provide real interconnection. You can argue that the view taken is too extreme and the conclusion is not wholly persuasive, but even so this is a tremendous, overwhelming work for serious filmgoers. See it and you'll be discussing it for days. (Original title: *Flandres*) MS

▶ Adelaïde Leroux, Samuel Boidin, Henri Crétel, Patrice Venant, David Poulain.
▶ *Dir* and *Screenplay* Bruno Dumont, *Pro* Jean

Daniel Craig in the underrated *Flashbacks of a Fool*.

Bréhat and Rachid Bouchareb, *Ph* Yves Cape, *Ed* Guy Lecorne, *Costumes* Cédric Grenapin and Alexandra Charles.

3B Productions/Arte France Cinéma/CRRAV/Nord-Pas-de-Calais etc-Soda Pictures.
92 mins. France. 2006. Rel: 6 July 2007. Cert 18.

Flashbacks of a Fool ★★★½

The last of this drama's three sections is less individual than those that precede it but nevertheless this film has been undervalued. The story of a Hollywood star in decline (Daniel Craig on good form) and of the seduction by a married woman of his younger self (Harry Eden in a star-making performance) is a most promising calling-card for writer/director Baillie Walsh. MS

▶ Daniel Craig, Harry Eden, Jodhi May, Miriam Karlin, Eve, Helen McCrory, Olivia Williams, Mark Strong, James D'Arcy, Claire Forlani, Emilia Fox, Keeley Hawes.
▶ *Dir* and *Screenplay* Baillie Walsh, *Pro* Lene Bausager, Damon Bryant, Claus Clausen and Genevieve Hofmeyr, *Ph* John Mathieson, *Pro Des* Laurence Dorman, *Ed* Struan Clay, *M* Richard Hartley, *Costumes* Stevie Stewart.

Left Turn Films/Sherezade Films/DRS Entertainment/Lipsync Productions/Visitor Pictures/A Mrs. Rogers

production-Buena Vista International (UK).
114 mins. UK/USA/South Africa. 2008. Rel: 18 April 2008. Cert 15.

Flight of the Red Balloon
★★½

Taiwan's Hou Hsiao Hsien visited Paris to make this film about a puppeteer (Juliette Binoche), her young son (Simon Iteanu) and the child's Taiwanese nanny (Fang Song). All three seem wonderfully real and it's well shot, but the film, which goes at the slowest pace imaginable, never draws us in. In any case, to combine this with echoes of Albert Lamorisse's famous short *The Red Balloon* (1955) seems wholly inappropriate. (Original title: *Le voyage du ballon rouge*) MS

▷ Juliette Binoche, Simon Iteanu, Hippolyte Girardot, Fang Song, Louise Margolin.
▷ *Dir* Hou Hsiao Hsien, *Pro* Francois Margolin and Kristina Larsen, *Screenplay* Hou and Margolin, *Ph* Mark Lee Ping Bing, *Art Dir* Paul Fayard and Hwarng Wern Ying, *Ed* Liao Ching Sung, *M* Camille, *Costumes* Jean-Charline Tomlinson.

3H Productions/Margo Films/Les Films du Lendemain etc-Park Circus Ltd.
115 mins. France/Taiwan. 2006. Rel: 14 March 2008. Cert PG.

Flood ★★★

London is about to be flooded unless our plucky band of heroes can stop the Thames Barrier from collapsing during a freak storm. Only weather expert Tom Courtenay has the answer and his estranged son (Carlyle) braves the wind and the rain. Meanwhile his ex-wife (Gilsig) and Crisis Control chief (Whalley) stand by biting their highly manicured nails and politician Suchet looks serious. Typical made-for-TV epic (given a limited cinema release) with some good flood action but dodgy-looking effects. Engrossing while it's on. MHD

▷ Robert Carlyle, Jessalyn Gilsig, Tom Courtenay, Joanne Whalley, David Suchet, Nigel Planer, David Hayman, Peter Wight, Moira Lister.
▷ *Dir* Tony Mitchell, *Pro* Judith Bodle and Peter McAleese, *Screenplay* Bodle, Matthew Cope and Nick Morley, based on the novel by Richard Doyle, *Ph* Pierre Jodoin, *Pro Des* Jonathan Lee, *Ed* Annie Ilkow and Simon Webb, *M* Debbie Wiseman, *Costumes* Kate Carin.

Powercorp/A Muse Productions/Moonlighting Films/ Flood Productions-Lionsgate.
111 mins. USA/South Africa/Canada. 2007. Rel: 24 Aug 2007. Cert 12A.

Matthew McConaughey is eclipsed by the scenery in *Fool's Gold*.

Fool's Gold ★½

Dead in the water romantic comedy-cum-treasure hunting adventure in a glamorous Caribbean setting. Matthew McConaughey and Kate Hudson as the estranged and tedious treasure hunting couple fail to create any sexual chemistry, while billionaire patron Donald Sutherland with a dodgy English accent looks justifiably embarrassed most of the time. Alexis Dziena as his airhead daughter and Kevin Hart as local gangster Bigg Bunny raise a smile but acting honours go to Australia's Gold Coast in the role of the Caribbean. CA

▷ Matthew McConaughey, Kate Hudson, Donald Sutherland, Alexis Dziena, Ewen Bremner, Ray Winstone.
▷ *Dir* Andy Tennant, *Pro* Donald De Line, Bernie Goldmann, Jon Klane, *Screenplay* Tennant, John Claflin and Daniel Zelman, *Ph* Don Burgess, *Pro Des* Charles Wood, *Ed* Troy Takaki and Tracey Wadmore-Smith, *M* George Fenton, *Costumes* Ngila Dickson.

Warner Bros Pictures/De Line Pictures-Warner Bros.
113 mins. USA. 2008. Rel: 18 Apr 2008. Cert 12A.

Forgetting Sarah Marshall
★★★

Peter, a struggling musician, is totally devastated when his girlfriend, television star Sarah Marshall, dumps him after six years of bliss. He takes an impulsive trip to Hawaii to get away from it all but to his horror Sarah is also there with her new boyfriend. Jason Segel is a likeable leading man, his script is clever but some of his comedy is not sharp enough. Overall an

Russell Brand struggles to recapture his old stand-up skills in Forgetting Sarah Marshall.

entertaining film with good performances and a fun cameo from Paul Rudd as the mad surf instructor. GS

▶ Jason Segel, Kristen Bell, Mila Kunis, Russell Brand, Bill Hader, William Baldwin, Paul Rudd.
▶ *Dir* Nicholas Stoller, *Pro* Judd Apatow and Shauna Robertson, *Screenplay* Jason Segel, *Ph* Russ T Alsobrook, *Pro Des* Jackson De Gova, *Ed* William Kerr, *M* Lyle Workman, *Costumes* Leesa Evans.

Apatow Productions-Universal Pictures International. 112 mins. USA. 2008. Rel: 25 Apr 2008. Cert 15.

Four Minutes ★★

It's a well-acted, competently directed award-winning film, but it's bosh all the same. Not camp enough to be fun, it offers a melodramatic blend featuring a piano teacher who works in a prison and her star female pupil groomed to enter a competition. It involves a paedophile who abuses his daughter, a lesbian lover betrayed, self-sacrifice for the crime of another and an acclaimed performance of the Schumann Piano Concerto without an orchestra but with modern discords defiantly added. It's absolutely bonkers. (Original title: *Vier Minuten*) MS

▶ Monica Bleibtreu, Hannah Kerzsprung, Sven Pippig, Jasmin Tabatabai.
▶ *Dir* and *Screenplay* Chris Kraus, *Pro* Meike Kordes and Alexandra Kordes, *Ph* Judith Kaufmann, *Pro Des* Silke Buhr, *Ed* Uta Schmidt, *M* Annette Focks, *Costumes* Gioia Raspé.

Kordes & Kordes Film/A Südwestrundfunk Bayerischer Rundfunk, Arte co-production etc-Peccadillo Pictures Ltd. 115 mins. Germany. 2006. Rel: 7 March 2008. Cert 15.

4 Months, 3 Weeks, 2 Days ★★★½

Abortion is the issue in this critically acclaimed Romanian film that takes place during twenty four hours. The acting is faultless, especially from Anamaria Marinca as the pregnant girl's friend trying to help her, but *Vera Drake* offered more of a story and more detailed background to its characters and Cristian Mungiu's direction often seems misjudged. Nevertheless, the setting is vividly realised (Romania in the 1980s under Communist control) and the film undoubtedly deserves to be seen. (Original title: *4 luni, 3 saptamâni si 2 zile*) MS

▷ Anamaria Marinca, Laura Vasilu, Vlad Ivanov, Alexandru Potocean.
▷ *Dir* and *Screenplay* Cristian Mungiu, *Pro* Oleg Mutu and Mungiu, *Ph* Mutu, *Pro Des* Mihaela Poenaru, *Ed* Dana Bunescu, *Costumes* Dana Istrate.

**Mobra Films/Saga Film etc-Artificial Eye.
113 mins. Romania/Netherlands/France/Germany. 2007. Rel: 4 Jan 2008. Cert 15.**

4:30 ★★★

If Royston Tan's previous feature *15* was Godardian in tone, this one in contrast embraces minimalism. It's a sympathetic study of a lonely boy in Singapore. Left alone with his absentee mother's depressed lodger, he turns him into a father figure and seeks to protect him. Too much detail is left obscure for too long, but there's a poetic tone and an admirably convincing performance by young Xiao Li Yuan. MS

▷ Xiao Li Yuan, Kim Young Jun.
▷ *Dir* Royston Tan, *Pro* Gary Goh, James Toh and Makota Ueda, *Screenplay* Liam Yeo and Tan from Tan's story, *Ph* Lim Ching Leong, *Art Dir* Daniel Lim, *Ed* Low Hwee Ling, *M* Hualampong Riddim and Vuchaya Vatanasapt.

**NHK/Singapore Film Commission/Zhao Wei Films-Peccadillo Pictures Ltd.
93 mins. Singapore/Japan. 2005. Rel: 23 Nov 2007. Cert 12A.**

1408 ★★½

Mikael Håfström's atmospheric thriller about paranormal events is adapted from a short story by Stephen King and takes place at the notorious Dolphin Hotel where horror novelist Mike Enslin (John Cusack) is determined to spend a night at the haunted 1408 suite despite warnings from the hotel manager (Samuel L Jackson). Both Cusack and Jackson are very watchable and are always good value for money, but they can't rescue this film from being just one simple but over-extended idea. GS

▷ John Cusack, Samuel L Jackson, Benny Urquidez,

Mary McCormack, Jasmine Jessica Anthony, Len Cariou.
▷ *Dir* Mikael Håfström, *Pro* Lorenzo di Bonaventura, *Screenplay* Matt Greenberg, Scott Alexander and Larry Karaszewksi, based on a story by Stephen King, *Ph* Benoit Delhomme, *Pro Des* Andrew Laws, *Ed* Peter Boyle, *M* Gabriel Jared, *Costumes* Natalie Ward.

**Dimension Films/Di Bonaventura Pictures-Paramount Pictures.
104 mins. USA. 2007. Rel: 31 Aug 2007. Cert 15.**

Fred Claus ★

Fred has always lived in the shadow of his famous brother Santa. He is now desperate for money and he reluctantly accepts a job at Santa's workshop in the North Pole. Predictably he creates chaos wherever he goes especially among the elves. Another silly, long and truly unfunny film for the festive season with an all-star cast totally wasted particularly Miranda Richardson as Mrs Claus and Rachel Weisz as Fred's long-suffering cockney girlfriend who unbelievably works as a traffic warden in New York (!) GS

▷ Vince Vaughn, Paul Giamatti, John Michael Higgins, Miranda Richardson, Rachel Weisz, Kathy Bates, Kevin Spacey.
▷ *Dir* David Dobkin, *Pro* Dobkin, Jessie Nelson and Joel Silver, *Screenplay* Dan Fogelman, from a story by Fogelman and Nelson, *Ph* Remi Adefarasin, *Pro Des* Allan Cameron, *Ed* Mark Livolsi, *M* Christophe Beck, *Costumes* Anna Sheppard.

**Warner Bros Pictures/Silver Pictures/David Dobkin Productions/Jessie Nelson Productions-Warner Bros.
116 mins. USA. 2007. Rel: 30 Nov 2007. Cert PG.**

Freebird ★

Jon Ivay's dull film tells the story of three London motorcycle couriers who set off from London to Wales in search of a hippy and his

Welsh bikers hit the road in *Freebird*.

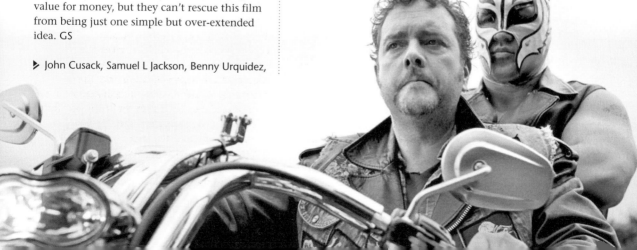

Karina Testa in
Frontiers.

cannabis farm. On the way they come into conflict with a group of Welsh-speaking bikers who are also out to get drunk and stoned. Ivay's muddled and badly written script tries hard to be eccentric and cool but fails miserably on both counts. GS

▶ Alun ap Brinley, Geoff Bell, Peter Bowles, Phil Daniels, Jon Ivay, Ian Ralph.
▶ *Dir and Screenplay* Jon Ivay, *Pro* Adam Bohling and David Reid, *Ph* Peter Wignall, *Pro Des* Richard Campling, *Ed* Celia Haining, *M* Martin Glover, *Costumes* Stephanie Collie.

Delanic Films (Distributors).
93 mins. UK. 2008. Rel: 1 Feb 2008. Cert 15.

Frontiers ★★★

In France a gang of small-time crooks takes advantage of an inner city riot to attempt a heist, but when it goes wrong they flee to the border and find refuge in a seedy hostel owned by a degenerate redneck family. This is slick, bravura filmmaking from Xavier Gens who goes to extreme lengths to shock and disgust his audience with his supremely violent, dirty and very nasty film. It makes *The Texas Chain Saw Massacre* look like *Mary Poppins*. (Original title: *Frontières*) GS

Funny Games US:
Tim Roth falls
victim in this
powerful remake.

▶ Karina Testa, Aurélian Wiik, Patrick Ligardes, David Saracino, Maud Forget, Samuel Le Bihan.

▶ *Dir and Screenplay* Xavier Gens, *Pro* Laurent Tolleron, Luc Besson etc, *Ph* Laurent Barès, *Pro Des* Jérémie Streliski, *Ed* Carlo Rizzo, *M* Jean-Pierre Taieb, *Costumes* Eléonore Dominguez.

BR Films/Pacific Films/Cartel Productions etc-Lionsgate.
108 mins. France/Switzerland. 2007. Rel: 14 Mar 2008.
Cert 18.

Funny Games US ★★★★½

This is Michael Haneke's re-make of his own 1997 feature about a family under threat from two strangers. It's now in English with a cast headed impressively by Naomi Watts but is close enough to the original to remain a brilliantly disquieting attack on the way in which many cinemagoers relish on-screen violence. The odd miscalculation apart, it's stunningly effective with little to choose between the two versions: whichever you see first will have the edge because it will take you by surprise. MS

▶ Naomi Watts, Tim Roth, Michael Pitt, Brady Corbet, Devon Gearhart.
▶ *Dir* and *Screenplay* Michael Haneke, *Pro* Chris Coen and Hamish McAlpine, *Ph* Darius Khondji, *Pro Des* Kevin Thompson, *Ed* Monika Willi, *M* Handel, Mascagni, Mozart and John Zorn, *Costumes* David Robinson.

Celluloid Dreams/Halcyon Pictures/Tartan Films/X Filme International/Lucky Red production etc-Tartan Films.

Madison Pettis and Dwayne Johnson in *The Game Plan*.

111 mins. France/UK/Germany/Italy/USA/Austria. 2007. Rel: 4 April 2008. Cert 18.

The Game Plan ★½

Superstar quarterback Joe Kingman's bachelor days are over when his precocious seven year old daughter he never knew he had arrives unannounced at his apartment. Dwayne Johnson is a likeable and a charismatic performer but here in Andy Fickman's bland and unimaginative film he is encouraged to overact and ultimately fails to deliver in this predictable, sugar-coated script. GS

▶ Dwayne 'The Rock' Johnson, Madison Pettis, Kyra Sedgwick, Roselyn Sanchez, Morris Chestnut.
▶ *Dir* Andy Fickman, *Pro* Mark Ciardi and Gordon Gray, *Screenplay* Nichole Millard and Kathryn Price from a story by Millard, Price and Audrey Wells, *Ph* Greg Gardiner, *Pro Des* David J Bomba, *Ed* Michael Jablow, *M* Nathan Wang, *Costumes* Genevieve Tyrrell.

Walt Disney Pictures/Mayhem Pictures/Sandman Studios-Walt Disney Studios Motion Pictures. 110 mins. USA. 2007. Rel: 7 Mar 2008. Cert U.

Gandhi, My Father ★★★

Feroz Khan's ambitious epic tells the little-known story of Gandhi's tragic relationship with the eldest of his four sons, Harilal, who rejected his father's principles, became an alcoholic and was later disowned. In the beginning it is difficult to get involved and care about the thinly sketched characters but as the film develops the strong acting and moving story take over aided by excellent production values and superb 'Scope photography. GS

▶ Akshaye Khanna, Darshan Jariwalla, Shefali Shah, Bhumika Chawla, Vinay Jain, Daniel Janks.
▶ *Dir and Screenplay* Feroz Abbas Khan, from the book by Chandulal Dalal and Neelamben Parikh, *Pro* Anil Kapoor, *Ph* David McDonald, *Pro Des* Nitin Chandrakant Desai, *Ed* A Sreekar Prasad, *M* Piyush Kanojia, *Costumes* Sujata Sharma.

Anil Kapoor Film Company-Eros Entertainment. 136 mins. India. 2007. Rel: 3 Aug 2007. Cert PG.

Garage ★★★½

Unless you are Irish you may not have heard of Pat Shortt, a comedian here playing it straight and doing it brilliantly. In this quiet, sensitive film he plays a loner running a roadside garage. This man seeks human contact – a girl in town, a youngster hired to help out – but fate is against him. It's a minimal, almost Beckettian work which just misses out in bringing home the tragedy at its heart, but connoisseurs of acting should not miss it. MS

▶ Pat Shortt, Anne-Marie Duff, Conor Ryan, John Keogh, Andrew Bennett.
▶ *Dir* Lenny Abrahamson, *Pro* Ed Guiney, *Screenplay* Mark O'Halloran, *Ph* Peter Robertson, *Pro Des* Padraig O'Neill, *Ed* Isobel Stephenson, *M* Stephen Rennicks, *Costumes* Sonya Lennon.

An Element Pictures production for Film4/Bord

Scannán na hÉireann/Irish Film Board etc-Soda Pictures.
85 mins. Ireland/UK. 2007. Rel: 7 March 2008. Cert 18.

Garbage Warrior ★★★½

Yes, there is something new to be said on film about environmental issues. This documentary feature is centred on the unconventional architect Mike Reynolds, an engaging presence as the film sets out his ideas for self-sufficient solar-powered buildings, records his troubles with the authorities in New Mexico and finally reveals his ability to help after the Asian tsunami of 2004. Slightly over-long, perhaps, but worth seeing. MS

❧ With Michael Reynolds, Chris Reynolds, Renni 'Zee' Zifferblatt, Dave Diciccio.
❧ *Dir* and *Ph* Oliver Hodge, *Pro* Rachel Wexler, *Ed* Phil Reynolds, *M* Patrick Wilson.

Open Eye Media UK/ITVS International/Sundance Channel etc-ICA Films.
86 mins. UK/USA/Finland/Denmark. 2007. Rel: 23 May 2008. No cert.

Ghosts of Cité Soleil ★★★★★

A milestone in cinema history, this truly remarkable film, shot in the criminal milieu of the slums of Port-au-Prince, features two brothers vying for the same woman. Required to support the dictator president Aristide, they become marked men when he falls and the tragedy so devastatingly depicted is both theirs and that of Haiti. What makes it extraordinary is that this is not a drama with actors but a documentary shot as events developed. The impact is greater than any fictional re-enactment could ever have achieved. It's something new in cinema and a major work of art. MS

❧ With Haitian 2pac, Bily, Lele, Franzo, JPB, Jean-Bertrand Aristide, Wyclef Jean.
❧ *Dir* Asger Leth with Milos Loncarevic, *Pro* Mikael Chr. Rieks, Tomas Radoor and Seth Kanegis, *Ph* Loncarevic, Frederik Jacobi and Leth, *Ed* Adam Nielsen, *M* Wyclef Jean and Jerry Wonder Duplessis.

Sony BMG Film/Nordisk Film/Sak Pasé Films/Sunset Production/Independent Pictures production etc-Revolver Entertainment.
89 mins. Denmark/USA. 2005. Rel: 20 July 2007. Cert 15.

The Go Master ★★★½

The director of *Horse Thief*, Tian Zhuangzhuang, returns with this biographical piece about Wu Qingyuan, famed exponent of the game of Go. As a narrative it tends to be elusive failing to bring characters and events fully into focus. However, its sense of Buddhist meditation (the atmosphere of the game rather than its moves is central here) is beautifully rendered and genuinely poetic. (Original title: *Wu Qingyuan*) MS

❧ Chang Chen, Sylvia Chang, Takayuki Inoue, Keiko Matsuzaka, Akira Emoto.

A rare moment of peace for Haitian 2-pac and Lele in *Ghosts of Cité Soleil*.

The Go Master: a truly poetic and meditative work.

▶ *Dir* Tian Zhuangzhuang, *Pro* Liu Xiaodian, *Screenplay* Ah Cheng, *Ph* Wang Yu, *Pro Des* Emi Wada, *Ed* Yang Hiongyu, *M* Zhao Li, *Costumes* Emi Wada.

Fortissimo Films/Century Hero Film Investment/etc-ICA Films.
104 mins. China/Hong Kong. 2006. Rel: 28 March 2008. No cert.

The Golden Compass ★★

Impressive as the spectacle of two armoured, talking, battling polar bears may be, Oscar-winning visual effects do not make a movie great. Burdened by largely amateurish performances, a leaden screenplay and over-complicated story, this regrettably routine fantasy struggles to bring novelist Philip Pullman's adventure to life. The tale of a girl on a magical quest to rescue kidnapped kids from a mysterious organisation, though only two hours long, it feels more like four. MJ

▶ Nicole Kidman, Daniel Craig, Dakota Blue Richards, Ben Walker, Eva Green, Derek Jacobi, Jim Carter, Tom Courtenay, Sam Elliott, Christopher Lee, Kristin Scott Thomas and the voices of Kathy Bates, Ian McKellen, Ian McShane, Freddie Highmore.
▶ *Dir and Screenplay* Chris Weitz, from the novel *Northern Lights* by Philip Pullman, *Pro* Bill Carraro and Deborah Forte, *Ph* Henry Braham, *Pro Des* Dennis Gassner, *Ed* Anne V Coates, Peter Honess

and Kevin Tent, *M* Alexandre Desplat, *Costumes* Ruth Myers.

New Line Cinema/Scholastic Productions/Depth of Field/Ingenious Film Partners/Rhythm and Hues-Entertainment Film Distributors.
113 mins. USA/UK. 2007. Rel: 5 Dec 2007. Cert PG.

Gone Baby Gone ★★★★

Featuring two private investigators, this Boston-set thriller about the kidnapping of a child carries several echoes of the *film noir* movies of the 1940s. That reduces our surprise as plot twists emerge but, under the direction of Ben Affleck, this is well done, atmospheric and persuasively performed. What does surprise is the sudden switch at the close which finds an intriguing moral question being raised. This enhances the film, and the more so because it refuses to manipulate the audience who are left to ponder for themselves the issue that emerges. MS

▶ Casey Affleck, Michelle Monaghan, Morgan Freeman, Ed Harris, Amy Ryan.
▶ *Dir* Ben Affleck, *Pro* Alan Ladd Jr, Dan Rissner and Sean Bailey, *Screenplay* Affleck and Aaron Stockard from Dennis Lehane's novel, *Ph* John Toll, *Pro Des* Sharon Seymour, *Ed* William Goldenberg, *M* Harry Gregson-Williams, *Costumes* Alix Friedberg.

Miramax Films present a Ladd Company

production-Buena Vista International (UK).
114 mins. USA. 2007. Rel: 6 June 2008. Cert 15.

Good Luck Chuck ★½

Thanks to a childhood curse, Chuck Logan
(Cook) is unable to find true love. Instead,
he's become an urban legend, attracting an
array of available women who believe that one
bonk with him will usher in the love of their
life – on their very next encounter. In keeping
with the recent trend for gross-out cinema, this
one presents us with the oral pleasuring of a
penguin and the sexual abuse of a grapefruit.
The rest is just obnoxious and far-fetched
detritus with a soggy centre. JC-W

▶ Connor Price, Dane Cook, Dan Fogler, Troy
Gentile, Caroline Ford, Natalie Morris, Ella English.
▶ *Dir* Mark Helfrich, *Pro* Mike Karz, Tracey E
Edmonds, Russell Hollander, Brian Volk-Weiss and
Barry Katz, *Screenplay* Josh Stolberg, from a short
story by Steve Glenn, *Ph* Anthony B Richmond,
Pro Des Mark S Freeborn, *Ed* Julia Wong, *M* Aaron
Zigman, *Costumes* Trish Keating.

Karz Entertainment/Lionsgate Films-Lionsgate.
101 mins. USA/Canada. 2007. Rel: 9 Nov 2007. Cert 15.

The Good Night ★

Gary (Martin Freeman) is a dissatisfied
commercial jingle writer whose relationship
with his girlfriend Dora (Gwyneth Paltrow) has
reached rock bottom. He only finds happiness
and true love in his dreams when he meets
the beautiful Anna (Pénelope Cruz). Martin
Freeman's wet and dull dream is a real bore
with a totally wasted Cruz who looks very
uncomfortable as the object of this loser's
desire. GS

▶ Pénelope Cruz, Danny De Vito, Martin Freeman,
Michael Gambon, Gwyneth Paltrow, Simon Pegg,
Keith Allen.
▶ *Dir and Screenplay* Jake Paltrow, *Pro* Donna
Gigliotti and Bill Johnson, *Ph* Giles Nuttgens,
Pro Des Eve Stewart, *Ed* Rick Lawley, *M* Alec Puro,
Costumes Verity Hawkes.

Destination Films/Good Night Productions/Grosvenor
Park Media etc-Momentum Pictures.
93 mins. USA/UK/Germany. 2008. Rel: 18 Jan 2008.
Cert 15.

Gypsy Caravan: When the Road Bends ★★★½

Half-way between Tony Gatliff's films about
gypsies and the much loved *Buena Vista Social
Club*, this well intentioned documentary shows
gypsy musicians from Romania, Macedonia,
India and Spain touring America in 2001 and
drawing closer in the process. There's interesting

Daniel Craig
in *The Golden
Compass.*

biographical material here but Jasmine Dellal has problems in shaping it all effectively. Nevertheless, those drawn to this subject matter will enjoy the film. (aka *When the Road Bends: Tales of a Gypsy Caravan*) MS

➤ With Antonio el Pipa, Esma Redzepova, Harish Kumar, Nicolae Ionita.
➤ *Dir, Pro* and *Screenplay* Jasmine Dellal, *Ph* Albert Maysles, Dellal and others, *Ed* Mary Myers and Dellal etc.

Little Dust Productions in association with ITVS, Fu Works & Fortissimo Films-ICA Films.
116 mins. USA/Netherlands. 2006. Rel: 28 Sept 2007. Cert PG.

Hairspray ★★★½

This is the film version of the musical derived from the John Waters movie of 1988. It's as nostalgic for the 1960s as *The Boy Friend* was for the '20s, but it is up to date in celebrating difference, the heroine being a plump 18 year old played by Nikki Blonsky. Through TV exposure in Baltimore, she gets to be Miss Teenage Hairspray. Its score is not the greatest and *Dreamgirls* was more memorable, but this is enjoyable enough. John Travolta's turn in drag as the heroine's mother includes an appealing duet with Christopher Walken as her father. MS

➤ John Travolta, Nikki Blonsky, Michelle Pfeiffer, Christopher Walken, Queen Latifah, Amanda Bynes, James Marsden, Brittany Snow.
➤ *Dir* and *Choreography* Adam Shankman, *Pro* Craig Zadan and Neil Meron, *Screenplay* Leslie Dixon from John Waters' 1988 screenplay and the 2002 musical stage play, *Ph* Bojan Bazelli, *Pro Des* David Gropman, *Ed* Michael Tronick, *M* Marc Shaiman and Scott Wittman, *Costumes* Rita Ryack.

New Line Cinema/Ingenious Film Partners/Offspring Entertainment-Entertainment Film Distributors Ltd.
116 mins. USA/UK. 2007. Rel: 20 July 2007. Cert PG

Half Moon ★★½

Lovers of magic realism may warm, as I did not, to this third feature by Bahman Ghobadi who gave us the splendid *A Time for Drunken Horses* (2000). It's a road movie about a musician journeying by way of Azerbaijan to perform in Kurdish Iraq and planning to include a female voice regardless of Iran's ban on that. The film's potential is great but an uneasy attempt to blend comedy and drama and to add a surreal element too results in a mix that did not work for me. (Original title: *Niwemang*) MS

➤ Ismail Ghaffari, Allah Morad Rashtiani,

Hedieh Tehrani, Golshifteh Farahani.
➤ *Dir* and *Pro* Bahman Ghobadi, *Screenplay* Ghobadi with Behnam Behzadi, *Ph* Nigel Bluck and Crighton Bone, *Pro Des* Mansooreh Yazdanjoo and Ghobadi, *Ed* Hayedeh Safiyari, *M* Hossein Alizadeh.

MiJ Films/Silkroad Production/New Crowned Hope Festival Vienna 2006 etc-ICA Films.
114 mins. Iran/Iraq/Austria/France/UK. 2006. Rel: 4 Jan 2008. No cert.

Hallam Foe ★★★

Echoes abound, from *Hamlet* to Hitchcock, but this Scottish tale of a troubled son (the ever excellent Jamie Bell) obsessed by his dead mother is too specific to invite audience identification through recognisable problems of adolescence. Eventually melodrama takes over which makes one question David Mackenzie's wisdom when choosing material, although his directorial skills remain impressive. Striking too is Sophia Myles in the central female role. MS

➤ Jamie Bell, Sophia Myles, Ciarán Hinds, Jamie Sives, Ewen Bremner.
➤ *Dir* David Mackenzie, *Pro* Gillian Berrie, *Screenplay* Ed Whitmore and Mackenzie based on the novel by Peter Jinks, *Ph* Giles Nuttgens, *Pro Des* Tom Sayer, *Ed* Colin Monie, *Costumes* Trisha Biggar.

Film4/Ingenious Film Partners/Scottish Screen/ Glasgow Film Finance Ltd/Independent Film Sales/ Sigma Films/Lunar Films etc-Buena Vista International (UK).
96 mins. UK. 2006. Rel: 31 Aug 2007. Cert 18.

Halloween ★★★½

Rather than simply remake John Carpenter's archetypal slasher flick, writer/director Rob Zombie adds an illuminating, new first act focusing on Michael Myers' journey from psycho boy to supernatural fiend. After that it's a pretty straight retelling of a film that was in no need of such treatment, but the extra gore's a laugh, the new Michael's agreeably massive, it's respectful to the source material and actually quite scary, bordering on disturbing. MJ

➤ Malcolm McDowell, Brad Dourif, Tyler Mane, William Forsythe, Sheri Moon Zombie, Udo Kier, Clint Howard.
➤ *Dir* and *Screenplay* Rob Zombie, based on the 1978 screenplay by John Carpenter and Debra Hill, *Pro* Zombie, Malek Akkad and Andy Gould, *Ph* Phil Parmet, *Pro Des* Anthony Tremblay, *Ed* Glenn Garland, *M* Tyler Bates, *Costumes* Mary McLeod.

Dimension Films/Nightfall Productions/Spectacle Entertainment Group/Trancas International Films/The

Weinstein Company-Paramount Pictures.
109 mins. USA. 2007. Rel: 28 Sep 2007. Cert 18.

Hannah Montana and Miley Cyrus Best of Both Worlds Concert Tour (3D) ★★★

This film was shot during Miley Cyrus and her alter ego Hanna Montana's 69-city concert tour called 'Best of Both Worlds'. The documentary also goes behind the scenes before the tour where Miley is rehearsing or composing some of the songs. Cyrus is a talented young lady and her enjoyable concert looks even better in gorgeous 3D. It is fun and young girls will certainly have a great time. GS

▶ Miley Cyrus, Billy Ray Cyrus, Paul Becker, Jaco Caraco, Joe Jonas.
▶ *Dir* Bruce Hendricks, *Pro* Hendricks, Kenny Ortega and Arthur F Repola, *Ph* Mitch Amundsen, *Ed* Michael Tronick, *Costumes* Dahlia Foroutan.

Pace-Walt Disney Pictures.
90 mins. USA. 2008. Rel: 14 Mar 2008. Cert U.

The Happening ★★★½

For no apparent reason the inhabitants of New York and Philadelphia start killing themselves. As the remaining populace floods into the countryside to escape the unseen cause, science teacher Elliot Moore (Mark Wahlberg) struggles to piece together the mystery. An accomplished cross between *The Mist and The Day of the Triffids*, *The Happening* is a return to form for M Night Shyamalan. Only the film's last third, which takes on a formulaic and maudlin air, lets the side down. JC-W

▶ Mark Wahlberg, Zooey Descanel, John Leguizamo, Ashlyn Sanchez, Betty Buckley, M Night Shyamalan.
▶ *Dir and Screenplay* M Night Shyamalan, *Pro* Shyamalan, Barry Mendel and Sam Mercer, *Ph* Tak Fujimoto, *Pro Des* Jeannine Claudia Oppewall, *Ed* Conrad Buff IV, *M* James Newton Howard, *Costumes* Betsy Heimann.

Blinding Edge Pictures/Barry Mendel Productions/Spyglass Entertainment etc/20th Century Fox Film Corporation.
91 mins. USA. 2008. Rel: 13 June 2008. Cert 15.

Happily N'ever After ★½

When the Wise Wizard of Fairyland goes on vacation, he leaves incompetent assistants Mambo and Muck in charge. But Wicked Stepmother (Sigourney Weaver) steals his magic staff and starts to change the plots of all our favourite tales. This animated feature sounds better on paper than in practice. The humour is forced and the visuals lack imagination. All in all an uninspired effort. CB

Zooey Deschanel and Mark Wahlberg in *The Happening*.

Mike Leigh
directs the
award-winning
Sally Hawkins in
Happy-Go-Lucky.

❧ Voices of George Carlin, Patrick Warburton, Sarah Michelle Gellar, Sigourney Weaver, Lisa Kaplan, Michael McShane, Freddie Prinze Jr, Wallace Shawn.
❧ *Dir* Paul J Bolger and Yvette Kaplan, *Pro* John H Williams, *Screenplay* Robert Moreland and Douglas Langdale, *Ph* David Dulac, *Pro Des* Deane Taylor, *Ed* Ringo Waldenburger, *M* Paul Buckley.

BAF Berlin Animation Film/ BFC Berliner Film Companie/Vanguard Films/Vanguard Animation Film-Odyssey Entertainment.
87 mins. USA/Germany. 2006. Rel: 3 Aug 2007. Cert U.

Happy-Go-Lucky ★★★

Acclaimed at Cannes but given a mixed reception here, Mike Leigh's latest has a fine cast headed by Sally Hawkins and Eddie Marsan and it's not the lightweight piece you may have been led to expect. If the schoolteacher Poppy adopts a bright surface to cope, the racist driving instructor she encounters is a tragicomic figure. Yet good scenes alternate with unpersuasive ones, the storyline is slender and Leigh's most engagingly optimistic female remains the one memorably incarnated by Ruth Sheen in *High Hopes* (1988). Nevertheless, all admirers of Leigh's work will want to judge for themselves. MS

❧ Sally Hawkins, Eddie Marsan, Alexis Zegerman, Sylvestra Le Touzel, Sarah Niles.
❧ *Dir* and *Screenplay* Mike Leigh, *Pro* Simon Channing-Williams, *Ph* Dick Pope, *Pro Des* Mark Tildesley, *Ed* Jim Clark, *M* Gary Yershon, *Costumes* Jacqueline Durran.

Summit Entertainment/Ingenious Partners/ Film4/UK Film Council/Thin Man Films etc-Momentum Pictures.
118 mins. UK/USA. 2007. Rel: 18 April 2008. Cert 15.

Harold and Kumar Escape from Guantanamo Bay ★½

If you saw the first Harold and Kumar outing (*H & K Get the Munchies* aka *H & K Go to White Castle*) you will know if you want to see the sequel in which the Indian and Korean pothead buddies head for cannabis bliss in Amsterdam but end up in a Guantamamo cell… but not for long. They manage to escape and on their journey back across the US get involved with the Ku Klux Klan, rednecks, whores and druggies, so it's much the same as before. If you thought *Borat* was in bad taste, you ain't seen nuthin' yet. CB

❧ John Cho, Kal Penn, Rob Orddry, Jack Conley, Roger Bart, Beverley D'Angelo.
❧ *Dir and Screenplay* Jon Hurwitz and Hayden

Schlossberg, *Pro* Nathan Kahane and Greg Shapiro, *Ph* Daryn Okada, *Pro Des* Tony Fanning, *Ed* Jeff Freeman, *M* George S Clinton, *Costumes* Shawn Holly Cookson.

Kingsgate Films/Mandate Pictures-New Line Cinema.
100 mins. USA. 2008. Rel: 30 May 2008. Cert 18.

Harry Potter and the Order of the Phoenix ★★★½

Part five of the Potter saga is the darkest yet and has Harry nearly getting expelled from Hogwarts for using his magic powers extramurally. The possible return of arch-enemy Voldemort (Fiennes) and a plot against Harry and his mentor Dumbledore (Gambon) are exacerbated by the arrival of Dolores Umbridge, a new broomstick sweeping her way through the Ministry of Magic like a mad version of Maggie Thatcher. It's the usual special effects and the still reliably good performances of the three young leads but even they are dwarfed by the killer instincts of Imelda Staunton's demented Dolores. MHD

❯ Daniel Radcliffe, Emma Watson, Rupert Grint, Fiona Shaw, Richard Griffiths, Ralph Fiennes, Imelda Staunton, Michael Gambon, Gary Oldman, Maggie Smith, Alan Rickman, Julie Walters, Robbie Coltrane, Jason Isaacs, Helena Bonham Carter.
❯ *Dir* David Yates, *Pro* David Barron and David

Heyman, *Screenplay* Michael Goldenberg, from the novel by J K Rowling, *Ph* Slawomir Idziak, *Pro Des* Stuart Craig, *Ed* Mark Day, *M* Nicholas Hooper, *Costumes* Jany Temime.

Warner Bros Pictures/Heyday Films/ Cool Music-Warner Bros.
138 mins. UK/USA. 2007. Rel: 12 Jul 2007. Cert 12A

Hatchet ★

During New Orleans' Mardi Gras two friends, Ben (Joel Moore) and Marcus (Deon Richmond), look for adventure, so they join a group of tourists on a haunted swamp tour. All the stereotypes are aboard this doomed boat – from the horrid misogynistic lecher who pretends he is a film director to the two very silly girls who want fame but spend the whole film screaming their heads off. It is a very nasty film, badly made and acted, which has no redeeming features whatsoever. GS

❯ Joel Moore, Tamara Feldman, Deon Richmond, Mercedes McNab, Parry Shen, Robert Englund.
❯ *Dir and Screenplay* Adam Green, *Pro* Sarah Elbert and Cory Neal, *Ph* Will Barratt, *Pro Des* Bryan McBrien, *Ed* Christopher Roth, *M* Andy Garfield, *Costumes* Heather Sladinski.

ArieScope Pictures/High Seas Entertainment/ Radioaktive Film-The Works.
85 mins. USA. 2006. Rel: 5 Oct 2007. Cert 18.

Rupert Grint, Daniel Radcliffe and Emma Watson in *Harry Potter and the Order of the Phoenix.*

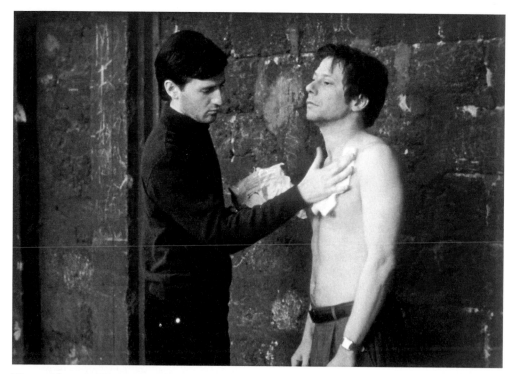

The ubiquitous Matthieu Amalric (right) in *La Question humaine* [*Heartbeat Detector*].

Heartbeat Detector ★★½

On paper it sounds intriguing: a view of the ruthless drive behind modern corporations that dares to suggest that they share the same lack of respect for human life associated with the Nazi concentration camps. Unfortunately, the treatment is slow and arty and, despite the potential of its challenging thesis, the film works well only at the close when Lou Castel's character reads a wartime letter also featured in Claude Lanzmann's *Shoah* (1985). That apart, this is one for eggheads. (Original title: *La Question humaine*) MS

▶ Matthieu Amalric, Michael Lonsdale, Jean-Pierre Kalfon, Lou Castel, Édith Scob.
▶ *Dir* Nicolas Klotz, *Pro* Sophie Dulac and Michel Zana, *Screenplay* Elisabeth Perceval based on François Emmanuel's novel *La Question humaine*, *Ph* Josée Deshales, *Pro Des* Antoine Platteau, *Ed* Rose-Marie Lausson, *M* Syd Matters, *Costumes* Dorothée Guiraud.

Sophie Dulac Productions/Centre national de la cinématographie etc-Trinity Filmed Entertainment. 140 mins. France. 2007. Rel: 16 May 2008. Cert 12A

The Heartbreak Kid ★★★

Sports store owner Eddie (Stiller) thinks he has met the perfect woman in Lila (Akerman), so he marries her but she turns out to be the bride from hell. On their disastrous honeymoon he meets Miranda (Monaghan), the real girl of his dreams, so how can he now break up with his new wife? A remake of the Elaine May-

Neil Simon comedy which was much funnier in 1972, the Farrellys' film broadens and very coarsely dumbs it down, but a good deal of the black fun survives in Stiller's performance. MHD

▶ Ben Stiller, Malin Akerman, Michelle Monaghan, Jerry Stiller, Carlos Mencia.
▶ *Dir* Bobby Farrelly and Peter Farrelly, *Pro* Ted Field and Bradley Thomas, *Screenplay* Bobby & Peter Farrelly, Scot Armstrong, Kevin Barnett, Leslie Dixon based on Bruce Jay Friedman's short story *A Change of Plan* and Neil Simon's 1972 screenplay, *Ph* Matthew F Leonetti, *Pro Des* Sydney Bartholomew and Jay Vetter, *Ed* Alan Baumgarten and Sam Seig, *M* Bill Ryan and Brendan Ryan, *Costumes* Louise Mingenbach.

DreamWorks Pictures/Conundrum Entertainment/ Davis Entertainment/Radar Pictures-DreamWorks SKG. 116 mins. USA. 2007. Rel: 5 Oct 2007. Cert 15.

Her Name is Sabine ★★★

Nothing could be more personal than Sandrine Bonnaire's first film as director, a documentary about her autistic sister Sabine. It allows Sabine to appear screen centre and tells her tragic story, albeit one not entirely without hope. Even so, for outsiders this sincerely felt film fails to illuminate and never gets to grips with anything that would make it a truly revealing and worthwhile exercise.

▶ With Sabine Bonnaire, Sandrine Bonnaire.
▶ *Dir* Sandrine Bonnaire, *Pro* Thomas Schmitt, *Ph* Bonnaire and Catherine Cabrol, *Ed* Svetlana

Vaynblat, *M* Jefferson Lembeye and Walter N'guyen.

A Mosaïque Films production etc-ICA Films.
90 mins. France/Switzerland/Belgium. 2007.
Rel: 20 June 2008. Cert 12A.

He Was a Quiet Man ★★★

This film's title comes from the not infrequently quoted response of those who learn that their respectable seeming neighbour is a killer. However, it's more of a black comedy than a thriller with Christian Slater playing a put-upon office worker. He's obsessed with the idea of killing his unfriendly colleagues but then finds himself greeted as a hero fit for promotion when he intervenes and shoots an employee who has acted out what he himself has only dreamed. Slater and lead actress Elisha Cuthbert are fine but the piece loses direction and doesn't really come off despite being interesting. MS

▶ Christian Slater, Elisha Cuthbert, William H Macy, Sascha Knopf.
▶ *Dir* and *Screenplay* Frank Cappello, *Pro* Michael Leahy and Cappello, *Ph* Brandon Trost, *Pro Des* Ermanno Di Febo-Orsini, *Ed* Kirk Morri, *M* Jeff Beal, *Costumes* Sarah Trost.

Quiet Man Productions, LLC-High Fliers Films.
95 mins. USA. 2007. Rel: 7 Dec 2007. Cert 15.

Helvetica ★★★★

Helvetica is the typeface designed in Switzerland which became ubiquitous. This well-judged documentary traces its origins and the ups and downs of its subsequent history which, being presented chronologically, gives shape to the piece. Gary Hustwit's film is also a comment on changing taste during recent decades and it makes you look afresh at the lettering of all the advertising that surrounds us. MS

▶ With David Carson, Matthew Carter, Massimo Vignelli, Erik Spiekermann.
▶ *Dir* and *Pro* Gary Hustwit, *Ph* Luke Geissbühler, *Ed* Shelby Siegel.

A Swiss Dots production in association with Veer-ICA Films.
80 mins. UK/USA. 2007. Rel: 7 Sept 2007. No cert.

Hitman ★★★

No one ever said an action movie couldn't be stupid. Indeed, in the right hands, or possibly the wrong ones, the correct amount of dumb can save a film from being terminally bog-standard. A case in point is this crazed but straight-faced, surprisingly stylish and inventive feature adaptation of a bloody video game. Timothy Olyphant plays a chrome-domed, genetically-engineered, world class assassin, inexplicably pricked by conscience and suddenly at war with both the goodies and the baddies. MJ

▶ Timothy Olyphant, Dougray Scott, Olga Kurylenko, Robert Knepper, Ulrich Thomsen, James Faulkner.
▶ *Dir* Xavier Gens, *Pro* Adrian Askarieh, Charles Gordon and Pierre-Ange Le Pogram, *Screenplay* Skip Woods, *Ph* Laurent Bares, *Pro Des* Jacques Bufnoir, *Ed* Carlo Rizzo and Antoine Vareille, *M* Geoff Zanelli, *Costumes* Olivier Beriot.

Twentieth Century Fox/Europa Corp/Anka Film/
Daybreak Productions/Dune Entertainment/Prime
Universe Productions-20th Century Fox.
100 mins. France/USA. 2007. Rel: 30 Nov 2007. Cert 15.

The Hoax ★★

This is the real-life tale of Clifford Irving's attempt to pass himself off as the authorised biographer of the reclusive millionaire Howard Hughes. However, the hoax perpetrated by writer William Wheeler and director Lasse Hallström is to persuade an audience that the excellent cast (Richard Gere is at his best as Irving) will render credible this fanciful take on reality. They simply can't, not when the script offers a mix that is one part naturalistic drama, one part exaggerated comedy and one part stylised hallucinations. MS

▶ Richard Gere, Alfred Molina, Marcia Gay Harden, Hope Davis, Julie Delpy, Eli Wallach, Stanley Tucci.
▶ *Dir* Lasse Hallström, *Pro* Bob Yari, Joshua D Maurer, Leslie Holleran etc, *Screenplay* William Wheeler based on the book by Clifford Irving,

The chrome-domed Timothy Olyphant in *Hitman*.

Rafal Fudalej and the altarpiece doomed to be stolen in *Hope*.

Ph Oliver Stapleton, *Pro Des* Mark Ricker, *Ed* Andrew Mondshein, *M* Carter Burwell, *Costumes* David Robinson.

Miramax Films/Bob Yari Productions/The Mark Gordon Company/Syndicate Films International etc-Momentum Pictures.
116 mins. USA. 2006. Rel: 3 Aug 2007. Cert 15.

Honeydripper ★★★½

Alabama in 1950 is the scene for John Sayles's latest film and music is the key: it's about the moment when, for many a guitarist, a new rhythm led them from jazz to what would become rock 'n' roll. Superbly photographed by Dick Pope and richly atmospheric, this is a film reflecting once again Sayles's warmth towards people and his social concerns. There is a debit side, however: the film is too long and the actual plot-line is surprisingly trite. MS

▶ Danny Glover, Yaya DaCosta, Gary Clark Jr, Charles S Dutton, Lisa Gay Hamilton, Stacy Keach, Mary Steenbergen, Vondie Curtis Hall, John Sayles.
▶ *Dir*, *Ed* and *Screenplay* John Sayles, *Pro* Maggie Renzi, *Ph* Dick Pope, *Pro Des* Toby Corbett, *M* Mason Daring, *Costumes* Hope Hanafin.

Anarchists' Convention/Emerging Pictures/Rainforest Films-Axiom Films Ltd.
124 mins. USA. 2007. Rel: 9 May 2008. Cert PG.

Hope ★★★

Krzysztof Piesiewicz wrote for the late Krzysztof Kieslowski and perhaps needs a collaborator to get his work into shape. Debutant director Stanislaw Mucha does an efficient job here but accepts a screenplay which, dealing with an idealistic youth and an art robbery, certainly intrigues one yet raises all sorts of unresolved questions about what it is trying to say. Consequently there's plenty to interest us but little real satisfaction despite a good cast. MS

▶ Rafal Fudalej, Wojciech Pszoniak, Kamilla Baar, Zbigniew Zapasiewicz.
▶ *Dir* Stanislaw Mucha, *Pro* Reinhard Brundig, Raimond Goebel and Zbigniew Dornagalski, *Screenplay* Krzysztof Piesiewicz, *Ph* Krzysztof Ptak, *Pro Des* Anna Wunderlich, *Ed* Jacek Tarasiuk, *M* Max Richter, *Costumes* Magdalena Biedrzycka.

Pandora Film & Studio Filmowe Kalejdoskop/ Telewizja Polska SA/Canal+ etc-Dogwoof Pictures.
101 mins. Germany/Poland. 2007. Rel: 18 April 2008. Cert 15.

Hot Rod ★★★

A likeable comedy about an amateur daredevil and his clueless entourage, *Hot Rod* sees *Saturday Night Live* regular Andy Samberg play a predictably lovable idiot forced by fate to attempt the jump of his life. Inspired by the showmanship and recklessness of 1970s icon Evel Knievel, *Hot Rod* plays like a Will Ferrell sports spoof, only cheaper, half as funny, and without Will Ferrell. It's watchable for sure, but hardly the main event. MJ

➤ Andy Samberg, Jorma Taccone, Bill Hader, Danny McBride, Isla Fisher, Ian McShane, Sissy Spacek.
➤ *Dir* Akiva Schaffer, *Pro* John Goldwyn and Lorne Michaels, *Screenplay* Pam Brady, *Ph* Andrew Dunn, *Pro Des* Stephen Altman, *Ed* Malcolm Campbell, *M* Trevor Rabin, *Costumes* Tish Monaghan.

Paramount Pictures/Broadway Video/The Lonely Island-Paramount Pictures.
88 mins. USA. 2007. Rel: 28 Sep 2007. Cert 12A.

Hotel Harabati ★★★

A post 9/11 view of paranoia in society, this French movie echoes a comparable take on an earlier period, Jacques Rivette's *Paris nous appartient* (1961). The story chosen to illustrate this is predictably offbeat although centred on a couple whose marriage is in danger of falling apart. Far too much here remains obscure however (as in Antonioni's celebrated *Blow-Up*), a fact that increasingly diminishes the impact of the piece. The veteran Anouk Aimée has a small role. (Original title: *De particulier à particulier*) MS

➤ Helene Fillières, Laurent Lucas, Julie Gayet, Anouk Aimée, Anthony Roth Costanzo.
➤ *Dir* Brice Cauvin, *Pro* Marc Irmer, *Screenplay* Cauvin, Jérôme Beaujour and Pierre Schöller, *Ph* Marc Tévanian, *Art Dir* Philippe van Herwijnen, *Ed* Agathe Cauvin, *Costumes* Eléonore Dominguez.

Mille et une productions/CNC/TPS Star etc-Soda Pictures.
93 mins. France. 2006. Rel: 7 Dec 2007. No cert.

The Hottie and the Nottie ★

Avoid this dire film and the talentless Paris Hilton. She plays Christabel, the 'perfect' woman (if you can believe it) who hangs out with her grotesque best friend June (Christine Lakin), so that any man who wants to seduce Christabel has to put up with June as well. Hilton is unable to look natural even when she walks, she looks ridiculous and resembles a man in drag in the wedding dress scene and her make-up and false eyelashes keep changing from scene to scene. She simply shouldn't be encouraged! GS

➤ Paris Hilton, Joel David Moore, Christine Lakin, Johann Urb, Adam Kulbersh.
➤ *Dir* Tom Putnam, *Pro* Neal Ramer, Hadeel Reda, Victoria Nevinny and Myles Nestel, *Screenplay* Heidi Ferrer, *Ph* Alex Vendler, *Pro Des* John Larena,

Paris Hilton and Christine Lakin are *The Hottie and the Nottie.*

Tre Armstrong (centre) in *How She Move*.

Ed Jeff Malmberg, *M* David E Russo, *Costumes* Christopher Lawrence.

Purple Pictures/Summit Entertainment-Pathé International. 90 mins. USA. 2008. Rel: 28 Mar 2008. Cert 12A.

How She Move ★★½

This film is very similar to *Step Up 2 –The Streets* but better. Raya (Rutina Wesley), a daughter of Jamaican immigrants, is thrilled when accepted to the exclusive Seaton Academy. But when her sister dies from a drug overdose, Raya is forced to leave school and re-examine her roots. Predictable to say the least but the strong step dancing choreography and Wesley's luminous performance carry the film effortlessly. GS

➤ Tre Armstrong, Rutina Wesley, Boyd Banks, Clé Bennett, Ardon Bess, DeRay Davis, Keyshia Cole.
➤ *Dir* Ian Iqbal Rashid, *Pro* Jennifer Kawaja and Julia Sereny, *Screenplay* Annmarie Morais, *Ph* André Pienaar, *Pro Des* Adrian Leroux, *Ed* Susan Maggi, *M* Andrew Lockington, *Costumes* Kimberley Ann Rush.

Celluloid Dreams/MTV Films/Sienna Films etc-Celluloid Dreams 94 mins. Canada. 2007. Rel: 4 Apr 2008. Cert 12A.

I Am Legend ★★★★

Immune from a deadly virus that has killed the entire population of New York, Will Smith plays the last man alive who sets out with his trusty dog to look for other survivors but also trying to avoid a species of mutant plague victims. A remake of the 1971 Charlton Heston starrer, this is a more polished affair, really spooky in the scenes of deserted desolation, but is Will Smith just too loveable for such a heavy ecological disaster? Obviously not, as a sequel is on the cards. MHD

➤ Will Smith, Alice Braga, Charlie Tahan, Salli Richardson, Willow Smith, Emma Thompson.
➤ *Dir* Francis Lawrence, *Pro* Akiva Goldsman David Heyman, James Lassiter and Neal Moritz, *Screenplay* Goldsman and Mark Protosevich, based on the novel *I Am Legend* by Richard Matheson, from the 1971 screenplay *The Omega Man* by John William Corrington and Joyce Corrington, *Ph* Andrew Lesnie, *Pro Des* Naomi Shohan, *Ed* Wayne Wahrman, *M* James Newton Howard, *Costumes* Michael Kaplan.

Warner Bros Pictures/Village Roadshow Pictures/Weed Road/Overbrook Entertainment/3 Arts Entertainment/ Heyday Films/Original Film-Warner Bros. 101 mins. USA. 2007. Rel: 26 Dec 2007. Cert 15.

I Do ★★★

Charlotte Gainsbourg has rarely been so engaging and it's a pleasure to see Bernadette Lafont again. Sadly, the piece they are in is rather silly and decidedly forgettable. It's about a bachelor's plan to avoid his family's demands that he marry by arranging a bogus engagement that will be broken off. Thanks to the players it's a tolerable way to pass an hour and a half, but that's all. (Original title: *Prête-moi ta main*) MS

▷ Alain Chabat, Charlotte Gainsbourg, Bernadette Lafont, Wladimir Yordanoff.
▷ *Dir* Eric Lartigau, *Pro* Alain Chabat, Amandine Billot and Christine Rouxel, *Screenplay* Chabat from his own idea with Laurent Zeltoun, Philippe Mechelen and others, *Ph* Régis Blondeau, *Pro Des* Sylvie Olivé, *Ed* Juliette Welfling, *M* Erwann Kermorvant, *Costumes* Anne Schotte.

Chez Wam/StudioCanal/ Script Associés/TFI Films/ Canal Plus-Optimum Releasing.
89 Mins. France. 2006. Rel: 2 Nov 2007. Cert 15.

I Don't Want To Sleep Alone
★★★

The current man of the moment in far eastern cinema seems to be the Malaysian born Taiwan based Tsai Ming-Liang. This piece of his set in Kuala Lumpur and made in 2006 is characteristic in its portrait of frustrated lives and loves. It's atmospheric with superb compositions, but less involving than one would wish. Furthermore, the ending, although hailed as a triumph by some, strikes me as kitsch with happiness being attained at last in a dreamlike image accompanied by Charles Chaplin's music from *Limelight*! (Original title: *Hei yan quan*) MS

▷ Lee Kang-Sheng, Chen Siang-Chyi, Norman Atun, Pearlly Chua.
▷ *Dir* and *Screenplay* Tsai Ming-Liang, *Pro* Bruno Pesery and Vincent Wang, *Ph* Liao Pen-Jung, *Pro Des* Lee Tian-Jue, *Ed* Chen Sheng-Chang, *Costumes* Sun Hui-Mey.

Soudaine Compagnie/Homegreen Films/New Crowned Hope etc-Axiom Films Ltd.
118 mins. France/Taiwan/Austria/China/UK/ Netherlands. 2006. Rel: 16 Nov 2007. Cert 15.

I for India ★★★★★

Modest, touching and immensely satisfying, this is a documentary in which Sandhya Suri tells the story of her family. Her father, who left India for England in 1965 and returned here after a later shortlived attempt to relocate to Delhi, is central, but she never takes sides, being fair to everyone. Family videos contribute to the story which emerges not just as a personal tale but as a piece of social history. This is a delightful film. MS

▷ With Yash Pal Suri, Sandhya Suri, Sheel Suri, Vanita Suri, Neeraj Suri.
▷ *Dir* and *Screenplay* Sandhya Suri, *Pro* Carlo Cresto-Dina, Kai Künnermann and Thomas Kufus, *Ph* Suri and Lars Lenski, *Ed* Cinzia Baldessari and Brian Tagg.

Fandango and zero west co-production with ZDF etc-ICA Films.
70 mins. Italy/Germany/Finland/South Africa/UK. 2005. Rel: 3 Aug 2007. No cert.

Lee Kang-Sheng has a less than ideal sleeping companion in *Hei yan quan* [*I Don't Want To Sleep Alone*].

I'm a Cyborg ★★★★

Rain and Su-Jeong Lim as institutional inmates who find their own way in *Saibogujiman kwenchana* [*I'm a Cyborg*].

Turning away most of the time from the violence of such past work as *Oldboy* (2003), Korea's Park Chan-wook comes up with the most bizarre of movies. It's a kind of fantastical comedy about inmates of an institution and their obsessive delusions. Some will hate it despite the wonderful images but, if I am puzzled, I am also intrigued by a film which evokes the work of Michel Gondry, Tim Burton, Stanley Kubrick and Roy Andersson. MS

▶ Rain, Su-Jeong Lim, Choi Hee-jin, Lee Yong-nyeo, Jung Ji-hoon, Sohn Young-soon.
▶ *Dir* Park Chan-wook, *Pro* Lee Chun-young, *Screenplay* Chung Seo-kyung and Park, *Ph* Chung Chung-hoon, *Pro Des* Ryu Seong-hie, *Ed* Kim Sang-bum and Kim Jae-bum, *M* Hong Dae-sung and Hong Yoo-jin, *Costumes* Cho Sang-kyung.

A Moho Film production/CJ Entertainment Inc etc-Tartan Films.
107 mins. Republic of Korea. 2006. Rel: 4 April 2008. Cert 15.

I'm Not There ★★★

Cate Blanchett as one of six Bob Dylans in *I'm Not There*.

Cards on the table: I'm not familiar with the life of Bob Dylan. Consequently I can respond to Todd Haynes's sense of cinema here but I can't pick up on all the oblique information in this uniquely unconventional impressionistic biopic. With six players representing Dylan including Cate Blanchett (she's as good as they say) this long film is by turns engaging and frustrating. But for Dylan fans it will provide a different experience altogether whatever their view of it. MS

▶ Christian Bale, Cate Blanchett, Richard Gere, Heath Ledger, Ben Whishaw, Marcus Carl Franklin, Charlotte Gainsbourg, Julianne Moore, Michelle Williams, Kris Kristofferson.
▶ *Dir* Todd Haynes, *Pro* Christine Vachon, James D. Stern, John Sloss and John Goldwyn, *Screenplay* Haynes and Oren Moverman from Haynes's idea, *Ph* Edward Lachman, *Pro Des* Judy Becker, *Ed* Jay Rabinowitz, *Costumes* John Dunn.

The Weinstein Company/Celluloid Dreams World Sales/Endgame Entertainment/Killer Films//VIP Medienfonds 4 etc-Paramount Pictures UK.
136 mins. Germany/USA. 2007. Rel: 21 Dec 2007. Cert 15.

I Now Pronounce You Chuck and Larry ★

Just when you've really started to admire Adam Sandler, up he comes with this old-fashioned stinker with naff attitudes we left behind in the bad old '70s. Sandler and Kevin James play firefighters who pose as a stereotype camp gay couple to pull a pensions scam in this laugh-free, bad-taste, homophobic, racist farce that also has endless jibes at James's weight while

In Bruges star Colin Farrell takes aim, with fatal consequences.

making Sandler out as a sex god (to women, of course!). Rob Schneider wears silly teeth, a fuzzy wig and comedy specs to play a thick Japanese man, Ving Rhames is extremely embarrassing as a camp gay African-American fireman and Richard Chamberlain is awful as the judge at the movie's supposedly heartwarming climax. Avoid! DW

▶ Adam Sandler, Kevin James, Jessica Biel, Dan Aykroyd, Ving Rhames, Steve Buscemi, Richard Chamberlain.
▶ *Dir* Dennis Dugan, *Pro* Michael Bostick, Adam Sandler, Tom Shadyac, Jack Giarraputo, *Screenplay* Barry Fanaro, Alexander Payne and Jim Taylor, from a treatment by Lew Gallo, *Ph* Dean Semler, *Pro Des* Perry Andelin Blake, *Ed* Jeff Gourson, *M* Rupert Gregson-Williams, *Costumes* Ellen Lutter.

Universal Pictures/Relativity Media/Happy Madison Productions/Shady Acres Entertainment/Universal Pictures.
110 mins. USA. 2007. Rel: 21 Sep 2007. Cert 12A.

In Bruges ★★★½

Not since *Trainspotting* (1996) has a British film

spoken so powerfully with a voice of its own. Martin McDonagh's first feature with its tale of two hit men in Bruges which blends thrills, drama (echoes of Graham Greene here) and cutting edge humour is a triumph – or would be if the last section did not topple into absurd contrivances. But nothing can detract from the perfect teaming of Colin Farrell and Brendan Gleeson, and Ralph Fiennes is great too. Seriously flawed but still not to be missed. MS

▶ Colin Farrell, Brendan Gleeson, Ralph Fiennes, Clémence Poésy, Jérémie Rénier.
▶ *Dir* and *Screenplay* Martin McDonagh, *Pro* Graham Broadbent and Pete Czernin, *Ph* Eigil Bryld, *Pro Des* Michael Carlin, *Ed* Jon Gregory, *M* Carter Burwell, *Costumes* Jany Temime.

Focus Features/Film4/A Blueprint Pictures production/ Scion Films-Universal Pictures International UK & Eire.
107 mins. USA/UK/Germany. 2007. Rel: 18 April 2008. Cert 18.

In Memory of Me ★★

Set in a Venetian monastery, this film offers none of the sense of meditation contained in that extraordinary documentary of 2005, *Into Great Silence*. Instead, this is a painfully slow drama about religious vocation which, largely lacking the cut and thrust on the issues that dialogue could have provided, is dead in the water despite fine photography. Film-maker Saverio Costanzo avers that he doesn't see himself as a religious person but tries to believe in something. Well, yes. (Original title: *In memoria di me*) MS

‣ Christo Jivkov, Filippo Timi, Marco Baliani, André Hennicke, Fausto Russo Alesi.
‣ *Dir* Saverio Costanzo, *Pro* Mario Gianani, *Screenplay* Costanzo inspired by the book *Lacrime impure: Il gesuita perfetto* by Furio Monicelli, *Ph* Mario Amura, *Pro Des* Maurizio Leonardi, *Ed* Francesca Calvelli, *M* Alter Ego, *Costumes* Antonella Cannarozzi.

A Medusa Film and Offside production in collaboration with Sky supported by MEDIA-Artificial Eye Film Company.
117 mins. Italy. 2007. Rel: 9 Nov 2007. Cert U

In Memory Of My Father ★★½

A father dying in LA requests that his son Chris film his demise. But that's just a MacGuffin (to use the Hitchcock term for the irrelevant excuse for a plot) and the film is a talkative affair about problematic relationships between tiresome people. It meanders on, only occasionally working either as comedy or drama: blame Christopher Jaymes involved on all levels. MS

‣ Christopher Jaymes, Jeremy Sisto, Judy Greer, Christine Lakin, Matt Keeslar.
‣ *Dir*, *Pro* and *Screenplay* Christopher Jaymes, *Ph* Abe Levy, *Pro Des* Leah Faust, *Ed* Eric Michael Cole and Jaymes, *M* Dan Teper.

Persona Film Company/Interspot Film Gesellschaft-Scanbox Entertainment UK Ltd.
96 mins. USA/Austria. 2005. Rel: 6 June 2008. No cert.

In Search of a Midnight Kiss
★★★★

Aimed like *Clerks* (1994) at a young audience and shot in black and white, this is a romantic film about relationships set in New York. As a first feature for writer/director Alex Holdridge, who makes the strong language seem natural, this is a bright debut. There's no strong plot but engaging characters, neat dialogue (often humorous) and an up-to-date concept in that the couple who may or may not hit it off meet through a website. A well acted, engaging film. MS

‣ Scoot McNairy, Sara Simmonds, Brian Matthew Maguire, Katie Luong.

‣ *Dir* and *Screenplay* Alex Holdridge, *Pro* Seth Caplan and Scoot McNairy, *Ph* Robert Murphy, *Ed* Jacob Vaughn and Frank Reynolds, *Music Supervisors* Roanna Gillespie and Joe Paganelli.

Distributed by Vertigo Films.
100 mins. USA. 2008. Rel: 13 June 2008. Cert 15.

In the Hands of the Gods
★★★½

Youngsters especially will readily identify with the central figures in this documentary: youths who, although virtually penniless, set out to make their way from England to Argentina in the hope of meeting their idol Diego Maradona. You don't need to be interested in football to respond to their chutzpah and determination. More about the background of these individuals would have added to the interest but, despite conflicts en route, this is an engaging portrait of modern youth. MS

‣ With Mike 'Mikey' Fisher, Sami Hall Bassam, Jeremy Lynch, Danny Robinson, Paul 'Woody' Wood, Diego Maradona.
‣ *Dir* Benjamin Turner and Gabe Turner, *Pro* Leo Pearlman, Ben Winston and Rebecca Green, *Ph* Matthew Beecroft and Diego Rodriguez, *Ed* Alastair Reid and Benjamin Turner, *M* Matthew Rozeik

A Fulwell 73/Green Wolf Films production in association with RTC Entertainment-Lionsgate UK.
106 mins. UK. 2007. Rel: 14 Sept 2007. Cert 15.

In the Shadow of the Moon
★★★★★

Beautifully judged and splendidly photographed, this is an uplifting documentary about the Apollo space missions and man's first landing on the moon. The reclusive Neil Armstrong may be absent but the film has real historical value including the engaging and

One small step against an epic backdrop – the awe-inspiring *In the Shadow of the Moon*.

remarkably humble comments of the other key astronauts now mainly in their seventies. The historical footage has been remastered and it's especially breathtaking when seen on the big screen. British director David Sington has done a fine job as has Philip Sheppard with his Copland-influenced music score. MS

▶ With Buzz Aldrin, Michael Collins, James Lovell, Edgar Mitchell, Alan Bean.
▶ *Dir* David Sington, *Pro* Duncan Copp, *Ph* Clive North, *Ed* David Fairhead, *M* Philip Sheppard.

Discovery Films/Channel Four/A DOX Productions film/Passion Pictures-Vertigo Films.
100 mins. UK. 2006. Rel: 2 Nov 2007. Cert U.

In the Valley of Elah ★★★★½

Tommy Lee Jones gives the performance of his life in this movie featuring a father with a military background seeking to trace and help his son who has reportedly gone AWOL on his return from Iraq. Like such Relph-Dearden pictures as *Sapphire* (1959) and *Victim* (1961) this uses a dramatic tale of investigation to comment on social issues, here the demands being made by the USA on its young soldiers. In passing, a few minor criticisms can be made,

Charlize Theron and Tommy Lee Jones *In the Valley of Elah.*

but this is a splendid film. Charlize Theron and Susan Sarandon are fine. MS

▶ Tommy Lee Jones, Charlize Theron, James Franco, Susan Sarandon, Josh Brolin.
▶ *Dir* Paul Haggis, *Pro* Patrick Wachsberger, Steven Samuels, Haggis and others, *Screenplay* Haggis from a story by Mark Boal and Haggis, *Ph* Roger Deakins, *Pro Des* Laurence Bennett, *Ed* Jo Francis, *M* Mark Isham, *Costumes* Lisa Jensen.

Warner Independent Pictures/Nala Films/Summit Entertainment/Samuels Media/A Blackfriar's Bridge production-Optimum Releasing.
121 mins. USA. 2007. Rel: 25 Jan 2008. Cert 15.

The Incredible Hulk ★★★

Ang Lee's *The Hulk* was, for most people, too arty a treatment of Marvel's not-so-jolly green giant. Considerably less complex and simply more entertaining is this second, more action-packed swipe at the franchise from *Transporter* director Louis Leterrier and weedy star Edward Norton. This time around, fugitive geneticist Bruce Banner is forced to embrace the beast within him to battle a bigger, scarier mutant. As silly and as exciting as it sounds, then easily forgotten. MJ

Cate Blanchett
and Harrison Ford
in *Indiana Jones
and the Kingdom
of the Crystal Skull*.

▶ Edward Norton, Liv Tyler, Tim Roth, William Hurt, Tim Blake Nelson, Ty Burrell, Christina Cabot.
▶ *Dir* Louis Leterrier, *Pro* Avi Arad, Kevin Feige and Gale Anne Hurd, *Screenplay* Zak Penn, *Ph* Peter Menzies Jr, *Pro Des* Kirk M Petruccelli, *Ed* Rick Shaine, Vincent Tabaillon and John Wright, *M* Craig Armstrong, *Costumes* Renee Bravene and Denise Cronenberg.

Marvel Enterprises/Marvel Studios/Valhalla Motion Pictures-Paramount Pictures.
114 mins. USA. 2008. Rel: 13 June 2008. Cert 12A.

Indiana Jones and the Kingdom of the Crystal Skull
★★★½

He might be drawing his pension and could soon need a walking frame, but there's still life in the old franchise yet as Harrison Ford revisits Indie territory some two decades on. The script may not be the best, but there's enough fun stuff and action along the way to keep the wheels turning on the old jalopy. Dr Jones stays one step ahead of the Russkies as they each vie to unearth a legendary crystal skull which has supernatural powers. Cate Blanchett is the Russian villainess, John Hurt plays another grizzled professor (*The Oxford Murders* qv) and Shia LaBeouf as Indie's young sidekick, Mutt, shows how good he will be when he takes over the leading role, as indeed he should. MHD

▶ Harrison Ford, Cate Blanchett, Karen Allen, Shia LaBeouf, Ray Winstone, John Hurt, Jim Broadbent.
▶ *Dir* Steven Spielberg, *Pro* Frank Marshall, Kathleen Kennedy and George Lucas, *Screenplay* David Koepp, from a story by George Lucas and Jeff Nathanson, *Ph* Janusz Kaminski, *Pro Des* Guy Hendrix Dyas, *Ed* Michael Kahn, *M* John Williams, *Costumes* Bernie Pollack and Mary Zophres.

Paramount Pictures/Lucasfilm-Paramount Pictures.
124 mins. USA. 2008. Rel: 22 May 2008. Cert 12A.

Infinite Justice ★★½

Arnold Silverman, a Jewish/American journalist is arrested and kept hostage in Karachi while investigating the financial network of Al-

Daniel Craig and Nicole Kidman brace themselves for the reviews of *The Invasion*.

Qa'ida. In captivity Silverman begins a strange relationship with one of his captors Kamal, a British Pakistani who has become a Muslim fundamentalist. This ambitious project by writer/producer/director Jamil Dehlavi is inspired by a true story and is similar to Michael Winterbottom's *A Mighty Heart*. It is not a bad film but it lacks fireworks and feels far too long despite its short (93 minutes) running time. GS

❯ Kevin Collins, Raza Jaffrey, Jennifer Calvert, Constantine Gregory, Irvine Iqbal, Jeff Mirza.
❯ *Dir, Pro and Screenplay* Jamil Dehlavi, *Ph* Nicholas D Knowland and Tony Miller, *Art Des* Lily Elms, Gareth Johnson and Marianne Stroyeva, *Ed* Angelica Landry, *M* Deborah Mollison, *Costumes* Jane Moxon.

Dehlavi Films-Miracle Communications.
93 mins. UK. 2006. Rel: 30 Nov 2007. Cert 15.

Interview ★★½

This is Steve Buscemi's remake in English of the film made in 2003 by Theo van Gogh who was murdered the next year by an Islamic fundamentalist. Virtually a two-hander, it's about a jaded journalist (Buscemi himself) interviewing an actress (Sienna Miller) brighter than her roles suggest. Unfortunately a promising concept is developed in ways that are totally unpersuasive. A pity, especially when

Miller proves her own abilities here. MS

❯ Steve Buscemi, Sienna Miller, Tara Elders, Michael Buscemi, David Schechter.
❯ *Dir* Steve Buscemi, *Pro* Bruce Weiss, Gijs van de Westelaken and Scott Hornbacher, *Screenplay* David Schechter and Buscemi based on Theodor Holman's original screenplay from an idea by Hans Teeuwin, *Ph* Thomas Kist, *Pro Des* Loren Weeks, *Ed* Kate Williams, *M* Evan Lurie, *Costumes* Vicki Farrell.

CinemaVault Releasing/A Column Film and Ironworks Productions etc-The Works UK Distribution Ltd.
84 mins. USA/Canada/Netherlands. 2006. Rel: 2 Nov 2007. Cert 15.

Intimate Enemies ★★★

Set in 1959 during the Algerian War, *Intimate Enemies* is a brutally tough action film that portrays war as the immoral last resort of the terminally desperate. Benoit Magimel plays a new commanding officer who has high-minded ideals about war and how to conduct it. He would rather play fair, without the need for torture or gratuitous killing. Writer-director Simi handles the material well, although with a largely unfamiliar cast, it is often confusing as to who has bitten the bullet or the dust. It really needs a George Clooney which it might get, should the US do a remake. (Original title: *L'ennemi intime*) MHD

▶ Benoit Magimel, Albert Dupontel, Aurélien Recoing, Marc Barbé, Eric Savin, Fellag.
▶ *Dir* Florent-Emilo Siri, *Pro* François Kraus and Denis Pineau-Valencienne, *Screenplay* Siri and Patrick Rothman, *Ph* Giovanni Fiore Coltellacci, *Pro Des* William Abello, *Ed* Christophe Danilo and Olivier Gajan, *M* Alexandre Desplat, *Costumes* Laetitia Harvey and Mimi Lempicka.

Les Films du Kiosque/France 2 Cinéma/SND/Canal + etc-Contender Entertainment Group.
108 mins. France. 2007. Rel: 25 Jan 2008. Cert 15.

Into the Wild ★★★½

This tells the true story of Christopher McCandless who turned his back on society and on his family to go out into the America wilds but died aged twenty four. It inspired director Sean Penn because of the way in which the life of McCandless embodied aspects of the American dream almost lost today. Emile Hirsch is ideal casting here, and there are admirable contributions from Catherine Keener and Hal Holbrook. The film is less sure-footed when portraying an individual's need for family and it feels seriously overlong, but when it's good it's very, very good and it looks great. MS

▶ Emile Hirsch, Marcia Gay Harden, William Hurt, Jena Malone, Catherine Keener, Brian Dierker, Hal Holbrook, Vince Vaughn.
▶ *Dir* and *Screenplay* Sean Penn from the book by Jon Krakauer, *Pro* Penn, Art Linson and Bill Pohlad, *Ph* Eric Gautier, *Pro Des* Derek Hill, *Ed* Jay Cassidy, *M* Michael Brook with Kaki King and Eddie Vedder, *Costumes* Mary Claire Hannan.

River Road Entertainment/Paramount Vantage/A Square One C.I.H/Linson Film production-Paramount Pictures UK.

148 mins. USA. 2007. Rel: 9 Nov 2007. Cert 15.

The Invasion ★★

Director Oliver Hirschbiegel's strangely uninvolving, flop update of the 1956 classic *Invasion of the Body Snatchers* moves Jack Finney's famous tale to Washington DC, where a crashed space shuttle unleashes an alien virus. Psychiatrist Nicole Kidman has to stay awake to avoid transformation to a soulless cipher and to trace her disease-immune son who's with her infected ex-hubby (Jeremy Northam). If a chilly Kidman makes little or no headway in the role, Daniel Craig is even worse off as her doctor friend – and the film is left relying on pointless car chases, violent clashes and CGI mutating cells on its way to a fudged finale. Soulless is the word. DW

▶ Nicole Kidman, Daniel Craig, Jeremy Northam, Jackson Bond, Jeffrey Wright, Veronica Cartwright, Roger Rees.
▶ *Dir* Oliver Hirschbiegel, *Pro* Joel Silver, *Screenplay* David Kajganich, from the novel *The Body Snatchers* by Jack Finney, *Ph* Rainer Klausmann, *Pro Des* Jack Fisk, *Ed* Hans Funck and Joel Negron, *M* John Ottman, *Costumes* Jacqueline West.

Warner Bros Pictures/Village Roadshow Pictures/ Oliver Pictures/Silver Pictures/Vertigo Entertainment-Warner Bros.
99 mins. USA/Australia. 2007. Rel: 12 Oct 2007. Cert 15.

Irina Palm ★★★

What is the audience for a non-porn film about a widowed grandmother (Marianne Faithfull) who takes a job masturbating men in a Soho sex club? She does it to raise money without which her grandson will not be able to fly out

Are her hands right for the job? Miki Manojlovic and Marianne Faithfull in *Irina Palm*.

Robert Downey Jr tests his firepower in *Iron Man*.

to Australia for a desperately needed operation available nowhere else. This bizarre work, which also incorporates a love story, veers uneasily between drama and comedy, but it's extremely well acted: by Miki Manojlovic, Kevin Bishop and Faithfull herself. MS

▶ Marianne Faithfull, Miki Manojlovic, Kevin Bishop, Siobhán Hewlett, Jenny Agutter.
▶ *Dir* Sam Garbarski, *Pro* Sébastien Delloye, *Screenplay* Martin Herron and Philippe Blasband, *Ph* Christophe Beaucarne, *Pro Des* Véronique Sacrez, *Ed* Ludo Troch, *M* Ghinzu, *Costumes* Anushia Nieradzik.

Entre Chien et Loup/Pallas Film/Samsa Film/Ipso Facto Films etc-Soda Pictures.
103 mins. Belgium/Germany/Luxembourg/UK/France. 2006. Rel: 13 June 2008. Cert 15.

Iron Man ★★★★½

Perfectly cast as a glib, bomb-making billionaire who learns the error of his ways and turns to superheroing as a means to make amends, Robert Downey Jr brings a believable edge and acerbic sense of humour to Marvel's most accomplished comicbook flick since *Spider-Man 2*. Dressed in a shiny, flying suit of armour, loaded with gadgets and dripping with justice-seeking weaponry, Downey Jr tackles terrorists and a giant robot man in this slick, exciting actioner. MJ

▶ Robert Downey Jr, Terrence Howard, Jeff Bridges, Gwyneth Paltrow, Leslie Bibb, Shaun Toub, Jon Favreau, and the voice of Paul Bettany.
▶ *Dir* Jon Favreau, *Pro* Avi Arad, Kevin Feige, *Screenplay* Mark Fergs, Art Marcum, Matt Holloway and Hawk Ostby, based on characters by Stan Lee etc, *Ph* Matthew Libatique, *Pro Des* J Michael Riva, *Ed* Dan Lebental, *M* Ramin Djawadi, *Costumes* Rebecca Bentjen and Laura Jean Shannon.

Dark Blades Films/Fairview Entertainment/Marvel Enterprises etc-Paramount Pictures.
126 mins. USA. 2008. Rel: 2 May 2008. Cert 12A.

I Served the King of England ★★★½

Now in his seventies Jirí Menzel returns with this adaptation of a novel by Bohumil Hrabal. It's decidedly Czech in character and very well staged. In telling the story of a young man on the make in the 1930s while also taking the tale into his old age, it blends the comic and the larger than life with serious drama that shows the repressive force of the Nazis and later of the Communists. Not all of it works, but it's never less than interesting. MS

▶ Ivan Barnev, Oldrich Kaiser, Julia Jentsch, Marián Labuda, Rudolf Hrusínsky.
▶ *Dir* and *Screenplay* Jirí Menzel from the novel by Bohumil Hrabal, *Pro* Robert Schaffer and Andrea

Metcalfe, *Ph* Jaromír Sofr, *Art Dir* Milan Bycek, *Ed* Jirí Brozek, *M* Ales Bezina, *Costumes* Milan Corba.

Bioscop/AQS/A TV Nova, Barrandov Studio, UPP, Magic Box Slovakia co-production etc-Arrow Film Distributors Ltd.
120 mins. Czech Republic/Slovakia. 2006. Rel: 9 May 2008. Cert 15.

The Italian ★★★★

In this engaging and award-winning Russian film the Italian is a nickname given to a six year old who runs away from a children's home where those in charge organise adoptions for profit. The boy's quest for his mother comes after an almost Dickensian portrayal of life in the institution although the movie has a contemporary setting. It's a well executed piece built around an excellent performance by child actor Kolya Spiridonov and it's no surprise to learn that debutant director Andrei Kravchuk is an admirer of De Sica. (Original title: *Italianetz*) MS

➤ Kolya Spiridonov, Denis Moiseenko, Sasha Sirotkin, Maria Kuznetsova.
➤ *Dir* Andrei Kravchuk, *Pro* Vladimir Husid, Vladimir Bogoyavlensky etc, *Screenplay* Andrei Romanov, *Ph* Alexander Burov, *Pro Des* Vladimir Svetozarov, *Ed* Tamara Lipartiya, *M* Alexander Kneiffel, *Costumes* Marina Nikolaeva.

Lenfilm Studios with the support of Russian Ministry of Culture-Soda Pictures.
99 mins. Russia. 2005. Rel: 25 Jan 2008. Cert12A.

The Jane Austen Book Club
★★★

Six protagonists – six books. A sextet of unlikely members of the eponymous cabal find themselves not unlike their literary counterparts. Each reader is assigned a Jane Austen tome and so, gradually, pride, sensibility, prejudice and sense all play their part. Set in contemporary California and based on the bestseller by Karen Joy Fowler (a Richard and Judy choice, to boot), this is about as contrived as they come. But it also has an accomplished cast and the result as goofy and engaging as a piece of top-drawer chicklit. JC-W

➤ Maria Bello, Emily Blunt, Kathy Baker, Amy Brenneman, Jimmy Smits, Lynn Redgrave.
➤ *Dir* Robin Swicord, *Pro* John Calley, Juliet Lynn and Diana Napper, *Screenplay* Swicord, from the novel by Karen Joy Fowler, *Ph* John Toon, *Pro Des* Rusty Smith, *Ed* Maryann Brandon, *M* Aaron Zigman, *Costumes* Johnetta Boone.

Mockingbird Pictures/John Calley Productions-Sony Pictures Releasing.
106 mins. USA. 2007. Rel: 16 Nov 2007. Cert 12A.

Another splendid child actor: Kolya Spiridonov as the boy searching for his mother in *The Italian*.

A vintage shot of Bernard Sumner, Ian Curtis, Peter Hook and Stephen Morris from the documentary *Joy Division*.

Jesus Camp ★★★★

A balanced, disturbing American documentary about one of that country's evangelical churches and its way of drawing children in. It's revealing and informative as it follows three children (the oldest being 13) who attend the annual camp run by the Rev. Becky Fischer, a proselytiser for God's army. Near the close a Methodist lawyer confronts this woman with a view of Christianity which she, alas, would never recognise. Recommended viewing. MS

▷ With Becky Fischer, Mike Papantonio, Levi, Rachael, Tory.
▷ *Dir* Heidi E. Ewing and Rachel Grady, *Pro* Grady, *Ph* Mira Chang and Jenna Rosher, *Ed* Enat Sidi, *M* J.J. McGeehan.

A & E Indie Films/A Loki Films production-ICA Films. 87 mins. USA. 2006. Rel: 23 Nov 2007. No cert.

John Waters: This Filthy World ★★★★

This is John Waters' celebrated one-man show where he talks about his life, his films and of course about Divine, the star of his early trashy and experimental films that gave the world a new definition of 'poor taste'. He, of course, discovered Johnny Depp in *Cry Baby* and hit the jackpot with *Hairspray* and *Polyester*. Waters is a brilliant personality and his abundance of energy is infectious in this hysterically funny film that will make you want to go and see his films all over again. GS

▷ John Waters, Alison Madwatkins.
▷ *Dir* Jeff Garlin *Pro* Garlin and Michele Armour, *Screenplay* John Waters, *Ph* Dan Shulman, *Pro Des* Vince Peranio, *Ed* Jared Gustadt and Rob Naylor, *M* Gustadt and Lukas Kaiser.

Filthy World-Revelation Films. 86 mins. USA. 2006. Rel: 28 Sep 2007. Cert 15.

Joy Division ★★★★

Grant Gee who last year photographed and edited the admirable *Scott Walker: 30 Century Man* here retains the former credit while also directing. His documentary on the history of Manchester's pop group Joy Division is no less expert and with its emphasis on the music the film is welcome as being complementary to Anton Corbijn's acted drama *Control* (qv). MS

▷ With Tony Wilson, Paul Morley, Annik Honoré, Peter Hook, Bernard Sumner.

▶ *Dir* and *filmed by* Grant Gee, *Pro* Tom Astor, Tom Atencio and Jacqui Edenbrow, *Writer* Jon Savage, *Ed* Jerry Chater.

A Hudson Productions Ltd. Production/Brown Owl Films-The Works UK Distribution Ltd.
100 mins. UK. 2008. Rel: 2 May 2008. Cert 15.

Jumper ★★

Hayden Christensen teleports around the world for fun and profit, pursued by a grumpy, grey-haired Samuel L Jackson, in this undercooked effort from *Mr and Mrs Smith* director Doug Liman. Though the effects are convincing, the actors are not. Merely the first instalment of what threatens to be a really lousy movie series, *Jumper* doesn't feel like a film in its own right, left incomplete, unresolved and, as a result, extremely unsatisfying. MJ

▶ Hayden Christensen, Samuel L Jackson, Diane Lane, Jamie Bell, Rachel Bilson, Michael Rooker.
▶ *Dir* Doug Liman, *Pro* Lucas Foster, Arnon Milchan, Simon Kinberg and Jay Sanders, *Screenplay* Simon Kinberg, Jim Uhls and David S Goyer from the novel by Steven Gould, *Ph* Barry

Peterson, *Pro Des* Oliver Scholl, *Ed* Saar Klein, Dean Zimmerman and Don Zimmerman, *M* John Powell, *Costumes* Magali Guidasci.

Twentieth Century Fox Film Corporation/New Regency Pictures/Dune Entertainment etc-20th Century Fox.
88 mins. USA. 2008. Rel: 14 Feb 2008. Cert 12A.

Juno ★★★½

More a comedy than a drama, this is a teenaged version of last year's *Knocked Up* told, as the title suggests, from the girl's point of view. The unwanted pregnancy, the rejection of abortion and a birth scene near the close underline the sense of déjà vu and the more dramatic side of the film doesn't always convince. There's a lot to enjoy, however, with particularly fine performances from Ellen Page as the spirited girl, Michael Céra as the gauche but engaging boy and JK Simmons as Juno's understanding father. MS

▶ Ellen Page, Michael Céra, Jennifer Garner, Jason Bateman, JK Simmons, Allison Janney.
▶ *Dir* Jason Reitman, *Pro* Lianne Halfon, John

Samuel L Jackson was reunited with his *Star Wars* co-star Hayden Christensen in *Jumper*.

Ellen Page and Olivia Thurlby in *Juno*, one of the year's big hits.

Malkovich, Mason Novick and Russell Smith, *Screenplay* Diablo Cody, *Ph* Eric Steelberg, *Pro Des* Steve Saklad, *Ed* Dana E. Glauberman, *M* Mateo Messina, *Costumes* Monique Prudhomme.

Fox Searchlight Pictures presents a Mandate Pictures/Mr Mudd production-20th Century Fox International (UK).
96 mins. USA. 2007. Rel: 8 Feb 2008. Cert 12A.

Kamikaze Girls ★★

Tetsuya Nakashima's stylish but totally OTT film is based on a Japanese graphic novel which tells the story of two young women's unlikely friendship. Momoko, who likes to dress like Lolita, abandons her boring life in a small town looking for adventure and meets her match in Ichigo, a moody and tough biker. The beginning is fun but the endless repetition and the almost incomprehensible surrealistic plot becomes tiresome by the end. (Original title: *Shimotsuma Monogatari*) GS

▶ Kyoko Fukada, Anna Tsuchiya, Hiroyuki Miyasako, Sadad Abe, Eiko Koike, Shin Yazawa, Kirin Kiki.
▶ *Dir* Tetsuya Nakashima, *Pro* Satoru Ogura, Takashi Hirano and Yuuji Ishida, *Screenplay* Nakashima, from the novel by Nobara Takemoto, *Ph* Masakazu Ato, *Pro Des* Towako Kuwashima,

Ed Yoshiyuki Koike and Chiaki Toyama, *M* Yoko Kanno.

Amuse Pictures/Hori Production/Shogakukan etc-Toho Company.
102 mins. Japan. 2004. Rel: 6 June 2008. No cert.

Kenny ★★★★

Spoof documentary about a thirtyish Melbourne toilet installer whose family does not approve of his chosen plumbing career. His mother is dead and his ex-wife has taken their son and left. His own life starts to change when he is sent to a US toilet trade fair in Nashville and meets an air hostess en route. On his return home to Oz he has to make a decision about his career and his life. This is a charming, funny and moving film about a 'real' person and his fight to be happy. As the outspoken but immensely loveable Kenny, Shane Jacobson is an absolute star. MHD

▶ Shane Jacobson, Ron Jacobson, Eve von Bibra, Chris Davis, Alf Scerri, Hayley Preusker, Jesse Jacobson.
▶ *Dir* Clayton Jacobson, *Pro* Clayton Jacobson and Rohan Timlock, *Screenplay* Clayton Jacobson and Shane Jacobson, *Ph* Alexander Bradley, *Ed* Clayton Jacobson and Sean Lander, *M* Richard Pleasance.

Thunderbox Films-Odeon Sky Filmworks.
103 mins. Australia. 2006. Rel: 28 Sep 2007. Cert 15.

The Killing of John Lennon
★★★½

Mark David Chapman killed John Lennon and now this compelling portrait of what happened told from the killer's viewpoint uses his own words to tell his story. The opening scenes are over-directed and one fears initially that this may prove to be an exploitation movie. But as the film proceeds this in-depth study of Chapman, however disquieting, becomes increasingly gripping and it's well played by Jonas Ball. A memorably individual work. MS

▶ Jonas Ball, Krisha Fairchild, Mie Ormori, Eric Takomoto.
▶ *Dir* and *Screenplay* Andrew Piddington, *Pro* Rakha Singh, *Ph* Roger Eaton, *Pro Des* Tora Peterson, *Ed* Tony Palmer, *M* Martin Kiszko, *Costumes* Michael Bevins and Lotus Yumiko Seki.

The Works/A Picture Players production-The Works UK Distribution Ltd.
114 mins. UK. 2007. Rel: 7 Dec 2007. Cert 15.

King of Kong ★★★

This documentary follows the men who tried to achieve the highest score at Donkey Kong, a favourite amusement arcade game. Steve Wiebe, out of work Boeing employee from Seattle, found an escape in the game and set out to beat the top score for the Guinness Book of World Records. He was challenging Billy Mitchell's record score of over 874,000 points. Steve finally hit one million points which only inspired Mitchell to try and outdo him. The battle of wits to see who could become the King of Kong makes for a fascinating insight into an unconventional way of achieving success. PL

▶ Steve Wiebe, Billy Mitchell, Walter Day, Mark Alpiger, Greg Bond.
▶ *Dir* Seth Gordon, *Pro* Ed Cunningham, *Ph* Ross Tuttle, Ty Clancey and Luis Lopez, *Ed* Jim Bruce, Luis Lopez and J Clay Tweel, *M* Craig Richey.

LargeLab-Revolver Entertainment.
79 mins. USA. 2007. Rel: 6 June 2008. Cert PG.

The Kingdom ★★½

The Kingdom is Saudi Arabia and suicide bombers have devastated an oil company compound, killing countless American women and children. Negotiating a five-day window to uncover crucial forensic evidence, a team of FBI specialists manoeuvre an incendiary path through Saudi bureaucracy. The Americans and local police both want to apprehend those responsible, but neither do themselves any favours. A self-consciously jagged, *cinéma-vérité* thriller, *The Kingdom* ventures into fascinating and topical territory – but is scuttled by incomprehensible plotting. JC-W

Video game addicts in *King of Kong*.

Friends across a divide: Zekeria Ebrahimi and Ahmad Khan Mahmoodzada in *The Kite Runner*.

▶ Jamie Foxx, Chris Cooper, Jennifer Garner, Jason Bateman, Jeremy Piven, Ali Sullivan.
▶ *Dir* Peter Berg, *Pro* Michael Mann and Scott Stuber, *Screenplay* Matthew Michael Carnahan, *Ph* Mauro Fiore, *Pro Des* Tom Duffield, *Ed* Colby Parker Jr and Kevin Stitt, *M* Danny Elfman, *Costumes* Susan Matheson.

Universal Pictures/Film 44/Forward Pass/Stuber/Parent/Relativity Media-Universal Pictures.
110 mins. USA/Germany. 2007. Rel: 5 Oct 2007. Cert 15.

The Kite Runner ★★★

In this film of the best-selling novel we are invited to identify with the sufferings of the Afghan people through a tale of childhood friends, one rich and one poor. What follows involves betrayal, rape and a family secret while the plotline takes us to America and to Pakistan. Through the quality of the writing the book conceals the extent to which the story sinks into the contrived and the unbelievable, but the film can't do this. Had it been a better film, it would have made for disturbing viewing so some audiences will like it as it is. MS

▶ Khalid Abdalla, Homayoun Ershadi, Zekiria Ebrahimi, Ahmad Khan Mahoodzada.
▶ *Dir* Marc Forster, *Pro* William Horberg, Walter Parkes and others, *Screenplay* Devid Benioff from the novel by Khaled Hosseini, *Ph* Roberto Schaefer, *Pro Des* Carlos Conti, *Ed* Matt Chessé, *M* Alberto Iglesias, *Costumes* Frank Fleming.

DreamWorks Pictures/Sidney Kimmel Entertainment/Participant Productions/Parkes-MacDonald etc-Paramount Pictures UK.
128 mins. USA/People's Republic of China. 2007. Rel: 26 Dec 2007. Cert 12A.

KM 31 ★★½

Popular on home ground in Mexico, this drama concerns twin sisters with an almost telepathic sense of each other's feelings. But it soon develops into a ghost story with the spirits of the dead at large and a living sacrifice the only way of seeing them off. Technically able, the piece lacks sufficient gore to please horror fans and becomes increasingly confusing in its storytelling, Hokum can be fun, but here it just becomes tiresome. MS

▶ Adrià Collado, Raúl Méndez, Iliana Fox, Carlos Aragón, Luisa Huertas.
▶ *Dir* and *Screenplay* Rigoberto Castañeda, *Pro* Billy Rovzar, Fernando Rovzar and Julio Fernández, *Ph* Alejandro Martínez, *Pro Des* Bernardo Trujillo, *Ed* Alberto de Toro, *M* Carles Cases, *Costumes* Mariestela Fernández.

Lemon Films/Santo Domingo Films/Filmax International/Castelao Productions etc-Yume Pictures Ltd.
103 mins. Spain/Mexico/Brazil. 2005. Rel: 7 Dec 2007. Cert 15.

Knocked Up ★★★½

It's a shame that at 129 minutes this youthful American comedy outstays its welcome. That fault apart, one can relish this admirably played piece which has the voice of today as it tells the tale of how Ben, a somewhat dumb near slacker, gets the attractive, ambitious Alison pregnant during a chance one-night stand. How they come to make a life together is a story blending crude popular comedy about sex and a real sense of warmth. Seth Rogen and Katherine Heigl play these central roles and the casting is perfect. MS

▶ Seth Rogen, Katherine Heigl, Paul Rudd, Leslie Mann, Jason Segel, Jonah Hill.
▶ *Dir* and *Screenplay* Judd Apatow, *Pro* Apatow, Shauna Robertson and Clayton Townsend, *Ph* Eric Edwards, *Pro Des* Jefferson Sage, *Ed* Brent White and Craig Alpert, *M* Loudon Wainwright and Joe Henry, *Costumes* Debra McGuire.

Universal Pictures/An Apatow production-Universal Pictures International UK & Eire.
129 mins. USA. 2007. Rel: 24 Aug 2007. Cert 15.

Lady Chatterley ★★★★½

It's DH Lawrence in French with subtitles, but how splendidly Pascale Ferran tells the familiar story. Her take on Lawrence is very long (168 minutes) but very sensitive. The developing relationship between Lady Chatterley (the splendid Marina Hands) and her gamekeeper (no hunk but a believable working class man in Jean-Louis Coulloc'h's performance) is beautifully treated, as explicit as the subject demands but full of emotional truth. Convincingly set in 1921 and superbly photographed, this is a film in which any minor misjudgments are quickly forgiven. MS

▶ Marina Hands, Jean-Louis Coulloc'h, Hippolyte Girardot, Hélène Alexandridis.
▶ *Dir* Pascale Ferran, *Pro* Gilles Sandoz, *Screenplay* Ferran and Roger Bohbot from the novel *John Thomas and Lady Jane* by D H Lawrence, *Ph* Julien Hirsch, *Pro Des* François-Renaud Labarthe, *Ed* Yann Dedet, *M* Béatrice Thiriet, *Costumes* Marie Claude Altot.

Maïa films/Arte France/Saga Films/Titre et Structure Production/Les Films du Lendemain etc-Artificial Eye Film Company.
168 mins. France/Belgium. 2006. Rel: 24 Aug 2007. Cert 18.

Lady Godiva ★

This dreadful film opens with the legendary medieval lady riding naked on a white horse before the action moves to modern day Oxford. Teacher Jemima wants to rebuild the Art Factory in memory of her dead brother and is even more determined to raise the cash after playboy Michael arranges a humiliating interview on national television. It is appallingly scripted and directed with very poor performances – a strong contender for the worst film of the year. GS

▶ Isabelle Amyes, Paul Ansdell, Eric Carte, James Wilby, Simon Williams, Marcia Warren, Phoebe Thomas, Nicholas Parsons, Matthew Chambers.
▶ *Dir and Screenplay* Vicky Jewson, *Pro* Adam Kempton and Rupert Whitaker, *Ph* George Stephenson, *Pro Des* Clive Crotty, *Ed* George Akers and Anthony Parker, *M* David Whitaker, *Costumes* Clare Harries.

Jewson Film Productions/Lady Godiva-Miracle Communications.
89 mins. USA. 2008. Rel: 25 Jan 2008. Cert 12A.

Lagerfeld Confidential ★★★

Fashion designer and photographer Karl Lagerfeld is good value: articulate, opinionated and offering an image that invites speculation. What a pity then that filmmaker Rodolphe Marconi doesn't dig more deeply and brings so little sense of shape or time to a movie that was shot over two years. Anyone besotted by the world of fashion may adore this movie, but for others it will come across as a rather wasted opportunity. MS

▶ With Karl Lagerfeld, Nicole Kidman, Princess Caroline of Monaco, Anna Wintour, Baz Luhrmann.
▶ *Dir* and *Ph* Rodolphe Marconi, *Pro* Grégory Bernard, *Ed* Laure Mercier.

Realitism Films/Backup Films and Coficup/Cinemao/Sindika Dokolo/Mélange etc-Revolver Entertainment.
89 mins. France. 2006. Rel: 26 Oct 2007. Cert 12A.

Lars and the Real Girl ★★★½

Much better than it sounds, this offbeat American film finds family and friends rallying round to support Lars by pretending to believe in the girl he insists is real but is actually a sex doll. Far from being sleazy, the piece is Capraesque and well acted (Patricia Clarkson as Lars' medical adviser is just perfect), but in the last analysis it's neither amusing enough nor touching enough to become truly memorable. Worth a look, nevertheless, and a further example of Ryan Gosling's versatility. MS

Ryan Gosling and his temperamental companion in *Lars and the Real Girl.*

▶ Ryan Gosling, Emily Mortimer, Paul Schneider, Patricia Clarkson, Kelli Garner.
▶ *Dir* Craig Gillespie, *Pro* Sidney Kimmel, John Cameron and Sarah Aubrey, *Screenplay* Nancy Oliver, *Ph* Adam Kimmel, *Pro Des* Arv Grewal, *Ed* Tatiana S Riegel, *M* David Torn, *Costumes* Kirston Mann and Gerri Gilan.

Metro-Goldwyn-Mayer Pictures/Sidney Kimmel Entertainment-Verve Pictures.
106 mins. USA. 2007. Rel: 14 March 2008. Cert 12A.

The Last Legion ★★

This is a mixture of Roman history and Arthurian legend. In ancient Rome the twelve-year-old Romulus Augustus' (Sangster) is about to be crowned emperor. However, wise man Ambrosinus (Kingsley) predicts trouble, so Romulus' father Orestes (Glen) makes Aurelius (Firth) his son's personal guard as the Barbarian hordes hit Rome again. Romulus and Aurelius are captured and taken to Capri where they find the mythical Excalibur sword. With the aid of a female Byzantine warrior and other heroes, they set off in search of the legendary last Roman legion. A sword and sandal epic with some dodgy re-writing of history, this one is only for fans of the genre. CB

▶ Colin Firth, Ben Kingsley, Peter Mullan, John Hannah, Iain Glen, Thomas Sangster, Aishwarya Rai.

▶ *Dir* Doug Lefler, *Pro* Dino De Laurentiis and Tarack Ben Ammar, *Screenplay* Jez Butterworth and Tom Butterworth, from a story by Carlo Carlei, Peter Rader and Valerio Manfredi, *Ph* Marco Pontecorvo, *Pro Des* Carmelo Agate, *Ed* Simon Cozens, *M* Patrick Doyle, *Costumes* Paolo Scalabrino.

Dino De Laurentiis Company/Ingenious Film Partners/ Quinta Communications/Zephyr Films-The Weinstein Company.
102 mins. UK/Italy/France/Slovakia. 2007. Rel: 19 Oct 2007. Cert 12A.

The Last Mistress ★★★½

It's a surprise to be comparing Catherine Breillat with Jacques Rivette but this 19th century Parisian drama from a novel by Barbey d'Aurevilly is reminiscent of *Don't Touch The Axe* (qv). The story charts a young man's obsession with his Spanish mistress extending beyond his marriage but the sex scenes avoid the extreme explicitness for which Breillat's films are famous. Production values are good, social comments are made, but the narrative, despite evading melodrama (just), fails to make you care about any of the characters. (Original title: *Une vieille maitresse*) MS

▶ Asia Argento, Fu'ad Aït Aattou, Roxane Mesquida, Claude Sarraute, Michel Lonsdale.
▶ *Dir* and *Screenplay* Catherine Breillat from the

novel by Jules Barbey d'Aurevilly, *Pro* Jean-François Lepetit, *Ph* Yorgos Arvantis, *Pro Des* François-Renaud Labarthe, *Ed* Pascale Chavance, *Costumes* Anaïs Romand.

Flach Film/CB Films/France 3 Cinema/StudioCanal/Buskin Film etc-Artificial Eye Film Company.
114 mins. France/Italy. 2007. Rel: 11 April 2008. Cert 15.

Leatherheads ★★

In 1925, a disastrous American football team, whose matches always end up with fist fights, loses its sponsor but their captain, Connelly (George Clooney), manages to convince big agent C C Frazier (Jonathan Pryce) to give the team another chance. The film looks good and the period is recreated with care and style but overall it lacks tension. The comedy scenes fail to work and the chemistry between Clooney and Renée Zellweger, as the reporter in search of a scandal, feels forced and uninspired. GS

❯ George Clooney, Renée Zellweger, John Krasinski, Jonathan Pryce, Stephen Root, Jack Thompson.
❯ *Dir* George Clooney, *Pro* Clooney, Grant Heslov and Casey Silver, *Screenplay* Duncan Brantley and Rick Reilly, *Ph* Newton Thomas Sigel, *Pro Des* James

D Bissel, *Ed* Stephen Mirrione, *M* Randy Newman, *Costumes* Louise Frogley.

Casey Silver Productions/Outlaw Productions/Road Rebel/Smoke House etc-Universal Pictures.
114 mins. USA. 2008. Rel: 11 Apr 2008. Cert PG.

Legacy ★★★

In 2005 Géla Babluani from Georgia featured his brother George in the thriller *13* (*Tzameti*) and now they are reunited, this time with their father Temor as co-director. Here French visitors to Tbilisi get caught up in a feud between two families. The slow first half is atmospheric, the second half more compelling, but even so it never seems to amount to much, although it won the 2007 Special Prize at the Sundance Festival. (Original title: *L'Héritage*) MS

❯ Sylvie Testud, Olga Legrand, Stanisas Merhar, Pascal Bongard, George Babluani, Leo Gaparidze, Augustin Legrand.
❯ *Dir* and *Screenplay* Temor and Géla Babluani, *Pro* Géla Babluani, Olivier Oursel and Jean Marie Delbary, *Ph* Tariel Meliava, *Pro Desr* Claude Billois and Teimuraz Khmaladze, *Ed* Géla Babluani and Noémie Moreau, *Costumes* Khatuna Tsrakaya.

Les Films de la Strada/Quasar Pictures/Premium Films/

Renée Zellweger and George Clooney in *Leatherheads*.

Solmane Productions etc-Revolver Entertainment.
83 mins. France. 2007. Rel: 14 Sept 2007. Cert PG.

Libero ★★★★

An unexpected double triumph for Italy's Kim
Rossi Stuart: this family drama was planned as
his directorial debut but when an actor dropped
out he additionally took over a leading role.
A sensitive, traditional work in the style of De
Sica, it centres on a boy of eleven being brought
up by a loving but sometimes misguided father
to whom the unreliable and unfaithful mother
periodically returns. Subtly characterised and
admirably unsentimental, it comes across as
a modest piece but then you realise that few
films have so successfully portrayed the way in
which members of a family affect one another's
psychology. There's not a false note in it.
(Original title: *Anche libero va bene*) MS

❧ Alessandro Morace, Barbora Bobulovi, Kim Rossi
Stuart, Marta Nobili.
❧ *Dir* Kim Rossi Stuart, *Pro* Carlo Degli Esposti with
Giorgio Magliulo and Andrea Costantini, *Story*
and *Screenplay* Linda Ferri, Federico Starnone,
Francesco Giammusso and Rossi Stuart, *Ph* Stefano
Falivene, *Pro Des* Stefano Giambanco, *Ed* Marco
Spoletini, *M* Banda Osiris, *Costumes* Sonu Mishra.

A Rai Cinema-Palomar production-Axiom Films Ltd.
109 mins. Italy. 2006. Rel: 25 Jan 2008. Cert 15.

Licence to Wed ★

Reverend Frank won't bless Ben and Sadie's
union until they attend his outrageous
'wedding-prep' classes and pass his never-ending
tests. Another unfunny comedy with Robin
Williams who gets worse with every film. He is
extremely irritating here giving an embarrassing
performance. However, John Krasinski and
Mandy Moore work well together and achieve
the impossible – to be real and keep their
dignity among such mediocrity and
overacting. GS

❧ Robin Williams, Mandy Moore, John Krasinski,
Christine Taylor, Peter Strauss.
❧ *Dir* Ken Kwapis, *Pro* Mike Medavoy, Nick
Osborne and Robert Simmonds, *Screenplay* Kim
Barker, Tim Rasmussen and Vince Di Meglio, from
a story by Kim Barker and Wayne Lloyd, *Ph* John
Bailey, *Pro Des* Gae S Buckley, *Ed* Kathryn Himoff,
M Christophe Beck, *Costumes* Deena Appel.

*Not a false
note: Allesandro
Morace in Anche
libero va bene
[Libero].*

Warner Bros Pictures/Village Roadshow Pictures/
Proposal Productions/Robert Simonds Productions/
Phoenix Pictures/Underground Films & Management-
Warner Bros.
91 mins. USA. 2007. Rel: 10 Aug 2007. Cert 12A.

Lions for Lambs ★★★

Three separate story threads unite in this drama
that questions the role of American soldiers
in Afghanistan as part of the so-called War on
Terror. The one segment involving action is
distractingly enveloped in darkness since it
takes place at night while the other parts are
talkative enough to suggest something better
suited to the stage. However the major names
involved – Redford, Streep and Cruise (the latter
on strong form) – should be respected for taking
on such serious material, even if there is less
depth and resonance than might have been
expected. MS

❧ Robert Redford, Meryl Streep, Tom Cruise,
Andrew Garfield, Derek Luke.
❧ *Dir* Robert Redford, *Pro* Redford, Matthew
Michael Carnahan, Andrew Hauptman and Tracy
Falco, *Screenplay* Carnahan, *Ph* Philippe Rousselot,
Pro Des Jan Roelfs, *Ed* Joe Hutshing, *M* Mark Isham,
Costumes Mary Zophres.

Metro-Goldwyn-Mayer Pictures/United Artists/
A Wildwood Enterprises/Brat Na Pont/Andell
Entertainment production-20th Century Fox
International (UK).
92 mins. USA. 2007. Rel: 9 Nov 2007. Cert 15.

Lonely Hearts ★★★★

This is based on the true story of serial killers
Martha Beck and Raymond Fernandez who
during the late 1940s travelled around the
country taking advantage of lonely and
vulnerable women, robbing them before killing
them. Detective Elmer C Robinson begins a
race against time in order to capture them
before they kill again. Todd Robinson's film
is extremely violent but captures the period
brilliantly with superb 'Scope photography.
Travolta is in good form here but Salma Hayek
steals the show as the ultimate *femme fatale*. GS

❧ John Travolta, James Gandolfini, Jared Leto,
Salma Hayek, Laura Dern, Scott Caan, Alice Krige.
❧ *Dir and Screenplay* Todd Robinson, *Pro* Boaz
Davidson and Holly Wiersma, *Ph* Peter Levy,
Pro Des Jon Gary Steele, *Ed* Kathryn Himoff,
M Mychael Danna, *Costumes* Jacqueline West.

Millennium Films/Emmett-Furla Films/Equity Pictures
Medienfonds/Holly Wiersma Productions/Nu Image
Entertainment-Entertainment Film Distributors.
108 mins. Germany/USA. 2006. Rel: 27 Jul 2007.
Cert 15.

Lonesome Jim ★★★

As a director Steve Buscemi is adept at
evoking small-town life in America without

condescension and here he has good players headed by Casey Affleck (whose presence may explain why this film from 2005 is being released here now). But ultimately success or failure turns on the screenplay by James C Strouse and his take on disillusioned siblings starts promisingly but seems to lose its way. MS

▷ Casey Affleck, Liv Tyler, Mary Kay Place, Kevin Corrigan, Seymour Cassel.
▷ *Dir* Steve Buscemi, *Pro* Gary Winnick. Jake Abraham, Galt Niederhoffer etc, *Screenplay by* James C Strouse, *Ph* Phil Parmet, *Pro Des* Chuck Voelter, *Ed* Plummy Tucker, *M* Evan Lurie, *Costumes* Victoria Farrell.

IFC Productions/An InDigEnt production/Plum Pictures-Lionsgate UK.
92 mins. USA. 2005. Rel: 11 April 2008. Cert 15.

The Lookout ★★★★

Joseph Gordon-Levitt is proving to be one of the best actors of his generation. Following *Mysterious Skin* and *Breach* he now provides a firm centre as the brain-damaged young man at the centre of Scott Frank's bank robbery thriller. It's a relatively modest piece but well acted by all. Because the characters are well established, the ensuing twists and turns of the plot are suspensefully engaging. MS

▷ Joseph Gordon-Levitt, Jeff Daniels, Matthew Goode, Greg Dunham, Carla Gugino.
▷ *Dir* and *Screenplay* Scott Frank, *Pro* Walter Parkes, Laurence Mark. Roger Birnbaum and Gary Barber, *Ph* Alar Kivilo, *Pro Des* David Briston, *Ed* JillSavitt, *M* James Newton Howard, *Costumes* Abram Waterhouse.

Miramax Films/Spyglass Entertainment etc-Buena Vista International (UK).
99 mins. USA. 2006. Rel: 2 Nov 2007. Cert 15.

Love in the Time of Cholera ★★★

The novel by Nobel Prize-winner Márquez is world famous but Ronald Harwood's adaptation suggests that it is the kind of work that sells well in airports. Its hero (well played by Javier Bardem who takes over from the younger and promising Unax Ugalde) lives in Colombia and loves but one inaccessible woman while bedding over six hundred others in order to forget his anguish! Mike Newell's direction keeps the film flowing but, even if you accept it on its own terms, the dialogue and the make-up eventually let it down. MS

▷ Javier Bardem, Giovanna Mezzogiorno,

Benjamin Bratt, Catalina Sandino Moreno, Liev Schreiber, Fernanda Montenegro, Hector Elizondo, Unax Ugalde. Laura Harring.
▷ *Dir* Mike Newell, *Pro* Scott Steindorff, *Screenplay* Ronald Harwood from the novel by Gabriel García Márquez, *Ph* Affonso Beato, *Pro Des* Wolf Kroeger, *Ed* Mick Audsley, *M* António Pinto, *Costumes* Marit Allen.

A Stone Village Pictures production/Grosvenor Park Media-Momentum Pictures.
138 mins. USA. 2007. Rel: 21 March 2008. Cert 15.

Lust, Caution ★★★★★

Set in China between 1938 and 1942 and subtitled, Ang Lee's latest film is probably his best. The story of a student (Tang Wei) drawn into politics and a plan to assassinate a collaborator aiding the Japanese (Tony Leung), it could have been a Hitchcockian thriller with sex added when the girl has to become the mistress of the collaborator for the scheme to work. Instead, the tale, long but engrossing, goes beyond that to attain tragic depths while also showing how in a crisis some people may succumb but others are able to grow as human beings. It's a masterpiece with a sensationally good debut performance from Tang Wei. MS

▷ Tang Wei, Tony Leung, Joan Chen, Leehom Wang, Chin Ka Lok.
▷ *Dir* Ang Lee, *Pro* Bill Kong, Lee and James Schamus, *Screenplay* Wang Hui Ling and Schamus based on the short story *Se, Jei* by Eileen Chang, *Ph* Rodrigo Prieto, *Pro Des* and *Costumes* Pan Lai, *Ed* Tim Squyres, *M* Alexandre Desplat.

Focus Features/River Road Entertainment/Haishang Films etc-Universal Pictures International UK & Eire.
158 mins. Taiwan/USA/Hong Kong/People's Republic of China. 2007. Rel: 4 Jan 2008. Cert 18.

Macbeth ★★★

This is Shakespeare modernised and relocated in Melbourne within a gangster milieu. In contrast to *Joe Macbeth* (1955) it retains Shakespeare's text but the stylised visuals work far better than the performances by players ill-attuned to the language. If you want a *Macbeth* for the pop video age with emphasis on gore and even nudity, then this is well done, but it's questionable as to what audiences will want to see the famous tragedy reduced to this. MS

▷ Sam Worthington, Victoria Hill, Lachy Hulme, Gary Sweet, Steve Bastoni.
▷ *Dir* Geoffrey Wright, *Pro* Martin Fabinyi, *Screenplay* Adapted from Shakespeare's play by Wright and Victoria Hill, *Ph* Will Gibson, *Pro Des*

David McKay, *Ed* Jane Usher, *M* John Clifford White, *Costumes* Jane Johnston.

Film Finance Corporation Australia/Film Victoria/ Arclight Films/Paradigm Hyde Films/Mushroom Pictures production etc-Revolver Entertainment. 109 mins. Australia. 2006. Rel: 13 July 2007. Cert 15.

Made of Honour ★★½

Philanderer Patrick Dempsey realises his best friend (Michelle Monaghan) is the one he loves, when she asks him to be a male maid of honour at her wedding. Initially likeable and pleasantly amusing, the film disintegrates into silliness and feeble jokes, which fall as flat as a dropped caber, when the scene shifts to Scotland for the nuptials with poor Kevin McKidd as the hapless bridegroom trying to convince in an American tourist's fantasy land of kilts and bagpipes. CA

▶ Patrick Dempsey, Michelle Monaghan, Kevin McKidd, Kadeem Hardison, Kathleen Quinlan, Sydney Pollack.
▶ *Dir* Paul Weiland, *Pro* Neil H Moritz, *Screenplay* Adam Sztykiel, Deborah Kaplan, Harry Elfont, *Ph* Tony Pierce-Roberts, *Pro Des* Kalina Ivanov, *Ed* Richard Marks, *M* Rupert Gregson-Williams, *Costumes* Penny Rose.

Columbia Pictures/Original Film/Relativity Media-Sony

Pictures Entertainment.
101 mins. USA/UK. 2008. Rel: 2 May 2008. Cert 12A.

The Magic Flute ★

An unintended advertisement for Ingmar Bergman's brilliant film of Mozart's opera made in 1975. Aiming at comprehensibility (it is performed in Stephen Fry's new English text), Kenneth Branagh achieves the opposite by forcing the work into a First World War setting that borrows from *Oh! What A Lovely War* and *Paths of Glory*. Ben Davis is a charmless and tiresome Papageno while Lyubov Petrova's Queen of the Night suggests a wicked witch from pantomime. Otherwise the musical performance is acceptable but the visuals and music are continually at odds. The only person to emerge with credit is Liz Smith appearing as the aged Papagena. MS

▶ Joseph Kaiser, Amy Carson, Benjamin Jay Davis, Sylvia Moi, Lyubov Petrova.
▶ *Dir* Kenneth Branagh, *Pro* Steve Clark-Hall and Simon Moseley, *Screenplay* Stephen Fry and Branagh, *Ph* Roger Lanser, *Pro Des* Tim Harvey, *Ed* Michael Parker, *M* Mozart, *Costumes* Christopher Oram.

Celluloid Dreams/ an Ideale Audience production for the Peter Moores Foundation-Revolver Entertainment. 139 mins. UK/France. 2006. Rel: 30 Nov 2007. Cert PG

Tang Wei and Tony Leung in Ang Lee's subtle masterpiece *Lust, Caution*.

Jack Black may be regretting taking on his role in *Margot at the Wedding*.

Man in the Chair ★★½

The total implausibility of his story undermines Michael Schroeder's attempt to appeal to film buffs through a tale in which two aged men of cinema (Christopher Plummer and M Emmet Walsh both on fine form) assist a troubled youngster to make a film about inadequate care homes. It's sentimental as well as silly but the intentions were obviously good. MS

▶ Christopher Plummer. Michael Angarano, M Emmet Walsh, Robert Wagner.
▶ *Dir* and *Screenplay* Michael Schroeder, *Pro* Schroeder, Randy Turrow and Sarah Schroeder, *Ph* Dana Gonzales, *Pro Des* Carol Strober, *Ed* Terry Cafaro, *M* Laura Karpman, *Costumes* Tricia Gray.

An Elbow Grease Pictures production-Transmedia Pictures.
109 mins. USA. 2006. Rel: 25 Jan 2008. Cert 12A.

Man of the Year ★★

Surprisingly ramshackle would-be satire on US methods of electing the President as television comedian Robin Williams manages to get to the White House on account of a computer error. Far from being the sharp comedy one might expect from writer-director Barry Levinson, the film soon gets lost in its own pretensions, leaving it to be yet another Robin Williams dud effort. CB

▶ Robin Williams, Christopher Walken, Laura Linney, Lewis Black, Jeff Goldblum.
▶ *Dir and Screenplay* Barry Levinson, *Pro* David Robinson and James G Robinson, *Ph* Dick Pope, *Pro Des* Stefania Cella, *Ed* Blair Daly and Steven Weisberg, *M* Graeme Revell, *Costumes* Delphine White.

Universal Pictures/Morgan Creek Productions-Morgan Creek International.
115 mins. USA. 2006. Rel: 2 Nov 2007. Cert 12A.

Manufactured Landscapes ★★★

This documentary feature linked to the work of photographer Edward Burtynsky is overshadowed by *Our Daily Bread* (qv). Both use fine images to comment on heartless industrial processes that increasingly mark modern life. Here it is not always clear what is the work of filmmaker Jennifer Baichwal and what is by Burtynsky and the film can be tiresomely demanding, as in the long panning shot inside a factory which opens the movie and seems endless. MS

▶ With Edward Burtynsky.
▶ *Dir* Jennifer Baichwal, *Pro* Nick de Pencier, Daniel Iron and Baichwal, *Ph* Peter Mettler, *Ed* Roland Schlimme, *M* Dan Driscoll.

Mercury Films/Foundry Films/The National Film Board of Canada etc-BFI Distribution.
87 mins. Canada. 2006. Rel: 9 May 2008. Cert U.

Manufacturing Dissent ★★★

Documentary filmmaker Michael Moore has the tables turned on him in Caine and Melnyk's attempt to get inside the mind of the champion of the US left and scourge of American right-wingers. However, although Moore's friends and associates are all too willing to talk about him, Moore himself is rather elusive and shy of the camera. The conclusion to draw is to ask whether any documentary can be totally fair to all sides. CB

▷ Michael Moore, Errol Morris, John Pierson, Roseanne Barr, Susan Sarandon, Quentin Tarantino, Ralph Nader, Albert Maysles, Christopher Hitchens, Noam Chomsky, Richard Gere.
▷ *Dir, Pro and Screenplay* Rick Caine and Debbie Melnyk, *Ph* Rick Caine, *Ed* Rob Ruzic and Bill Towgood, *M* Michael White.

Persistence of Vision Productions-Liberation Entertainments.
97 mins. Canada. 2007. Rel: 5 Nov 2007. Cert 12A.

Margot at the Wedding ★★★

Less a forward-moving tale than a series of character studies, this new film by Noah Baumbach of last year's *The Squid and the Whale* has a sibling relationship at its centre. Nicole Kidman plays Margot, an unscrupulous writer who, invited to the marriage of her sister (Jennifer Jason Leigh), takes against the uncouth bridegroom (Jack Black) and tries to wreck things. It's an interesting attempt to present characters far from one-sided but it's more ambitious than successful and Black is ill at ease when he attempts pathos. MS

▷ Nicole Kidnman, Jennifer Jason Leigh, Jack Black, John Turturro, Zane Pais.
▷ *Dir* and *Screenplay* Noah Baumbach, *Pro* Scott Rudin, *Ph* Harris Savides, *Pro Des* Anne Ross, *Ed* Carol Littleton, *Music Supervisor* George Drakoulias, *Costumes* Ann Roth.

Paramount Vantage-Paramount Pictures UK.
93 mins. USA. 2007. Rel: 29 Feb 2008. Cert 15.

Marigold ★★

American actress Marigold Lexton arrives in India to make a small Hollywood film. Her bad attitude gets worse when the film is cancelled and she is stranded in Goa. She ends up doing a small part in a Bollywood musical where she falls for the charming choreographer Prem. The film boasts strong production values with fun musical numbers but the lazy script and direction finally disappoint. Also the chemistry between the two leads is forced and unbelievable. GS

▷ Salman Khan, Ali Larter, Nandana Sen, Ian Bohen, Shari Watson.
▷ *Dir and Screenplay* Willard Carroll, *Pro* Charles Salmon and Tom Wilhite, *Ph* Anil Mehta, *Pro Des* Jon Bunker and Nitin Chandrakant Desai, *Ed* Anuradha Singh, *M* Shankar Mahadevan, Graeme Revell, Loy Mendonsa and Ehsaan Noorani, *Costumes* Rocky S and Holly Faircrest.

Hyperion Pictures/Firewall Entertainment/Becker Films-Adlabs Films UK.
110 mins. USA/UK/India. 2007. Rel: 17 Aug 2007. Cert PG.

Mee Shee: The Water Serpent ★★

Ten-year-old Mac reluctantly accompanies his father on an emergency salvage mission at a remote Canadian lake instead of their planned holiday to Florida. But when he discovers that the lake is famous for a mythical creature, he is determined to find it – and does. It is a fun idea, decently acted – particularly from Daniel Magder – but it is poorly executed with unsophisticated special effects and directed in a predictable and unimaginative way. GS

▷ Bruce Greenwood, Daniel Magder, Joel Tobeck, Rena Owen, Phyllida Law, Shane Rimmer.
▷ *Dir* John Henderson, *Pro* Barry Authors, Ken Tuohy, Rainer Mockert and Gary Hannam, *Screenplay* Barry Authors , *Ph* John Ignatius, *Pro Des* Chris Wheatley, *Ed* Bill Jones and David Yardley, *M* Pol Brennan, *Costumes* Pauline Bowkett.

MBP (Germany)/Ogopogo Productions Ltd-The Works.
94 mins. UK/Germany. 2005. Rel: 17 Aug 2007. Cert PG.

Meet the Spartans ★

From the makers of *Epic Movie* and *Date Movie*, here's another one you may care to avoid – this

Sean Maguire and Ken Davitian struggle for laughs in *Meet the Spartans*.

Tom Wilkinson and George Clooney in superior legal thriller *Michael Clayton*.

just appalling parody of the 2007 hit *300* has Sean Maguire doing a fair vocal impersonation of Gerard Butler as the Spartan king Leonidas, who leads a paltry band of warriors against the mighty Persians under camp king Xerxes (Borat's Ken Davitian). Lame, crude, unfunny and plain pathetic, it just mirthlessly follows the plot of *300* and, in a desperate bid to pad out its puny running time, adds in a pointless and incredibly feeble spoof of celebrity culture from Paris Hilton to Simon Cowell and from Sylvester Stallone to Tom Cruise – all horribly mean spirited. DW

▶ Sean Maguire, Carmen Electra, Ken Davitian, Kevin Sorbo, Diedrich Bader.
▶ *Dir and Screenplay* Jason Friedberg and Aaron Seltzer, *Pro* Friedberg and Peter Safran, *Ph* Shawn Maurer, *Pro Des* William A Elliott, *Ed* Peck Prior, *M* Christian Lennertz, *Costumes* Frank Helmer.

New Regency Pictures/Regency Enterprises-20th Century Fox.
84 mins. USA. 2008. Rel: 21 Mar 2008. Cert 12A.

Memories of Matsuko ★★★★

This is a visual treat and much superior to Nakashima's earlier *Kamikaze Girls* (q.v). When Shou's father asks him to clean the apartment of his murdered aunt Matsuko, he is intrigued and wants to find out more about the circumstances and why she abandoned her life as a teacher and

became a tramp in her last years. It's a fascinating and very colourful journey in the style of a Douglas Sirk melodrama with an amazing performance from Miki Nakatani as Matsuko. (Original title: *Kiraware Matsuko no Isshô*). GS

▶ Miki Nakatani, Eita, Yusuke Iseya, Teruyuki Kagawa, Mikako Ichikawa.
▶ *Dir and Screenplay* Tetsuya Nakashima, from the novel by Muneki Yamada, *Ph* Masakazu Ato, *Pro Des* Towako Kuwashima, *Ed* Yoshiyuki Koike, *M* Gabrielle Roberto.

Tokyo Broadcasting System/Amuse Soft Entertainment-Toho Company.
130 mins. Japan. 2006. Rel: 13 June 2008. No cert.

Michael Clayton ★★★★

Latest in the line of legal thrillers in which the bad guys are generally the lawyers. Clooney plays the title role, a fixer for a law firm, who has to get his employers off the hook when one of their personnel goes off his nut during an expensive lawsuit against a powerful corporation. It's heady, thrilling stuff with excellent performances by Clooney, Wilkinson as the nutcase, Pollack as a fellow lawyer and Swinton as a corporation big cheese. MHD

▶ George Clooney, Tom Wilkinson, Michael O'Keefe, Sydney Pollack, Tilda Swinton, Denis O'Hare.
▶ *Dir and Screenplay* Tony Gilroy, *Pro* Jennifer Fox,

Kerry Orent, Sydney Pollack and Steve Samuels, *Ph* Robert Elswit, *Pro Des* Kevin Thompson, *Ed* John Gilroy, *M* James Newton Howard, *Costumes* Sarah Edwards.

Clayton Productions/Castle Rock Entertainment/ Mirage Enterprises/Samuels Media-Pathé Distribution. 119 mins. USA. 2007. Rel: 28 Sep 2007. Cert 15.

Midnight Talks ★★★

Although agreeably cast, this Polish rom-com lacks any distinctive features. A woman wanting a child advertises in the lonely hearts column but the man who applies doesn't realise that she's not seeking a romantic attachment. The rest you could write yourself, but those audiences content to accept a formula movie may well find it tolerably entertaining. (Original title: *Rozmowy noca*) MS

▶ Magdalena Rózczka, Marcin Dorocinski, Weronika Ksiazkiewicz.
▶ *Dir* Maciej Zak, *Pro* Agata Janicka, Matrcin Jaworski and Piotr Reisch, *Screenplay* Karolina Szymczyk Majchrzak, *Ph* Michal Englert, *Pro Des* Joanna Macha, Marcelina Poczatek-Kunikowska and Tomasz Stasinski, *Ed* Jaroslaw Pietraszek, *M* Piotr 'Miki' Mikolajczak, *Costumes* Agata Culak.

Telewizja Polsat SA/SPI Internationmal Polska/50/50 Films etc-Dogwoof Pictures. 95 mins. Poland. 2008. Rel: 15 Feb 2008. Cert 12A.

A Mighty Heart ★★★★

Michael Winterbottom's fine film about the kidnapping of journalist Daniel Pearl in Karachi in 2002 and his consequent death plays like a cross between *United 93* and *Zodiac*: the former because a real-life tragedy is here handled with sensitivity and restraint and the latter because this is a complex, detailed record of an investigation. The casting is fine (Angelina Jolie's contribution is heartfelt), the location shooting splendidly atmospheric and the final dedication touching. MS

▶ Angelina Jolie, Dan Futterman, Irrfan Khan, Denis O'Hare. Will Patton.
▶ *Dir* Michael Winterbottom, *Pro* Brad Pitt, Dede Gardner and Andrew Eaton, *Screenplay* John Orloff based on the book by Marianne Pearl, *Ph* Marcel Zyskind, *Pro Des* Mark Digby, *Ed* Peter Christelis, *M* Molly Nyman and Harry Escott, *Costumes* Charlotte Walter and Lee Hunsaker.

Paramount Vantage presents a Plan B Entertainment/ Revolution Films production-Paramount Pictures UK. 108 mins. USA/UK. 2007. Rel: 21 Sept 2007. Cert 15.

Mister Lonely ★★½

Samantha Morton as Marilyn Monroe? Not really: she plays someone who impersonates Monroe just as Diego Luna portrays a Michael Jackson imitator. Both players respect the theme of loneliness and inadequacy in Harmony Korine's film but, despite beginning well with a moody title song from Bobby Vinton, it soon becomes over-extended and improbable. There's potential here and the right players, but it's off-target all the same. MS

▶ Diego Luna, Samantha Morton, Denis Lavant, James Fox, Werner Herzog.
▶ *Dir* Harmony Korine, *Pro* Nadja Romain,

A barely recognisable Angelina Jolie in the moving *A Mighty Heart*.

No longer John Wayne as the conqueror but Asano Tadanobu in *Mongol*.

Screenplay Harmony and Avi Korine, *Ph* Marcel Zyskind, *Pro Des* Richard Campling, *Ed* Paul Zucker and Valdís Óskarsdóttir, *M* Jason Spaceman and The Sun City Girls, *Costumes* Judy Shrewsbury.

agnes b. and Jeremy Thomas/ Dreamachine/Gaga/ Film4 etc-Tartan Films.
113 mins. UK/France/Ireland/USA/Japan. 2006.
Rel: 14 March 2008. Cert 15.

Molière ★★★

With an echo of *Becoming Jane*, the life of the French playwright Molière is refashioned to carry echoes of situations portrayed in his works and to provide a tragic love story. Here, however, much of the emphasis is on farce. If, despite good production values and strong performances, I found this over-long film neither affecting nor satisfyingly comic, it may be because to appreciate it you need to be more familiar than I am with Molière's plays. MS

▶ Romain Duris, Fabrice Luchini, Laura Morante, Edouard Baer, Ludivine Sagnier.
▶ *Dir* Laurent Tirard, *Pro* Olivier Delbosc and Marc Missonnier, *Screenplay* Tirard and Grégoire Vigneron, *Ph* Gilles Henry, *Pro Des* Françoise Dupertuis, *Ed* Valérie Deseine, *M* Frédéric Talgorn, *Costumes* Pierre-Jean Larroque.

Fidélité/Virtual Films/Wild Bunch/France 3 Cinéma etc-Pathé Distribution.
121 mins. France. 2006. Rel: 13 July 2007. Cert 12A.

Mongol ★★★★

The rating above ignores my own wish that Sergei Bodrov of *Freedom is Paradise* (1989) had made this into a serious, well written study of the early life of the 12th-century warrior who became Genghis Khan. Accept it for what it is, however, and you have a modern, bloodthirsty, boys' own adventure yarn which, if nothing more, is stunningly shot and looks great on the big screen. MS

▶ Asano Tadanobu, Sun Honglei, Khulan Chuluun, Odnyam Odsuren, Ba Sen.
▶ *Dir* Sergei Bodrov, *Pro* Sergey Selyanov, Bodrov and Anton Melnik, *Screenplay* Arif Ailyev and Bodrov, *Ph* Sergey Trofimov and Rogier Stoffers, *Pro Des* Dashi Namdakov, *Ed* Zach Staenberg and Valdís Oskarsdóttir, *M* Tuomas Kantelinen, *Costumes* Karin Löhr.

CTB Film Company/Andreyevsky Flag Film Company/ X Filme Creative Pool/Kinofabrika/Eurasia Film/ Eco-Finance/Cinetools Film etc-The Works UK Distribution Ltd.
125 mins. Russia/Germany/Switzerland/Kazakhstan/ Mongolia. 2007. Rel: 6 June 2008. Cert 15.

Mouth to Mouth ★★

Ellen Page's presence may explain the belated release of this drama. It's about a group that offers an alternative lifestyle but not one that is a religious cult despite proving to be despotic. Such groups do exist, but the film quite fails to explain their lure. Consequently we are left thinking that if only the characters had come to their senses earlier we would have escaped the boredom of this film. Only director Alison Murray's skill in matching music and visuals compensates. MS

▶ Eric Thal, Ellen Page, Natasha Wightman, August Diehl, Maxwell McCabe-Lokos.
▶ *Dir* and *Screenplay* Alison Murray, *Pro* Anne Beresford and Judy Tossell, *Ph* Barry Stone, *Pro Des* Ulrika Andersson, *Ed* Christian Lonk, *M* Rowan Oliver, *Costumes* Jemima Cotter.

M2M Films/Egoli Tossell Film/Hellround etc-Dogwoof Pictures.
103 mins. UK/Germany. 2004. Rel: 9 May 2008. Cert 15.

Mr Brooks ★★★

Kevin Costner is on great form in the title role. He is playing a schizophrenic who is a model citizen as businessman and philanthropist but also a compulsive serial killer with an alter ego in the form of William Hurt. The main thrust of this piece may be preposterous, but it's fun. Unfortunately the film is too long and incorporates two sub-plots which in any case overegg the pudding. MS

▶ Kevin Costner, Demi Moore, Dane Cook, Marg Helgenberger, William Hurt.
▶ *Dir* Bruce A Evans, *Pro* Jim Wilson, Kevin Costner and Raynold Gideon, *Screenplay* Evans and Gideon, *Ph* John Lindley, *Pro Des* Jeffrey Beecroft, *Ed* Miklos Wright, *M* Ramin Djawadi, *Costumes* Judianna Makovsky.

Element Films/Relativity Media/Eden Rock Media/A TIG Production-Verve Pictures.
120 mins. USA/Australia. 2007. Rel: 12 Oct 2007. Cert 18.

Mr Magorium's Wonder Empire ★★★

This Willy Wonka derived children's film has toy store owner Dustin Hoffman set to retire (i.e. die) and pass his magical business empire on to his protégé – store manager Natalie Portman whose heart lies elsewhere, in composing music. Arresting art direction makes great use of first colour then monochrome. Cast and crew appear to have had fun making it and this spills over onto the screen. Commendably, the piece never talks down to its child audience. JC

▶ Dustin Hoffman, Zach Mills, Natalie Portman, Ted Ludzik, Paula Boudreau.
▶ *Dir* and *Screenplay* Zach Helm, *Pro* James

Garavente and Richard N Gladstein, *Ph* Roman Osin, *Pro Des* Thérèse DePrez, *Ed* Sabrina Plisco and Steven Weisberg, *M* Alexandre Desplat, *Costumes* Christopher Hargadon.

Mandate Pictures/FilmColony/Walden Media/Gang of Two Productions-Icon Film Distribution.
93 mins. USA. 2007. Rel: 14 Dec 2007. Cert U.

Mr Woodcock ★★★

A patchy comedy with Seann William Scott as an author of bestselling self-help books, who sets out to destroy the wedding plans of his widowed mother (Susan Sarandon) and the sadistic gym teacher Mr Woodcock (Billy Bob Thornton) who terrorised him as a child. Thornton is of course typecast, but he performs his nasty role perfectly, and is hilarious whenever the weak script allows him a funny line, Scott is a naturally infectious comic actor who's always good for a laugh, and a largely wasted Sarandon battles her odd casting with a steely will. There's a far, far better film trying to squeeze out of this, but it's still a watchably amusing entertainment that, with its suspiciously short running time, doesn't outstay it welcome. DW

▶ Billy Bob Thornton, Susan Sarandon, Seann William Scott, Melissa Sagemiller, Ethan Suplee.
▶ *Dir* Craig Gillespie, *Pro* Bob Cooper and David Dobkin, *Screenplay* Michael Carnes and Josh Gilbert, *Ph* Tami Reiker, *Pro Des* Alison Sadler, *Ed* Alan Baumgarten and Kevin Tent, *M* Theodore Shapiro, *Costumes* Wendy Chuck.

Avery Pictures/Landscape Pictures/MACRON Film Produktion Projekt 1 KG-New Line Cinema.
87 mins. USA. 2007. Rel: 28 Sep 2007. Cert 12A.

Mrs Ratcliffe's Revolution ★½

Frank Ratcliffe, an idealist teacher and head of the Bingley Communist Party, transports his family from the north of England to East Germany. But when the oppressive bureaucracy and brutal system turn his dreams sour, it is up to Mrs Ratcliffe to get her family back to England. The strong script based on a true story from the late '60s is let down by unimaginative direction and a mixture of acting styles. Iain Glen is always good value for money but Catherine Tate appears to be in a different film altogether. GS

▶ Catherine Tate, Iain Glen, Brittany Ashworth, Heike Makatsch, Jessica Barden, Christian Brassington
▶ *Dir* Bille Eltringham, *Pro* Leslee Udwin, *Screenplay* Bridget O'Connor and Peter Straughan, *Ph* Sean

Bobbit, *Pro Des* Malcolm Thornton, *Ed* John Wilson, *M* Robert Lane, *Costumes* Andrea Flesch.
Assassin Films/Pioneer Pictures/UK Film Council-Warner Bros.
102 mins. UK/Hungary. 2007. Rel: 28 Sep 2007. Cert 12A.

My Blueberry Nights ★★½

Being a film by Wong Kar-Wai (his first in English in fact), this looks great, but this episodic piece set in America never grips as a narrative. Norah Jones (her acting debut) and Jude Law play the leads, people whose troubled past relationships mean that they could find solace together. However, she takes to the road instead because otherwise there would be no film. This is empty, meretricious fluff that wastes the actors who cannot overcome a screenplay that seems banal throughout. MS

❥ Norah Jones, Jude Law, David Strathairn, Rachel Weisz, Natalie Portman.
❥ *Dir* Wong Kar-Wai, *Pro* Wong, Jean-Louis Piel and Wang Wei and Jacky Pang Yee Wah, *Screenplay* Wong and Lawrence Block from Wong's story, *Ph* Darius Khondji, *Pro Des* and *Ed* William Chang Suk-Ping, *Costumes* William Chang Suk-Ping and Sharon Globerson.

Block 2 Pictures/Studio Canal/A Jet Tone Films /Lou Yi Ltd production etc-Optimum Releasing.
95 mins. Hong Kong/France/China. 2007. Rel: 22 Feb 2008. Cert 12A.

My Brother is an Only Child ★★★

One of the most Italianate films ever made, this blends a family saga with historical events in Italy during the 1960s and the 1970s. Two contrasted brothers growing to manhood are central and both fall for the same girl. But equally key to the tale are the political issues involving Fascists, Communists and terrorist activities. It's ably presented but Italian audiences have the advantage, both because they will be more *au fait* with the politics and because many of them will find in this material a nostalgia trip. (Original title: *Mio fratello è figlio unico*) MS

❥ Elio Germano, Riccardo Scamarcio, Angela Finocchiaro, Diane Fleri.
❥ *Dir* Daniele Luchetti, *Pro* Riccardo Tozzi, Giovanni Stabilini and Marco Chimenz, *Screenplay* Sandro Petraglia, Stefano Rulli and Luchetti from Antonio Pennacchi's novel *Il fasciocomunista*, *Ph* Claudio Collepiccolo, *Pro Des* Francesco Frigeri, Giovanni Stabilini and Riccardo Tozzi, *Ed* Mirco Garrone, *M* Franco Piersanti, *Costumes* Maria Rita Barbera.

Elio Germano and Riccardo Scamarcio in *My Brother Is An Only Child.*

Warner Bros Pictures/Cattleya/Babe Films etc-Revolver Entertainment.
104 mins. Italy/France. 2006. Rel: 4 April 2008. Cert 15.

My Kid Could Paint That ★★★★

This absorbing documentary tells the story of an acclaimed painter of abstracts whose talent was applauded when she was all of four years old. Film-maker Amir Bar-Lev had already started to record her story when in 2005 a TV programme hinted that her father might have lent a hand. In addition to allowing you to decide for yourself what you take to be the truth of the matter, this is a fascinating comment on the art world and on art interacting with commerce – plus there's the director having to decide what his duties were when the subject he had chosen took such a different turn. It's splendidly thought-provoking on many levels. MS

❥ With Marla Olmstead, Laura Olmstead, Mark Olmstead, Amir Bar-Lev.
❥ *Dir* and *Pro* Amir Bar-Lev, *Ph* Matt Boyd, Nelson Hume and Bill Turnley, *Ed* Michael Levine, *M* Rondo Brothers.

Sony Pictures Classics/A&E IndieFilms/BBC/Axis Films/ Passion Pictures-Sony Pictures Releasing.
83 mins. USA/UK. 2007. Rel: 14 Dec 2007. Cert 12A.

My Nikifor ★★★★

Although lacking the impact of the Russian film *Pirosmani* (1969), this study of the eccentric naïve artist Nikifor will certainly appeal to Polish audiences familiar with his work. Concentrating on Nikifor's last years when his health was failing, the film almost becomes a buddy movie since it puts much emphasis on the less adept professional artist who is made responsible for Nikifor and then finds his initial irritation turning to friendship. The casting of the role of Nikifor is quirky but successful (I won't say more). Slight, perhaps, but sincere. MS

❥ Krystyna Feldman, Roman Gancarczyk, Jerzy Gudejko, Lucyna Malec.
❥ *Dir* Krzysztof Krauze, *Pro* Juliusz Machulski, *Screenplay* Joanna Kos and Krauze, *Ph* Krzysztof Ptak, *Pro Des* Magdalena Dipont, *Ed* Krzysztof Szpetmanski, *M* Bartlomiej Gliniak, *Costumes* Dorota Roqueplo.

Best Film/TVP Telewizja Polska SA/Canal+ production-Dogwoof Pictures.
100 mins. Poland. 2004. Rel: 14 Sept 2007. Cert 12A.

Diane Kruger and Nicolas Cage in *National Treasure: Book of Secrets*.

Nancy Drew ★★★

Nancy, the bright teenage detective, has to leave her old school and friends behind in River Heights when she moves with her father to Los Angeles. She enrols at Hollywood High School and is determined to solve the case involving the mysterious death of famous actress Dehlia Draycott who lived in their mansion years earlier. Based on the popular graphic novel, the film is fun (although it drags in the middle) boasting clever designs, which anachronistically suggest the 1950s. Emma Roberts is perfectly cast as the eponymous heroine. GS

▶ Emma Roberts, Rich Cooper, Max Thieriot, Amy Bruckner, Kay Panabaker, Tate Donovan.
▶ *Dir* Andrew Fleming, *Pro* Jerry Weintraub, *Screenplay* Fleming and Tiffany Paulsen, from a story by Paulsen based on characters by Carolyn Keene, *Ph* Alexander Gruszynski, *Pro Des* Tony Fanning, *Ed* Jeff Freeman, *M* Ralph Sau, *Costumes* Jeffrey Kurland.

Jerry Weintraub Productions/Warner Bros Pictures/Virtual Studios-Warner Bros.
99 mins. USA. 2007. Rel: 10 Oct 2007. Cert PG.

Nanhe Jaisalmer ★★★½

In Rajasthan ten-year-old Nahne is obsessed with actor Bobby Deol. He makes his sister write a letter to him every day and his room is full with his idol's photographs. So, when it is announced that Deol is coming to town to make another film, Nahne can't believe his luck. It is a charming tale with strong production values aided by a mature performance from Dwij Yadav who carries the film effortlessly. The scenes where the obsessive boy and the Bollywood star meet in the middle of the night have an uneasy feel about them but overall this is very entertaining. GS

▶ Dwij Yadav, Karan Arora, Sukhwinder Chahal, Bobby Dheol, Katrina Kaif, Bina Kak.
▶ *Dir* Samir Karnik, *Pro* Jaswant Khera and Bashir Sayyad, *Screenplay* Aseem Aora from a story by Karnik and Eklavya Singh Bhati, *Ph* Binod Pradhan, *Pro Des* Sunil Nigvekar, *Ed* Sanjay Sankla, *M* Himesh Reshammiya, *Costumes* Tanya Deol.

Dharam Motion Pictures/K Sera Sera/Top Angle Productions-Eros International
129 mins. India. 2007. Rel: 14 Sep 2007. Cert U.

The Nanny Diaries ★½

Number one on *The New York Times* bestseller list, Emma McLaughlin and Nicola Kraus' 2002 novel was a celebrated critique of Manhattan society. Inspired by the authors' own experiences as babysitters, the story sees college graduate Annie Braddock (Johansson) land a potentially cushy nannying job on the Upper East Side. Of course, the position is anything but and Braddock has to take a long, hard look at herself before combatting a world in which children are merely accessories. Considering that co-writer-directors Berman and Pulcini previously brought us the original, hilarious and touching *American Splendor*, their second outing is a major letdown. Ms Johansson is a lacklustre presence, her ward a tiresome brat and the other characters exasperating stereotypes. JC-W

▷ Scarlett Johansson, Laura Linney, Donna Murphy, John Henry Cox, Paul Giamatti, Alicia Keys.
▷ *Dir and Screenplay* Shari Springer Berman and Robert Pulcini, from the novel by Emma McLaughlin and Nicola Kraus, *Pro* Richard S Gladstein and Dany Wolf, *Ph* Terry Stacey, *Pro Des* Mark Ricker, *Ed* Robert Pulcini, *M* Mark Suozzo, *Costumes* Michael Wilkinson.

The Weinstein Company/FilmColony-Paramount Pictures.
106 mins. USA. 2007. Rel: 12 Oct 2007. Cert 12A.

National Treasure: Book of Secrets ★½

Failing to capture the fun, adventurous spirit and sense of wonder present in the flawed but entertaining original, director Jon Turteltaub delivers a bloated, charmless, by-the-numbers sequel full of stars who, unlike the characters they play, must only have done it for the money, among them Nic Cage and Helen Mirren. A mess of unconvincing production design, muddled set-pieces and flat, forced humour, this mythical treasure hunting tale in search of secrets about past US Presidents, should never have been unearthed. MJ

▷ Nicolas Cage, Ed Harris, Harvey Keitel, Justin Bartha, Jon Voight, Helen Mirren, Diane Kruger.
▷ *Dir* John Turteltaub, *Pro* Turteltaub and Jerry Bruckheimer, *Screenplay* Marianne and Cormac Wibberley, from a story by The Wibberleys, Gregory Poirier, Ted Elliott and Terry Rossio, based on characters by Oren Aviv, Jim Kouf and Charles Segars, *Ph* Amir Mokri and John Schwartzman, *Pro Des* Dominic Watkins, *Ed* William Goldenberg and David Rennie, *M* Trevor Rabin, *Costumes* Judianna Makovsky.

Jerry Bruckheimer Films/Walt Disney Pictures/Sparkler Entertainment etc-Walt Disney Motion Pictures.
124 mins. USA. 2007. Rel: 8 Feb 2008. Cert PG.

Never Apologise: A Personal Visit with Lindsay Anderson ★★★★

This filmed version of Malcolm McDowell's one-man stage tribute to the filmmaker Lindsay Anderson rewardingly incorporates extracts from Anderson's own writings. It also shows McDowell on his best form performing the material for an audience, but the neat editing and placing of close-ups make it cinematic too. It's honest and informative about Anderson and

highly entertaining. It may not be what you expect of a film but that matters not a jot. MS

▷ With Malcolm McDowell.
▷ *Dir* Mike Kaplan, *Pro* Kaplan and Malcolm McDowell, *Conceived by* McDowell, *Ph* Matt Walla, Jesse Hagy and others, *Ed* Eric Foster and Kate Johnson.

Travis Productions/Circle Associates Ltd-Lagoon Entertainment.
112 mins. USA. 2007 Rel: 2 Nov 2007. Cert 15.

Never Back Down ★

Jake, a football star from Iowa moves with his mother and siblings to Orlando, Florida, but now he is like a fish out of water. He is a total outsider still trying to cope with the recent death of his father until he unwillingly enters the world of Mixed Martial Arts when school bully Ryan provokes him into a fight. *Fight Club* goes to High School in this pointless and violent film. GS

▷ Sean Faris, Amber Heard, Cam Gigandet, Evan Peters, Leslie Hope.
▷ *Dir* Jeff Wadlow, *Pro* Craig Baumgarten, *Screenplay* Chris Hauty, *Ph* Lukas Ettlin, *Pro Des* Ida Random, *Ed* Victor DuBois and Debra Weinfeld, *M* Michael Wandmacher, *Costumes* Judy Ruskin Howell.

Mandalay Pictures/Summit Entertainment/BMD Films etc-Momentum Pictures.
110 mins. USA. 2008. Rel: 4 Apr 2008. Cert 15.

Night Bus ★★★★

Receiving a limited release in the UK, Davide Marengo's *Night Bus* certainly shows promise, an offbeat thriller that is a cut above the usual *film noir* genre. In the course of her work,

Amber Heard watches Sean Faris kick off in *Never Back Down*.

Abigail Breslin looks for help on *Nim's Island*.

Nim's Island ★★★

Charming and imaginative comedy with Abigail Breslin as 12 year old Nim, living on a remote Pacific island with her father. When he's lost at sea she calls on Alex Rover, hero and writer of her favourite *Indiana Jones* style adventure novels, not knowing that Alex is really neurotic, agoraphobic novelist Alexandra (Jodie Foster). It runs out of steam towards the end but Gerald Butler is fun in the dual roles of dad and the fictional Alex, and Breslin too is delightful. CA

▶ Abigail Breslin, Jodie Foster, Gerald Butler, Michael Carman, Mark Brady.
▶ *Dir* Jennifer Flackett and Mark Levin, *Pro* Paula Mazur, *Screenplay* Flackett, Levin, Mazur and Joseph Kwong from the novel by Wendy Orr *Ph* Stuart Dryburgh, *Pro Des* Barry Robison, *Ed* Stuart Levy, *M* Patrick Doyle, *Costumes* Jeffrey Kurland.

Walden Media-Universal Pictures.
96 mins. USA. 2008. Rel: 2 May 2008. Cert U.

The Nines ★★★½

This film offers three distinct pieces in each of which the same players appear in roles that echo one another somewhat. This unusual structure seems to promise an eventual revelatory tie-up but that never really happens and you may well feel that you have been sold short. Nevertheless, this is a pleasingly original piece in which the principal characters are writers, agents and actors. This becomes a way of commenting on the worlds they create and on their responsibilities. The stand-out player here is the little-known Melissa McCarthy. MS

▶ Ryan Reynolds, Hope Davis, Melissa McCarthy, Elle Fanning.
▶ *Dir* and *Screenplay* John August, *Pro* Dan Etheridge, Dan Jinks and Bruce Cohen, *Ph* Nancy Schreiber, *Art Dir* Colleen Saro, *Ed* Douglas Crise, *M* Alex Wurman, *Costumes* Molly Elizabeth Grundman.

Distribution Company presents a Jinks/Cohen Company production-Optimum Releasing.
100 mins. USA. 2006. Rel: 30 Nov 2007. Cert 15.

female thief Leila (Giovanna Mezzogiorno), who drugs and robs her victims, obtains a valuable microchip hidden in a passport. Pursued by two hitmen, she boards a bus and befriends the driver, Franz (Valerio Mastandrea), a lonely soul dragged down by gambling debts. Together they form an odd friendship. Marengo directs with a style that demonstrates a true mastery of film technique. (Original title: *Notturno Bus*) CB

▶ Giovanna Mezzogiorno, Valerio Mastandrea, Ennio Fantastichini, Anna Romantowska, Roberto Citran.
▶ *Dir* Davide Marengo, *Pro* Sandra Silvestri and Maura Vespini, *Screenplay* Giampiero Rigosi and Fabio Bonifacci, based on a novel by Rigosi, in collaboration with Vespini, Isotta Toso, Maria Grazzi Perria and Cesare Cicardini, *Ph* Amaldo Catinari, *Ed* Patrizio Marone, *M* Gabriele Coen and Mario Rivera, *Costumes* Eva Coen.

Emme/Rai Cinema etc-01 Distribuzione.
105 mins. Italy. 20087. Rel: 6 June 2008. No cert.

No Country for Old Men ★★★★★

Basically this is a very superior chase movie. When hunter Josh Brolin discovers an abandoned truck littered with dead bodies, he grabs the loot, leaving a drugs haul behind. Soon he is pursued by psychopath Javier Bardem and subsequently local sheriff Tommy Lee Jones. The Coen brothers strike a rich seam, the result being one of the best films of the year which took four Oscars at the Academy Awards. Great performances from Brolin, Jones and the award-winning Bardem. Roger Deakins' pellucid, widescreen cinematography received a gong from BAFTA but also deserved an Oscar. MHD

▶ Tommy Lee Jones, Javier Bardem, Josh Brolin, Woody Harrelson, Kelly Macdonald, Tess Harper.
▶ *Dir and Screenplay* Ethan and Joel Coen, from the novel by Cormac McCarthy, *Pro* The Coens and Scott Rudin, *Ph* Roger Deakins, *Pro Des* Jess Gonchor, *Ed* Roderick Jaynes (The Coens), *M* Carter Burwell, *Costumes* Mary Zophres.

Paramount Vantage/Miramax Films/Scott Rudin Productions/Mike Ross Productions-Paramount Pictures. 122 mins. USA. 2007. Rel: 18 Jan 2008. Cert 15.

No Reservations ★★★½

In the words of her employer, Kate Armstrong (Zeta-Jones) is one of the better chefs in New York City. She's also exceptionally beautiful although she puts exotic recipes before personal commitments. Then her sister is killed and she finds herself the sole guardian of her nine-year-old niece. Adapted from the critically acclaimed German film *Mostly Martha* (2002), *No Reservations* is a slick, efficient soapser, albeit terribly predictable. But thanks to sharp performances from an excellent cast, it manages to be both hugely engaging and affecting. JC-W

▶ Catherine Zeta-Jones, Aaron Eckhart, Abigail Breslin, Patricia Clarkson, Jenny White, Bob Balaban, John McMartin, Dearbhla Molloy.
▶ *Dir* Scott Hicks, *Pro* Sergio Aguero and Kelly Heysen, *Screenplay* Carol Fuchs and Sandra Nettelbeck from Nettelbeck's 2001 screenplay *Mostly Martha*, *Ph* Stuart Dryburgh, *Pro Des* Barbara Ling, *Ed* Pip Karmel, *M* Philip Glass, *Costumes* Melissa Toth.

Warner Bros Pictures/Village Roadshow Pictures/Castle Rock Entertainment/WV Films III-Warner Bros. 104 mins. USA/Australia. 2007. Rel: 31 Aug 2007. Cert PG.

Once ★★★★

In Dublin a street musician develops an intimate as well as a professional relationship with a single mother from the Czech Republic, who inspires him to pursue his songwriting dreams. There is an effortless chemistry between Glen Hansard and Markéta Irglova who deliver lovely performances and complement each other beautifully in John Carney's charming film. They deservedly won the Oscar for one of their original and harmonious songs. GS

▶ Glen Hansard, Markéta Irglova, Hugh Walsh, Gerry Hendrick, Alastair Foley.

Javier Bardem in *No Country for Old Men*, one of the outstanding films of the year.

Glen Hansard and Markéta Irglova in the poignant and surprising *Once*.

▶ *Dir and Screenplay* John Carney, *Pro* Martina Niland, *Ph* Tim Fleming, *Pro Des* Tamara Conboy, *Ed* Paul Muller, *M* Glen Hansard and Irglova, *Costumes* Tiziana Corvisieri.

Bord Slannán Na hÉireann/Radio Telfis Éireann/Samson Films/ Summit Entertainment-Icon Film Distribution 85 mins. Ireland. 2007. Rel: 19 Oct 2007. Cert 15.

One Missed Call ★½

This is another unnecessary Japanese horror remake about a series of friends who meet gruesome deaths, having previously received voicemails from themselves detailing the time of their death. It is an intriguing premise but this remake is unimaginatively directed with a wasted Shannyn Sossamon and a wooden Edward Burns as the bemused detective attempting to solve the mystery. (Remake of the 2003 Japanese film *Chakushin Ari*) GS

▶ Shannyn Sossamon, Edward Burns, Ana Claudia Talancón, Ray Wise, Azura Skye, Margaret Cho.
▶ *Dir* Eric Valette, *Pro* Broderick Johnson, Scott Kroopf, Andrew A Kosove, Jennie Lew Tugend etc , *Screenplay* Andrew Klavan, from the novel Chakushin Ari by Yasushi Akimoto and the 2003 screenplay by Miwako Dair, *Ph* Glen MacPherson, *Pro Des* Laurence Bennett, *Ed* Steve Mirkovich, *M*

Reinhold Heil and Johnny Klimek, *Costumes* Sandra Hernandez.

Kakokawa Pictures/Missed Call Productions etc-Warner Bros.
87 mins. Japan/USA/Germany. 2008. Rel: 4 Apr 2008. Cert 15.

Opera Jawa ★★★★

You ain't seen nothing like it! That's hardly surprising given that this is a mix of Indonesian music and dance blended with art installations. The story told (a triangle drama drawing on the *Ramayana*) could at times be clearer and it's all of specialised appeal. However, it's wonderfully colourful and possessed of choreography so closely allied to camera movement that it never seems like a photographed stage piece. Add that all the words are sung and that the work has a strong erotic charge and you have a one-off. Love it or hate it, it's the real thing. MS

▶ Martinus Miroto, Artika Sari Devi, Eko Supriyanto, Siompo Pui.
▶ *Dir* and *Pro* Garin Nugroho, *Screenplay* Garin Nugropho Armantono based on *The Abduction of Sinta*, *Ph* Teoh Gay Hian, *Pro Des* Nanang Rakhmat Hidayat, *Ed* Andy Pulung Waluyo, *M* Rahayu Supanggah, *Costumes* Samuel Watimena.

SET Film production/New Crowned Hope Festival Vienna 2006 etc-Yume Pictures Ltd.
120 mins. Indonesia/Austria/Netherlands/Sweden/UK. 2006. Rel: 7 Sept 2007. Cert 12A.

The Orphanage ★★★★

It's a sign of how successful *Pan's Labyrinth* was that this ghost story has been promoted by using the fact that Guillermo del Toro was its executive producer. In fact this tale involving a mother (Belén Rueda) and a young son who disappears is very ably handled by its director J A Bayona. This Spanish film lacks the wider imaginative range of *Pan's Labyrinth* and carries echoes of other pieces (*The Innocents*, *The Others*) but it's atmospheric, tense and always adroit. MS

‣ Belén Rueda, Fernando Cayo, Roger Príncep, Mabel Rivera, Geraldine Chaplin.
‣ *Dir* J A Bayona, *Pro* Mar Targarona, Joaquin Padró and Álvaro Augustín, *Screenplay* Sergio G. Sánchez, *Ph* Óscar Faura, *Pro Des* Josep Rosell, *Ed* Elena Ruiz, *M* Fernando Velázquez, *Costumes* Maria Reyes.

Guillermo del Toro presents a Rodar y Rodar and Telecinco Cinema production/Warner Bros Pictures España-Optimum Releasing.
106 mins. Spain/France. 2006. Rel: 21 March 2008. Cert 15.

The Other Boleyn Girl ★★½

Those who enjoyed *Elizabeth: The Golden Age* may applaud this adaptation of Philippa Gregory's novel about Henry VIII and the two Boleyn girls, Anne and Mary. But it also offers us the other Peter Morgan, the one who, despite writing *The Queen* and being a brilliant playwright, becomes insipid when handling historical drama of an earlier age. Odd direction, convincing accents from the non-Brits but not much impact except, perhaps, from Kristin Scott Thomas. MS

‣ Natalie Portman, Scarlett Johansson, Eric Bana, Ana Torrent, Kristin Scott Thomas, Mark Rylance, David Morrissey, Jim Sturgess, Benedict Cumberbatch.
‣ *Dir* Justin Chadwick, *Pro* Alison Owen, *Screenplay* Peter Morgan from the novel by Philippa Gregory, *Ph* Kieran McGuigan, *Pro Des* John Paul Kelly, *Ed* Paul Knight and Carol Littleton, *M* Paul Cantelon, *Costumes* Sandy Powell.

Columbia Pictures/Focus Features/BBC Films/Relativity Media/A Ruby Films/ Scott Rubin production-Universal Pictures International UK & Eire.
115 mins. USA/UK. 2008. Rel: 7 March 2008. Cert 12A.

Our Daily Bread ★★★½

Quite wordless, this extraordinary documentary from Germany offers a disturbing look at food production methods and related issues. It's a plus that the film's visual quality is magnificent – pristine photography, superb compositions – but there's a minus too: the film seems excessively over-long for its material. Furthermore, it follows such comparatively recent pieces as *Fast Food Nation* and *Super Size Me* which had similar or parallel themes – but it is remarkable. MS

‣ With Claus Hansen Petz, Arkadiusz Rydellek, Barbara Hinz.
‣ *Dir* and *Ph* Nikolaus Geyrhalter, *Pro* Geyrhalter, Markus Glaser, Michael Kitzberger and Wolfgang Widerhofer, *Screenplay* Geyrhalter and Widerhofer, *Ed* Widerhofer.

A Nikolaus Geyrhalter Filmproduktion GmbH production etc-ICA Films.
86 mins. Austria/Germany. 2005. Rel: 25 Jan 2008. Cert 12A.

Out of the Blue ★★★

Set in November 1990, this film tackles a portrayal of what remains New Zealand's

Ana Claudia Talancón gets the creeps in the uninspiring *One Missed Call*.

Eva Longoria Parker comes back to life in *Over Her Dead Body*.

most notorious case of a man running amok and gunning down innocents. The film is not exploitative but surreal touches hardly blend with the dominating documentary-style approach. Since the real-life story is too harrowing to be entertaining, you look for insights to justify the enterprise, yet nothing special surfaces. MS

▶ Karl Urban, Matt Sunderland, Lois Lawn, Simon Ferry, Tandi Wright.
▶ *Dir* Robert Sarkies, *Pro* Tim White and Steve O'Meagher, *Screenplay* Graeme Tetley and Sarkies from Bill O'Brien's book *Aramoana*, *Ph* Greig Fraser, *Pro Des* Phil Ivey, *Ed* Annie Collins, *M* Victoria Kelly, *Costumes* Lesley Burkes-Harding.

New Zealand Film Commission/New Zealand On Air/TV3/A Southern Light Films, Desert Road Films production-Metrodome Distribution Ltd.
103 mins. New Zealand. 2006. Rel: 14 March. Cert 15.

Outpost ★½

A group of mercenaries led by Hunt, an engineer searching for mineral wealth, find much more than they bargained for in a deserted World War II bunker in Eastern Europe. Steve Barker's direction is slick and efficient but is let down by the routine script. It is also difficult to care about the one-dimensional characters in this over familiar horror film with a plot almost identical to *The Bunker* (2001). GS

▶ Ray Stevenson, Julian Wadham, Richard Brake, Paul Blair, Brett Fancy.
▶ *Dir* Steve Barker, *Pro* Arabella Page Croft and Kieron Parker, *Screenplay* Rae Brunton, *Ph* Gavin Struthers, *Pro Des* Max Berman and Gordon Rogers, *Ed* Chris Gill and Alastair Reid, *M* James Brett, *Costumes* Ali Mitchell.

Black Camel Pictures/Cinema One/Productions/

Matador Pictures etc-Vertigo Films.
90 mins. U. 2008. Rel: 16 May 2008. Cert 18.

Over Her Dead Body ★★

The exceedingly demanding and controlling Kate dies accidentally on her wedding day. Her ghost tries everything to keep her fiancé Henry single. It is a reasonable idea but the script is more like a first draft and it is difficult, despite the strong presence of Eva Longoria Parker and Paul Rudd, to feel involved when the characterisations are so thin. This is a far cry from the wit of, say, *Blithe Spirit*. GS

▶ Eva Longoria Parker, Paul Rudd, Lake Bell, Jason Biggs, Lindsay Sloane.
▶ *Dir and Screenplay* Jeff Lowell, *Pro* Paul Brooks and Peter Safran etc, *Ph* John Bailey, *Pro Des* Cory Lorenzen, *Ed* Matt Friedman, *M* David Kitay, *Costumes* Tracy Tynan.

Gold Circle Films/The Safran Company/Dead Fiancée Productions-Entertainment Film Distributors.
95 mins. USA. 2008. Rel: 1 Feb 2008. Cert 12A.

The Oxford Murders ★★★

This is a real oddity, a murder mystery hinging on philosophical speculations on mathematics. Elijah Wood plays Martin, an American graduate at Oxford under the guidance of John Hurt's Professor of Logic. When Martin's landlady (Anna Massey), a former cracker of the Enigma Code, is murdered, Wood and Hurt try to solve a number of serial killings linked by mathematical symbols. Although it doesn't all add up, it's nicely shot in Oxford, but from a script that feels as if it's been translated from another language. This one really needs Inspector Morse on the job. MHD

▶ Elijah Wood, John Hurt, Leonor Watling, Julie Cox, Anna Massey, Jim Carter, Alan David, Alex Cox.
▶ *Dir* Alex de la Iglesia, *Pro* Iglesia, Alvaro Augustin, Gerardo Herrero, Mariela Besuievski and Elena Manrique, *Screenplay* Iglesia and Jorge Guerricaechevarria, based on the novel by Guillermo Martinez, *Ph* Kiko de la Rica, *Pro Des* Cristina Casali, *Ed* Alejandro Lázaro and Cristina Pastor, *M* Roque Baños, *Costumes* Paco Delgado.

Eurimages/La Fabrique de Films/Telecinco Cinema/ Tornasol Films SA-Odeon Sky Filmworks.
107 mins. Spain/France. 2008. Rel: 24 Apr 2008. Cert 15.

Paranoid Park ★★★½

This is Gus Van Sant's best film for some time. It's centred on a teenager (the well cast non-professional Gabe Nevins) growing up

in Portland, Oregon. We enter his world (the narrative not necessarily fully reliable is his own) and, although events lead to a shocking death, there's far more here than in *Hallam Foe* (qv) for teenagers in general to identify with. It tails off a bit as side issues start to dominate but it's an interesting film. MS

▶ Gabe Nevins, Taylor Momsen, Jake Miller, Dan Liu, Lauren McKinney.
▶ *Dir, Ed* and *Screenplay* Gus Van Sant from the novel by Blake Nelson, *Pro* Neil Kopp and David Cress, *Ph* Christopher Doyle and Rain Kathy Li, *Art Dir* John Pearson-Denning, *Costumes* Chapin Simpson.

Marin Karmitz and Nathanael Karmitz present an MK2 production/A Meno Film Company production etc-Tartan Films.
85 mins. France/USA. 2007. Rel: 26 Dec 2007. Cert 15.

Pathology ★

The prognosis on this one is not good. A gang of medical school students play at pathology, a game in which they have to outdo each other in the let's fake a murder department. Trying to create the perfect killing without any forensic evidence is the aim but of course it all goes horribly wrong, while along the way there's enough blood and guts to turn the strongest stomach. The final diagnosis is that this unruly patient is not worth reviving since it was dead on arrival. PL

▶ Milo Ventimiglia, Michael Weston, Alyssa Milano, Lauren Lee Smith. Johnny Whitworth.
▶ *Dir* Marc Schoelermann, *Pro* Gary Gilbert, Gary Lucchesi, Mark Neveldine, Tom Rosenberg, Brian Taylor and Skip Williamson, *Screenplay* Neveldine and Taylor, *Ph* Ekkehart Pollack, *Pro Des* Jerry Fleming, *Ed* Todd E Miller, *M* Johannes Kobilke and Robert Williamson, *Costumes* Frank Helmer.

Camelot Pictures/Lakeshore Entertainment-Entertainment Film Distributors.
93 mins. USA. 2008. Rel: 11 Apr 2008. Cert 18.

Penelope ★½

Penelope is afflicted by a secret family curse that has turned her face into that of a pig so that the countless suitors lusting after her inheritance run a mile when they see her face. Only true love can restore her beauty. Christina Ricci looks suitably uncomfortable in this uneven, badly scripted and muddled family comedy. Surprisingly James McAvoy and Peter Dinklage manage to look reasonably believable despite Mark Palansky's weak and unfocused direction. GS

▶ Christina Ricci, James McAvoy, Catherine O'Hara, Reese Witherspoon, Peter Dinklage, Richard E Grant, Lenny Henry, Russell Brand.
▶ *Dir* Mark Palansky, *Pro* Dylan Russell, Jennifer Simpson, Scott Steindorff and Reese Witherspoon, *Screenplay* Leslie Caveny, *Ph* Michel Amathieu, *Pro Des* Amanda McArthur, *Ed* Jon Gregory, *M* Joby Talbot, *Costumes* Jill Taylor.

John Hurt and Elijah Wood think of a number in *The Oxford Murders*.

Vincent Paronnaud and Marjane Satrapi's *Persepolis* is a world of its own.

Stone Village Pictures/Grosvenor Park Productions etc-Momentum Pictures.
104 mins. UK/USA. 2006. Rel: 1 Feb 2008. Cert U.

Persepolis ★★★★

Working with Vincent Paronnaud, Marjane Satrapi here brings to the screen her own graphic novel about life in Tehran where she was born in 1969. Despite humorous touches, this animated feature is essentially serious as one would expect (its images are mainly in black and white) and the family tale related is virtually autobiographical. The love-life of the adolescent heroine is rather banal but the presentation of Iran's tragedy gains from such a fresh approach and this is a masterpiece, albeit a flawed one. My assessment does, however, ignore my misfortune in seeing a dubbed print (very American in tone) and not the subtitled version also available but much less widely shown. MS

▶ With the voices of Chiara Mastroianni, Catherine Deneuve. English version also features Gena Rowlands, Sean Penn and Iggy Pop, French version Danielle Darrieux and Simon Abkarian.
▶ *Dir* and *Screenplay* Vincent Paronnaud and Marjane Satrapi, *Pro* Marc-Antoine Robert and Xavier Rigault, *Ph* François Girard, *Ed* François Nabos, *M* Olivier Bernet, *Animation Dir* Christian Desmares.

24.7 Films/ France 3 Cinema/The Kennedy/Marshall Company/Franche Connection Animations/Diaphana Distribution etc-Optimum Releasing.
96 mins. France/USA. 2007. Rel: 25 April 2008. Cert 12A.

Planet Terror ★★★½

Robert Rodriguez' deliciously over the top fantasy horror was originally made to accompany Tarantino's *Death Proof* (qv) as part of the *Grindhouse* double bill. The preposterous but fun story takes place in a small Texas town. A poisonous gas is accidentally released and thousands are turned into zombies. When go-go dancer Cherry loses her leg in a road accident she replaces it with a machine gun and joins forces with a group of warriors in their attempt to exterminate the infected. A scream! GS

▶ Rose McGowan, Freddy Rodriguez, Josh Brolin, Marley Shelton, Quentin Tarantino, Jeff Fahey, Michael Biehn, Naveen Andrews, Bruce Willis, Cheech Marin, Michael Parks.
▶ *Dir, Screenplay, Ph and M* Robert Rodriguez, *Pro* Rodriguez, Elizabeth Avellán and Quentin Tarantino, *Pro Des* Steve Joyner, *Ed* Rodriguez and Ethan Maniquis, *Costumes* Nina Proctor.

The Weinstein Company/Dimension Films/Rodriguez International Pictures/Troublemaker Studios-Momentum Pictures.
105 mins. USA. 2007. Rel: 9 Nov 2007. Cert 18.

Priceless ★★

Well mounted but profoundly unengaging, this romantic comedy set on the Côte d'Azur is about a gold-digger (Audrey Tautou) and the hotel barman who falls for her. Believing him to be a rich guest, she plays up to him. It's a cold film about cold people that would like to think of itself as the new *Breakfast at Tiffany's*: some hope. MS

▶ Audrey Tautou, Gad Elmaleh, Vernon Dobtcheff, Marie-Christine Adam.
▶ *Dir* Pierre Salvadori, *Pro* Philippe Martin, *Screenplay* Salvadori and Benoît Graffin, *Ph* Gilles Henry, *Art Dir* Yves Fournier, *Ed* Isabelle Devinck, *M* Camille Bazbaz, *Costumes* Virginie Montel.

Les Films Pelléas/France 2 Cinéma/France 3 Cinéma/ Tovo Films/KS2 Productions etc-Icon Film Distribution. 106 mins. France. 2006. Rel: 13 June 2008. Cert 12A.

Princess ★★★

This feature debut from Denmark by Anders Morgenthaler is not that good, but it's certainly different. It's a tale of revenge on the part of a clergyman whose sister had become a porn star. After her death he had recognised the potential corruption of her five year old daughter brought up in this environment. The story might have appealed to Michael Winner, but he could never have made it with 20 per cent live action and 80 per cent animation. There are many flaws (improbable plotting, sentimentality at the close) but the project is strange enough never to bore. MS

▶ Isabella Thomsen, Valdemar Jacobsen and voice cast headed by Thure Lindhardt, Stine Fischer Christensen and Tommy Kenter.
▶ *Dir* Anders Morgenthaler, *Pro* Sarita Christensen, *Screenplay* Morgenthaler and Mette Heeno, *Ph* Kasper Tuxen Andersen, *Pro Des* Rune Fisker,

Ed Mikkel EG Nielsen, *M* Mads Brauer and Casper Clausen, *Costumes* Sofia Astby, *Animation Dir* Mads Juul and Kristjan Møller.

Zentropa GRRRR ApS/Shotgun Pictures GmbH/New Danish Screen-Tartan Films. 81 mins. Denmark/Germany. 2006. Rel: 19 Oct, 2007. Cert 18.

Private Fears in Public Places ★★★

This is Alain Resnais' latest attempt to bring to the screen the work of playwright Alan Ayckbourn. Thankfully it's better than the disastrous duo comprising *Smoking* and *No Smoking*. This time the switch to a French setting works and he has a talented cast that enables him to bring out the sadness beneath the humour in this complex take on relationships. However, some of the plotting simply doesn't convince and touches of stylisation (such as snow indoors as well as out) prove tiresome. Uneven. (Original title: *Coeurs*) MS

▶ Sabine Azéma, Isabelle Carré, André Dussollier, Laura Morante, Pierre Arditi, Lambert Wilson, Claude Rich.
▶ *Dir* Alain Resnais, *Pro* Bruno Pesery, *Screenplay* Jean-Michel Ribes from the play by Alan Ayckbourn, *Ph* Eric Gautier, *Pro Des* Jacques Saulnier and Solange Zeitoun, *Ed* Hervé de Luze, *M* Mark Snow, *Costumes* Jackie Budin.

Rose McGowan models the latest in prosthetic limbs on *Planet Terror*.

Soudaine Compagne/StudioCanal/France 2 Cinéma/
SFp Cinéma/BIM Distribuzione etc-Artificial Eye Film
Company.
126 mins. France/Italy. 2006. Rel: 20 July 2007. Cert 12A.

Private Property ★★★½

No plot-driven drama but a study of family
life, this film from Joachim Lafosse features
two immature twin brothers who as adults are
still living with their divorced mother in rural
Belgium. The two young men and their mother
(the ever excellent Isabelle Huppert) are all
characters who have their faults, but they are
very much bound together even though the
mother is now trying to break away to make
a new life with a lover. The response elicited
is thoughtful rather than emotional, but an
interesting film breaks off with an ill-defined
conclusion that one regrets. (Original title: *Nue
propriété*) MS

▶ Isabelle Huppert, Jérémie Renier, Yannick Renier,
Kris Cuppens.
▶ *Dir* Joachim Lafosse, *Pro* Joseph Rouschop,
Screenplay Lafosse and François Pirot with Philippe
Blasband, *Ph* Hichame Alaouié, *Pro Des* Anna
Falguère, *Ed* Sophie Vercruysse, *M* Gustav Mahler,
Costumes Nathalie du Roscoät.

Hilary Swank and
Gerard Butler
check their post
in *PS I Love You*.

Tarantula and Mact productions/ RTBF (Télévision
belge) etc-Soda Pictures.
95 mins. Belgium/France/Luxembourg. 2006. Rel: 18
April 2008. Cert 15.

Prom Night ★½

Another pointless remake of yet another average
1970s horror – haven't they remade them all by
now? Donna's psychopath stalker, who brutally
killed her entire family, escapes from prison and
comes looking for her on prom night. Curiously
Donna and her friends spend more time in the
hotel's suite powdering their noses and arguing
than on the dance floor, thus giving the psycho
plenty of opportunity for slashing. It is routine
and lacking in thrills. GS

▶ Brittany Snow, Scott Porter, Jessica Stroup, Dana
Davis, Collins Pennie, Kelly Blatz.
▶ *Dir* Nelson McCormick, *Pro* Neal H Moritz,
Screenplay J S Cardone, *Ph* Checo Varese, *Pro
Des* Jon Gary Steele, *Ed* Jason Ballantine, *M* Paul
Haslinger, *Costumes* Lyn Paolo.

Alliance Films/Newmarket Films/Original Film- Sony
Pictures Releasing.
88 mins. USA/Canada. 2008. Rel: 6 June 2008. Cert 15.

Protégé ★★★

Narcotics agent Nick spends eight years
undercover as the protégé of the 'Banker' in order
to gather enough information to indict him.
But when he gets close to fulfilling his mission,
he receives an order to remain undercover and
expose the man behind the Banker as well as
bring down the entire organisation. Derek Yee's

tight film paints a clear and violent picture of the drug culture in modern day Hong Kong but is too similar to the superior *Infernal Affairs*. (Original title: *Moon to*). GS

▶ Andy Lau, Daniel Wu, Louis Koo, Jingchu Zhang, Anita Yuen, Nirut Sirichanya.
▶ *Dir and Screenplay* Derek Yee, *Pro* Peter Ho-Sun Chan, *Ph* Venus Keung, *Pro Des* Kenneth Mak, *Ed* Kong Chi Leung, *M* Peter Kam, *Costumes* William Fung.

Artforce International/Mediacorp Pictures/Global Entertainment Group/ Film Unlimited etc-Arm Distribution.
106 mins. Hong Kong. 2007. Rel: 18 Apr 2008. Cert 18.

PS I Love You ★★★½

Reviled by the critics but loved by audiences (especially by women, I would guess), this is an uneven but often engaging rom-com. It dares to make death central, but only to show how by pre-planning a dying man can support his bereaved wife and help her find a new life. It's done by arranging for encouraging letters to be delivered at intervals after his death. This escapist piece is genuinely romantic popular fare with Hilary Swank cast against type providing a strong centre. MS

▶ Hilary Swank, Gerard Butler, Lisa Kudrow, Harry Connick Jr, Kathy Bates.
▶ *Dir* Richard LaGravenese, *Pro* Wendy Finerman, Broderick Johnson, Andrew A, Kosove and Molly Smith, *Screenplay* LaGravenese and Steven Rogers from Cecilia Ahern's novel, *Ph* Terry Stacey, *Pro Des* Shepherd Frankel, *Ed* David Moritz, *M* John Powell, *Costumes* Cindy Evans.
Alcon Entertainment/Grosvenor Park Films LLP etc-Momentum Pictures.
126 mins. USA/UK. 2007. Rel: 4 Jan 2008. Cert 12A.

P2 ★★★★

Three cheers for this nail-biting, first class horror thriller, in which Rachel Nichols (from TV's *Alias*) is brilliant as a late-working corporate high-flier who fights back when she's targetted by a mad security guard after being locked deep in her firm's empty underground car park on Christmas Eve. Wes Bentley (from *American Beauty*) makes an equally great job of the psychopath, an Elvis fan, who just doesn't want to be lonely this Christmas. It's Tension City throughout this creepy, really well-made movie, with several big scares and frightening shock moments. Sheer terror throughout. DW

▶ Wes Bentley, Rachel Nichols, Simon Reynolds, Philip Akin, Miranda Edwards.

Rachel Nichols is locked underground in the excellent *P2*.

Strong stuff: Sylvester Stallone revives the *Rambo* franchise.

▶ *Dir* Franck Khalfoun, *Pro* Alexandre Aja, Erik Feig, Gregory Levasseur and Patrick Wachsberger, *Screenplay* Khalfoun, Levasseur and Aja, *Ph* Maxime Alexandre, *Pro Des* Oleg M Savytski, *Ed* Patrick McMahon, *M* tomandandy, *Costumes* Ruth Secord.

P2 Productions/Summit Entertainment-Tartan Films. 98 mins. USA. 2007. Rel: 2 May 2008. Cert 18.

Rambo ★★★

Sixtysomething writer, director and old school action icon Sylvester Stallone returns to the role he first played more than a quarter of a century ago, slaughtering genocidal Burmese soldiers with an outrageous arsenal of bone-splintering, flesh-tearing, blood-spraying weaponry. One of the most violent actioners ever made, it's gorier than most horror films and treads a fine line between illuminating the plight of the war-torn Burmese, and totally exploiting them. A nasty, guilty pleasure. MJ

▶ Sylvester Stallone, Julie Benz, Matthew Marsden, Graham McTavish, Rey Gallegos.
▶ *Dir* Sylvester Stallone, *Pro* Kevin King-Templeton, Avi Lerner and John Thompson , *Screenplay* Stallone and Art Monterastelli, *Ph* Glen MacPherson, *Pro Des* Franco-Giacomo Carbone, *Ed* Sean Albertson, *M* Brian Tyler, *Costumes* Lizz Wolf.

The Weinstein Company/Emmett/Furla Films/ Lionsgate/Millennium Films etc-Sony Pictures Releasing. 91 mins. USA/Germany. 2008. Rel: 22 Feb 2008. Cert 18.

Ratatouille ★★★★

Remy is a French provincial rat with a taste and a nose for good food. Evicted from his humble country abode, he fetches up in a sewer near to the restaurant of famous chef Auguste Gusteau. When restaurant critic Anton Ego gives Auguste a bad review, the chef dies of shame and, to prevent the restaurant from further ignominy, Remy pals up with the kitchen porter and secretly takes over the cooking to great success. Brilliant CGI animation and good voice-work (particularly O'Toole's lugubrious food critic) make this a terrific addition to Bird's Pixar CV. However, it's too adult to be a children's cartoon. MHD

▶ Voices of Patton Oswalt, Ian Holm, Lou Romano, Brian Dennehy, Peter O'Toole, James Remar, Brad Garrett, Peter Sohn.
▶ *Dir and Screenplay* Brad Bird and Jan Pinkava, from an original screenplay and story by Bird and Jim Capobianco, *Pro* Brad Lewis, *Pro Des* Harley Jessup, *Ed* Darren T Holmes, *M* Michael Giacchino.

Pixar Animation Studios/Walt Disney Pictures-Buena Vista International. 111 mins. USA. 2007. Rel: 12 Oct 2007. Cert U.

Razzle Dazzle ★★★★

Ben Miller makes an ideal job of the plum role in this Aussie gem as gay dance teacher Mr Jonathon, whose kids' dance academy (The Jazzketeers) prepares his amazingly talented little moppets for Australia's most prestigious dance competition. Dance school rivalry and pushy stage mothers threaten to get in the way of Mr Jonathon's daft vision to reflect the world's injustices via dance, and his sly ambition to get his kids to win the all-important competition. There are laughs all the way through this thoroughly entertaining mockumentary: the dancing's great, the routines and costumes marvellous and both adults and kids are spot on. A super little show. DW

❧ Ben Miller, Kerry Armstrong, Shayni Notelovitz, Sheridan Rynne, Kerry-Ann Thoo, Tara Morice, Barry Crocker, Paul Mercurio, Leo Sayer, Michael Peschardt.
❧ *Dir* Darren Ashton, *Pro* Andrena Finlay and Jodi Matterson, *Screenplay* Robin Ince and Carolyn Wilson, *Ph* Garry Phillips, *Pro Des* Karen Harborow, *Ed* Julie-Anne De Ruvo, *M* Roger Mason, *Costumes* Ariane Weiss.

A Wild Eddie Production/Film Finance Corporation Australia/NSW Film & TV Office-Palace Films.
95 mins. Australia. 2007. Rel: 19 Oct 2007. Cert PG.

Rebellion: The Litvinenko Case ★★★

One for the specialists. This documentary about the poisoning in London in 2006 of the Russian dissident Alexander Litvinenko features his discussions with the filmmaker who knew him personally. As an analysis of Russia and its ideologies today it is wide-ranging but, moving around in time and place, it may well prove rather confusing for viewers not already conversant with the ground it covers. MS

❧ With Alexander Litvinenko, Andrei Nekrasov, Marina Litvinenko, Vladimir Putin.
❧ *Dir* Andrei Nekrasov, *Pro* Olga Konskaya, *Ed* and *Conceived by* Nekrasov and Konskaya, *Ph* Marcus Winterbaum, Sergei Tsikhanovich etc, *M* Irina Bogushevskaya and Oleg Lipatov.

Dreamscanner-Soda Pictures.
103 mins. Russia. 2007. Rel: 23 May 2008. No cert.

[Rec] ★★★★

Manuela Velasco stars as an over-cheery presenter of a Spanish TV reality show filming work at a busy Madrid firehouse. But the smile's soon wiped off her face when she joins an emergency team responding to a call from a city centre apartment building where one of the occupants takes a bite out of a cop's neck. Panic, shocks, ever-increasing tension and finally sheer terror ensue in best horror film style, culminating in a brilliant, nail-biting ten-minute finale. Extremely scary, nightmarish and full-on, it's a very, very good stab at putting

new blood into the old zombie/*Blair Witch*/*Cloverfield* videocam formulas. Unsurprisingly, the US remake is already planned. DW

❧ Manuela Velasco, Javier Botet, Manuel Bronchud, Martha Carbonell, Claudia Font, Vicente Gil.
❧ *Dir* Jaume Balagueró and Paco Plaza, *Pro* Julio Fernández, *Screenplay* Balagueró, Plaza and Luis Berdejo, *Ph* Pablo Rosso, *Pro Des* Gemma Fauria, *Ed* David Gallart, *Costumes* Gloria Viguer.

Filmax-Odeon Sky Filmworks.
80 mins. Spain. 2007. Rel: 11 Apr 2008. Cert 18.

Redacted ★★★★

Brian De Palma's take on Iraq draws on a real-life incident involving rape and murder by American soldiers. It's powerful stuff albeit lacking the depth that Nick Broomfield brought to *Battle for Haditha* (qv) and its style of presentation makes use of modern technology to create a sense of raw immediacy. Thus much footage is supposedly a video shot by one of the characters and blogs on websites feature alongside scenes which are presented as documentary film and newscasts. Imperfect, perhaps, but absorbing and succinct. MS

❧ Patrick Carroll, Rob Devaney, Izzy Diaz, Mike Figueroa, Ty Jones, Kel O'Neill.
❧ *Dir* and *Screenplay* Brian De Palma, *Pro* Jennifer Weiss, Simone Urdl, Jason Kliot and Joana Vicente, *Ph* Jonathon Cliff, *Pro Des* Phillip Barker, *Ed* Bill Pankow, *Costumes* Jamila Aladdin.

HDNet Films/A Film Farm production Jordan Production-Optimum Releasing.
91 mins. USA/Canada. 2007. Rel: 14 March 2008. Cert 15.

Rendition ★★★★

It's a pity that a plot twist of an unnecessary kind disfigures what is otherwise an admirable

Nail-biting suspense in the inventive Spanish horror [Rec].

film, a work more compelling and coherent than *Babel* as it interconnects events around the globe. When her husband, an Egyptian chemical engineer, disappears, his American wife unearths evidence that he has been extradited as a suspected terrorist. His fate will ultimately hang on the actions that a disillusioned CIA man is prepared to take. A gripping entertainment touching on serious issues, but why add that manipulative twist? MS

‣ Jake Gyllenhaal, Reese Witherspoon, Meryl Streep, Alan Arkin, Peter Sarsgaard, Omar Metwally, Igal Naor, JK Simmons, Hadar Ratzon, Simon Abkarian.
‣ *Dir* Gavin Hood, *Pro* Steve Golin and Marcus Viscidi, *Screenplay* Kelley Sane, *Ph* Dion Beebe, *Pro Des* Barry Robinson, *Ed* Megan Gill, *M* Paul Hepker and Mark Kilian, *Costumes* Michael Wilkinson.

New Line Cinema/Level 1 Entertainment/An Anonymous Content production etc-Entertainment Film Distributors Ltd.
122 mins. USA. 2007. Rel: 19 Oct 2007. Cert 15.

Reprise ★★★★

Forget the bogus *Dans Paris*, this Norwegian feature debut by Joachim Trier is the film that offers a genuine and delightful homage to the French *nouvelle vague*. It's about friends who are rivals as writers. If their story comes across as a *jeu d'esprit* (the film contains stylisation and *Tristram Shandy*-like digressions) it also offers serious reflections on the literary world in which trendy popularity can win through at the expense of real talent. This is a stimulating and pleasingly individual film. MS

‣ Espen Klouman Høiner, Anders Danielsen Lie, Viktoria Winge, Pål Stokka.
‣ *Dir* Joachim Trier, *Pro* Karin Julsrud, *Screenplay* Eskil Vogt and Trier, *Ph* Jakob Ihre, *Pro Des* Roger Rosenberg, *Ed* Oliver Bugge Coutté, *M* Ola Fløttum, *Costumes* Maria Bohlin.

4½/Filmlance AB/Nordisk Film Post Production/Norsk Filmstudio etc-Diffusion Pictures Ltd.
107 mins. Norway/Sweden. 2006. Rel: 7 Sept 2007. Cert 15.

Rescue Dawn ★★★

Werner Herzog returns to the story of Dieter Dengler, the subject of an earlier documentary of his. Now it's an acted drama that could easily have been called *Prison Camp Story* with Christian Bale giving another committed performance. As Dengler he makes a bid to escape through the jungle to Thailand, after being imprisoned following a plane crash in Laos at a time when tensions would lead to the

Vietnam War. If you're drawn to the material, you won't be let down by the film, but the scenes in the camp seem over-familiar and there's nothing very fresh here. MS

‣ Christian Bale, Steve Zahn, Jeremy Davies, Zach Grenier, Toby Huss.
‣ *Dir* and *Screenplay* Werner Herzog, *Pro* Steve Marlton, Elton Brand and Harry Knapp, *Ph* Peter Zeitlinger, *Art Dir* Arin 'Aoi' Pinijvararak, *Ed* Joe Bini, *M* Klaus Badelt, *Costumes* Annie Dunn.

Metro-Goldwyn-Mayer Pictures/Top Gun Productions/ Thema Production/A Gibraltar Films production-Pathé Distribution.
125 mins. USA/Luxembourg. 2006. Rel: 23 Nov 2007. Cert 12A.

Resident Evil: Extinction ★★★

In part three of writer Paul WS Anderson's pounding video-game-based trilogy, the incredible Milla Jovovich is back again as action babe Alice, out to finally put paid to those pesky killer zombies rampaging in a virus-infested world. A cover-girl star in cool suspenders and lip-gloss, Jovovich kicks non-stop mean zombie butt, though the highlights this time are the brand new zombie crows! Even more preposterous and zesty than before, this flashy item is surprisingly likeable, and pumped up to bursting point by director Russell Mulcahy. It's junk but the action's often astounding and Iain Glen overacts to perfection as the baddie. DW

‣ Milla Jovovich, Oded Fehr, Ali Larter, Iain Glen, Ashanti, Christopher Egan.
‣ *Dir* Russell Mulcahy, *Pro* Paul W S Anderson, Jeremy Bolt, Samuel Hadida Robert Kulzer and Bernd Eichinger, *Screenplay* Paul W S Anderson, *Ph* David Johnson, *Pro Des* Eugenio Caballero, *Ed* Niven Howie, *M* Charlie Clouser, *Costumes* Joseph A Porro.

Resident Evil Productions/Constantin Film Produktion/ Davis-Films/Impact Pictures-Sony Pictures Releasing.
95 mins. France/Austria/Germany/UK/USA. 2007. Rel: 12 Oct 2007. Cert 15.

RFK Must Die: The Assassination of Bobby Kennedy ★★★★

Shane O'Sullivan's admirable documentary is a well set out account that aims to show that there are as many disturbing questions to be asked about the official version of the killing of Bobby Kennedy as in the case of his brother. The film doesn't hide facts that go against the thesis being developed, but the point is to show the pertinence of questions not to offer a neat answer. Recommended. MS

▶ With Haynes Johnson, Munir Sirhan, Dr Herbert Spiegel, Ruben 'Rocky' Carbajal.
▶ *Dir, Pro* and *Ed* Shane O'Sullivan, *Ph* George Dougherty, *M* Pyratek.

Distributed by Soda Pictures.
102 mins. UK. 2007. Rel: 16 May 2008. No cert.

The Right of the Weakest
★★★★

When the steel mill in Liège closes, three friends become unemployed and spend most of their time in the pub playing cards and getting drunk. And then Marc, a mysterious loner, provides them with the perfect plan to escape from their boring lives. Belvaux has created believably affable characters in his gritty depiction of a society in decline. The acting is excellent and the film, which starts as a heavy social drama, develops into an exciting thriller boasting strong production values. (Original title: *La raison du plus faible*). GS

▶ Eric Caravaca, Claude Semal, Lucas Belvaux, Patrick Deschamps, Natacha Régnier.
▶ *Dir and Screenplay* Lucas Belvaux, *Pro* Patrick Sobelman, *Ph* Pierre Milon, *Pro Des* Frédérique Belvaux, *Ed* Ludo Troch, *M* Riccardo Del Fra, *Costumes* Nathalie Raoul.

Agat Films et Cie/Entre Chien et Loup-Tartan Films
116 mins. Belgium/France. 2006. Rel: 28 Sep 2007. Cert 15.

Rise of the Foot Soldier ★

Incredibly violent and foul-mouthed British gangster drama based on a true story – the real-life Rettendon Range Rover murders. It follows the career of Essex football thug Carlton Leach (Ricci Harnett) who turns to drug dealing and becomes a gangland hatchet man, a career culminating in a bloodbath. Admittedly the acting and direction are powerful, but this is repellent stuff done with sadistic gusto and numbing realism. DW

▶ Ricci Harnett, Terry Stone, Craig Fairbrass, Roland Manookian, Coralie Rose.
▶ *Dir* Julian Gilbey, *Pro* Mike Loveday, *Screenplay and Ed* Julian and Will Gilbey, *Ph* Ali Asad, *Pro Des* Matthew Button, *M* Sandy McLelland, Ross Cullum and Nigel Champion, *Costumes* Hayley Nebauer.

Carnaby International/Hanover Films-Optimum Releasing.
119 mins. UK. 2007. Rel: 7 Sep 2007. Cert 18.

River Queen ★★★½

Conflicts during production may have weakened this sometimes rushed epic about an Irish girl and her young son by a Maori who are both caught up in the colonial dramas engulfing New Zealand in the 1860s. Despite being uneven, this film offers yet another fine performance by Samantha Morton and director Vincent Ward, however chequered his career,

River Queen: Samantha Morton in Vincent Ward country.

Laura Ramsey explores the darkness in *The Ruins*.

Nicholas D'Agosto, Anna Kendrick, Reece Daniel Thompson, Margo Martindale, Vincent Piazza, Denis O'Hare.

Dir and Screenplay Jeffrey Blitz, *Pro* Sean Welch, *Ph* Jo Willems, *Pro Des* Rick Butler, *Ed* Yana Gorskaya, *M* Eef Barzelay, *Costumes* Ernesto Martinez.

B & W Films/Duly Noted Inc/HBO Films/Rocket Science Inc-Optimum Releasing.
101 mins. USA. 2007. Rel: 28 Sep 2007. Cert 15.

Ruby Blue ★★

The promise of 2005's *Gypo* is sadly not maintained in Jan Dunn's second feature. It again utilises Kent locations but simply attempts too much by trying to tackle so many issues. These range from bereavement to disaffected adolescents and from living as a transsexual to injustice resulting from wrongly suspected paedophilia. With too many plot contrivances as well, the film sinks despite its obvious good intentions. MS

Bob Hoskins, Josiane Balasko, Jody Latham. Josef Altin, Jessica Stewart, Ashley McGuire.
Dir and *Screenplay* Jan Dunn, *Pro* Elaine Wickham, *Ph* Ole Bratt Birkeland, *Pro Des* Stevie Stewart, *Ed* Emma Collins, *M* Janette Mason.

Old Vic Productions/Pink Sands Films/Medb Films-Target Entertainment.
108 mins. UK. 2007. Rel: 25 April 2008. Cert 15.

The Ruins ★★★

Carter Smith's horror film based on Scott Smith's novel follows a group of friends who, while on holiday in Mexico, visit some ancient Mayan ruins deep in the jungle but end up fighting for their lives. The film works quite well because Smith takes his time in establishing the characters. It may not be very scary, but it is well made and is decently acted by the young cast. GS

Jonathan Tucker, Jena Malone, Laura Ramsey, Shawn Ashmore, Joe Anderson, Dimitri Baveas.
Dir Carter Smith, *Pro* Chris Bender, Ben Stiller, Stuart Cornfeld and Jeremy Kramer, *Screenplay* Scott B Smith, based on his own novel, *Ph* Darius Khondji, *Pro Des* Grant Major, *Ed* Jeff Betancourt, *M* Graeme Revell, *Costumes* Lizzy Gardiner.

BenderSpink/DreamWorks SKG/Red Hour Films/Spyglass Entertainment-Paramount Pictures International.
91 mins. Australia/USA. 2008. Rel: 20 June 2008. Cert 18.

Run Fatboy Run ★½

Having dumped his pregnant girlfriend at the altar many years ago, Dennis (Pegg) suddenly

proves that he still has a great eye for visuals. MS

Samantha Morton, Cliff Curtis, Kiefer Sutherland, Stephen Rea.
Dir Vincent Ward, *Pro* Don Reynolds and Chris Auty, *Screenplay* Ward, Kely Lyons and Toa Fraser from Ward's story, *Ph* Alun Bollinger, *Pro Des* Rick Kofoed, *Ed* Ewa J Lind, *M* Karl Jenkins, *Costumes* Barbara Darragh.

Silverscreen Films/The Film Consortium/ Endgame Entertainment etc-The Works UK Distribution Ltd.
114 mins. New Zealand/UK/USA. 2005. Rel: 15 Feb 2008. Cert 15.

Rocket Science ★★★★

Jeffrey Blitz, the director of the excellent *Spellbound*, effortlessly makes the transition from documentaries to features. Here he visits similar territory but goes a step further when his hero Hal, a teenager with a stutter, has ambitions of entering his school's public debate team. Blitz elicits excellent performances from his young cast especially from Reece Daniel Thompson, as the troubled teenager determined to succeed against all odds. It is a likeable and perfectly judged piece of work. GS

realises that his ex-fiancée is the love of his life. So, how does an under-achieving slob win back the woman he has so terribly slighted? Thanks to Simon Pegg's native popularity and an aggressive marketing campaign, *Run, Fat Boy, Run* was a considerable success at the UK box-office. More fool the public. While director Schwimmer ignores the fundamental rules of comedy, Pegg must hold the record for the number of times a star has fallen over in one movie. Otherwise it's all rather mechanical and contrived. JC-W

▶ Simon Pegg, Thandie Newton, Hank Azaria, Dylan Moran, Stephen Merchant, Simon Day, Ruth Sheen, Chris Hollins, Denise Lewis, David Walliams.
▶ *Dir* David Schwimmer, *Pro* Sarah Curtis and Robert Jones, *Screenplay* Michael Ian Black and Simon Pegg, from a story by Black, *Ph* Richard Greatrex, *Pro Des* Sophie Belcher, *Ed* Michael Parker, *M* Alex Wurman, *Costumes* Annie Hardinge.

Entertainment Films/Material Entertainment-Entertainment Film Distributors.
100 mins. UK. 2007. Rel: 7 Sep 2007. Cert 12A.

Running Stumbled ★★½

In this documentary John Maringouin turns the camera on his own family, in particular on his father and the latter's common-law wife with whom he lives in a love/hate relationship. This might have been a fascinating take on life as tragicomedy but the filming is self-indulgent and no framework is supplied that would help the audience to feel involved. MS

▶ With Johnny Roe Jr, Virgie Marie Pennoui,

Stanley Laviolette, John Maringouin.
▶ *Dir* and *Ph* John Maringouin, *Pro* Maringuin and Molly Lynch, *Ed* Maringouin and Lynch.

Self Pictures-Self Films.
83 mins. USA. 2006. Rel: 27 July 2007. No cert.

Rush Hour 3 ★★

How anyone can stomach the caustic comedy stylings of Chris Tucker is a mystery that rivals the Bermuda Triangle, but if you have a strong enough constitution, and you actually liked the preceding chapters, this third instalment of odd couple action is just about watchable. A characteristically mediocre Brett Ratner effort, it brings nothing new to the series beyond the Parisian locations, but the action's moderately decent and Jackie Chan, at least, has some charisma. MJ

▶ Chris Tucker, Jackie Chan, Max von Sydow, Hiroyuki Sanada, Yvan Attal, David Niven Jr
▶ *Dir* Brett Ratner, *Pro* Roger Birnbaum, Arthur Sarkissian, Jay Stern, Andrew Z Davis and Jonathan Glickman, *Screenplay* Jeff Nathanson, based on characters created by Ross LaManna, *Ph* J Michael Muro, *Pro Des* Ed Verreaux, *Ed* Mark Helfrich, Dean Zimmerman and Don Zimmerman, *M* Lalo Schifrin, *Costumes* Betsy Heimann.

New Line Cinema/Roger Birnbaum Productions/Arthur Sarkissian Productions-Entertainment Film Distributors.
91 mins. USA/Germany. 2007. Rel: 10 Aug 2007. Cert 12A.

The Savages ★★★½

Old age and senility providing problems for estranged siblings who have to look after their

Laura Linney and Philip Seymour Hoffman play siblings in *The Savages*.

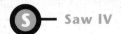

elderly father are at the heart of this piece which tries to handle the subject with a fair measure of humour. The actors (just check out that cast list) could not be better, but the tone often seems wrong as the screenplay by director Tamara Jenkins attempts to lighten essentially serious subject matter. MS

➤ Philip Seymour Hoffman, Laura Linney, Philip Bosco, Cara Seymour, Peter Friedman.
➤ *Dir* and *Screenplay* Tamara Jenkins, *Pro* Ted Hope, Anne Carey and Erica Westheimer, *Ph* Mott Hupfel, *Pro Des* Jane Ann Stewart, *Ed* Brian A Kates, *M* Stephen Trask, *Costumes* David Robinson.

Fox Searchlight Pictures/Lone Star Film Group/This Is That Production etc-20th Century Fox International (UK).
114 mins. USA. 2007. Rel: 25 Jan 2008. Cert 15.

Saw IV ★★

Preposterous, muddled and not in the least bit scary but still quite tense, agreeably gory and moderately illuminating, *Saw IV* explores Jigsaw's (Tobin Bell) tragic origins and witnesses him messing with a fresh batch of not-so-innocent victims from beyond the grave. Though not a patch on the original, between the hokey dialogue and tepid performances there are at least a few good ideas and some horrifying set pieces. MJ

➤ Tobin Bell, Costas Mandylor, Scott Patterson, Betsy Russell, Lyriq Bent.
➤ *Dir* Darren Lynn Bousman, *Pro* Mark Burg, Oren Koules and Gregg Hoffman, *Screenplay* Patrick Melton and Marcus Dunstan, from a story by Melton, Dunstan and Thomas Fenton, *Ph* David A Armstrong, *Pro Des* David Hackl, *Ed* Kevin Greutert and Brett Sullivan, *M* Charlie Clouser, *Costumes* Alex.Kavanagh.

Lions Gate Films/TwistedPictures-Lionsgate.
95 mins. USA. 2007. Rel: 26 Oct 2007. Cert 18.

Sea Monsters 3D: A Prehistoric Adventure ★★★½

We've all met the dinosaurs and T Rex and their friends, but until now we haven't encountered the tylosaur, the pleiososaur and, biggest and most savage of all, the dolichorhynchops, an underwater monster that ravaged the late Cretaceous period. The National Geographic people look at the fossils found in Kansas and Texas to recreate this brutal denizen of the deep. The IMAX screen and 3D bring the monster to more than extraordinary life in this fascinating and at times scary documentary. MHD

➤ Jerry Hoffman, Jennifer Aguilar, Michael Ashcroft, Paul Burmaster, Albert Burnet, Toni Dodd.
➤ *Dir* Sean MacLeod Phillips, *Pro* Jini Burr and Lisa Truitt, *Screenplay* Mose Richards, *Ph* T C Christensen, *Pro Des* Diana Goodwin, *Ed* Jonathan P Shaw, *M* Richard Evans, David Rhodes and Peter Gabriel.

Day's End Pictures/National Geographic Giant Screen Films.
40 mins. USA. 2007. Rel: 19 Oct 2007. Cert PG.

A Secret ★★½

This tale of a boy growing up in a Jewish family in the decade after the Second World War pivots on a no longer discussed family secret linked to persecution by the Nazis. The Jewish subject matter makes this a personal project for filmmaker Claude Miller and the cast is good. However, the film's structure is often clumsy and the key moment when eventually revealed involves behaviour that I didn't believe in for a second. (Original title: *Un secret*) MS

➤ Cécile de France, Patrick Bruel, Ludivine Sagnier, Julie Depardieu, Mathieu Amalric.
➤ *Dir* Claude Miller, *Pro* Yves Marmion, *Screenplay* Miller and Natalie Carter from Philippe Grimbert's novel, *Ph* Gérard de Battista, *Art Dir* Jean-Pierre Kohut-Svelko, *Ed* Véronique Lange, *M* Zbigniew Preisner, *Costumes* Jacqueline Bouchard.

UGC YM/Integral Film/France 3 Cinéma co-production etc-Arrow Film Distributors Ltd.
106 mins. France /Germany. 2007. Rel: 9 May 2008. Cert 15.

Semi-Pro ★

Jackie Moon is the owner, coach and player of a basketball team, the Michigan Tropics of the ABA league, and is determined to prove that his team has what it takes when the opposing NBA announces a plan to merge with the ABA. It is hard to find anything positive to say about this miserable and totally unfunny comedy which is another strong contender for the worst film of the year. To be avoided! GS

➤ Will Ferrell, Woody Harrelson, André Benjamin, DeRay Davis, Patti LaBelle.
➤ *Dir* Kent Alterman, *Pro* Jimmy Miller, *Screenplay* Scot Armstrong, *Ph* Shane Hurlbut, *Pro Des* Clayton Hartley, *Ed* Debra Neil Fisher, *M* Theodore Shapiro, *Costumes* Susan Matheson.

Donners' Company/Mosaic Media/Road Rebel/MFP Semi-Pro-New Line Cinema.
91 mins. USA. 2008. Rel: 29 Feb 2008. Cert 15.

Seraphim Falls ★★★½

Pierce Brosnan is terrific in this unusual western set in New Mexico and Oregon in the post civil war era. Liam Neeson with four aides is a man pursuing Brosnan but the film cleverly takes its time in revealing where our sympathies should lie. What a pity that the last section in seeking profundity goes badly awry. Until then the film is splendid, impressively directed (a debut by David Von Ancken) and marvellously photographed (by John Toll). MS

▷ Pierce Brosnan, Liam Neeson, Michael Wincott, Wes Studie, Anjelica Huston.
▷ *Dir* David Von Ancken, *Pro* Bruce Davey and David Flynn, *Screenplay* Von Ancken and Abby Everett Jaques, *Ph* John Toll, *Pro Des* Michael Hanan, *Ed* Conrad Buff, *M* Harry Gregson-Williams, *Costumes* Deborah L Scott.

Icon Productions-Icon Film Distribution.
111 mins. USA. 2006. Rel: 24 Aug 2007. Cert 15.

The Serpent ★★★★

Vincent, a successful French photographer going through a nasty divorce, becomes a prime suspect for murder. His old classmate Joseph, who now works as a private detective, suddenly appears on the scene offering to help but unbeknown to Vincent he wants revenge for events that happened in their childhood. Barbier's perfectly crafted and suitably atmospheric thriller is immaculately acted especially by Attal as the desperate man running out of time. It is definitely worth seeing before the inevitable American remake. GS

▷ Clovis Cornillac, Yvan Attal, Pierre Richard, Simon Abkarian, Jean-Claude Bouillon.
▷ *Dir* Eric Barbier, *Pro* Olivier Delbosc, Pierre Rambaldi, Eric Jehelmann and Marc Missonier, *Screenplay* Barbier and Tran-Minh Nam, from the novel *Plender* by Ted Lewis, *Ph* Jérôme Robert, *Pro Des* Pierre Renson, *Ed* Véronique Lange, *M* Renaud Barbier, *Costumes* Claire Gerard-Hirne.

Fidélité Productions/Big World/Canal+/France 2 Cinéma-Wild Bunch Distributors.
119 mins. France. 2006. Rel: 14 Sep 2007. Cert 15.

Sex and the City ★★★★

This surprisingly successful transition of the television series from the small to the big screen sees the four girls several years on from their TV incarnation. Carrie Bradshaw, the New York journalist who writes only one sentence a week, has moved in with her on-off, off-on boyfriend Mr Big. They decide to get married and start planning. Samantha, a woman for all sexual seasons, has difficulty in committing; Charlotte is still trying to get pregnant; Miranda, living with Steve, finds out he has been unfaithful, so tries to stop Mr Big from marrying Carrie. Still packed with good, down and dirty gags, the fun

Seraphim Falls: Liam Neeson finds himself in a tight spot, but does he deserve our sympathy?

rarely stops and, even if the result seems like
five TV episodes stitched together, it still
works beautifully as a clever comedy of
modern manners. All four girls get their own
story, so more power to their perfectly formed
elbows. MHD

▶ Sarah Jessica Parker, Kim Cattrall, Kristin Davis,
Cynthia Nixon, Chris Noth, Mario Cantone,
Candice Bergen.
▶ *Dir* Michael Patrick King, *Pro* Michael Patrick
King, Sarah Jessica Parker, Darren Star and John
Melfi, *Screenplay* Candace Bushnell and Michael
Patrick King, *Ph* John Thomas, *Pro Des* Jeremy
Conway, *Ed* Michael Berenbaum, *M* Aaron Zigman,
Costumes Patricia Field.

New Lion Cinema/Home Box Office-Entertainment
Film Distributors.
145 mins. USA. 2008. Rel: 28 May 2008. Cert 15.

Sharkwater ★★★★

Rob Stewart's striking underwater documentary
is very enlightening but also deeply upsetting.
It is a labour of love which took him four years
to finish and his passionate plea to save his
beloved sharks from extinction comes straight
from the heart. He swims, touches and caresses
these incredible creatures and with fellow
activists he chases illegal poachers around the

world in order to put a stop to their horrific
slaughter. A work of great beauty. GS

▶ Patrick Moore, Rob Stewart, Erich Ritter, Paul
Watson, Boris Worm.
▶ *Dir, Screenplay and Ph* Rob Stewart, *Pro* Brian
Stewart and Rob Stewart, *Ed* Rob Stewart, Michael
Clarke, Rik Morden and Jeremy Stuart, *M* Jeff Rona.

SW Productions/Sharkwater Productions-Show Box
Media Group.
89 mins. Canada. 2006. Rel: 22 Feb 2008. Cert PG.

Sherrybaby ★★½

This movie belongs to a sub-genre, the one
that features a drug-taking mother and her
child. With the talented Maggie Gyllenhaal as
the mother in question, you get good acting,
but the screenplay is sadly unpersuasive. In
particular, we are offered a conclusion that
suggests disaster ahead despite being passed
off as an optimistic resolution. It's sincere
undoubtedly, but not a film that really
tackles the conflicts inherent in the central
situation. MS

▶ Maggie Gyllenhaal, Brad William Henkie,
Giancarlo Esposito, Ryan Simpkins.
▶ *Dir* and *Screenplay* Laurie Collyer, *Pro* Marc
Turtletaub and Lenore Syvan, *Ph* Russell Lee Fine,

Pro Des Stephen Beatrice, *Ed* Curtiss Clayton and Joe Landauer, *M* Jack Livesey, *Costumes* Jill Newell.

A Big Beach production/Elevation Filmworks etc-Metrodome Distribution Ltd.
95 mins. USA. 2006. Rel: 27 July 2007. Cert 15.

Shine a Light ★★★★

For this concert documentary Martin Scorsese recruited an incredible team of celebrated cinematographers in order to capture the Rolling Stones in action at the Beacon Theatre in New York in 2006. There are far too many discussions about designs and camera positions before the concert, but once Mick Jagger walks on stage the film commands attention. The legendary group perform many of their favourite songs including the very first number they ever wrote, 'As Tears Go By'. The rest, as they say, is history. GS

▶ Mick Jagger, Keith Richards, Charlie Watts, Ron Wood, Christina Aguilera, Buddy Guy, Jack White III, Martin Scorsese.
▶ *Dir* Martin Scorsese, *Pro* Steve Bing, Michael Cohl, Victoria Dearman and Zane Weiner, *Ph* Robert Richardson, *Pro Des* Star Theodos, *Ed* David Tedeschi.

Concert Promotions International/Shangri-La Entertainment-20th Century Fox.
122 mins. USA/UK. 2008. Rel: 11 Apr 2008. Cert 12A.

Shoot 'Em Up ★★★★

Quietly eating a carrot on a bench, 'Smith' (Clive Owen) witnesses a heavily pregnant woman running for her life. Minutes later, Smith is emptying gun cartridges onto the woman's belly as she gives birth. For some reason, some very nasty men want the baby dead and so Smith feels beholden to protect it. One of the guiltiest pleasures of the year, *Shoot 'Em Up* is a B-movie with wit, style and dynamism to spare. Knowingly preposterous and unashamedly nasty, the film zips along while spilling out great visual gags and priceless one-liners. Pulp fiction *par excellence*. JC-W

▶ Clive Owen, Paul Giamatti, Monica Bellucci, Stephen McHattie, Greg Bryk, Daniel Pilon.
▶ *Dir and Screenplay* Michael Davis, *Pro* Rick Benattar, Don Murphy and Susan Montford, *Ph* Peter Pau, *Pro Des* Gary Frutkoff, *Ed* Peter Amundson, *M* Paul Haslinger, *Costumes* Denise Cronenberg.

New Line Cinema/AngryFilms-Entertainment Film Distributors.
86 mins. USA. 2007. Rel: 14 Sep 2007. Cert 18.

Shotgun Stories ★★★★½

In his feature debut set in Alabama and superbly photographed, writer/director Jeff Nichols has created one of the few films in which the characters, the setting and the story seem inextricably bound together and at one. Sadly the ending doesn't fully convince, but this comment on the difficulty of escaping from family feuds is genuine in its dislike of violence and the piece is a thoughtful work that comes close to being a minor masterpiece. MS

▶ Michael Shannon, Douglas Ligon, Barlow Jacobs, Travis Smith, Glenda Pannell.
▶ *Dir and Screenplay* Jeff Nichols, *Pro* David Gordon Green, Lisa Muskat and Nichols, *Ph* Adam Stone, *Ed* Steven Gonzales, *M* Ben Nichols Lucero and Pyramid, *Costumes* Rachel Worthen.

Upload Films/Muskat Film Properties/A Lucky Old Sun production-Vertigo Films.
90 mins. USA. 2007. Rel: 23 May 2008. Cert 12A.

Michael Shannon in *Shotgun Stories*, an Alabama movie of rare authenticity.

Rachael Taylor makes a shocking discovery in *Shutter*.

Saraf, *Ed* Jake Roberts and Mermin, *M* James Burrell. **Storyville & Sundance Channel present a Little Bird production-Moviehouse Entertainment (ICA Films). 99 mins. UK/USA. 2007. Rel: 18 Jan 2008. No cert.**

Shrooms ★★

Paddy Breathnach's horror film boasts a strong visual style but a totally implausible plot. A group of American teenagers, who totally hate each other, take up their friend Jake's invitation for a 'trip' of a lifetime in Ireland. On arrival they head straight for the forest determined to try as many (magic mu)shrooms as possible. Predictably things go wrong when the hallucinations begin. The film fails to raise the temperature despite an unexpected twist. GS

‣ Lindsey Haun, Jack Huston, Max Kasch, Maya Hazen, Alice Greczyn, Robert Hoffman.
‣ *Dir* Paddy Breathnach, *Pro* Paddy McDonald and Robert Walpole, *Screenplay* Pearse Elliott, *Ph* Nanu Segal, *Pro Des* Mark Geraghty, *Ed* Dermot Diskin, *M* Dario Marianelli, *Costumes* Rosie Hackett.

Capitol Films/Treasure Entertainment Ltd/ Potboiler Productions/Northern Ireland Film & Television Commission-Vertigo Films. 84 mins. Ireland. 2006. Rel: 23 Nov 2007. Cert 18.

Shutter ★★★

Seemingly nice, clean-cut American newlyweds Joshua Jackson and Rachael Taylor head for Japan, but apparently run down a young woman on a lonely country road. When she goes missing, ghostly images appear in photographs they develop. While hubby works on his doomed fashion shoot, Taylor sets out to find the truth – big mistake! – about the photos, which she thinks are spirit pictures of the dead girl who now wants revenge. Remake of a fine Thai film from 2004, this unexpectedly polished and suspenseful US chiller is spooky and startling throughout, the pacing's perfect and both score and photography are classy, adding a freshness to the old situations. DW

‣ Joshua Jackson, Rachael Jackson, Megumi Okina, David Denman, John Hensley, Maya Hazen.
‣ *Dir* Masayuki Ochiai , *Pro* Doug Davison, Takashige Ichise and Roy Lee, *Screenplay* Luke Dawson, *Ph* Katsumi Yanagishima, *Pro Des* Norifumi Ataka, *Ed* Tim Alvrson and Michael N Knue *M* Nathan Barr, *Costumes assistant* Stevie Sterman.

Ozla Pictures/Regency Enterprises/Vertigo Entertainment-20th Century Fox. 85 mins. USA. 2008. Rel: 16 May 2008. Cert 15.

Shot in Bombay ★★★

A documentary about the Bollywood film industry might well be interesting but here Liz Mermin chooses to concentrate on the making of one atypical Bollywood movie, the real-life crime thriller *Shootout at Lokhandwala*. Its star, Sanjay Dutt, was caught up in delayed court proceedings after being accused of owning an illegal weapon, but the consequence for this film is that inadequately investigated issues about India's criminal justice system sit uneasily alongside footage, sometimes amusing, about the shooting of what looks to be a poor movie. MS

‣ With Apoorva Lakhia, Sanjay Dutt, Vivek Oberoi, AA Khan, Iqbal Skaikh.
‣ *Dir* Liz Mermin, *Pro* Nahrein Mirza, *Ph* Vikash

Sicko ★★★★

Acclaimed by many at Cannes but less well received here by our critics, this documentary takes a while to find its feet. Soon however it finds Michael Moore on characteristic form exposing the terrible flaws in health care in America while lauding medical facilities in Canada, France and, yes, England. OK, we know that the NHS has serious imperfections, but let's enjoy it being praised since the principle behind it is deserving of that. And, of course, Moore is fun, especially in his response to someone who attacked him on the internet: this is one-upmanship that the late Stephen Potter would have relished. MS

▶ With Michael Moore.
▶ *Dir* and *Screenplay* Michael Moore, *Pro* Moore and Meghan O'Hara, *Ph* Tony Hardmon, Peter Nelson and others, *Ed* Dan Swietlik, Geoffrey Richman and Christopher Seward, *M* Erin O'Hara.

The Weinstein Company presents a Dog Eat Dog Films production-Optimum Releasing.
123 mins. USA. 2007. Rel: 26 Oct 2007. Cert 12A.

Silent Light ★★★★

Carlos Reygadas's third feature is a highly demanding work by a rigorous artist. Like Bresson (but far less succinctly) he creates an inner drama. Here it's that of a husband, part of a Mennonite family, who, being concerned for his wife and children, is anguished on falling deeply in love with a woman who becomes his mistress. Exceedingly slow, exquisitely photographed, it places the human drama in the context of the wider world, not excluding a religious dimension. You have to work at it, but it's the real thing. (Original title: *Stellet licht*). MS

▶ Cornelio Wall, Miriam Toews, Maria Pankratz, Peter Wall, Jacobo Klassen.
▶ *Dir* and *Screenplay* Carlos Reygadas, *Pro* Jaime Romandía and Reygadas, *Ph* Alexis Zabé, *Art Dir* Nohemi González, *Ed* Natalie López.

NoDream/Mantarraya/BAC Films/Foprocine/Arte France Cinéma etc-Tartan Films.
136 mins. Mexico/France/Netherlands. 2007. Rel: 7 Dec 2007. Cert 15.

Silk ★

Silk is a multi-national adaptation of the Alessandro Baricco novel, in which Hervé Joncour (Michael Pitt) journeys to Japan to find a new supply of silkworms. Due to his regular source in Africa having been wiped out by disease, Joncour settles long enough in the East to fall for the charms of a local concubine. The year's most soporific movie, *Silk* attempts to make up for its lethargy by unfurling a series of chocolate box tableaux. But this doesn't make up for the incongruous American accents or the black hole of Pitt's performance. JC-W

▶ Sei Ashina, Michael Pitt, Tony Vogel, Toni Bertorelli, Keira Knightley, Alfred Molina.
▶ *Dir* François Girard, *Pro* Domenico Procacci, Sonoko Sakai, Niv Fichmann and Nadine Luque, *Screenplay* Girard and Michael Goldner, from the novel by Alessandro Baricco, *Ph* Alain Dostie, *Pro Des* François Séguin, *Ed* Pia di Ciaula, *M* Ryuichi Sakamoto, *Costumes* Kazuko Kurosawa and Carlo Poggioli.

Bee Vine Pictures/Astral Media/Medusa Film/Odeon Film/Vice Versa Film-Entertainment Film Distributors.
107 mins. UK/Japan/Canada/France. 2007.
Rel: 9 Nov 2007. Cert 15.

The Simpsons Movie ★★★★

"I can't believe we're paying to see something everybody can see free on TV," blurts an outraged Homer (Dan Castellaneta) at a screening of *The Itchy and Scratchy Movie*, setting the mocking, satirical tone of a film that combines sophisticated swipes at everything from religion to the environment and, at the same time, knows the value of a classic sight gag. Essentially an extended episode of the show, though hardly genius it's still very funny. MJ

▶ Voices of Dan Castellaneta, Julie Kavner, Nancy Cartwright, Yeardley Smith, Hank Azaria, Harry Shearer, Tom Hanks, Joe Mantegna.
▶ *Dir* David Silverman, *Pro* James L Brooks, Matt Groening, Al Jean, Mike Scully, Richard Sakai, *Screenplay* Groening, Jean, Scully, Jon Vitti, Ian Maxtone-Graham, George Meyer, David Mirkin, Mike Reiss, Matt Selman and John Schwartzwelder, *Pro Des* Dima Malanitchev, *Ed* John Carnochan, *M* Hans Zimmer.

Twentieth Century Fox Film Corporation/Gracie Films-20th Century Fox.
87 mins. USA. 2007. Rel: 25 July 2007. Cert PG.

The Singer ★★★

Most appropriately Gérard Depardieu's brilliant performance here has been acclaimed. He plays a once popular singer past his prime who convincingly becomes involved with a much younger woman (Cécile de France) with a troubled history. Half of the film is splendid in its delicacy and sensitivity, but then it

Michael Caine and Jude Law in the poorly received remake of *Sleuth*.

outstays its welcome and goes round in circles for the second hour. The film flounders but not the players, a comment that applies also to Christine Citti, superb in support. MS

▶ Gérard Depardieu, Cécile de France, Mathieu Amalric, Christine Citti.
▶ *Dir* and *Written by* Xavier Giannoli, *Pro* Edouard Weil and Pierre-Ange Le Pogam, *Ph* Yorick Le Saux, *Pro Des* François-Renaud Labarthe, *Ed* Martine Giordano, *M* Alexandre Desplat, *Costumes* Nathalie Benros.

A EuropaCorp/Rectangle Production/France 3 Cinèma co-production-Artificial Eye Film Company.
113 mins. France/Belgium. 2006. Rel: 28 Sept 2007. Cert 12A.

Sleuth ★★★★

Absurdly undervalued, Kenneth Branagh's film, in which Harold Pinter offers a fresh slant on Anthony Shaffer's stage play filmed by Joseph L Mankiewicz in 1972, teases us engagingly. When an author (Michael Caine) is visited by his wife's lover (Jude Law) to discuss the possibility of a divorce, power games and humiliations ensue. Satisfying thriller twists lead to a section centred on issues of sexuality that recall, and better, the pretentious pseudo-classic *Performance* (1970). No masterpiece but a well-acted offbeat entertainment. MS

▶ Michael Caine, Jude Law, Harold Pinter.
▶ *Dir* Kenneth Branagh, *Pro* Jude Law, Simon

Halfon, Branagh and others, *Screenplay* Harold Pinter adapted from Anthony Shaffer's play, *Ph* Haris Zambarloukos, *Pro Des* Tim Harvey, *Ed* Neil Farrell, *M* Patrick Doyle, *Costumes* Alexandra Byrne.

Sony Pictures Classics/Castle Rock Entertainment/A Riff Raff production/A Timnick Films production-Paramount Pictures UK.
88 mins. USA/UK. 2007. Rel: 23 Nov 2007. Cert 15.

Small Engine Repair ★★★★

In Northern Ireland Doug spends most of his time boozing with his fellow forestry workers, still hoping to make it as a country singer. His best friend Bill, a mechanic of the small engine repair garage, encourages him to take his demo to the local radio station. Niall Heery makes an impressive debut with his low-key depiction of an unfriendly and solitary land, coaching outstanding and mature performances from both Glen as the frustrated singer and Mackintosh as the not so bright but likeable mechanic. GS

▶ Iain Glen, Steven Mackintosh, Stuart Graham, Laurence Kinlan, Tom Murphy, Kathy Kiera Clarke, Gary Lydon, David Hayman.
▶ *Dir and Screenplay* Niall Heery, *Pro* Dominic Wright and Tristan Orphen-Lynch, *Ph* Tim Fleming, *Pro Des* Mark Lowry, *Ed* Emer Reynolds, *M* Niall Byrne, *Costumes* Hazel Webb-Crozier.

Subotica Entertainment-Guerilla Films.
98 mins. Ireland. 2006. Rel: 7 Sep 2007. Cert 15.

Smart People ★★½

Desperately wanting to be another *Sideways* (it's erudite about literature rather than about wine), this piece centres on largely unpleasant characters in Philadelphia including an insensitive professor played by Dennis Quaid. Had Jack Nicholson taken the role he just might have made me believe in his redemption through a former pupil still in love with him. As it is, this tragicomedy fails to realise its potential, becoming pretentious and sentimental in turn. Ellen Page displays the same assurance as in *Juno* (qv). MS

➤ Dennis Quaid, Sarah Jessica Parker, Thomas Haden Church, Ellen Page.
➤ *Dir* Noam Murro, *Pro* Bridget Johnson, Michael Costigan, Michael London and Bruna Papandrea, *Screenplay* Mark Jude Poirier, *Ph* Toby Irwin, *Pro Des* Patti Podesta, *Ed* Robert Frazen and Yana Gorskaya, *M* Nuno Bettencourt, *Costumes* Amy Westcott.

Miramax Films/Groundswell Productions/Corduroy Films/Table Top Films etc-Icon Film Distribution.
95 mins. USA/Hungary. 2007. Rel: 16 May 2008.
Cert 15.

Someone Else ★★

David is a thirty something photographer who dumps his girlfriend Lisa for Nina. He gets what he deserves when Nina tells him that she is in love with someone else. Proctor's well observed script – extended from his 16-minute short *New Year's Eve* – about confused and anxious males is let down by the leading man. Mangan should be the perfect anti-hero for romantic comedy but here he is simply irritating, failing to obtain our sympathy. GS

➤ Stephen Mangan, Susan Lynch, Lara Belmont, Chris Coghill, Sean Dingwall, Bridget Fry.
➤ *Dir* Col Spector, *Pro* Radha Chakraborty, *Screenplay* Spector and Chakraborty, *Ph* Trevor Forrest, *Pro Des* Clive Howard, *Ed* Matthew McKinnon, *Costumes* Greg Fay.

A Col Spector Film-Soda Pictures.
78 mins. USA. 2006. Rel: 7 Sep 2007. Cert 15.

Son of Man ★★★½

From the people who made the wonderful *U Carmen eKhayelitsa* comes a contemporary story of Christ which is simply told in a very effective and powerful way. It takes place in the state of Judea in southern Africa, where a divine child is born at the time when civil war reaches a new level with imminent threats from the neighbouring dictatorship. It is a brutal but extraordinarily beautiful film and sadly this violent conflict is still relevant to what is happening to the world today. GS

➤ Andile Kosi, Pauline Malefane, Andries Mbali, Mvuyisi Mjali, Zorro Sidloyi.
➤ *Dir* Mark Dornford-May, *Pro* Dornford-May and Camilla Driver, *Screenplay* Dornford-May, Pauline Malefane and Andiswa Kedama, *Ph* Giulio Biccari, *Pro Des* Ernie Seegers, *Ed* Ronelle Loots and Anne Sopel, *M* Charles Hazlewood, Pauline Malefane and Sibulele Mjali, *Costumes* Jennifer Dornford-May.

Spier Films-Spier Films.
86 mins. South Africa. 2006. Rel: 7 Mar 2008. Cert 12A.

Son of Rambow ★★★½

Brought up in a Plymouth Brethren household,

Son of Man: The story of Christ retold in a modern setting.

Will Proudfoot (Bill Milner) is a rather isolated ten-year-old. It is 1982 in suburban England and Will is forbidden to watch television, listen to music or even spend time in his late father's garden shed. Then he's recruited by the school bully to star in a home video inspired by Sylvester Stallone's morally dubious *Rambo: First Blood*. Utterly charming, inventive and often very funny, this disarming original has the nous to appeal to children of all ages. If Ken Loach had a sense of humour… JC-W

➤ Neil Dudgeon, Bill Milner, Jessica Stevenson, Anna Wing, Will Poulter, Tallulah Evans, Adam Godley.
➤ *Dir* and *Screenplay* Garth Jennings, *Pro* Nick Goldsmith, *Ph* Jess Hall, *Pro Des* Joel Collins, *Ed* Dominic Leung, *M* Joby Talbot, *Costumes* Harriet Cawley.

Hammer & Tongs/Celluloid Dreams/Reason Pictures etc-Optimum Releasing.
96 mins. UK/France/Germany. 2007. Rel: 4 Apr 2008. Cert 12A.

Southland Tales ★½

The follow-up to the cult classic *Donnie Darko* comes as a major disappointment. After a nuclear attack in Texas in 2008 the aftermath is felt in Los Angeles, where Boxer Santaros, an actor stricken by amnesia after being stranded in the desert, and Krysta Now, an adult film star who is developing her own television show, are trying to make sense of their lives. And so do the audience with this terribly confusing and incomprehensible plot. Some good ideas but overlong and a total mess. GS

➤ Carlos Amezcua, Curtis Armstrong, Robert Benz, Todd Berger, Joe Campana, Christopher Lambert, John Larroquette, Justin Timberlake, Miranda Richardson.
➤ *Dir* and *Screenplay* Richard Kelly, *Pro* Bo Hyde, Sean McKittrick, Kendall Morgan and Matthew Rhodes, *Ph* Steven B Poster, *Pro Des* Alec Hammond, *Ed* Sam Bauer, *M* Moby, *Costumes* April Ferry.

Universal Pictures/Eden Roc Productions/Darko Entertainment-Universal International Pictures.
145 mins. USA/Germany/France. 2007. Rel: 7 Dec 2007. Cert 15.

Sparkle ★★★½

A risky title for an engaging but flawed film. Following *Boyfriends* and *Lawless Heart* Neil Hunter and Tom Hunsinger seem to have aimed at something more mainstream in this tale of a young Liverpudlian on the make in London. Some performances are spot on (note Ellie

Haddington in a small part) but some roles are miscast. Also the overtly upbeat resolution doesn't really fit with the subtleties and complexities of characterisation that mark the best work of this team. MS

➤ Stockard Channing, Shaun Evans, Anthony Head, Bob Hoskins, Lesley Manville, Amanda Ryan, John Shrapnel.
➤ *Dir* and *Screenplay* Neil Hunter and Tom Hunsinger, *Pro* Martin Pope and Michael Rose, *Ph* Sean Van Hales, *Pro Des* Cristina Casali, *Ed* Martin Brinkler, *M* Adrian Johnston, *Costumes* Alexandra Caulfield.

Isle of Man Film/Baker Street/UK Film Council/ North West Vision/BBC Films/Magic Light Pictures etc-Vertigo Films.
104 mins. UK. 2006. Rel: 17 Aug 2007. Cert 15.

Speed Racer ★

Even more tedious and over-produced than the second and third *Matrix* movies, this monstrous Wachoswki Brothers effort is based on an obscure 1960s toon about a boy named Speed (*Into the Wild's* Emile Hirsch) who loves to race. Despite the title, quick cut cartoon visuals and frequent bouts of auto action, it's oddly slow, drawn out and tedious. Much like watching someone you don't like playing a video game you're not interested in. MJ

➤ Emile Hirsch, Nicholas Elia, Christina Ricci, John Goodman, Susan Sarandon, Richard Roundtree.
➤ *Dir* and *Screenplay* Andy and Larry Wachowski, based on the animated series by Tatsuo Yoshida, *Pro* The Wachowskis, Grant Hill and Joel Silver, *Ph* David Tattersall, *Pro Des* Owen Paterson, *Ed* Roger Barton and Zach Staenberg, *M* Michael Giacchino, *Costumes* Kym Barrett.

Warner Bros Pictures /Silver Pictures/Village Roadshow Pictures etc-Warner Bros.
135 mins. USA. 2008. Rel: 9 May 2008. Cert PG.

The Spiderwick Chronicles ★★★★★

Based on a series of children's novels, this has Arthur Spiderwick (David Strathairn) disappear after building a magic circle round his isolated country home. Generations later, his descendants (single mum, three kids) move in unaware of the invisible nasties who want to get hold of his book chronicling their unseen world. When one of the twin brothers (Freddie Highmore) unwittingly opens the book, mayhem ensues. Terrific, character-driven screenplay. Released in both regular and IMAX formats. JC

▶ Freddie Highmore, Sarah Bolger, Nick Nolte, Mary-Louise Parker, Joan Plowright.
▶ *Dir* Mark Waters, *Pro* Mark Canton, Albie Hecht, Larry J Franco, Karey Kirkpatrick, Ellen Goldsmith-Vein, Julia Pistor etc, *Screenplay* Kirkpatrick, David Berenbaum and John Sayles, *Ph* Caleb Deschanel, *Pro Des* James D Bissell, *Ed* Michael Kahn, *M* James Horner, *Costumes* Odette Gadoury and Joanna Johnston.

The Kennedy/Marshall Company/ Nickelodeon Movies/Spiderwick Productions/Mark Canton Productions/Gotham Group-Paramount Pictures. 107 mins. USA. 2008. Rel: 21 Mar 2008. Cert PG.

St Trinian's ★½

Pointless sequel to what was once an entertaining original but whose subsequent sequels never matched the 1954 original. This one sees the schoolgirl horrors trying to save their alma mater from closure by the bank. Rupert Everett plays the headmistress rather like Camilla but is no match for Alastair Sim and Russell Brand as Flash Harry is no replacement for George Cole. What Colin Firth is doing in it is a mystery. Is this the best the British film industry can offer? If so, it doesn't deserve to be an Ealing Studios film as it besmirches the very name. Michael Balcon must really be in a spin. MHD

▶ Rupert Everett, Colin Firth, Jodie Whittaker, Mischa Barton, Russell Brand, Anna Chancellor, Cheryl Cole, Stephen Fry, Lena Headey, Celia Imrie.
▶ *Dir and Pro* Oliver Parker and Barnaby Thompson, *Screenplay* Piers Ashcroft and Nick Moorcroft, Jamie Minoprio and Jonathan M Stern, based on cartoons by Ronald Searle, *Ph* Gavin Finney, *Pro Des* Amanda McArthur, *Ed* Alex Mackie, *M* Charlie Mole, *Costumes* Rebecca Hale and Penny Rose.

Ealing Studios/Fragile Films-Entertainment Film Distributors. 97 mins. UK. 2007. Rel: 21 Dec 2007. Cert 12A.

Freddie Highmore and David Strathairn peruse the pages of *The Spiderwick Chronicles.*

Abbie Cornish and Mamie Gummer in *Stop-Loss*, a woman's take on today's US military undertakings.

Stardust ★★★

Adapted from a Neil Gaiman novel set in the 19th century, this has youth Charlie Cox breach the wall beyond which lies a magical kingdom where he meets and falls for fallen star Claire Danes. In pursuit are aging witch Michelle Pfeiffer hoping to restore her lost youth, and the kingdom's princes, killing each other to validate their claim to the throne. However, this enjoyable enough fantasy effects romp somehow fails to rise above the average. JC

‣ Ian McKellen, Ben Barnes, Charlie Cox, Sienna Miller, Michelle Pfeiffer, Robert De Niro, Nathaniel Parker, Ricky Gervais, Peter O'Toole, Rupert Everett, David Walliams.
‣ *Dir* Matthew Vaughn, *Pro* Vaughn, Lorenzo di Bonaventura, Michael Dreyer and Neil Gaiman, *Screenplay* Vaughn and Jane Goldman, from the novel by Gaiman, *Ph* Ben Davis, *Pro Des* Gavin Bocquet, *Ed* Jon Harris, *M* Ilan Eshkeri, *Costumes* Sammy Sheldon.

Paramount Pictures/Di Bonaventura Pictures/ Ingenious Film Partners/ Marv Films/True North-Paramount Pictures.
127 mins. UK/USA. 2007. Rel: 19 Oct 2007. Cert PG.

Step Up 2: The Streets ★★

The original was a surprise hit a couple of years ago and now the same story is more or less repeated but with a female lead and a touch of *8 Mile*. Andie (Briana Evigan), who comes from the streets, is the total outsider in the elite Maryland School of the Arts but is determined to prove herself with her raw talent. There is some strong choreography but the story and script are predictable, lacking the charm of the original. GS

‣ Briana Evigan, Robert Hoffman, Adam G Sevani, Will Kemp, Cassie Ventura, Danielle Polanco.
‣ *Dir* Jon M Chu, *Pro* Erik Feig, Jennifer Gibgot, Adam Shankman, Patrick Wachsberger, *Screenplay* Toni Ann Johnson and Karen Barna, based on characters created by Duane Adler, *Ph* Max Malkin, *Pro Des* Devorah Herbert, *Ed* Andrew Marcus, *M* Aaron Zigman, *Costumes* Luca Mosca.

Touchstone Pictures/Offspring Entertainment/Summit Entertainment-Universal Pictures.
98 mins. USA. 2008. Rel: 21 Mar 2008. Cert PG.

Still Life ★★★

Elem Klimov's *Farewell* (1983) told a moving story of a township flooded for a dam to be built, and that is echoed in this Chinese piece about Fengjie on the Yangtze River. Here two strangers arrive in search of their former partners, but in each case the tale moves slowly and atmosphere counts for more than plot or characters. There's none of the involvement achieved by Klimov despite this film's meaningful sense of place. MS

▸ Zhao Tao, Han Sanming, Wang Hongwei, Li Zhubin.
▸ *Dir* and *Screenplay* Jia Zhangke, *Pro* Xu Pengle, Wang Tianyun and Zhu Jiong, *Ph* Yu Likwai, *Pro Des* Wang Yu, *Ed* Kong Jinlei, *M* Lim Giong.

Xstream Pictures-BFI Distribution.
113 mins. Hong Kong/China. 2006. Rel: 1 Feb 2008. Cert PG.

Stop-Loss ★★★½

The title refers to the procedure whereby American soldiers due for discharge can find themselves posted back and returned to Iraq. Ryan Philippe is on good form as a soldier who finds himself in this situation and wants out and Kimberly Peirce (of *Boys Don't Cry*) directs well. Nevertheless echoes of other films – not least the splendid *In the Valley of Elah* (qv) – make for a sense of déjà vu and the later stages are less sure-footed in any case. MS

▸ Ryan Philippe, Abbie Cornish, Channing Tatum, Joseph Gordon-Levitt, Ciarán Hinds.
▸ *Dir* Kimberly Peirce, *Pro* Peirce, Mark Roybal, Scott Rudin and Gregory Goodman, *Screenplay* Mark Richard and Peirce, *Ph* Chris Menges, *Pro Des* David Wasco, *Ed* Claire Simpson, *M* John Powell, *Costumes* Marlene Stewart.

Paramount Pictures/MTV Films-Paramount Pictures UK.
112 mins. USA. 2007. Rel: 25 April 2008. Cert 15.

Strange Wilderness ★

The son of a celebrated naturalist, Peter Gaulke (Steve Zahn) presents his own nature show, making statements like, "monkeys make up over 80 per cent of the world's monkey population." Inevitably, his ratings are in decline, so Peter hits on the idea of shooting Bigfoot. A one star rating is too good for this execrable mess. Offensive, amateur and moronic, it challenges one's concept of what can be released in mainstream cinemas – until one realises that Adam Sandler executive produced it. JC-W

▸ Steve Zahn, Allen Covert, Jonah Hill, Kevin Heffernan, Ashley Scott, Peter Dante, Harry Hamlin, Robert Patrick, Joe Don Baker, Ernest Borgnine.
▸ *Dir* Fred Wolf, *Pro* Allen Covert and Peter Gaulke, *Screenplay* Gaulke and Wolf, *Ph* David Hennings, *Pro Des* Perry Andelin Blake, *Ed* Tom Costain, *M* Waddy Wachtel, *Costumes* Maya Lieberman.

Pelican Productions/Happy Madison Productions/Level 1 Entertainment-Paramount Pictures.
87 mins. USA. 2008. Rel: 11 Apr 2008. Cert 15.

Street Kings ★★½

Somewhat routine and occasionally melodramatic drama about police corruption in LA. Keanu Reeves plays a cop with a drinking problem, who comes to realise his mentor (Forest Whitaker) and all his mates – the 'street kings' of the title who write their own rules – are as bent as corkscrews. It has good action sequences, a high level of violence and an underwritten role for Hugh Laurie as the man from Internal Affairs, but the subject matter cries out for a deeper and more thought-provoking movie. CA

Steve Zahn is menaced by Bigfoot in the staggering *Strange Wilderness*.

➤ Keanu Reeves, Forest Whitaker, Hugh Laurie, Chris Evans, Cedric the Entertainer, John Corbett.
➤ *Dir* David Ayer, *Pro* Lucas Foster, Alexandra Milchan, Erwin Stoff, *Screenplay* James Ellroy, Kurt Wimmer and Jamie Moss, from a story by Ellroy, *Ph* Gabriel Beristain, *Pro Des* Alec Hammond, *Ed* Jeffrey Ford, *M* Graeme Revell, *Costumes* Michele Michel.

Regency Enterprises/Yari Film Group/3 Arts Entertainment/Emmett-Furla Films-Fox Searchlight Pictures
109 mins. USA. 2008. Rel: 18 Apr 2008. Cert 15.

Sugarhouse ★★

East London is the relatively unfamiliar setting but this violent tale of criminal dealing offers nothing new save for a script so over the top that the cast struggle to bring any conviction at all to the story. Despite the valiant efforts of all save Andy Serkis who simply succumbs to the excess, *Sugarhouse* can only be described as a ludicrous waste of effort. MS

➤ Steven Mackintosh, Ashley Walters, Andy Serkis, Adam Deacon, Tolga Safer.
➤ *Dir* Gary Love, *Pro* Michael Riley, Rachel Connors, Arvind Ethan and others, *Screenplay* Dominic Leyton, *Ph* Daniel Bronks, *Pro Des* Caroline Story, *Ed* Peter Davies, *M* Michael Price, *Costumes* Guy Speranza.

Drake Bell and Sarah Paxton spoof *Spider-Man* in *Superhero Movie*.

Slingshot Studios/Lunar Films/A Wolf Committee film-Slingshot.
90 mins. UK. 2007. Rel: 24 Aug 2007. Cert 15.

Superbad ★½

It is now official – Hollywood is ruled by nerds and their latest products are strictly for people with similar taste. The team behind *Knocked Up* are recycling the same ideas and this time a group of teenage losers are endlessly dreaming of having it off with beautiful women. All they want to do is to get drunk and end up with the objects of their desire in this misogynistic and unfunny comedy. GS

➤ Jonah Hill, Michael Cera, Christopher Mintz-Plasse, Martha MacIsaac, Emma Stone, Aviva.
➤ *Dir* Greg Mottola, *Pro* Shauna Robertson and Judd Apatow, *Screenplay* Seth Rogers and Evan Goldberg, *Ph* Russ Alsobrook, *Pro Des* Gerald Sullivan, *Ed* William Kerr, *M* Lyle Workman, *Costumes* Debra McGuire.

Columbia Pictures/Apatow Productions-Sony Pictures Releasing.
118 mins. USA. 2007. Rel: 14 Sep 2007. Cert 15.

Superhero Movie ★★½

Cheap, cheerful and not nearly as terrible as most other quickfire spoofs, *Superhero Movie* sees

Drake Bell bitten by a radioactive dragonfly, develop incredible powers, then do the hero thing. Making fun of just about everything going but sticking most closely to Sam Raimi's first *Spider-Man* adventure, it's crass and uneven, peppered with dated cultural references, and a little too reliant on potty humour. Regardless, if you're a fan of superhero cinema, it's still worth a look. MJ

▶ Drake Bell, Sarah Paxton, Christopher McDonald, Leslie Nielsen, Kevin Hart, Robert Hays, Charlene Tilton, Pamela Anderson.
▶ *Dir and Screenplay* Craig Mazin, *Pro* Mazin, Robert K Weiss and David Zucker, *Ph* Thomas E Ackerman, *Pro Des* Bob Ziembicki, *Ed* Andrew S Eisen, Craig P Herring and Daniel A Schalk, *M* James L Venable, *Costumes* Carol Ramsey.

Dimension Films-Momentum Pictures.
85 mins. USA. 2008. Rel: 6 June 2008. Cert 12A.

Surf's Up ★★★★

Far superior to the cute kiddie fare you'd expect, this CG animated surfing penguin tale cleverly presents itself as a mockumentary, brilliantly recreating live action camera movements and more. Think *Creature Comforts*, think *A Bug's Life* spoof outtakes, only this keeps it up for the entire movie. It simultaneously and brilliantly satirises competitive sports TV coverage, sleazy promoters, hippie surfers and more. Much too smart for kids, although they'll love it. Groundbreaking in its own way. JC
▶ Voices of Shia LaBeouf, Jeff Bridges, Zooey

Deschanel, Jon Heder, James Woods, Mario Cantone, Jane Krakowski.
▶ *Dir* Ash Brannon and Chris Buck, *Pro* Christopher Jenkins, *Screenplay* Brannon, Buck, Jenkins and Don Rhymer, from a story by Jenkins and Christian Darren, *Ph* Sylvain Deboissy, *Pro Des* Paul Lasaine, *Ed* Ivan Bilancio and Nancy Frazen, *M* Mychael Danna.

Sony Pictures Animation-Sony Pictures Releasing.
85 mins. USA. 2007. Rel: 10 Aug 2007. Cert PG.

Sweeney Todd: The Demon Barber of Fleet Street ★½

Although it carries a seal of approval from Stephen Sondheim, Tim Burton's film of his 'musical thriller' does not translate well to the cinema. Essentially a theatrical, not to say operatic, piece, the resulting film, despite its gothic appearance, lacks real atmosphere. Johnny Depp as Sweeney and Helena Bonham Carter as Mrs Lovett seem detached from the action. They lack good singing voices and, since most of the choruses have been cut, an air of flatness hangs over the film, whereas the original stage show tingles with excitement. Supporting players Alan Rickman, Timothy Spall and Sacha Baron Cohen try to save a piece that was sold more as a horror film than a musical. A major disappointment. MHD

▶ Johnny Depp, Helena Bonham Carter, Alan Rickman, Timothy Spall, Laura Michelle Kelly, Sacha Baron Cohen, Jamie Campbell Bower.
▶ *Dir* Tim Burton, *Pro* John Logan, Richard

Surf's Up: Why would a penguin p-p-p-pick up a board like that?

Sweeney Todd:
Johnny Depp is
reunited with
his razor sharp
'friends' above
Helena Bonham
Carter's pie shop.

D Zanuck, Laurie MacDonald and Walter Parkes,
Screenplay John Logan, based on the musical by
Stephen Sondheim and Hugh Wheeler and a
musical adaptation by Christopher Bond,
Ph Dariusz Wolski, *Pro Des* Dante Ferretti, *Ed* Chris
Lebenzon, *M* Stephen Sondheim, *Costumes* Colleen
Atwood.

DreamWorks Pictures/Warner Bros Pictures/The
Zanuck Company/Parkes MacDonald Productions-
Warner Bros.
116 mins. USA/UK. 2007. Rel: 25 Jan 2008. Cert 18.

Syndromes and a Century
★★★

To admire the films of Thailand's Apichatpong
Weerasethakul you need to be an egghead.
That said, this two-part film is at least beautiful
to look at and not quite as impenetrable as
its pretentious predecessor, *Tropical Malady*.
Here each part offers a tale that is a variant
of the other, one set in a country hospital
and the other in a modern urban location.
There's a contemplative Buddhist tone with
music playing a key role, but this poetic film is
frustratingly obscure as to meaning. MS

▶ Nantarat Sawaddikul, Jaruchai Iamaram, Sophon
Pukanok, Jenjira Pongpas.
▶ *Dir, Pro* and *Screenplay* Apichatpong
Weerasethakul, *Ph* Sayombhu Mukdeeprom,
Art Dir Akekarat Homlaor, *Ed* Lee Chatametikool,
M Kantee Anantagant, *Costumes* Virasinee
Tipkomol and Askorn Sirikul.

New Crowned Hope/Fortissimo Films/Back Up Films
etc-BFI Distribution.
106 mins. Thailand/France/Austria/Netherlands. 2006.
Rel: 21 Sept 2007. Cert 15.

Tales from Earthsea ★★★

Originally the great Hayao Miyazaki was to
direct this adaptation of the work of the cult
American author Ursula K Le Guin. In the event,
his son has picked up the paintbrush to create
this dream-like, imaginary world of dragons,
wizards and truant princes. Largely based on
the third book in the *Earthsea* series, the film
follows the adventures of the 17-year-old Prince
Arren, who teams up with the mysterious and
omnipotent sorcerer Sparrowhawk. At times
ponderous and static, the film has to work
hard to maintain our interest. Yet the power
of the original narrative, and the simplicity of
Miyazaki's approach, do win through in the
end. (Original title: *Gedo Senki*). JC-W

▶ Voices of Timothy Dalton, Mariska Hargitay,
Matt Levin, Cheech Marin, Blaire Restaneo.
▶ *Dir* Goro Miyazaki, *Pro* Javier Ponton and Toshio
Suzuki, *Screenplay* Miyazaki and Keiko Niwa, based
on the novel by Ursula K Le Guin and a concept by
Hayao Miyazaki, *Pro Des* Yogi Takeshige, *Ed* Takeshi
Seyama, *M* Tamiya Terajima, *Animation Dir* Takeshi
Imamura.

Buena Vista Home Entertainment/Mitsubishi Shoji
Co/NTV/Toho Company-Optimum Releasing.
115 mins. Japan. 2007. Rel: 3 Aug 2007. Cert PG.

Talk to Me ★★★

Don Cheadle and Chiwetel Ejiofor make a great team here portraying respectively the ex-con and DJ Petey Greene and the radio station executive Dewey Hughes who put Petey on the air in Washington D.C. in the 1960s. It's a true story that reflects an era, but its potential is undermined by an inconsistent approach. With the killing of Dr Martin Luther King the film turns dramatic but much of it plays as exaggerated comedy bordering on farce. MS

▶ Don Cheadle, Chiwetel Ejiofor, Cedric The Entertainer, Taraji P Henson, Mike Epps, Vondie Curtis Hall, Martin Sheen.
▶ *Dir* Kasi Lemmons, *Pro* Mark Gordon, Sidney Kimmel and others, *Screenplay* Michael Genet and Rick Famuyiwa from a story by Genet, *Ph* Stéphane Fontaine, *Pro Des* Warren Alan Young, *Ed* Terilyn A Shropshire, *M* Terence Blanchard, *Costumes* Gersha Phillips.

Focus Features/Sidney Kimmel Entertainment/Mark Gordon Company/Pelagius Films-Verve Pictures.
118 mins. USA. 2007. Rel: 23 Nov 2007. Cert 15.

Taxi to the Dark Side ★★★½

Alex Gibney's documentary, unlike John Pilger's *The War on Democracy* (2007), ladles on the music and favours creating a dramatic effect. In addition it moves back and forth in time distractingly. But, while this is not to my mind particularly good filmmaking, what it reveals about the Bush administration and about torture in Bagram Air Force Base in Afghanistan, in Abu Ghraib and at Guantanamo Bay make it an indictment that should not be ignored. MS

▶ Maan Kaassamani, Greg D'Agostino, Brian Keith Allen, Karyn Plonsky.
▶ *Dir* and *Screenplay* Alex Gibney, *Pro* Gibney, Eva Orner and Susannah Shipman, *Ph* Maryse Alberti and Greg Andracke, *Ed* Sloane Klevin, *M* Ivor Guest and Robert Logan.

Jigsaw Productions/Tall Woods, LLC and Wider Film Projects-Revolver Entertainment.
106 mins. USA. 2007. Rel: 13 June 2008. Cert 15.

Taxidermia ★★★★

This story of obsession follows three generations of a family in Hungary beginning with the bizarre sexual fantasies of the dim grandfather during World War II. Years later we follow the obese father's obsession for food and his desire to succeed as an athlete (many scenes of throwing up), leading to the son's addiction to taxidermy (a shocking climax). Palfi is a unique and highly original talent whose work may be grotesque and repulsive but also very poetic and is definitely not for people with a sensitive stomach. GS

▶ Csaba Czene, Gergely Trócsányi, Piroska Molnár, Adél Stanczel, Marc Bischoff, Gábor Máté.
▶ *Dir* György Pálfi, *Pro* Alexander Dumreicher-Ivanceanu, Emilie Georges, Gabriele Kranzelbinder and Alexandre Mallet-Guy, *Screenplay* Pálfi and Zsófia Ruttkay, based on the short stories of Lajos Parti Nagy, *Ph* Gergely Pohárnok, *Pro Des* Adrienn Asztalos, *Ed* Réka Lemhényi, *M* Amon Tobin, *Costumes* Julia Patkos.

Amour Fou Film Produktion/Eurofilm Studio/Katapult Film/La Cinéfacture/Memto Films Production-Tartan Films.
91 mins. Hungary/Austria/France. 2006. Rel: 13 Jul 2007. Cert 18.

10,000 BC ★★

As brainless a spectacle as virtually every other Roland Emmerich movie, this derivative combination of *Quest for Fire*, *One Million Years BC*, *Conan the Barbarian* and *The Prince of Egypt* follows a prehistoric warrior's efforts to rescue his people from a band of pyramid-building

Camilla Belle faces prehistoric peril in *10,000 BC*.

The Oscar-winning Daniel Day-Lewis in the superb *There Will Be Blood*.

warlords. No surprises here, or acting talent for that matter, but the creature effects are cool, and the action, when it comes, has a little spirit. MJ

▶ Steven Strait, Camilla Belle, Cliff Curtis, Joel Virgel, Mona Hammond, Tim Barlow, Omar Sharif.
▶ *Dir* Roland Emmerich, *Pro* Emmerich, Mark Gordon and Michael Winner, *Screenplay* Emmerich and Harald Kloser, *Ph* Ueli Steiger, *Pro Des* Jean-Vincent Puzos, *Ed* Alexander Berner, *M* Kloser and Thomas Wander, *Costumes* Renee April and Odile Dicks-Mireaux.

Warner Bros Pictures/Legendary Picures/Mark Gordon Productions/Centropolis Entertainment etc-Warner Bros.
109 mins. USA/New Zealand. 2008. Rel: 14 Mar 2008. Cert 12A.

Terror's Advocate ★★★½

No doubt Barbet Schroeder's documentary will fascinate those already intrigued by the enigmatic figure of lawyer Jacques Vergès who went missing for eight years in the 1970s and won't talk about where he was. But he will talk about his fame (notoriety?) as a defender of freedom fighters, terrorists and those accused of being Nazi war criminals. Interesting certainly, but rather long at 137 minutes especially when so many questions inevitably remain unanswered. MS

▶ With Jacques Vergès, Pol Pot, Carlos, Jean-Paul Sartre, Djamila Bouhired.
▶ *Dir* Barbet Schroeder, *Pro* Rita Dagher, *Ph* Caroline Champetier and Jean-Luc Perréard, *Ed* Nelly Quettier, *M* Jorge Arriagada.

A Wild Bunch, Yalla Films co-production etc-Artificial Eye Film Company.
137 mins. France. 2007. Rel: 16 May 2008. Cert 12A.

There Will Be Blood ★★★★½

Texas: 1898-1927. Daniel Plainview is a ruthless, ambitious oil prospector who uses charm, grit and intimidation to push his way to the top of his profession. A masterclass in filmmaking, Anderson's fifth feature is a piece that is as timeless as it is unforgettable. From its smallest gestures and muscular quirks to its moments of *grand guignol*, it asserts its originality. And Daniel Day-Lewis, appropriating the voice of John Huston, is an extraordinary spectacle: bowed, bloodied but amorally determined. Besides, any film that dares not utter a word for its first 15 minutes deserves respect. JC-W

▶ Daniel Day-Lewis, Martin Stringer, Barry Del Sherman, Paul F Tompkins, Paul Dano, Ciarán Hinds.
▶ *Dir and Screenplay* Paul Thomas Anderson, based on the novel *Oil!* by Upton Sinclair, *Pro* Anderson, Daniel Lupi, JoAnne Sellar, *Ph* Robert Elswit, *Pro Des* Jack Fisk, *Ed* Dylan Tichenor, *M* Jonny Greenwood, *Costumes* Mark Bridges.

Ghoulardi Film Company/Paramount Vintage/Miramax Films-Walt Disney Studios Motion Pictures.
158 mins. USA. 2007. Rel: 15 Feb 2008. Cert 12A.

Things We Lost in the Fire ★★

The fact that this piece about overcoming bereavement was made in Hollywood by Denmark's Susanne Bier only serves to stress the fictional tone that contrasts with her wonderful *Open Hearts* (2002). In any case her directorial style has become increasingly mannered and in addition she uses 'Scope without persuading Benicio Del Toro to adjust an outsize performance. Halle Berry fares better, but it's terribly drawn out and unpersuasive. MS

▶ Halle Berry, Benicio Del Toro, David Duchovny, Alison Lohman, John Carroll Lynch, Omar Benson Miller.
▶ *Dir* Susanne Bier, *Pro* Sam Mendes and Sam Mercer, *Screenplay* Allan Loeb, *Ph* Tom Stern, *Pro Des* Richard Sherman, *Ed* Pernille Bech Christensen and Bruce Cannon, *M* Gustavo Santaolalla and Johan Söderqvist, *Costumes* Karen Matthews.

DreamWorks Pictures/A Neal Street production etc-Paramount Pictures UK.
118 mins. USA/UK/Canada. 2007. Rel: 1 Feb 2008. Cert 15.

30 Days of Night ★★★

Adapted from a graphic novel, the story takes place in the isolated town of Barrow, Alaska, where a group of bloodthirsty vampires have a field day – or should I say a field month – when the winter cycle begins and the daylight sinks into darkness for 30 days. The countdown commences and Sheriff Eben, his estranged wife Stella and a group of locals try against all odds to stay alive. Similar to last year's *Frostbite* from Sweden, this is also a suitably tight and stylishly designed film that will satisfy fans of the genre. GS

▶ Josh Hartnett, Melissa George, Danny Huston, Ben Foster.
▶ *Dir* David Slade, *Pro* Sam Raimi, *Screenplay* Steve Niles, Stuart Beattie and Brian Nelson, based on the comic strip by Steve Niles and Ben Templesmith, *Ph* Joe Willems, *Pro Des* Paul Denham Austerberry, *Ed* Art Jones, *M* Brian Reitzell, *Costumes* Jane Holland.

Columbia Pictures/Dark Horse Entertainment/Ghost House Pictures-Columbia Pictures.
113 mins. USA. 2007. Rel: 1 Nov 2007. Cert 15.

This Christmas ★½

We join the Whitfield family for their first Christmas together in four years. Ma'Dere is delighted that her three sons and three daughters come to her LA home but soon the emotional reunion turns into a time of dispute where deep secrets are revealed. The story and the actors are not bad, but Whitmore's heavy-handed direction and reluctance to cut even a single line from his overextended script make *This Christmas* a lame and utterly forgettable affair. GS

▶ Delroy Lindo, Idris Elba, Loretta Devine, Chris Brown, Keith Robinson, Sharon Leaf.
▶ *Dir and Screenplay* Preston A Whitmore II, *Pro* Whitmore and William Packer, *Ph* Alexander Gruszynski, *Pro Des* Dawn Snyder, *Ed* Paul Seydor, *M* Marcus Miller, *Costumes* Francine Jamison-Tanchuck.

Facilitator Films/Rain Forest Films/Screen Gems-Sony Pictures Releasing.
117 mins. USA. 2007. Rel: 30 Nov 2007. Cert 12A.

Three and Out ★½

Mackenzie Crook is unappealing as the hard-up London Tube driver who thinks he's in for a huge pay-off if he can persuade a third person inside a month to fall in front of his train. While not as tasteless as it sounds,

Halle Berry and David Duchovny in *Things We Lost in the Fire*.

this is woefully unfunny and, when it attempts a bit of tragedy too, falls flat on its face. Colm Meaney as a potential suicide and Imelda Staunton as his estranged wife add a bit of class. CA

❯ Mackenzie Crook, Colm Meaney, Imelda Staunton, Gemma Arterton, Annette Badland, Mark Benton, Kerry Katona, Antony Sher.
❯ *Dir* Jonathan Gershfield, *Pro* Wayne Marc Godfrey and Ian Harries, *Screenplay* Steve Lewis and Tony Owen, *Ph* Richard Greatrex, *Pro Des* Amanda McArthur, *Ed* Jon Gregory, *M* Trevor Jones, *Costumes* Annie Hardinge.

Rovinge Picture Motion Picture Company-Worldwide Bonus Entertainment.
106 mins. UK. 2008. Rel: 25 Apr 2008. Cert 15.

3.10 to Yuma ★★★

Made to appeal to a modern audience, James Mangold's re-make of Delmer Daves' classic western of 1957 is much longer and much more violent. The tale still pivots on the changing relationship between an outlaw (Russell Crowe) and the married man (Christian Bale) delivering him to the train which will take him to trial – unless of course he is rescued en route. Admirers of the original will miss the succinct subtle interplay but find good acting here, especially from Peter Fonda in support. However as a western for today *Seraphim Falls* (qv) is much more interesting. MS

❯ Russell Crowe, Christian Bale, Logan Lerman, Ben Foster, Peter Fonda, Gretchen Mol, Dallas Roberts.
❯ *Dir* James Mangold, *Pro* Cathy Konrad, *Screenplay* Stuart Beattie, Michael Brandt, Derek Haas and Mangold based on Halsted Welles's screenplay from the short story by Elmore Leonard, *Ph* Phedon Papamichael, *Pro Des* Andrew Menzies, *Ed* Michael McCusker, *M* Marco Beltrami, *Costumes* Arianne Phillips.

Lionsgate/Relativity Media/A Tree Line Film production-Lionsgate UK.
122 mins. USA. 2007. Rel: 14 Sept 2007. Cert 15.

Timber Falls ★★½

This is a slightly different take on the "young people being kidnapped by weirdo hillbillies in West Virginia" story. It involves some very peculiar preserves, a man with a horribly disfigured face, a creepy distortion of Christian teaching and a bizarre plot to give a childless couple the baby they desperately crave. Beth Broderick as the deceptively gentle, God-fearing kidnapper is very scary. Some effective shocks and red herrings, sickening torture and violence lead to a buckets of gore climax. CA

❯ Josh Randall, Brianna Brown, Nick Searcy, Beth Broderick, Sascha Rosemann.
❯ *Dir* Tony Giglio, *Pro* Christopher Eberts, Steve Markoff, Kia Jam and Arnold Rifkin, *Screenplay* Giglio and Dan Kay, *Ph* Tobian Moore, *Pro Des* John Welbanks, *Ed* Peter Mergus, *M* Henning Lohner, *Costumes* Bobbie Read.

Rifkin-Eberts/Ascendant Pictures/A-Mark Entertainment-Scanbox Entertainment.
100 mins. USA. 2007. Rel: 23 May 2008. Cert 18.

Tough Enough ★★★½

Berlin is a grim and violent place in this German movie. It's about a fifteen year old boy with a flighty mother who is lured by school friends into truancy and petty crime before getting caught up with drug dealers. The film is let down by an unpersuasive resolution, but until then it is powerfully done. Younger audiences could well be drawn in and have the advantage that for them the storyline is probably less familiar. MS

❯ David Kross, Jenny Elvers-Elbertzhagen, Erhan Emre, Inanç Oktay Özdemir.
❯ *Dir* Detlev Buck, *Pro* Claus Boje, *Screenplay* Zoran Drvenkar and Gregor Tessnow from Tessnow's novel *Knalhart*, *Ph* Kolja Brandt, *Pro Des* Udo Kramer, *Ed* Dirk Grau, *M* Bert Wrede, *Costumes* Jale Kustaloglu.

A Boje Buck production with WDR, Arte etc-Dogwoof Pictures.
99 mins. Germany. 2005. Rel: 21 Sept 2007. Cert 15.

Tovarisch I Am Not Dead ★★★★½

Being a documentary about the filmmaker's father which utilises home movies and tells a personal story that reflects much wider issues, this is comparable to the wonderful *I For India* (qv). Stuart Urban's father was a formidable figure whose courage and determination enabled him to make several wartime escapes including one from a gulag. That mysteries remain about him is a fact that should have been signalled early on but, that apart, this is an absorbing piece with an immaculate mix of material. Highly recommended. MS

❯ With Stuart Urban, Garri S Urban, Noka Alekseyevna Kapranova.
❯ *Dir Pro* and *Screenplay* Stuart Urban, *Ph* Urban, Shai Peleg and Ben Nicolosi Endo, *Ed* Emily Harris, *M* Dirk Campbell.

Cyclops Vision-Cyclops Vision Distribution.
83 mins. UK. 2006. Rel: 2 May 2008. Cert 15.

Transformers ★

A film that bludgeons the casual observer with explosive special effects and very little else, Michael Bay's *Transformers* is a fans-only thrill ride about an ancient war that resumes on earth between two tribes of alien robots. Remaining true to the shoddy commercial spirit of the original, this product-heavy Hasbro production is little more than a bloated, feature-length advert for dodgy movie merchandise that nobody needs. Expect sequels. MJ

▶ Shia LaBeouf, Megan Fox, Josh Duhamel, Tyrese Gibson, Rachael Taylor, Jon Voight, John Turturro, Kevin Dunn
▶ *Dir* Michael Bay, *Pro* Tom De Santo, Don Murphy, Ian Bryce and Lorenzo di Bonaventura, *Screenplay* Roberto Orci and Alex Kurtzman, from a story by Orci, Kurtzman and John Rogers, *Ph* Mitchell Amundsen, *Pro Des* Jeff Mann, *Ed* Thomas A Muldoon, Glen Scantlebury and Paul Rubell, *M* Steve Jablonsky, *Costumes* Deborah L Scott.

DreamWorks SKG/Paramount Pictures/Hasbro/Di Bonaventura Pictures-Paramount Pictures.
144 mins. USA. 2007. Rel: 27 Jul 2007. Cert 12A.

Transylvania ★★

Tony Gatlif has made a speciality of creating films that feature the lives of gypsies. This, however, is one of his least satisfactory efforts since its story is tiresomely melodramatic and unengaging. It follows its foolish heroine (Asia Argento) who has travelled from Paris to Transylvania to seek the Romanian musician who has made her pregnant. Later she links up with another man. That it carries echoes of Fellini's masterpiece *La Strada* only serves to underline how feeble and uninvolving this is. MS

▶ Asia Argento, Amira Casar, Birol Unel, Alexandra Beaujard, Marco Castoldi.
▶ *Dir* Tony Gatlif, *Screenplay* Gatlif with Marco Castoldi, *Ph* Céline Bozon, *Art Dir* Brigitte Brassart, *Ed* Monique Dartonne, *M* Gatlif and Delphine Mantoulet, *Costumes* Rose-Marie Melka.

Princes Films/Pyramide Productions/DMG Films etc-Peccadillo Pictures Ltd.
102 mins. France/Romania. 2007. Rel: 10 Aug 2007. Cert 15.

True North ★★½

A well intentioned misfire from writer/director Steve Hudson, this is a drama about a Scottish trawler which, as part of a desperate gamble to pay off the skipper's debts, is used to smuggle illegal Chinese immigrants into the UK. It's well acted but the story lurches from contrivance to melodrama until it sinks in a sea of improbability. MS

▶ Martin Compston, Peter Mullan, Gary Lewis, Steven Robertson, Angel Li.
▶ *Dir* and *Screenplay* Steve Hudson, *Pro* Sonja Ewers, Benjamina Mirnik, David Collins and Edie Dick, *Ph* Peter Robertson, *Pro Des* John Hand and Bettina Schmidt, *Ed* Andrea Mertens, *M* Edmund Butt, *Costumes* Carole K.Millar.

BBC Films/Filmstiftung NRW/FFA/Ariel films/Makar Productions/Samson Films etc-Cinefile Ltd.
96 mins. Germany/UK/Ireland. 2006. Rel: 14 Sept 2007 Cert 15.

One of the impressive CGI sequences from the otherwise disappointing *Transformers*.

Katherine Heigl shows off one of the *27 Dresses*.

12.08 East of Bucharest ★★★★

Of the recent Romanian movies released here, this is the only one that is essentially a comedy – and even then it has a serious theme. The host of a local TV show finds speakers to discuss the day when Ceausescu was defeated, but their tailored recollections often clash with the memories of those who participate by phoning in. Influenced by Jarmusch but warm-hearted like Satyajit Ray, this gentle, subtle piece resonates by questioning how much 'history' as handed down is made up of subjective and sometimes doctored views. MS

▸ Mircea Andreescu, Teodor Corban, Ion Sapdaru, Mirela Cioaba, Cristina Ciofu.
▸ *Dir* and *Screenplay* Corneliu Porumboiu, *Ph* Marius Panduru, *Art Dir* Daniel Raduta, *Ed* Roxana Szel, *M* Grupul Rotaria, *Costumes* Monica Raduta.

42km Film supported by Racova Com-Agro-Pan Grup, Mopan, Vio, Ulerom and Cinéfondation-Artificial Eye Film Company.
89 mins. Romania/France. 2006. Rel: 17 Aug 2007. Cert 15.

21 ★★★

Twenty-one-year-old Ben is desperate to find money for medical school, so he agrees to join a group of students trained by their maths professor Micky to become experts in blackjack. Micky then lets them loose at the Las Vegas casinos for a share of the winnings. The setting is over familiar but surprisingly the film works thanks to British actor Jim Sturgess's confident and strong presence. He makes a credible hero with a convincing American accent to match. GS

▸ Jim Sturgess, Kevin Spacey, Kate Bosworth, Aaron Yoo, Lawrence Fishburne.
▸ *Dir* Robert Luketic, *Pro* Dana Brunetti, Michael De Luca and Spacey, *Screenplay* Peter Steinfeld and Allan Loeb, from the book *Bringing Down the House: the inside story of six M I T students who took Vegas for millions* by Ben Mezrich, *Ph* Russell Carpenter, *Pro Des* Missy Stewart, *Ed* Elliot Graham, *M* David Sardy, *Costumes* Luca Mosca.

Michael De Luca Productions/Relativity Media/Trigger Street Productions-Sony Pictures Releasing.
123 mins. USA. 2008. Rel: 11 Apr 2008. Cert 12A.

27 Dresses ★★½

Jane Nichols just loves weddings – she's been a bridesmaid 27 times. Now she's beginning to have feelings for her boss, a man who admits that he couldn't function without her. Then Jane's sister comes to stay and sweeps the latter off his feet. In spite of some good lines, the plot is about as prefabricated as a frock from Primark. Still, Katherine Heigl is a winning presence, making up for a deficit of charm and originality. JC-W

▸ Brian Kerwin, Charli Barcena, Jane Pfitsch, Katherine Heigl, Anne Fletcher, Kevin Doyle, Edward Burns.
▸ *Dir* Anne Fletcher, *Pro* Gary Barber, Jonathan Glickman and Roger Birnbaum, *Screenplay* Aline Brosch McKenna, *Ph* Peter James, *Pro Des* Shepherd Frankel, *Ed* Priscilla Nedd-Friendly, *M* Randy Edelman, *Costumes* Catherine Marie Thomas.

Fox 2000 Pictures/Spyglass Entertainment-20th Century Fox.
107 mins. USA. 2008. Rel: 23 Mar 2008. Cert 12.

Two Days in Paris ★★★½

Reminiscent at times of Woody Allen's work but with a French sensibility, this comedy is the creation of Julie Delpy who is writer, star, director, editor and composer. Julie's character is that of a girl in Paris visiting her parents (played by Julie's own parents) in order to introduce them to her American boy friend (Adam Goldberg). It's an engaging movie but the story is a mite too insubstantial to make a memorable feature length film. MS

▶ Adam Goldberg, Julie Delpy, Marie Pillet, Albert Delpy, Adan Jodorowsky.
▶ *Dir*, *Screenplay*, *Ed*, and *M* Julie Delpy, *Pro* Christophe Mazodier, Delpy and Thierry Potok, *Ph* Lubomir Bakchev, *Art Dir* Barbara Marc, *Costumes* Stephen Rollot.

Polaris Film Production & Finance/Tempete sous un crane production/3L Filmproduktion GmbH etc-The Works UK Distribution Ltd.
101 mins. France/Germany. 2006. Rel: 31 Aug 2007. Cert 15.

U, Me Aur Hum ★½

This strange, overlong Bollywood film about a doomed love affair begins on a sea cruise. The first half is badly acted and directed and its silly and superficial script is difficult to take seriously. And then miraculously it changes gear half way through and becomes a serious film about Alzheimer's. The performances are also totally transformed as if the actors are performing in a completely different film. A real oddity. GS

▶ Shyam Adhatrao, Ramu Bashyal, Richa Bhattacharya, Robin Bhatt.
▶ *Dir and Pro* Ajay Devgan, *Screenplay* Robin Bhatt, Sutanu Gupta, Akarsh Khurana, based on a story by Ajay Devgan, *Ph* Aseem Bajaj, *Pro Des* Samir Chanda, *Ed* Dharmendra Sharma, *M* Vishal Bharadwaj, *Costumes* Anil Cherian, Manish Malhotra and Anna Singh.

Devgan Films-Eros International.
157 mins. India. 2008. Rel: 11 Apr 2008. Cert 12A.

U2 3D ★★★★

Directors Catherine Owens and Mark Pellington have made history with the first-ever live-action digital 3D film which is even more breathtaking if seen on a giant IMAX screen.

Bono reaches out to his audience in *U2 3D*.

War-torn Beirut as it really is in Philippe Aractingi's compelling *Sous les bombes* [*Under the Bombs*].

The film captures the wonderful U2 in concert in Argentina towards the end of their Vertigo tour. This is an amazing cinematic experience where you truly believe you are right there in the crowd with the best seat in the house. GS

▶ Bono, Adam Clayton, The Edge, Larry Mullen Jr.
▶ *Dir* Catherine Owens and Mark Pellington, *Pro* Owens, John Modell, Jon Shapiro and Peter Shapiro, *Ph* Peter Anderson and Tom Krueger, *Ed* Olivier Wicki, *M* U2 and Peter Anderson.

3ality Digital Entertainment-Revolver Entertainment
85 mins. USA. 2007. Rel: 2 Feb 2008. Cert U.

The Ugly Duckling and Me
★★★

This is an enjoyable and imaginative animated feature from Denmark based on Hans Christian Andersen's classic. Ratso, is a city rat who has reached rock bottom as a theatrical agent but believes he can hit the big time when he comes across Ugly, a baby duckling. He pretends he is Ugly's father and takes him to a countryside carnival hoping to cash in on his ugliness. The characters are clearly drawn, it is colourful and fun. GS

▶ Voices of Morgan C Jones, Paul Tylack, Anna Olson, Gary Hetzler, Danna Davis.
▶ *Dir* Michael Hegner and Karsten Kiilerich, *Pro* Moe Honan , Gladys Morchoisne and Irene Sparre

Hjorthøj, *Screenplay* Mark Hodkinson, from a story by Hodkinson, Hegner and Kiilerich, *Pro Des* Sten Mesterton, *Ed* Thorbjørn Christoffersen, Virgil Kastrup and Per Risager, *M* Jacob Groth.

A Film Company/Magma Films/Ulysses Film Productions etc-Warner Bros.
90 mins. France/Germany/UK/Ireland/Denmark. 2006. Rel: 3 Aug 2008. Cert U.

Under the Bombs ★★★★

A quarter of a century or so after Volker Schlöndorff's *Circle of Deceit* featured footage of war-torn Beirut, Philippe Aractingi's admirable film was shot in comparable conditions. The harsh reality is vividly conveyed in a work that acutely blends professional players with non-professionals. It utilises a narrative about the growing sympathy between a Christian taxi driver and his Shiite passenger who is desperately seeking the child she had left with her sister who, it turns out, has died during a bomb attack. Without sentimentality the film brings out the common humanity of its protagonists and the continuing tragedy of the conflict. (Original title: *Sous les bombes*) MS

▶ Georges Khabbaz, Nada Abou Farhat, Rawya El Chab, Bshara Atallah.
▶ *Dir* Philippe Aractingi, *Pro* Hervé Chabalier, François Cohen-Séat, Paul Raphael and Aractingi, *Screenplay* Michel Léviant and Aractingi, *Ph* Nidal

Abdel Khalek, *Ed* Deena Charara, *M* René Aubry and Lazare Boghossian.

Capa Cinéma/Starfield Productions/Art'mell/ Fantascope Production etc-Artificial Eye Film Company. 99 mins. France/UK/Lebanon/Belgium. 2007. Rel: 21 March 2008.Cert 15.

Underdog ★★

What is it with Jim Belushi and canines? After the *K-9* comedies, he gets a new dog as a pal when he plays ex-cop Dan Unger whose teenage son Jack (Alex Neuberger) persuades a beagle called Underdog to use his talking and flying super-powers to fight crime in the city. Belushi deserves better material, but he makes the most of what's going, though the 4'5" Peter Dinklage (so good in *The Station Agent*) is wasted as crazed scientist Dr Barsinister, who has injected the beagle with a DNA cocktail. Based on a 1960s animated TV series, it's all very silly – but then that's the whole point! DW

➤ Jason Lee, Peter Dinklage, Jim Belushi, Patrick Warburton, Taylor Momsen, Alex Neuberger.
➤ *Dir* Frederick Du Chau, *Pro* Gary Barber, Roger Birnbaum, Jonathan Glickman and Jay Polstein, *Screenplay* Adam Rifkin, Joe Piscatella and Craig A Williams based on their own story from the television series by W Watts Biggers, *Ph* David Eggby, *Pro Des* Garreth Stover, *Ed* Tom Finan, *M* Randy Edelman, *Costumes* Gary Jones.

Walt Disney Pictures/Have No Fear Productions/ Maverick Film Company etc-Buena Vista International 84 mins. USA. 2007 Rel: 1 Feb 2008. Cert U.

Untraceable ★★★½

FBI Special Agent Marsh (Diane Lane) and her partner Griffin Dowd (Colin Hanks) are in charge of cracking down on credit card fraud and sexual predators on the internet. But they begin to run out of time when a new untraceable website called killwithme.com appears out of nowhere and a series of gruesome murders are committed online. The more people visit the site, the sooner the victims will die. Gregory Hoblit's suitably dark and atmospheric film delivers with an excellent central performance from the wonderful Miss Lane. GS

➤ Diane Lane, Billy Burke, Colin Hanks, Mary Beth Hurt, Peter Lewis, Joseph Cross.
➤ *Dir* Gregory Hoblit, *Pro* Andy Cohen, Hawk Koch, Steven Pearl, Tom Rosenberg and Gary Lucchesi, *Screenplay* Robert Fyvolent, Mark R Brinker and Allison Burnett, *Ph* Anastas Michos, *Pro Des* Paul Eads, *Ed* Gregory Plotkin and David Rosenbloom, *M* Christopher Young, *Costumes* Elisabetta Beraldo.

Cohen-Pearl Productions/Lakeshore Entertainment-Universal Pictures.
101 mins. USA. 2008. Rel: 29 Feb 2008. Cert 18.

Vantage Point ★★★

This is a contemporary assassination drama set in Salamanca where the American president (William Hurt) is the target. Forget the talk of *Rashomon* since this film's series of narratives each revisiting the incident from a different viewpoint don't conflict as in the Japanese classic – they merely elaborate as in the recent *11.14*. It's slick, popular fodder that nevertheless wastes a good cast (Whitaker, Weaver, Quaid etc) and eventually becomes absurdly contrived as its coincidences mount. MS

➤ Dennis Quaid, Matthew Fox, Forest Whitaker, William Hurt, Sigourney Weaver.
➤ *Dir* Pete Travis, *Pro* Neal H Moritz, *Screenplay* Barry L Levy, *Ph* Amir Mokri, *Pro Des* Brigitte Broch, *Ed* Stuart Baird, *M* Atli Örvarsson, *Costumes* Luca Mosca.

The excellent Diane Lane arms herself in *Untraceable*.

Dennis Quaid gets the picture, but not the whole story, in *Vantage Point*.

Columbia Pictures/Relativity Media/An Original Film production etc-Sony Pictures Releasing.
90 mins. USA. 2008. Rel: 7 March 2008. Cert 12A.

A Very British Gangster ★★★½

Donal MacIntyre's documentary about Dominic Noonan, his brothers and his family, notorious figures in Manchester, is a very well made film (genuinely cinematic it should be said). But it's often disturbing for the wrong reasons. Dominic, both Catholic and gay, is a man to be feared but he's also charismatic and this film gives no voice to the police or to those who might wish to speak out on behalf of victims. As a successful gangster who is a thorn in the side of the establishment, Dominic could become for some the most dangerous of role models. MS

▶ With Donal MacIntyre, Dominic Noonan, Bugsy Noonan, Sean Noonan.
▶ *Dir* Donal MacIntyre, *Pro* MacIntyre and Lil Cranfield, *Ph* Nick Manleya nd Mike Turnbull, *Ed* Sally Hilton.

Dare Films with Five/Extreme Productions (Belfast)-Contender Entertainment.
102 mins. UK. 2007. Rel: 7 Dec 2007. Cert 15.

Vexille ★★★★

This is another case of Japanese animation being up there with the best of Hollywood. An action tale set in the future, it features a heroine, Vexille, who leads an American investigative unit to penetrate Japan. That's after that country has defied an international ban on biotechnological research and set up a magnetic shield to keep observers out. The plot is conventional enough for this genre, one which allows a film to be dubbed without grating. But what counts are the visuals, and there's great stuff here in this undervalued film. MS

▶ With voices of Kuroki Meisa, Tanihara Shosuke, Matsuyuki Yasuko, Pak Romi.
▶ *Dir* and *Ed* Sori, *Pro* Nakazawa Toshiaki, Yoshihara Yumiko and Takase Ichiro, *Screenplay* Handa Haruka, *Pro Des* Hishiyama Toru, *M* Paul Oakenfold, *CGI Supervisor* Matsuno Tadao.

Shochiko Co Ltd, and FUNimation Entertainment/An Oxybot production-Momentum Pictures.
110 mins. Japan. 2007. Rel: 9 May 2008. Cert 12A.

El Violin ★★★★

Despite the specific Mexican setting, this tale of poor people fighting an oppressive regime has a wider timeless quality. Unusually the prime figure among those resisting is not a strong handsome hero but a violin-playing grandfather. He is magnificently embodied by the award winning Don Ángel Tavira now in his eighties. Shot in black and white this modest work has a myth-like resonance. Recommended. MS

▶ Don Ángel Tavira, Dagoberto Gama, Gerardo Taracena, Mario Garibaldi.
▶ *Dir*, *Pro* and *Screenplay* Francisco Vargas Quevedo, *Ph* Martín Boege Paré, *Art Dir* Claudio 'Pache' Contreras, *Ed* Quevedo and Ricardo Garfias Méndez, *M* Cuauhtémoc Tavira and Armando Rosas, *Costumes* Rafael Ravello.

Camára Carnal Films/Fondo de Inversión y Estímulos al Cine FIDECINE/ Centro de Capacitación Cinematografica CONACULTA etc-Soda Pictures.
98 mins. Mexico/Spain/France. 2006. Rel: 4 Jan 2008. Cert 15.

The Waiting Room ★★½

Roger Goldby's debut feature finds him misunderstanding his own work (he's writer as well as director). Set in South London (which has never looked more suited to a rom-com thanks to James Aspinall's colour photography), the story told is of tangled relationships. It needed to be treated as a tragicomedy in the manner of Mike Leigh and not as a rom-com. With this misjudged tone and material about old age that mixes uneasily with a rather candid portrait of sexual betrayals, the film misfires badly. MS

▷ Anne-Marie Duff, Ralf Little, Rupert Graves, Frank Finlay, Phyllida Law.
▷ Dir and Screenplay Roger Goldby, Pro Sarah Sulick, Ph James Aspinall, Pro Des Ana Viana, Ed David Thrasher, M Edmund Butt, Costumes Ralph Holes.

A Bright Pictures production-Lionsgate UK.
105 mins. UK. 2007. Rel: 6 June 2008. Cert 15.

Waitress ★★★½

A film stamped with a feminine sensibility, this is the legacy of the delightful Adrienne Shelley, actress turned director and writer, who, after completing this work, became a murder victim in New York. The film, however, is a comedy about a put-upon woman (Keri Russell) finding her own way. There are moments of whimsy and sentimentality but at its best this film has a voice of its own and it's splendidly played (how good to see Andy Griffith again). MS

▷ Keri Russell, Nathan Fillion, Cheryl Hines, Adrienne Shelley, Andy Griffith.
▷ Dir and Screenplay Adrienne Shelley, Pro Michael Roiff, Ph Matthew Irving, Pro Des Ramsey Avery, Ed Annette Davey, M Andrew Hollander, Costumes Ariyela Wald-Cohain.

Fox Searchlight Pictures/ Night & Day Pictures-20th Century Fox.
108 mins. USA. 2007. Rel: 10 Aug 2007. Cert 12A.

Walk Hard: The Dewey Cox Story ★★★★

Hilarious spoof biopic about imaginary musician Dewey Cox who, as a successful rock 'n'roller progresses through every decade from the 1950s onwards, meeting and befriending everybody from Elvis, Buddy Holly and the Temptations to the Beatles, Jackson Browne and Lyle Lovett, singing in every possible style imaginable. He sleeps with every woman he meets, has three wives, countless kids and gets hooked on every known drug but finally ends up with the woman of his dreams. John C Reilly actually makes Dewey believable and the script and direction of Jake Kasdan make the film truly funny and, daft as it is, it has its own sense of reality. MHD

▷ John C Reilly, Tim Meadows, Connor Rayburn,

Vexille: A dazzling and undervalued example of Japanese animation.

Chip Horness, Raymond J Barry, Jack White, Frankie Muniz, Jenna Fischer.
▶ *Dir* Jake Kasdan , *Pro* Kasdan, Judd Apatow and Clayton Townsend, *Screenplay* Kasdan and Apatow, *Ph* Uta Briesewitz, *Pro Des* Jefferson D Sage, *Ed* Tara Timpone and Steve Welch, *M* Michael Andrews, *Costumes* Debra McGuire.

Columbia Pictures/Apatow Productions/Nominated Films/Relativity Media/GH Three-Sony Pictures Releasing.
96 mins. USA. 2007. Rel: 18 Jan 2008. Cert 15.

The Walker ★★★½

In this drama echoing the private eye thrillers of the 1940s, it's a gay man who becomes the story's investigator and moral compass. He moves beyond his role as a companion of socialite women to protect one of their number who, consequent on a murder, could find herself involved in a scandal. The potential of Paul Schrader's piece is unrealised due to the miscasting of Woody Harrelson in the central role but it's an intriguing film nevertheless. MS

▶ Woody Harrelson, Kristin Scott Thomas, Lauren Bacall, Ned Beatty, Moritz Bleibtreu, Mary Beth Hurt, Lily Tomlin, Willem Dafoe.
▶ *Dir* and *Screenplay* Paul Schrader, *Pro* Deepak Nayar, *Ph* Chris Seager, *Pro Des* James Merifield, *Ed* Julian Rodd, *M* Anne Dudley, *Costumes* Nic Ede.

Kintop Pictures/Ingenious Film Partners/Asia Pacific Films/Isle of Man Film etc-Pathé Distribution.
108 mins. UK/Germany. 2007. Rel: 10 Aug 2007. Cert 15.

Wanted ★★★

Wesley (James McAvoy) is a put-upon loser of an office worker under the thumb of his gross, female boss, his girlfriend and his duplicitous best friend. One day he learns that his estranged father, a professional assassin, has been murdered. To prevent his own death he is engaged by Fox (Angelina Jolie), a mysterious woman from the Fraternity, a secret group of assassins. During Wesley's training by Fox and Sloan (Morgan Freeman), leader of the Fraternity, his latent powers surface and he sets out to avenge his father's death. This is high-tone action tosh with unbelievably complex special effects that enable bullets to fly around corners. Try not to think about it and you might enjoy the po-faced seriousness of it and a beefed-up McAvoy with his newly-acquired abs and pecks. MHD

▶ James McAvoy, Morgan Freeman, Angelina Jolie, Terence Stamp, Marc Warren, David O'Hara.

▶ *Dir* Timur Bekmambetov, *Pro* Jim Lemley, Jason Netter, Iain Smith and Marc E Platt, *Screenplay* Derek Haas, Michael Brandt and Chris Morgan, based on a story by Brandt and Haas, from the comic book series by Mark Millar and J G Jones, *Ph* Mitchell Amundsen, *Pro Des* John Myhre, *Ed* David Brenner, *M* Danny Elfman, *Costumes* Varvara Avdyushko

Universal Pictures/Kickstart Productions/Bazeleys Production/Marc Platt Productions/Relativity Media etc-Universal Pictures.
110 mins. USA. 2008. Rel: 25 June 2008. Cert 18.

War ★★½

When FBI agent John Crawford (Statham) learns that his partner and family have been killed by a notorious assassin called Rogue, he seeks revenge by initiating a gang war between the Chinese Triads and the Japanese Yakuzas. What might have been a good actioner is marred by formula writing and characterisation. Despite Jet Li and some scenes of car chases, explosions and other nonsense, the film fails to catch fire. CB

▶ Jet Li, Jason Statham, John Lone, Devon Aoki, Luis Guzman, Saul Rubinek.
▶ *Dir* Philip G Atwell, *Pro* Steve Chasman, Christopher Petzel and Jim Thompson, *Screenplay* Lee Anthony Smith and Gregory J Bradley, *Ph* Pierre Morel, *Pro Des* Chris August, *Ed* Scott Richter, *M* Brian Tyler, *Costumes* Cynthia Ann Summers.

Lionsgate Films/Current Entertainment/Fierce Entertainment/Mosaic Media Group-Lionsgate.
103 mins. USA. 2007. Rel: 29 Sep 2007. Cert 18.

The Water Horse ★★★½

Set in Scotland in 1942, this original take on the Loch Ness monster offers a story with echoes of *The Railway Children* and *E.T.* and with a child as the central human character. Incorporating good animation work but rather wasting the talents of Emily Watson, it's an unexceptional but generally appealing tall tale aimed first and foremost at young children and their grandparents who can explain why a German invasion was expected and why a bulldog should be called Churchill. MS

▶ Emily Watson, Alex Etel, Ben Chaplin, David Morrissey, Joel Tobeck, Brian Cox.
▶ *Dir* Jay Russell, *Pro* Robert Bernstein, Douglas Rae, Barrie M Osborne and Charlie Lyons, *Screenplay* Robert Nelson from the book by Dick King-Smith, *Ph* Oliver Stapleton, *Pro Des* Tony

Burrough, *Ed* Mark Warner, *M* John Newton
Howard, *Costumes* John Bloomfield.
Revolution Studios/Walden Media/Beacon Pictures/
Ecosse Films-Sony Pictures Releasing.
112 mins. USA/UK. 2007. Rel: 8 Feb 2008. Cert PG.

Water Lilies ★★★½

There's an individual stamp to this first feature
from France's Céline Sciamma. It is a study of
three teenage girls, adolescence seen from a
female perspective and wonderfully persuasive
for at least two thirds of its length. Thereafter
plot-lines come more to the fore and not
always convincingly. Elements of burgeoning
lesbianism emerge but only as part of an overall
view of female adolescents which, if lacking
a satisfying conclusion, will nevertheless be
appreciated by those drawn to the subject-
matter. MS

▶ Pauline Acquart, Louise Blachère, Adèle Haenel,
Warren Jacquin.
▶ *Dir* and *Screenplay* Céline Sciamma, *Pro*
Bénédicte Couvreur and Jérôme Dopffer,
Ph Crystel Fournier, *Art Dir* Gwendal Bescond,
Ed Julien Lacheray, *M* Para One, *Costumes* Marine
Chauveau.

Les Productions Balthazar/Centre National de la
Cinématographie/Canal+ etc-Slingshot.
84 mins. France. 2007. Rel: 14 March 2008. Cert 15.

The Wayward Cloud ★★★

Dating from 2004/5 and released here belatedly,
this film with songs comments on our frequent
failures in the quest for love, something also
reflected in the films of Jacques Demy. But
nothing could be less Demy-like than the
sexual explicitness of Tsai's beautifully designed
but bizarre work which plays against the
background of the porn industry in Taipei.
Many critics have found it very funny, but that's
an odd response overall when the crucial last
scene is quite intentionally deeply shocking. MS

▶ Lee Kang-Sheng, Chen Shiang-Chyi,
Lu Yi-Ching, Yang Kuei-Mei.
▶ *Dir* and *Screenplay* Tsai Ming-Liang, *Pro* Bruno
Pesery, *Ph* Liao Pen-Jung, *Pro Des* Yip Kam-Tim,
Ed Chen Sheng-Chang, *Choreography* Peggy Wu,
Costumes Sun Hui-Mey.

Aréna Films/Homegreen Films/Arte France Cinéma
etc-Axiom Films Ltd.
114 mins. France/Taiwan/China. 2004.
Rel: 16 Nov 2007. Cert 18.

Waz ★★

Detective Argo (Stellan Skarsgard) and his
new partner Westcott (Melissa George) try to
solve the mystery behind a series of mutilated
bodies with the equation 'waz' carved into
their flesh. First-time director Tom Shankland's

The Loch Ness
Monster is tended
by Alex Etel and
Priyanka Xi in
The Water Horse.

Stellan Skarsgard interrogates a witness in *W Delta Z* [*Waz*].

thriller, filmed in Belfast and New York, aims to be another *Seven* but unfortunately it lacks its sophistication and style. The leads are fine and Selma Blair is well used in a role against type. However, most of the British actors in the supporting roles fail to convince with their American accents. (Original title: *W Delta Z*). GS

▶ Stellan Skarsgard, Melissa George, Ashley Walters, Tom Hardy, Selma Blair, Paul Kaye.
▶ *Dir* Tom Shankland, *Pro* Allan Niblo and James Richardson, *Screenplay* Clive Bradley, *Ph* Morten Søborg, *Pro Des* Ashleigh Jeffers, *Ed* Tim Murrell, *M* David Julyan, *Costumes* Maggie Donnelly.

Ingenious Film Partners/UK Film Council/Northern Ireland Film & Television Commission-Vertigo Films. 104 mins. UK. 2007. Rel: 22 Feb 2008. Cert 18.

We're All Christs ★★★

Tough-going but deeply committed, this Polish drama is concerned with alcoholism. Its truthfulness and lack of sentimentality could well mean that alcoholics will applaud the realism of this study, for it shows how one man's life is ruined by drink, causing the break-up of his marriage and the alienation of his son. The emphasis on religion may come as a surprise, but it works – the drawback is that to appreciate this film fully you probably need to be a Polish alcoholic Catholic! (Original title: *Wszyscy jestesmy Chrystusami*) MS

▶ Marek Kondrat, Michal Koterski, Andrzej Chyra, Janina Traczykówna.
▶ *Dir* and *Screenplay* Marek Koterski, *Pro* Wlodzimierz Otulak, *Ph* Edward Klosinski,

Pro Des Przemyslaw Kowalski, *Ed* Ewa Smal, *M* Jerzy Satanowski, *Costumes* Magdalena Biedrzycka and Justyna Stolarz.

Vision Film supported by Polski Instytut Sztuki Filmowej (Polish Film Institute)-Dogwoof Pictures. 110 mins. Poland. 2006. Rel: 17 Aug 2007. Cert 15.

We Are Together ★★★★

It's no surprise that this documentary feature has won awards at festivals all over the world. Paul Taylor made it to help the Agape orphanage in South Africa where he had been a volunteer helper. He was encouraged to do so not only by its valiant work in helping children, many of whom had lost parents to AIDS, but by the fact that he found the children's choir there inspirational. Indeed his film confronts the social issues honestly but is also immensely uplifting and it's a film, simple but heartfelt, that deserves the widest possible audience. MS

▶ With Slindile Moya, Sifiso Moya, 'Grandma' Zodwa Mqadi, Alicia Keys.
▶ *Dir* and *Ph* Paul Taylor, *Pro* Teddy Leifer and Taylor, *Screenplay* Slindile Moya and Taylor, *Ed* Masahiro Hirakubo and Ollie Huddleston.

EMI/Shooting People Films/HBO Documentary Films/ Channel 4 British Documentary Film Foundation/Rise Films-EMI/Shooting People. 87 mins. UK/USA. 2007. Rel: 7 March 2008. Cert PG.

We Own the Night ★★★½

As in *Little Odessa* and *The Yards*, James Gray blends a crime story with a study of family life and tensions. Here the latter elements somewhat lose out as the piece proceeds, but it remains a characteristic work. This time it's set in Brooklyn in 1988 where one brother has followed dad into the NYPD while the more rebellious sibling has connections with criminals. Overall more ambitious than *American Gangster* (qv) but less good although well acted. MS

‣ Joaquin Phoenix, Mark Wahlberg, Eva Mendes, Robert Duvall, Alex Veadov.
‣ *Dir* and *Screenplay* James Gray, *Pro* Nick Wechsler, Marc Butan, Mark Wahlberg and Joaquin Phoenix, *Ph* Joaquin Baca-Asay, *Pro Des* Ford Wheeler, *Ed* John Axelrad, *M* Wojciech Kilar, *Costumes* Michael Clancy.

2929 Productions/Nick Wechsler/-Universal Pictures.
117 mins. USA. 2007. Rel: 14 Dec 2007 Cert 15.

The Wedding ★★

This Polish comedy doesn't lead to a marriage but begins with one. The wedding party that ensues provides an opportunity for black comedy exposing everybody as materialistic and calculating. The targets are lined up but in such an obvious way – there's far more comic invention in *Death at a Funeral* (qv) – that the film drags. Of the players only Iwona Bielska creates an effective comic character. (Original title: *Wesele*) MS

‣ Marian Dziedziel, Iwona Bielska, Tamara Arciuch, Marciej Stuhr.
‣ *Dir* and *Screenplay* Wojtek Smarzowski, *Pro* Anna Iwaszkiewicz, Dariusz Pietrykowski and Bartlomiej Topa, *Ph* Andrzej Szulkowski, *Pro Des* Barbara Ostapowicz, *Ed* Pawel Laskowski, *M* Ryszard Tymon Tymanski, *Costumes* Magdalena Maciejewska.

Telewizja Polska SA/Agencja Produkcji Filmowej etc–Dogwoof Pictures.
105 mins. Poland. 2004. Rel: 14 Dec 2007. Cert 15.

Weirdsville ★★½

Willem Wennekers' fun but silly script tells the story of friends Dexter and Royce who are desperate to find a way of paying their debts to their violent drug dealer. Royce's girlfriend Matilda suggests robbing a house she knows but after she has an overdose things go from bad to worse. Director Allan Moyle keeps the pace and energy going while the actors have fun with their OTT roles but the implausible plot becomes more and more preposterous. GS

‣ Scott Speedman, Wes Bentley, Taryn Manning, Matt Frewer, Greg Bryk, Maggie Castle.
‣ *Dir* Allan Moyle, *Pro* Nicholas Tabarrok,

Screenplay Willem Wennekers, *Ph* Adam Swica, *Pro Des* Oleg M Savytski, *Ed* Michael Doherty, *M* John Rowley, *Costumes* Alex Kavanagh.

Darius Films/Darius-Weirdsville Productions-Contender Entertainment Group
91 mins. USA. 2007. Rel: 3 Aug 2007. Cert 15.

Welcome Home Roscoe Jenkins ★

Roscoe Jenkins is a popular TV talk-show personality who has abandoned his Georgian roots. But, when his parents invite him back home for their 50th wedding anniversary, he decides to return with his arrogant new fiancée and ten-year-old son. He is then forced to re-examine the true values of life. This is a dreadful and totally unfunny comedy with a smug Martin Lawrence contributing further to the decline of his career. Avoid! GS

‣ Martin Lawrence, James Earl Jones, Margaret Avery, Joy Bryant, Cedric the Entertainer.
‣ *Dir and Screenplay* Malcolm D Lee, *Pro* Charles Castaldi, Mary Parent and Scott Stuber, *Ph* Greg Gardiner, *Pro Des* William A Elliott, *Ed* George Bowers and Paul Millspaugh, *M* David Newman, *Costumes* Danielle Hollowell.

Universal Pictures/Spyglass Entertainment/Stuber-Parent-Universal Pictures.
114 mins. USA. 2008. Rel: 30 May 2008. Cert 12A.

Welcome to the Sticks ★★★★

Philippe Abrams, the manager of the post office in Salon-de-Provence, is desperate for a transfer to the Côte d'Azur but, when he tries to cheat the system, he is sent to Bergues, a small town in the dreaded North. Actor/director Dany Boon's delightfully funny satire on the prejudices of the French boasts delicious performances and Kad Merad's sheer enjoyment as the reluctant manager is infectious. It is a story that could easily be transported anywhere. (Original title: *Bienvenue chez les Ch'tis*). GS

‣ Kad Merad, Dany Boon, Zoé Félix, Lorenzo Ausilia-Foret, Anne Marivin, Line Renaud, Michel Galabru.
‣ *Dir* Dany Boon, *Pro* Claude Berri and Jérôme Seydoux, *Screenplay* Boon, Franck Magnier and Alexandre Charlot, *Ph* Pierre Aim, *Pro Des* Alain Veyssier, *Ed* Luc Barnier and Julie Delord, *M* Philippe Rombi, *Costumes* Florence Sadaune.

Pathé Renn Productions/Les Productions du Chicon/ TF1 Films Productions/Canal+ etc-Pathé Distribution.
106 mins. France. 2008. Rel: 4 Apr 2008. Cert 12A.

What Happens in Vegas... perhaps should have stayed between Cameron Diaz and Ashton Kutcher.

What Happens in Vegas ★★

This is a romantic comedy of ill-matched strangers who get drunk and marry in Vegas and are forced to stay together by an unexpected jackpot and a preachy judge. There are some funny scenes as the uptight Cameron Diaz and slobby Ashton Kutcher come into conflict, but really good gags are thin on the ground. That they will eventually fall in love is inevitable. The interest is in how they get there and frankly it isn't interesting enough. CA

▶ Cameron Diaz, Ashton Kutcher, Rob Corddry, Lake Bell, Treat Williams, Queen Latifah.
▶ *Dir* Tom Vaughan, *Pro* Michael Aguilar, Shawn Levy and Jimmy Miller, *Screenplay* Dana Fox, *Ph* Matthew E Leonetti, *Pro Des* Stuart Wurtzel, *Ed* Matt Friedman, *M* Christophe Beck, *Costumes* Renée Ehrlich Kalfus.

21 Laps Entertainment/Musak Media Group/Penn Station Entertainment/Dune Entertainment III/Regency Enterprises-20th Century Fox.
99 mins. USA. 2008. Rel: 9 May 2008. Cert 12A.

Where in the World is Osama Bin Laden? ★★

With this silly, jokey piece about searching for Bin Laden, Morgan Spurlock squanders all the goodwill he gained when he made the splendid *Super Size Me*. Neglecting his pregnant wife to make the movie in many countries, Spurlock claims he's doing it out of concern for the world his unborn child will inherit, but it looks more like an attempt to cash in on the earlier success. MS

▶ With Morgan Spurlock, Alexandra Jamieson, Hossam Bahgat, Khalil Al-Khalil.
▶ *Dir* Morgan Spurlock, *Pro* Jeremy Chilnick, Stacey Offman and Spurlock, *Screenplay* Chilnick and Spurlock from a story by them and others, *Ph* Daniel Marracino, *Ed* Gavin Coleman and Julie 'Bob' Lombardi, *M* Jon Surney.

The Weinstein Company/Wild Bunch/Non Linnear Films/Warrior Poets production-Optimum Releasing.
90 mins. USA/France. 2008. Rel: 9 May 2008. Cert 12A.

Wind Chill ★★★

Two characters get stuck in a snow drift on their way home for Christmas. This corny cliché of a situation is deftly handled by director Gregory Jacobs as the screenplay strands them inside the car with only each other for company. The relationship develops between the snooty college girl and her nerdy boy companion who turns out not to be all that he seems. Stuck miles from anywhere, the girl starts to imagine ghosts and the film becomes a horror thriller and falls apart. With George Clooney and Steven Soderbergh as executive producers, one might have expected something better. CB

▶ Emily Blunt, Ashton Holmes, Martin Donovan, Ian Wallace, Donny Lucas, Linden Banks.
▶ *Dir* Gregory Jacobs, *Pro* Graham Broadbent and

Peter Czernin, *Screenplay* Joseph Gangemi and Steven Katz, *Ph* Dan Lautsen, *Pro Des* Howard Cummings, *Ed* Lee Reilly, *M* Clint Mansell, *Costumes* Trish Keating.

Blueprint Pictures/Section Eight-Sony Pictures Releasing. 91 mins. UK/USA. 2007. Rel: 3 Aug 2007. Cert 15.

The Witnesses ★★★★

One of André Téchiné's best films, this is a very French take – non-judgmental and civilised – on issues of sex and sexuality. It's set in the 1980s both before and after AIDS appeared on the scene. It involves heterosexual and gay characters – and, indeed, bisexual ones too – and it's beautifully acted (Michel Blanc has his best role since *Monsieur Hire* in 1990). There are minor flaws but this is a very fine film that gained less attention than it deserved. (Original title: *Les témoins*) MS

▷ Michel Blanc, Emmanuelle Béart, Sami Bouajila, Johan Libéreau, Julie Depardieu.
▷ *Dir* André Téchiné, *Pro* Saïd Ben Saïd, *Screenplay* Téchiné with Laurent Guyot and Vivane Zingg, *Ph* Julien Hirsch, *Art Dir* Michèle Abbe, *Ed* Martine Giordano, *M* Philippe Sarde, *Costumes* Khadija Zeggaï.

UGC/SBS Films/France 2 Cinéma etc-Artificial Eye Film Company.
114 mins. France/Spain. 2006. Rel: 19 Oct 2007. Cert 15.

Wristcutters: A Love Story ★★★

What a pity that this black comedy loses its way in the last third when fanatical religion irrelevantly raises its ugly head. Until then Goran Dukic's film is engagingly original. The main characters are suicides who find themselves in hell – hell proving to be just like the world that had driven them to take their lives. In this context a love story develops between a genuine suicide (Patrick Fugit) and a girl named Mikal (Shannyn Sossamon) who claims she shouldn't be there because her death had been accidental. Fugit and Sossamon play together beautifully. MS

▷ Patrick Fugit, Shannyn Sossamon, Shea Whigham, Leslie Bibb, Tom Waits.
▷ *Dir* and *Screenplay* Goran Dukic from Etgar Keret's novella *Kneller's Happy Campers*, *Pro* Adam Sherman, Chris Coen, Tatiana Kelly and Mikal P. Lazarev, *Ph* Vanja Cernjul, *Pro Des* Linda Sena, *Ed* Jonathan Alberts, *M* Bobby Johnston, *Costumes* Erica Nocotra.

Halcyon Pictures Ltd./Crispy Film/Adam Sherman Inc/ No Matter Pictures-Miracle/Halcyon Pictures.
88 mins. USA. 2006. Rel: 23 Nov 2007. Cert 15.

XXY ★★★★

This sensitive feature from Argentina is the work of Lucía Puenzo who tells a story that explores the plight of those born with both male and female sex organs. It's never didactic. Instead this personal drama about a teenager in this state explores the uncertainties of the parents over turning to surgery having recognised that their child now has a boyfriend. Rather than promoting some single solution as always being the right one, the film leaves matters open

Morgan Spurlock embarks on a fruitless search in *Where in the World is Osama Bin Laden?*

for consideration. Not a subject to interest all admittedly, but those drawn to the film won't be disappointed by this well-acted piece. MS

❯ Inés Efrón, Martín Piroyansky, Ricardo Darin, Valeria Bertuccelli, Germán Palacios, Carolina Peleritti.
❯ *Dir* and *Screenplay* Lucía Puenzo based on Sergio Bizzio's short story *Cinismo*, *Pro* Puenzo and José María Morales, *Ph* Natasha Braier, *Pro Des* Roberto Samuelle, *Ed* Alex Zito and Hugo Primero, *M* Andrés Goldstein and Daniel Tarrab.

Historias Cinematográficas/Wanda Visión etc-Peccadillo Pictures.
91 mins. Argentina/Spain/France. 2007. Rel: 9 May 2008. Cert 15.

The Yacoubian Building ★★★½

Managing to sustain a length of 172 minutes, this film version of the novel of the same name is something of a triumph for director Marwan Hamed making his first feature. The Cairo block of the title, once luxurious but now decayed, is symbolic of life in the city as illustrated by a range of stories that connect up with the building and its inhabitants. There's brave social comment but also in the last third especially elements of soap opera. Original title: *Omaret yakobean*). MS

❯ Adel Imam, Youssra, Hend Sabri, Khaled El Sawy, Ahmed Rateb, Isaad Younis, Nour El Sherif, Mohamed Imam.
❯ *Dir* Marwan Hamed, *Pro* Emad El Din Adeeb, *Screenplay* Waheed Hamed based on the novel by Alaa Al Aswany, *Ph* Sameh Selim, *Art Dir* Fawzy El Awamry, *Ed* Khaled Marei, *M* Kheled Hammad, *Costumes* Nahed Nasrallah.

Good News 4 Film & Music-ICA Films.
172 mins. Egypt. 2006. Rel: 14 Sept 2007. Cert 15.

Year of the Dog ★★

This is an attempt by Mike White as writer and director to bring us a film about dogs that is more sophisticated and insightful than the typical family-orientated movies that feature pets. So much for good intentions because the movie is totally misjudged, be it the relentless chirpiness of its opening or the inability to find the right transitions in tone necessary for tragicomedy. Here the elements never come together. MS
❯ Molly Shannon, Laura Dern, Regina King, John C Reilly, Peter Sarsgaard.
❯ *Dir* and *Screenplay* Mike White, *Pro* White, Ben Leclair and Dede Gardner, *Ph* Tim Orr, *Pro Des* Daniel Bradford, *Ed* Dody Dorn, *M* Christophe Beck, *Costumes* Nancy Steiner.

Paramount Vantage/Rip Cord/Plan B-Paramount Pictures UK.
97 mins. USA. 2007. Rel: 31 Aug 2007. Cert PG.

Yella ★★★

Critics are often asked not to give away plot twists but this overpraised film ends up with one of the oldest and corniest in the business. What a pity, because this tale of a young female accountant seeking a fresh start in life – she takes up a new job following the break-up of her marriage – is admirably played by Nina Hoss and the supporting cast. There is an individual tone here, but you just hope that the story won't lead to the obvious cliché only to find that it does. MS

❯ Nina Hoss, Hinnerk Schönemann, Birghart Klaußner, Devid Striesow.
❯ *Dir* and *Screenplay* Christian Petzold, *Pro* Florian Koerner von Gustorf and Michael Weber, *Ph* Hans Fromm, *Pro Des* Kade Gruber, *Ed* Bettina Böhler, *M* Stefan Will, *Costumes* Anette Guther and Lotte Sawatzki.

Schramm Film Koerner & Weber/ZDF/Arte/FFA etc-Artificial Eye.
90 mins. Germany. 2007. Rel: 21 Sept 2007. Cert 12A.

You Kill Me ★★★

Ben Kingsley is great here, and so too is Téa Leoni, but John Dahl's latest finds him forsaking noir-ish thrillers for a piece about an alcoholic assassin that is closer to black comedy. However, when Kingsley's workaholic killer and Leoni's lonely loner are drawn to one another we are meant to feel sympathy. Predictably the mix is uneasy – the man is, after all, a professional killer – but if the material seems unworthy the performances certainly aren't. MS

❯ Ben Kingsley, Téa Leoni, Luke Wilson, Philip Baker Hall, Bill Pullman, Dennis Farina.
❯ *Dir* John Dahl, *Pro* Carol Baum, Mike Marcus, Zvi Howard Rosenman and others, *Screenplay* Christopher Markus and Stephen McFeely, *Ph* Jeffrey Jur, *Pro Des* John Dondertman, *Ed* Scott Chestnut, *M* Marcelo Zarvos, *Costumes* Linda Madden.

Code Entertainment/Baum/Echo Lake/Rosenman/ Bipolar etc-Revolver Entertainment.
93 mins. USA/Canada. 2007. Rel: 7 Dec 2007. Cert 15.

You, the Living ★★★★

No less than with Jacques Tati, Roy Andersson's films could be the work of no other man. Like Kaurismäki, he deals in comic miserabilism, but he pushes it even further and his visual style, as earlier shown in his masterpiece *Songs from the*

You, The Living:
Roy Andersson's
bleakly comic
universe is
unique.

Second Floor (2000), is uniquely his own. With vignettes replacing a story, this view of modern life will divide audiences into those who respond and those who are bored. Sometimes the misery outweighs the humour, but I have to admire what is one of the most personal visions in cinema today. (Original title: *Du levande*) MS

▷ Elisabet Helander, Jugge Nohall, Jan Wikblad, Björn Englund, Jessika Lundberg.
▷ *Dir* and *Screenplay* Roy Andersson, *Pro* Pernilla Sandström, *Ph* Gustav Danielsson, *Art Dir* Magnus Renfors and Elin Segerstedt, *Ed* Anna Märta Waern, *M* Robert Hefter, *Costumes* Sophia Frykstam.

Studio 24/Roy Andersson/Filmproduktion AB/
Thermidor Filmproduktion etc-Artificial Eye Film
Company.
93 mins. Sweden/Germany/France/Denmark/Norway/
Japan. 2007. Rel: 28 March 2008. Cert 15.

Youth without Youth ★★½

Francis Ford Coppola's first film in years is a personal undertaking likened by him to what an independent young filmmaker might produce. It is, however, more reminiscent of Powell and Pressburger. We accept as a given that when struck by lightning Tim Roth's elderly character will not die but discover that he now has the body of a forty year old. This leads to a meditation on the conflict between creative ambition and loving relationships. Alexandra Maria Lara turns up more than once as Roth's perfect woman. But there's serious overloading – the film also brings in Nazi Germany, Indian philosophy and reincarnation – while the female roles suffer from inferior writing and there's no chemistry at all between Roth and

Lara. Ambitious undeniably, but also very disappointing. MS

▷ Tim Roth, Alexandra Maria Lara, Bruno Ganz, André M Hennicke.
▷ *Dir*, *Pro* and *Screenplay* Francis Ford Coppola based on the writing of Mircea Eliade, *Ph* Mihai Malaimaire Jr, *Pro Des* Calin Papura, *E* Walter Murch *M* Osvaldo Golijov, *Costumes* Gloria Papura.

American Zoetrope/SRG Atelier (Romania)/Pricel
(France)/BIM Distribuzione (Italy)-Pathé Distribution.
125 mins. Romania/France/Italy/USA. 2007.
Rel: 14 Dec 2007. Cert 15.

Zoo ★★

The fine poetic photography here is totally at odds with what is needed since Robinson Devor's taboo-breaking documentary feature is concerned with zoophiles – those who have sex with animals. Instead of being informative about this form of sexuality which could have added to our understanding and helped us to draw our own conclusions, it's a largely one-sided plea by 'zoos' that it's all harmless. "But they would say that, wouldn't they?" is the likely response. MS

▷ With Coyote, Jenny Edwards, John Edwards, John Paulsen, Ron Carrier.
▷ *Dir* Robinson Devor, *Pro* Alexis Ferris and Peggy Case, *Story by* Charles Mudede and Devor, *Ph* Sean Kirby, *Pro Des* Jeanne Cavenaugh, *Ed* Joe Shapiro, *M* Paul Matthew Moore.

Cook Ding/Think Film/Northwest Film Forum-Revolver
Entertainment.
76 mins. USA. 2007. Rel: 30 May 2008. Cert 18.

Faces of the Year

By James Cameron-Wilson

Casey Affleck

CASEY AFFLECK

Born: 12 August 1975, in Falmouth, Massachusetts, USA

For many years Casey Affleck had coasted his way through a number of high-profile films in the shadow of his more-famous brother. He was in *To Die For*, *Good Will Hunting*, *American Pie* and *Ocean's Eleven*. He even played Gerry in Gus Van Sant's *Gerry* – opposite Matt Damon. Then, just as Ben Affleck's star began to wane, Casey stepped into the limelight. This was due to two movies: *Gone Baby Gone* and *The Assassination of Jesse James by the Coward Robert Ford*. In the latter, he played the coward, the central role in an epic Western that some considered to be the best film of 2007. Casey himself was nominated for an Oscar in the best supporting category, even though he had a bigger part than Brad Pitt. In *Gone Baby Gone* he was in more heroic form, as a private investigator hired to track down a

missing four-year-old girl. Under the direction of his brother Ben, he revealed a surprising intensity contained within a minimalist mien, which has become something of a trademark. So, after all these years, Casey has emerged as one of the most interesting actors currently working in Hollywood. He was certainly the leading light in two of the best films to emerge from America in 2007, although his range has still to be fully proven.

ABBIE CORNISH

Born: 7 August 1982, in Lochinvar, New South Wales, Australia

Abbie Cornish first caught the attention of international critics with her starring role in Cate Shortland's *Somersault*. A poetic and deeply affecting portrait of a 16-year-old runaway, the film won best feature, director and actress trophies from the Australian Film Critics' Circle. As Heidi, Cornish was a total natural, her helplessness underpinned by the instinctive doggedness of the teenage psyche. However, it wasn't until she played a very English lady-in-waiting to Cate Blanchett's domineering monarch in *Elizabeth: The Golden Age* that her versatility proved unmistakable. She was also a heroin addict in the little-seen *Candy*, opposite Heath Ledger, and a strapping Texan army wife in Kimberly Peirce's hard-hitting *Stop-Loss*. A natural blonde, the Australian shares

Abbie Cornish

Marion Cotillard

the same coquettish smile of her compatriot Nicole Kidman and is big enough to welcome the comparison. With another contrasting role in Ridley Scott's *A Good Year* (as the plucky Californian daughter of Albert Finney), Cornish follows a line of incredibly versatile ladies from Down Under, including her idol, Ms Blanchett. And, like Kidman, she started out as something of a tomboy, learning to drive at eleven and entering her first rally aged 15. She's also backpacked across Morocco, Brazil, Italy and France, but is now determined to settle down as a serious actress. Next, she'll be seen as the muse and fiancée of John Keats (Ben Whishaw) in Jane Campion's *Bright Star* and in the Viking drama *Last Battle Dreamer*, opposite her *Stop-Loss* co-star Ryan Phillippe.

MARION COTILLARD

Born: 30 September 1975, in Paris, France

Marion Cotillard is no newcomer. However, prior to 2007, only the most dedicated *cineaste* knew who she was. Now she's starring opposite Johnny Depp in Michael Mann's *Public Enemies* and Daniel Day-Lewis in the big-budget musical *Nine*. Still, when she flew to California to promote her Oscar chances for *La Vie En Rose*, she was overawed when she met the latter at

the Palm Springs International Film Festival. "I really think he's one of the greatest actors ever," she gushed. As Edith Piaf in *La Vie En Rose*, Mlle Cotillard gave a performance of astonishing transformation. Playing the singer from *ingénue* to premature old age (Piaf died at 47), Cotillard captured the pain, bravado and crankiness with a prodigious hand. But what was truly remarkable is that the actress looks nothing like the icon she has reinvented for a new generation, being both a very attractive woman and a foot taller than Piaf. The performance she gives is certainly the stuff of glittering prizes but it also came with subtitles and a modest budget, even by French standards. So, understandably, Cotillard was genuinely stunned when she won the London Film Critics' Circle award for best actress, followed two days later by the BAFTA and then two weeks after that by the Oscar itself. Yet the actress is no stranger to awards. She received a César nomination for playing ill-fated twins in *Pretty Things* (2001) and won the award as a disconsolate and deadly prostitute in *A Very Long Engagement*. She also found local fame as Lili Bertineau in Luc Besson's trio of action-packed Taxi films and was chosen by Ridley Scott to play the headstrong waitress Fanny Chenal opposite Russell Crowe in *A Good Year*.

Anne-Marie Duff

ANNE-MARIE DUFF

Born: 8 October 1970, in Southall, London, England

Anne-Marie Duff is not an overnight star. An actress of gradient capacities, Ms Duff has been steadily building an impressive resumé over the last few years. On film, she scored as the pitiful Margaret (condemned for being raped by her cousin) in Peter Mullen's tough and masterful *The Magdalene Sisters*. On television, she made a name for herself as the charitable if choleric Fiona Gallagher in *Shameless* – and then as Elizabeth I in the BBC's *The Virgin Queen*. And on stage, she wowed audiences and critics alike with her portrayals of Mona in *Days of Wine and Roses* and as Shaw's *Saint Joan*. The director Howard Davies once said of her that, "she throws herself at parts as if bruising herself on them." She has certainly proved her versatility, revealing an astonishing array of colours in all mediums. But it wasn't until this year that her stature as a film actress really began to take shape. She is simply incandescent and heart-breaking as the single mum in Roger Goldby's sweet and observant *The Waiting Room*. And she was nominated Best Supporting Actress in the Irish Film and Television Awards for *Garage*. Meanwhile, she has hurled herself into a string of upcoming movies: starring opposite Michael Caine in the nostalgic drama *Is There Anybody There?*, headlining the romantic comedy *French Film*, and playing Tolstoy's daughter Sasha in Michael Hoffman's all-star *The Last Station*. For a while, Anne-Marie Duff may have been eclipsed by the fame of her husband James McAvoy, but she is currently proving to be very much his equal.

KATHERINE HEIGL

Born: 24 November 1978, in Washington DC

Katherine Heigl simmered nicely under the radar for 15 years before exploding across the multiplex in *Knocked Up*. In the latter, she played an ambitious, career-focused TV presenter who ends up being impregnated by a beer-swilling slacker played by Seth Rogen. Yet another hit from the gross, gilded stable of Judd Apatow, the film was the surprise success of the year, a touching, honest, disgusting and very funny comedy about what it means to be male and female – and pregnant. It also grossed $219 million and transformed Ms Heigl into one of the hottest female stars in Tinseltown. To prove it, she was paid $6 million for her next film, *27 Dresses*, which took in over $159m worldwide, further adding to her commercial lustre. However, Ms Heigl has been appearing in films since the age of 14, when she played the part of Kathryn in *That Night*, starring C Thomas Howell and Juliette Lewis. Nevertheless, it was her role as Gérard Depardieu's contrary daughter Nicole in *My Father the Hero* – a remake of *Mon Père, Ce Héros* – that first hiked her into the limelight. Yet her celebrity was short-lived

Katherine Heigl

and films such as *Under Siege 2: Dark Territory*, *Prince Valiant* and *Bride of Chucky* failed to raise her profile. Now, finally, she's a bona fide star, has won an Emmy for her role as intern Dr Isabel 'Izzie' Stevens in ABC TV's *Grey's Anatomy* and will next be seen opposite Gerard Butler in the romantic comedy *The Ugly Truth*.

SHIA LaBEOUF

Born: 11 June 1986, in Los Angeles, USA

Shia LaBeouf never seemed destined for superstardom. Ordinary looking and even slightly nerdish, he has been quoted as saying that *Dumb and Dumber* is his favourite movie. Musically, his tastes range from Jack Johnson to 50 Cent. OK, so he's a *kid*. The son of a Franco-Cajun clown (his father) and a ballet dancer, he had showbusiness – sort of – in his blood. Indeed, his mother's father was a comedian and his father's mother a lesbian Beatnik poet. Shia (pronounced 'shyer') says that he "was acting when I came out of the womb." Doing stand-up comedy aged ten, he found himself an agent through the Yellow Pages and made a name for himself as the mischievous Louis Stevens in the Disney Channel's *Even Stevens*. He cropped up on TV in *The X Files*, *Freaks and Geeks* and *ER*, before landing the lead in Andrew Davis's lively, engaging *Holes*, adapted from Louis Sachar's cult novel. The latter grossed a handsome $67 million in the US and Shia found himself lending support in *Charlie's Angels:*

Full Throttle, *I, Robot* and *Constantine*. However, the last three years have seen his career step into high gear. He was excellent in *A Guide to Recognising Your Saints* and had a good part in Emilio Estevez' *Bobby* and then pulled off an astonishing hat trick. He was the voice of the pushy penguin Cody in the quirky cartoon *Surf's Up* (which grossed $149 million worldwide) and, in *Disturbia*, played a teenager under house arrest who thinks he witnesses a murder. Steven Spielberg was instrumental in casting him in the latter – which was a surprise hit – and repeated the favour with *Transformers*, the third highest grossing film of 2007. Shia then played Harrison Ford's sidekick in Spielberg's *Indiana Jones and the Kingdom of the Crystal Skull*, which has also done rather well.

Shia LeBoeuf

Sam Riley

SAM RILEY

Born: 8 January 1980, in Menston, West Yorkshire, England

Both Jude Law and Cillian Murphy were up to play Ian Curtis in *Control* while Sam Riley was still folding shirts for a living. Riley heard about the film and auditioned three times, while director Anton Corbijn re-mortgaged his house to meet the budget. Eventually, Riley got the part and Corbijn's efforts were rewarded with some of the best reviews to greet a British biopic since *Gandhi*. A gritty, black-and-white portrait of the epileptic, self-destructive lead singer of Joy Division, *Control* went on to win best film prizes from the London Film Critics' Circle, the Evening Standard Awards, the Hamburg Film Festival and the British Independent Film Awards. Riley himself took home trophies from the London Critics, the Chicago International Film Festival and the Edinburgh Film Festival, as well as a BAFTA nomination for 'rising star'. A gangly, brooding presence, Riley managed to capture the look and essence of Ian Curtis – and his singing prowess – that astonished the latter's devotees. As it happens, Riley was lead singer with the Leeds band 10,000 Things after he'd dabbled with the National Youth Theatre. When the band folded following a nasty review in the NME, Riley found himself on his uppers, hence the shirt-folding gig. Now he's in huge demand and has already completed a role opposite Ryan Phillippe in the sci-fi thriller *Franklyn*. Meanwhile, he's biding his time with his girlfriend Alexandra Maria Lara (who played Annik in *Control*) in Berlin, far from the international limelight. He remains phlegmatic about his future: "I don't want not to work, but I don't want to work for the sake of it," he says.

SETH ROGEN

Born: 15 April 1982, in Vancouver, British Columbia, Canada

Seth Rogen was not your likely leading man. But then neither was John Candy or Jack Black. The difference with Rogen is that, like Woody Allen, he writes his own material. He was a staff writer on *Da Ali G Show* with Judd Apatow, when the latter encouraged him to take up a film career. So, he not only played the part of Steve Carell's

Saoirse Ronan

cohort Cal in Apatow's directorial debut, *The 40-Year-Old Virgin*, but also co-produced the film, a resounding hit. He then took the lead in Apatow's *Knocked Up*. It went on to gross $219 million. Slovenly, unshaven and portly, Rogen's Ben Stone was Quasimodo to Katherine Heigl's Esmeralda, but there was an endearing candour and earnestness in his immaturity that audiences connected with. Rogen also co-scripted the semi-autobiographical *Superbad*, another box-office titan ($170m), and co-penned the Owen Wilson comedy *Drillbit Taylor*. Next, Rogen starred in the Apatow-produced *Pineapple Express* – from his own screenplay – and took the lead in Kevin

Smith's *Zack and Miri Make a Porno*. After that, he played a security guard in *Observe and Report* and wrote the screenplay to *The Green Hornet*, in which he'll take the title role.

SAOIRSE RONAN

Born: 12 April 1994, in New York City, USA

Like Mel Gibson, Saoirse Ronan was born in New York City. And like Mel Gibson, Saoirse Ronan is a master of accents. Unlike Mel Gibson, though, Ms Ronan is just 14 years old. When she was nominated for her first Oscar, she was 13. And when she was signed up to play the key role of Briony Tallis in the award-laden *Atonement*, she was twelve. In the interim, the County Carlow-raised actress has played the daughter of Catherine Zeta-Jones in *Death Defying Acts*, is the central character in the fantasy *City of Ember* – with Bill Murray – and is starring in Peter Jackson's *The Lovely Bones*, based on the critically acclaimed, best-selling novel by Alice Sebold. In the last-named, Ms Ronan plays a girl who, in the book's first chapter, is raped, murdered and dismembered, later coming to terms with her own death. Considering the performance that Peter Jackson coaxed out of a 19-year-old Kate Winslet in *Heavenly Creatures*, Saoirse is unlikely to disappoint her fans in what is her biggest showcase yet. The daughter of the Mancunian actor Paul Ronan – who allowed her to be carried around by Brad Pitt on the set of *The*

Seth Rogen

Channing Tatum

Devil's Own – Saoirse started out in a couple of Irish TV series, *The Clinic* and *Proof*. However, she really revealed her acting chops when she played Michelle Pfeiffer's daughter in the little-seen *I Could Never Be Your Woman*. With a pitch-perfect American accent, she played a street-savvy 13-year-old who feeds her scenarist mother dialogue for the latter's TV show *You Go Girl*. Saoirse's transformation into the upper crust, sexually confused Briony in *Atonement* confirmed the depth of her talent. Other than the ongoing debate about the sheer scale of her thespian prowess, the main question seems to be the pronunciation of Saoirse. Clever clogs insist on pronouncing it the traditional way of 'seer-sha', although Saoirse prefers to call herself 'sur-shuh' as in 'inertia'.

CHANNING TATUM

Born: 26 April 1980, in Cullman, Alabama, USA

A school football star and ex-model, Channing Tatum ticks all the requisite boxes to be a mid-league movie luminary. Tall, strikingly handsome and built like a Trojan demigod, the Alabama native made his film debut as a basketball jock in *Coach Carter*. But it was his turn as a high school soccer stud in *She's the Man* – opposite Amanda Bynes – that got him noticed and which duly accelerated the pulse rate of female viewers. He capitalised on this with the central role of street dancer Tyler Gage in *Step Up*, an engaging slice of formulae that went on to gross $114 million worldwide. Having proved himself as an actor of some physical heft – basketball, football, motorcross racing in *Supercross: The Movie* – Channing (Chan to his fans) revealed greater thespian depths in something even as cliché-blown as *Step Up*. Here were rumblings, if not mumblings of early Brando, with the charisma to match. Chan's career stepped up a gear when decent filmmakers requested his services: in the edgy indie *A Guide to Recognising Your Saints* Tatum responded to the autobiographical material of first-time director Dito Montiel. The director then signed up the actor to headline his second film, *Fighting*. Before then, though, Chan joined Ryan Phillippe and Abbie Cornish in the hard-hitting drama *Stop-Loss*, directed by none other than Kimberley Peirce. The first woman director to tackle the subject of Iraq, Peirce steered Hilary Swank to an Oscar in her first film, *Boys Don't Cry*. Here, Peirce tapped into Tatum's reserves of testosterone while dredging up something a little more uncomfortable and exposed. Since then, he's played Pretty Boy Floyd for Michael Mann – in *Public Enemies* – and snared the central role in *GI Joe*, co-starring Dennis Quaid and Sienna Miller.

So What's New?

Mansel Stimpson identifies two significant trends
in Britain's recent cinema history.

It's always true that, as Bob Dylan said, the times they are a-changin', but sometimes we notice it and sometimes we don't. Consequently it's no surprise that this applies in the case of cinemagoing in Britain over the year covered by this annual. The change that must have been noticed by every ordinary cinemagoer is the increased cost of cinema tickets. However, no announcement about seat prices stood out like the one that came to my notice earlier this year. What it said was that the cost for an adult of certain seats at the Odeon Leicester Square would usually be £19 each. That, of course, was the new going rate for the best seat in the house offering luxury in the royal circle and we are dealing here with what is now the leading cinema in the Square. But, even so, it is an example that takes the breath away – after all it means that a couple would be paying £38 and a family unit

even more. The fact is that cinemas around the country keep raising their prices at not infrequent intervals and, if the levels do not compare with those in London's West End, they are high enough to deter many potential customers.

That is, of course, in line with so much today as the cost of living rises, but for cinemas such price increases could prove particularly risky. We live in an age when big films, if aided by hype, are often safe from any critical reservations that may be expressed about them: this applies to such summer blockbusters as *Mamma Mia!* which weathered some over-harsh criticisms and *The Dark Knight* which pleased both critics and public. Despite the pirates out there anxious to sell you a DVD copy, most people do indeed want to see these major attractions as soon as possible and on a cinema screen. Here price increases are unlikely to have much effect, but the moment you turn to other areas, to enjoyable but

Heath Ledger
as the psychotic
Joker in the
acclaimed
The Dark Knight.

The versatile
Meryl Streep
toasts the success
of ABBA musical
Mamma Mia!

unexceptional fare or to a film with no known names attached as star or director but with strong backing from the critics, then it is another story. The public can all too easily regard such films as less tempting and more of a gamble with the cost of an evening out being the factor that could weigh against going out to see them.

At this point another key factor comes into play. Fifty years ago it was television that was seen as a threat to cinema (in 1953 an understandably forgotten Ealing comedy, *Meet Mr Lucifer*, recognised this fact by satirising the public's obsession with television). Now, far more seriously one suspects, cinemagoing is threatened by the popularity of DVDs, and it's not just a case of new films being challenged by old ones. While the fear of television persisted, film distributors would ensure that the arrival of a film on TV was delayed until it had well and truly used up its potential in cinemas. There's no such rigid approach as to how quickly a film may pass from cinemas onto DVD. The most extreme recent example involved Nick Broomfield's splendid *Battle for Haditha*. At the national press show for its cinema release the publicity sheets announced that it would be issued on DVD within a few days. Purists will, of course, declare that the cinema is the best place to see a film, and I could not argue with that. But, if I were a parent seeking a movie for the whole family to view, I would certainly find myself balancing the cost of cinema tickets against the price of purchasing or hiring a DVD. This is a situation unlikely to go away and it could become all too pertinent to the question of the survival of our cinemas.

Regular cinemagoers will also be aware on some level of the other marked change that has crept up on us, but they may not have considered its implications fully. I refer now to the unexpected increase in the number of cinema releases. Treated simply as a statistic, this could be regarded as wholly beneficial: the fact that more films are coming out suggests a wider range of material and a greater choice for the viewer. But when the facts are given full consideration the picture that emerges is a disturbing one. We have moved on from the days when in most weeks a mere handful of films could be expected to open and we now inhabit a world in which the emergence in London of between seven and ten titles a week is no longer unusual. This trend reached what one assumes is likely to be its peak in May 2008 when within the space of two weeks 23 new titles and one re-issue appeared.

So, what's bad about that? Well, one answer is that with so many titles appearing, some of them are likely to find very few screens available for them (some films open in London on one screen only and that screen may be in Mile End or Hammersmith, thus making the film far from easy to access for many potential viewers). Another answer is that, with so many titles lined up, the length of time for which a film will run is in many cases diminishing (some, indeed, last only a week). This kind of situation is as far removed as

could be imagined from those distant days when the Academy Cinema in Oxford Street would virtually guarantee long runs of films, usually of an art-house kind. That cinema belonged to the Hoellering family headed by George who produced the film version of *Murder in the Cathedral* and who died in 1980. What was special was that they would nurse a film that failed initially to click at the box-office and, because they screened works that they loved, they would keep such movies on for as many weeks as possible. It's more reasonable, business-wise, to follow the current pattern which decrees that if a film that opens on Friday does not perform well on its first three days then, unless pressurised by it being a movie from a major distributor, you arrange on Monday to replace it the following Friday. It makes sense, but how one misses the attitude which characterised the Academy.

However, I have yet to point out the worst consequence that flows from so many new films appearing each week. Many newspapers are unwilling to devote substantially more space than before to cinema, so the inevitable result is that a large number of new films get a review that is no more than a paragraph in length – indeed, it is not unknown for a review to consist of one sentence. Of course, plenty of these films are unworthy, but many an editor will insist on the latest big mainstream films being given the main slot and, because of that, it is not uncommon to find work that is more independent or art-house in character getting coverage so brief that it is inadequate.

Foreign films in particular can suffer in this way, which is one reason why in my survey of this year's world cinema highlight many outstanding titles that passed almost unnoticed. They were not necessarily unpraised by the critics, but how can a critic with limited space expect to convey to readers the nature of a film, its plot and its special qualities in a way that will make them decide to rush out and see it? In the past with more space available it was possible to convey enthusiasm clearly and to help a film at the box-office as a result. Now it's more difficult to achieve that, not only because of shortage of space but for another reason too. If a critic does indeed succeed in making readers want to see something out of the ordinary then, if those readers can't fit it in immediately, there is a good chance that, by the time they are free to go, the film has already come off.

Overall, then, despite the increased range of material coming our way, the state of cinema today is far from satisfactory. Ironically, though, it's a situation that can make this annual more valuable to its readers than ever before. With so much around, so much missed or overlooked, there is a greater chance than ever before for the reviews here to draw to your attention films of real merit that you have yet to see. Most cinema releases become available here on DVD and can at least be seen that way. It may be second best to a cinema viewing, but at least it's an opportunity to keep these films alive when, without the DVD market, they might disappear forever.

Cinemagoing: Aren't

*Going to the cinema in Britain can be depressing and expensive. **Michael Darvell** wonders how we can once again enjoy saying 'let's go to the pictures!'*

A tantalising promise from the days when trailers were something to look forward to.

Of course, anything we used to do was always better than the way it is now. There's always a downside to everything, entertainment-wise, be it going to the cinema, the theatre, the opera, music gigs, eating out or just trying to get on public transport. Everything is so much more expensive now, including the cost of getting there and all the penalties you have to suffer, such as congestion charges and parking fees, before you can even start to enjoy yourself. Going out becomes a major operation thereby making entertainment a special event. Whereas film-going used to be a regular habit, now just visiting your local cinema can be difficult and costly. Admittedly, local cinema prices are lower than those in the big cities, but even these are creeping ever upwards. Then there are all the extras if you are taking the family with you – the buckets of popcorn, the nachos and the hot dogs, the bags of sweets and chocolate bars, the drinks and the ice creams, all on sale at inflated prices.

Once you're inside the cinema there is the problem of noisy neighbours. Young people brought up in the MTV age are used to chatting constantly and now that we're in the age of the mobile phone, nobody thinks twice about not answering it when it rings mid-film. It happens in spite of on-screen warnings to switch off. A classic response once came when I complained to a couple of girls sitting next to me who were having a full-on conversation. Looking at the

screen, one of them said: 'It's all right, mate, they're only talking.'

Apart from those extraneous noises, there are also the sounds of patrons chomping and slurping their way through all the food and drink they have slavishly bought at the kiosk, all in giant-size packs, presumably to last through a two-hour film show. The rank odour of popcorn, nachos and hot dogs that nowadays pervades even often quite small cinemas becomes at the least distracting and at the most downright sickening. Officially cinema customers are not allowed to bring their own refreshments in with them, mainly because the circuits rely on their own sales of food and drink to swell their meagre profit margins. Surely this is against our human rights and, anyway, how would or could, say, pensioners fork out for these edibles at exorbitant prices? According to a British Film Institute report, popcorn in cinemas is the most expensive product on the planet. It beats plutonium and heroin with its 10,000 per cent mark-up. In fact the cardboard container for the popcorn costs more to produce than the edible rubbish inside it. This year the Picturehouse circuit tried a no-food policy at certain performances to gauge public reaction and by now have extended the experiment to further performances at more cinemas.

Apart from the high cost of going to the pictures, the actual cinema buildings are ever more soulless. These days multiplex screens, which is where most of the UK's cinema patrons see their films, are purely functional and often just an adjunct to a boring shopping mall. Many cinemas do not display what's on today in a viewer-friendly way and going to the pictures usually involves a long hike up escalators and along corridors with rarely any staff to greet or show you where to find Screen 14. And when you get there, you are in a dank and dismal hangar, badly-lit and with no sense of style (whatever happened to cinema tabs which opened and closed at every possible eventuality?) and there is certainly no showmanship in cinemas now. You may then be welcomed by an on-screen voice but only to tell you to switch off your mobile and suggest you go and get another gallon of Coke. After that there are acres of commercials to plough

You Sick Of It?

through and the inevitable trailers that pass for today's Future Attractions.

One has to assume that when the Cineworld circuit announced pre-tax profts of £25.7m for the year 2007, against a loss of £7.7m in 2006, it was due to their taking over Carlton Screen Advertising. My local cinema is a Cineworld multiplex and the audience regularly has to sit through a half hour or more of ads and trailers. This, I assume, constitutes what we used to call a Full Supporting Programme and it would appear that Cineworld are making sure they get their money's worth out of their patrons. Having paid over the odds for a cinema ticket and perhaps something from the kiosk, why should cinemagoers have to endure all those commercials anyway? They could stay home and watch the ads on television.

Another cavil is why are film trailers for forthcoming attractions now so deadly dull? They tell you nothing and, like the ads, they are played at full blast and yet they fall short of what they are supposed to do, which is to make you want to come back next week. If filmmaking in general is not what it used to be,

then the art of the trailer is a lost one. We all remember the heyday of the film trailer when the star names and other legends came right at you in your seat. Every film, good or bad, was always Exciting!!, Colossal!!, Stupendous!! So that, even if the double-bill features were not up to scratch, there were always the trailers to look forward to… and the newsreel… and the short subject… or a cartoon maybe… all lost and gone now to today's lacklustre screen presentation.

If you want to see what trailers used to be like, check out any DVD of a vintage classic and the extras will invariably include the original trailer. I also recommend you seek out the DVD of *Grindhouse Trailer Classics* (Nucleus Films, £14.99, Cert 18), a two-hour trip into the gory, glory days of cult and exploitation cinema, in theatrical promos for a slew of titles you would find labelled under the sub-genre of Grindhouse. For a further taste of old trailers try to catch up with the two films that originally formed the *Grindhouse* double-bill of Quentin Tarantino's *Death Proof* and Robert Rodriguez's *Planet Terror* which includes hilarious spoof trailers of the same ilk. They're exciting, colossal

Marley Shelton in Robert Rodriquez's exploitation homage *Planet Terror*.

Cinemagoing: Aren't You Sick Of It?

Quentin Tarantino collaborated with Robert Rodriquez on the *Grindhouse* double-bill of movies designed to evoke the drive-in exploitation films of the 1950s and 60s.

ABC Film Review – yours for six old pence.

and stupendous and should be coming to a DVD player near you sooner or later.

Even the physical screening of a film can have its problems. Either the sound is too soft or too loud or, in one case, non-existent. With no staff around on the top floor of a multiplex, who do you ask? With only one projectionist buried somewhere in the middle of the building not keeping his or her eye on every screen, it's no wonder that the art of film exhibition has deteriorated. When the sound failed to come on at the beginning of a screening in a West End cinema, I had to ask a passing builder to tell someone several flights downstairs in the foyer that there was no sound. Eventually a member of staff appeared, mobile phone in hand, talking to the projection suite. The film is running, they claimed. Yes, but the amplifier had not been switched on.

Another experience involved seeing the first 20 minutes of *Wanted* condensed from widescreen to standard ratio. The racking was all wrong, and obviously so, from the beginning when the Universal logo was oval in shape and didn't fit the screen. James McAvoy and his co-stars all appeared like LS Lowry matchstick men. Eventually somebody took notice of the complaints made by the public and rectified it. But really, in these days of computer programming of projection facilities, it really shouldn't happen. At least, in the good old (bad

old?) days, if the film broke or the sound went off at the changeover, then we all whistled at the projectionist who would get the message immediately.

When I first went to the cinema in the 1950s, I was an ABC Minor and received one shilling and twopence (about six new pence) for Saturday Morning Pictures – six old pence for admission, six old pence for an ice cream and one old penny each way on the bus. When I went to the cinema with my parents, there was a sweet kiosk but for anything else, mainly ice cream in tubs, choc ices and Lyons Maid iced lollies and perhaps a small bag of Butterkist, you waited to be served in your seat. Remember... 'The girl with the tray is coming your way' and there was always a Flavour of the Month such as Blackcurrant Sundae. I believe studies were made to determine whether the girl with the ice cream tray sold more product walking from the front of the cinema (stage end) up the aisle to the back, or backwards down the aisle to the screen end.

When my parents went to the cinema by themselves in the evening, my treat was to receive on their return a tub of ice cream and a copy of the *ABC Film Review* (no relation). Now, with the Odeon Leicester Square charging record prices (their previews of *Mamma Mia!* cost £24 including goody bag – see Mansel Stimpson's 'So, What's New?' feature for more on this), is it any wonder that DVD sales are rocketing? For £24 I could get the train to Edinburgh and buy the DVD! Looking back to the 1950s, those certainly were the days when it was a pleasure to say 'let's go to the pictures'. But today...?

Bigger, Better and Back with a Vengeance

*Our current comic book heroes have been part and parcel of the cinemagoing experience for some 30 years. **Marshall Julius** pays tribute to the coming of age of the comic book superhero.*

The poster promised a lot: that we'd believe a man could fly. It seemed unlikely, given the poor quality of all previous superhero films, shows, cartoons and serials. But *Superman: The Movie* (1978) had a secret weapon: a director who respected the source material. As the comics themselves began to mature, so too did the movies they inspired, and in Richard Donner's hands, a film that could so easily have been self-consciously camp became instead an honest-to-goodness American epic. It was the film that made believers of us all, a genre-defining classic that set the standard for superhero cinema so high, it wasn't actually bettered until Christopher Nolan's *Batman Begins* (2005).

With its blend of humour, adventure and romance, *Superman: The Movie* established a framework for superflicks from which few have dared to deviate. Proving that there was an adult audience for superpowered entertainment, Donner's blockbuster guaranteed that everything that followed had a healthy budget. Though this ensured top notch visuals, it failed to rescue the following 20 years of superhero movies from directors who appeared self-conscious about their subject matter, keeping things light and jokey in order to hide both their embarrassment and the fact that they didn't understand the genre, and had no particular knowledge of the comics they were adapting.

The 1980s saw four additions to the franchise, although they were anything but super. *Superman II* (1980) was the best of a bad bunch, with *Superman III* (1983) dashing itself on the rocks of slapstick, *Supergirl* (1984) turning out tired and bland, and, with a reduced budget and zero confidence in the project, *Superman IV: The Quest for Peace* (1987) was just awful.

By the late 1980s, as Alan Moore's *Watchmen* and Frank Miller's *The Dark Knight Returns* proved that comic books could be every bit as sophisticated as any other art form, director Tim Burton turned his eye to *Batman* (1989). Heralded by months of expensive publicity, the movie played to capacity crowds, merchandising flew off the shelves and the world was a better place for all but a precious few who knew Bob

Christian Bale made his superhero debut in *Batman Begins*.

173

Tobey Maguire does whatever a spider can in *Spider-Man 2*.

Opposite top: Edward Norton meddles with mysterious forces in the 2008 version of *The Incredible Hulk*.

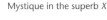

Rebecca Romijn-Stamos as Mystique in the superb *X2*.

Kane's creation too well to be palmed off with Burton's flashy interpretation which, though it looked the part, managed to trash the entire Batman myth. It just didn't feel right, and with each Batsequel the problems grew until Joel Schumacher's *Batman and Robin* (1997) choked the life out of the franchise.

Cut to the noughties, when the situation finally started to improve, firstly because a new generation of filmmakers joined the party. They were people raised on comic books who knew them back to front and loved them just as much as movies, and secondly because advances in special effects, particularly in the digital world, meant that anything could now be realistically portrayed on screen, no matter how outrageous. If the filmmakers could dream it, the special effects wizards could do it.

A hot property in Hollywood after making *The Usual Suspects* (1995), Bryan Singer kicked the decade off in style with *X-Men* (2000), the first decent Marvel Comics movie ever, and a solid introduction to a franchise that reached its full potential with the masterful *X2* (2003). Then

there was *Darkman* director Sam Raimi with a gripping, realistic *Spider-Man* (2002), although it was *Spider-Man 2* (2004) that truly captured the magic, a perfect, live action representation of the wall crawler and his complex private life.

Superhero movies were back with a vengeance, bigger and better than ever before, but nothing that we had seen up to that point prepared us for *Batman Begins* (2005). Thanks to *Memento* (2000) director Christopher Nolan and an amazing cast headed by Christian Bale, the Caped Crusader's epic live action losing streak finally came to an end. Blessed with an uncommonly smart screenplay – no surprise considering it was co-written by Nolan and *Blade* scribe David S Goyer – *Batman Begins* was a serious and entirely successful attempt to finally get inside Batman's head and explore his obsessions and the demons that drive him. For the first time on film, Bruce Wayne was a fully realised, well-rounded character. More grown up still was Nolan's 2008 sequel *The Dark Knight*, more a complex crime thriller than a straight action adventure, the first serious evolution of the superflick since Superman's inaugural 1978 adventure, and one of the most successful films ever made.

Recent examples of superhero cinema include the traditional but polished *Fantastic Four: Rise of the Silver Surfer* (2007), the neatly edgy *Iron Man* (2008), directed by Jon Favreau with Robert Downey Jr commanding in

the lead, elevating the project to must-see status; *The Incredible Hulk* (2008), a watchable reimagining of a story that director Ang Lee overcooked with his more cerebral *Hulk* (2003); and *Superhero Movie* (2008), a cheap, cheerful and surprisingly watchable spoof, although not nearly as funny as earlier comic effort *Mystery Men* (1999).

Today, thanks to Sam Raimi, Bryan Singer, David Goyer, Christopher Nolan and a handful of others, the superhero movie is finally coming of age, no longer restricted to the action adventure genre. These days they are just as likely to be funny (namely 2006's *My Super Ex-Girlfriend* and 2008's *Hancock*), scary (the *Blade* and *Hellboy* series), animated (2004 Pixar sensation *The Incredibles*) or darkly dramatic (*The Dark Knight*). One day soon, we may even see as much variety in superhero movies as we do in superhero comics.

As for the future, expect a full slate of Batsequels, more Supermen, Iron Men, a new Punisher, movies focusing on X-Men characters Magneto and Wolverine, blockbuster vehicles for Green Lantern, Ant Man, Flash, Green Arrow and Wonder Woman, and, from *300* director Zack Snyder, the feature adaptation that nobody believed was possible, *Watchmen* (2009).

Rather than running out of juice, the superhero genre is actually just beginning to realise its true potential. Step back because great things are coming.

Christian Bale and Heath Ledger in *The Dark Knight*.

Film It Again, Sam!

It seems that today's cinema comprises mainly remakes of classic movies, sequels to box-office blockbusters and those ever-continuing series, from 007 to Carry On. However, says **Michael Darvell**, *it has been ever thus.*

Will Smith walks a well-trodden path in *I Am Legend*.

Nothing succeeds like success, so they say, or in the film industry, nothing succeeds like excess. And, according to film producers, you can't have too much of a good thing, especially if it has made a mint of money at the box office: hence the remakes and sequels industry. In this past year alone we have had remakes of *3:10 to Yuma*, *Halloween* and *I Am Legend*, plus the umpteenth version of *Macbeth* and another version of *The Magic Flute*. Sequels that appeared over the last year include *The Bourne Ultimatum, Die Hard 4.0, Elizabeth: the Golden Age, Harry Potter and the Order of the Phoenix, Rambo, Rush Hour 3, St Trinian's, Asterix at the Olympic Games, The Chronicles of Narnia: Prince Caspian, Diary of the Dead, The Incredible Hulk, Indiana Jones and the Kingdom of the Crystal Skull, National Treasure: Book of Secrets, The Mummy: Tomb of the Dragon Emperor* and *Aliens vs Predator: Requiem*. This last title is the sequel to two crossbred movie series, *Aliens* and *Predator*. Presumably with a title like *Requiem*, it means that this is the final chapter and that there won't be any more... or will there? If the producer thinks another sequel will make money, then off we go again.

This is quite a cross section of film titles and the original films were all once successful the first time around. But how do the remakes fare? It's difficult to imagine anybody improving on Delmer Daves' original *3:10 to Yuma* from 1957 or John Carpenter's 1978 *Halloween*, even if your name happens to be Rob Zombie, director of the 2007 remake. Among the sequels *The Bourne Ultimatum* was inevitable, as there were already three books available for filming. The same goes for the Harry Potter films which have a finite life with seven books. *The Chronicles of Narnia* will carry on until all the books are filmed (cf *The Lord of the Rings*). *I Am Legend* is a remake of *The Last Man on Earth* (1964) with Vincent Price as the sole survivor of a worldwide plague. It was remade as *The Omega Man* in 1971 with Charlton Heston and this year resurfaced under the title of the original Richard Matheson novel on which it was based. Starring Will Smith, this has been so successful that a sequel is planned!

As for the rest, time must surely be running out for the *Rush Hour*

Malcolm McDowell follows in the footsteps of Donald Pleasence in Rob Zombie's remake of *Halloween*.

films, although there seems to be no end to George A Romero's *Day of the Dead* sequels, which have never eclipsed the original film. Did we need another *Hulk* so soon after Ang Lee's none too popular effort? Probably, yes, because this year's film is more like the Marvel comic hero and with better, scarier action sequences. *Die Hard 4.0* was an improvement on the previous sequel, so has earned its place in cinema history. Dare it go for five? *Elizabeth: The Golden Age* came a cropper and seems to have been as bad as the original *Elizabeth* was good. Wrong move, there, as it probably didn't need a sequel.

St Trinian's tried to reinvent the Ealing Studios comedy style but failed miserably. Only the 1954 original was any good in this series, with Alastair Sim giving two great comedy performances. The earlier sequels (*Blue Murder, Great Train Robbery, Pure Hell* and *Wildcats*) could not match the original, so to try and revive the genre decades later was folly indeed.

It was nearly 20 years since the last *Indiana Jones* movie, so it was a risk to bring Harrison Ford back at pensionable age to recreate the action hero once more, but he just about managed to make it work without a walking frame and an oxygen tent and it scooped up many millions at the box office, which is all that matters.

Remakes are nothing new but most of the time you wonder why they bother. If they get it right first time around, why remake a film, as you cannot improve on a classic. What possessed Gus Van Sant to reshoot Hitchcock's *Psycho*, frame by frame, with Bernard Herrmann's score, but in colour, I cannot begin to fathom. Hitchcock's *Rear Window* was even remade for television with the paralysed Christopher Reeve in the James Stewart role. It had a certain interest because

of its star, but was not a patch on the Hitchcock. Of course Hitchcock wasn't averse to remaking his own films. *The Man Who Knew Too Much* first appeared in 1934 but Hitch returned to it in 1956. Both versions have their moments although they are entirely different except in basic plot points.

Hitchcock's *The Lady Vanishes* (1938) was also reshot in 1979 but not generally made welcome. Hitchcock also didn't remake his version of *The 39 Steps* (1935) but many others have: unfortunately neither Ralph Thomas's 1959 version with Kenneth More and Taina Elg, nor Don Sharp's 1978 version with Robert Powell and Karen Dotrice could match Robert Donat and Madeleine Carroll in Hitchcock's original which has now been adapted very successfully for the stage and is playing in live theatres all over the world. BBC Television is filming a new version with Rupert Penry Jones as Richard Hannay, to be shown at Christmas 2008, which only goes to show that you can't keep a good remake down.

Some properties seem made for a remake over and over again. *The Shop Around the Corner*, Ernst Lubitsch's charming rom-com with James Stewart and Margaret Sullavan, based on the play *Parfumerie* by Miklos Laszlo, first appeared in 1940. It was then remade in 1949 as *In the Good Old Summertime*, a musical for Judy Garland and Van Johnson. Then it reappeared as *You've Got Mail* in 1998 with Tom Hanks and Meg Ryan. In between it found time to be turned into a stage musical, *She Loves Me*, with Barbara Cook and Daniel Massey. The London stage revival a few years ago starred Ruthie Henshall and John Gordon Sinclair.

Talking of musicals, *A Star is Born* began life as *What Price Hollywood?* with Constance Bennett as a

The sixth *St Trinian's* film was a remake of Ealing's classic original.

Bruce Willis was back for yet more in *Die Hard 4.0*.

young actress finding success in the movie industry, and directed by George Cukor in 1932. It then appeared as *A Star is Born* in 1937, with William A Wellman directing Janet Gaynor. In 1954 Cukor came back to the subject and directed Judy Garland in another version which ultimately became the best film ever made about Hollywood. In 1976 Barbra Streisand took the lead in Frank Pierson's version which moved the subject from the movies to the music business. Garland's film, however, remains the definitive version.

George Cukor again: his 1939 film of Clare Boothe Luce's play *The Women* was one of the funniest comedies of its time, a tale of divorced women played by an all-female cast including Norma Shearer, Joan Crawford and Rosalind Russell. Less successful was the 1956 musical remake, *The Opposite Sex*, with June Allyson, Dolores Gray and Joan Collins. It has now been remade again this year under its original title with Meg Ryan, Annette Bening, Eva Mendes and Bette Midler.

Classic texts are always ripe to be remade. There have been three versions of *Little Women*, in 1933, 1949 and 1994. Similarly *Great Expectations* has appeared three times in 1934, 1946 1998, but it is the middle version by David Lean we all remember. *King Solomon's Mines* has been made three times, as has *The Four Feathers*, beginning in 1929. The most famous version from 1939 was directed by Zoltan Korda who, in 1955, remade it as *Storm Over the Nile* and plundered the action footage from his earlier, better version.

The Maltese Falcon is a much filmed property but it's not the first film version of Dashiell Hammett's novel that we remember. Roy Del Ruth directed Ricardo Cortez and Bebe Daniels in the 1931 version. Then, in 1936, William Dieterle had Bette Davis and Warren William star in another version of the same story, re-titled as *Satan Met a Lady*. Finally, in 1941 John Huston's definitive version with Humphrey Bogart, Mary Astor, Peter Lorre and Sydney Greenstreet appeared under the book's original title.

There are many remakes and sequels on the horizon in the near future. I trust we have had all we need from the *Pirates of the Caribbean* triple-bill, and the same goes for *Ocean's 11* and its followers. There surely won't be an *Ocean's 14?* Maybe not, but we can look forward (or not) to such remakes as another *Papillon*, *Robin Hood*, *The Rocky Horror Picture Show*, *The Seven Samurai*, *The Day the Earth Stood Still*, *Rosemary's Baby*, *Clash of the Titans*, *The Secret Life of Walter Mitty*, *Carousel*, *Jesus Christ Superstar*, *Meatballs* and even, already, *The Lives of Others*. Oh, and Quentin Tarantino has begun shooting a remake of *The Dirty Dozen*, to be called *Inglorious Bastards* for a June 2009 release.

On the sequels front look out for *RoboCop 3-D*, *Resident Evil 4*, *Iron Man 2*, *Spawn 2*, *I Robot 2*, *Wanted 2*, *Beverly Hills Cop 4*, *Sin City 2* and *3*, *National Treasure 3*, *Scream 4*, *Alvin and the Chipmunks 2*, *Toy Story 3* and *Shrek Goes Fourth* among many others. You can be sure that Hollywood will never run out of ideas for films, not while they still have their back catalogue to draw on.

The World View

Mansel Stimpson looks at the most recent crop of film
releases not in the English language.

In the absence of any desire to challenge the convention, I will lead off this survey of the year's foreign releases by listing what I regard as the ten best. Right at the top of my list is the remarkable documentary *Ghosts of Cité Soleil* made in Haiti. It's unique in capturing both a social and personal tragedy that developed and took shape while the cameras were running and it deserves a place in cinema history. The other nine titles, wide ranging in their sources, are all dramas: *Libero* from Italy, Ang Lee's *Lust, Caution*, Pascale Ferran's *Lady Chatterley*, the devastating *Flanders*, André Téchiné's *The Witnesses*, *El Violín* from Mexico, *Under The Bombs* filmed in Beirut, *The Italian* which, despite the title, comes from Russia and *The Edge of Heaven* which takes place both in Germany and in Turkey.

There are also plenty of runners-up fighting for a place on this list, one of them being the French thriller *Tell No-one* and another the Spanish drama of the supernatural *The*

Orphanage. Both did very well at the box-office in this country and because of that and also because of the earlier success of the Edith Piaf bio pic *La Vie en Rose* there has been a growing tendency to release more popular-style foreign movies here. It's more usual to find art-house offerings geared towards audiences seeking something thought-provoking or even challenging but now we are getting quite a number of genre pictures.

In particular we have had rom-coms from France but the likes of *Priceless*, *I Do* and *Change of Address* have only served to prove that foreign takes on the genre are not necessarily better – Julie Delpy's *Two Days in Paris* was probably the best of a rather disappointing bunch. We have also had what can be thought of as a follow-up to the success of *Black Book* in the form of films from Europe that, technically adroit, take serious historical events but belittle them by treating them as popular-style melodramas. If you admire Louis Malle's *Au Revoir les Enfants* or *Lacombe Lucien* or even Herbert Wilcox's *Odette*, it's difficult to feel that *Female Agents* (dealing with wartime resistance agents) and *Children of Glory* (portraying the Hungarian Uprising of

Ghosts of Cité Soleil: Life and death in Haiti caught in Asger Leth's extraordinary documentary.

The Kite Runner:
A serious subject,
a popular hit.

Karl Markovics
strikes a difficult
bargain with his
captors in
Die Fälscher [The
Counterfeiters].

1956) are adequate treatments of their subjects. Imperfect but much better was *The Kite Runner* which proved commercially successful despite or because of the way in which the happy ending indulges the audience. The German prisoner of war drama *The Counterfeiters* was arguably nearer the mark, while of Sergei Bodrov's *Mongol* it could be said that, if unpersuasive as history, it did at least match the epic blood and thunder and yet more blood of the Hollywood action movies it was seeking to emulate.

Yet another area in which commercially-orientated foreign movies were to be found in British cinemas stemmed from the enterprise of Dogwoof Pictures. The company has set up a subsidiary, Polish Connection, to distribute films from that country, which will have pleased the many Poles now residing in England. It was just a pity that for the most part the standard of these films was not higher. In contrast – and it has been a very marked contrast – we have also been offered many titles from what counts as avant-garde cinema. Not all of them were extreme examples of the genre but most audiences would find them hard going. Most striking here were the attempts – successful with some – to promote as major directors such figures as Apachatpong Weerasethakul (*Syndromes and a Century*) and Tsai Ming-Liang (*The Wayward Cloud* and *I Don't Want to Sleep Alone*). All of these films contained striking images but, as also to some extent with Bahman Ghobadi's *Half Moon* and Jia Zhangke's *Still Life*, one felt that the artiness was allowed to override the desirability of involving the audience in an effective narrative. When given a season at the National Film Theatre, Apachatpong was rechristened 'Joe' but even then I doubt that many other than eggheads found it easy to respond positively to the experience of watching his films.

Lest the above should suggest that I am unable to enjoy cinema that is adventurous and demanding, I should add that for those ready to face challenges of this kind there were at least four titles in this category which, just

El Violín featured the remarkable acting debut of octogenarian Don Ángel Tavira.

outside my Top Ten, struck me as well worth investigating: I refer to Carlos Reygadas's supremely beautiful *Silent Light*, Esteban Sapir's homage to silent cinema in *La Antena*, Roy Andersson's continuing exploration of life's painful comedy in *You, the Living* and Park Chan-wook's totally off-beat *I'm A Cyborg*.

With the widening number of releases, it is impossible to touch here on the full range of foreign cinema presented to us during the year. I haven't, for example, managed to mention either *The Diving Bell and the Butterfly* or *The Band's Visit* both of which have their passionate admirers. Nevertheless all releases are covered in our Releases of the Year section. Sadly, a large number of them were less good than one had hoped. Although they had their supporters, I myself would include in this category the latest works of Resnais (*Private Fears in Public Places*), Rivette (*Don't Touch the Axe*), Hou (*Flight of the Red Balloon*) and Claude Miller (*A Secret*). Altogether more interesting were three films that I don't feel quite belong in this context: the wonderful documentary *I for India*, a touchingly honest portrayal of the director's family who came to England from India (English is the main language here) and two animated films from France. *Persepolis* used that form to tell of life in Iran but was mainly seen here in a dubbed print and Michel Ocelot's *Azur & Asmar: The Princes' Quest* was released only in a dubbed version although in its case the character of the piece, its beauty and its wisdom survived largely intact.

In surveying this period it would be wrong not to make mention of the continuing impact of work from Romania. Following the breakthrough of *The Death of Mr Lazarescu* released here in July 2006, we had three further films from that country which were of substantial interest. The most famous is Cristian Mungiu's *4 Months, 3 Weeks, 2 Days*, a drama about abortion which is also part of a planned series of films looking at life in Romania during the 1980s, but I actually prefer Corneliu Porumboiu's *12.08 East of Bucharest* (another runner–up to my Top Ten) which combines humour with serious comment on how history is remembered. Less good but very effective in parts was *California Dreamin' (Endless)* by the late Cristian Nemescu.

If length was the undoing of *California Dreamin'*, it was more confusion of narrative that

Tuncel Kurtiz, another remarkable older actor, appeared in *The Edge of Heaven*.

A debut performance of sheer perfection by Tang Wei in *Lust, Caution*.

Gérard Depardieu has no need to hide behind those glasses in *The Singer*.

marred another often strikingly long movie, the French *Couscous*. But length, albeit hazardous in any film that lasts well over two hours, did not weaken the impact of the longest films in my Top Ten, *Lady Chatterley* and *Lust, Caution*. As it happens, both performed disappointingly at the box-office here. I would have predicted the opposite for Pascale Ferran's beautifully judged take on DH Lawrence but possibly younger audiences regarded the material as too old hat while for many older people dislike of sexual explicitness in films discouraged them from

going. There was strong sex too in *Lust, Caution* which being the work of Ang Lee was marketed widely but without stress on its being a sub-titled film. Those who were looking for the sex scenes and for violent action as the *raison d'être* of this tale of assassination seemed to be unready for the depth and subtlety of the moral drama at the heart of the story: a shame because this is quite possibly Lee's best film.

Several of the other titles in my Top Ten suffered from very limited exposure for reasons discussed in my article So What's New? written for this annual. I very much hope that readers will make a point of looking up my comments on these titles in the Releases section since there is no space to elaborate further here. There is, however, just enough room to end with a word about performances. Having started off with my Top Ten films, I end with my choice of top actor and top actress. In the former category, despite strong competition from unexpected sources – the non-professional octogenarian Don Ángel Tavira in *El Violín* and Tuncel Kurtiz in Fatih Akin's *The Edge of Heaven* – my choice has to fall on the veteran Gérard Depardieu. Although the second half of the film in which he appears fails to sustain itself, his touching performance in *The Singer* ranks with his finest work. And actress? Well here we go to the other extreme: Wei Tang who is the female lead in *Lust, Caution* had never made a film before, but her performance is absolutely extraordinary and unmatched by any I have seen during the year.

Awards and Festivals

The 80th American Academy of Motion Picture Arts and Sciences Awards ('The Oscars') and Nominations, Kodak Theatre, Los Angeles, 24 February 2008

▶▶ **Best Film**: *No Country for Old Men*. Nominations: *Atonement, Juno, Michael Clayton, There Will Be Blood*

▶▶ **Best Director**: Ethan Coen and Joel Coen for *No Country for Old Men*. Nominations: Paul Thomas Anderson for *There Will Be Blood*; Tony Gilroy for *Michael Clayton*; Jason Reitman for *Juno*; Julian Schnabel for *Le Scaphandre et le papillon (The Diving Bell and the Butterfly)*

▶▶ **Best Actor**: Daniel Day-Lewis for *There Will Be Blood*. Nominations: George Clooney for *Michael Clayton*; Johnny Depp for *Sweeney Todd: The Demon Barber of Fleet Stree;*, Tommy Lee Jones for *In the Valley of Elah*; Viggo Mortensen for *Eastern Promises*

▶▶ **Best Actress**: Marion Cotillard for *La Môme*. Nominations: Cate Blanchett for *Elizabeth: The Golden Age;* Julie Christie for *Away from Her;*

Laura Linney for *The Savages;* Ellen Page for *Juno*

▶▶ **Best Supporting Actor**: Javier Bardem for *No Country for Old Men*. Nominations: Casey Affleck for *The Assassination of Jesse James by the Coward Robert Ford*; Philip Seymour Hoffman for *Charlie Wilson's War*; Hal Holbrook for *Into the Wild*; Tom Wilkinson for *Michael Clayton*

▶▶ **Best Supporting Actress**: Tilda Swinton for *Michael Clayton*. Nominations: Cate Blanchett for *I'm Not There*; Ruby Dee for *American Gangster*; Saoirse Ronan for *Atonement*; Amy Ryan for *Gone Baby Gone*

▶▶ **Best Animated Feature**: *Happy Feet*. Nominations: *Cars; Monster House*

▶▶ **Best Original Screenplay**: Diablo Cody, for *Juno*. Nominations: Nancy Oliver, for *Lars and the Real Girl*; Tony Gilroy for *Michael Clayton*; Brad Bird, Jan Pinkava and Jim Capobianco for *Ratatouille*; Tamara Jenkins for *The Savages*

▶▶ **Best Adapted Screenplay**: Joel Coen and Ethan Coen for *No Country for Old Men*. Nominations: Christopher Hampton for *Atonemen;*, Sarah Polley for *Away from Her*; Ronald Harwood for *Le Scaphandre et le papillon (The Diving Bell and the Butterfly)*; Paul Thomas Anderson for *There Will Be Blood*

▶▶ **Best Cinematography**: Robert Elswit for *There Will Be Blood*. Nominations: Roger Deakins for *The Assassination of Jesse James by the Coward Robert Ford*; Seamus McGarvey for *Atonement*; Roger Deakins for *No Country for Old Men*; Janusz Kaminski for *Le Scaphandre et le papillon (The Diving Bell and the Butterfly)*

▶▶ **Best Editing**: Christopher Rouse, for *The Bourne Ultimatum*. Nominations: Juliette Welfling for *Le Scaphandre et le papillon (The Diving Bell and the Butterfly)*; Jay Cassidy for *Into the Wild*, Ethan Coen and Joel Coen for *No Country for Old Men*; Dylan

Ethan and Joel Coen pictured during the filming of the Oscar-winning *No Country for Old Men*.

Philip Seymour Hoffman and Albert Finney in *Before the Devil Knows You're Dead.*

Tichenor for *There Will Be Blood*

>> **Best Original Score**: Dario Marianelli for *Atonement.* Nominations: Alberto Iglesias for *The Kite Runner;* James Newton Howard for *Michael Clayton;,* Michael Giacchino for *Ratatouille;* Marco Beltrami for *3:10 to Yuma*

>> **Best Original Song**: Glen Hansard and Markéta Irglová for 'Falling Slowly' from *Once.* Nominations: Jamal Joseph, Charles Mack and Tevin Thomas for 'Raise It Up' from *August Rush;* Alan Menken and Stephen Schwartz for 'Happy Working Song' from *Enchanted;* Alan Menken and Stephen Schwartz for 'So Close' from *Enchanted;* Alan Menken and Stephen Schwartz for 'That's How You Know', from *Enchanted*

>> **Best Art Direction:** Dante Ferretti and Francesca Lo Schiavo for *Sweeney Todd: The Demon Barber of Fleet Street.* Nominations: Arthur Max, Beth A Rubino for *American Gangster;* Sarah Greenwood and Katie Spencer for *Atonement;* Dennis Gassner and Anna Pinnock for *The Golden Compass;* Jack Fisk and Jim Erickson for *There Will Be Blood*

>> **Best Costume Design:** Alexandra Byrne for *Elizabeth: The Golden Age.* Nominations: Albert Wolsky for *Across the Universe;* Jacqueline Durran for *Atonemen;,* Marit Allen for *La Môme;* Colleen Atwood for *Sweeney Todd:*

The Demon Barber of Fleet Street

>> **Best Sound**: Scott Millan, David Parker and Kirk Francis for *The Bourne Ultimatum.* Nominations: Skip Lievsay, Craig Berkey, Greg Orloff and Peter F Kurland for *No Country for Old Men;* Randy Thom, Michael Semanick and Doc Kane for *Ratatouille;* Paul Massey, David Giammarco and Jim Stuebe for *3:10 to Yuma;* Kevin O'Connell, Greg P Russell and Peter J Devlin for *Transformers*

>> **Best Sound Editing**: Karen M Baker and Per Hallberg for *The Bourne Ultimatum.* Nominations: Skip Lievsay for *No Country for Old Men;* Randy Thom and Michael Silvers for *Ratatouille;* Matthew Wood for *There Will Be Blood;* Mike Hopkins and Ethan Van der Ryn for *Transformers*

>> **Best Makeup**: Didier Lavergne and Jan Archibald for *La Môme.* Nominations: Rick Baker and Kazuhiro Tsuji for *Norbit;* Ve Neill and Martin Samuel for *Pirates of the Caribbean: At World's End*

>> **Best Visual Effects**: Michael L Fink, Bill Westenhofer, Ben Morris and Trevor Wood for *The Golden Compass.* Nominations: John Knoll, Hal T Hickel, Charlie Gibson and John Frazier for *Pirates of the Caribbean: At World's End;* Scott Farrar, Scott Benza, Russell Earl and John Frazier for *Transformers*

>> **Best Animated Feature Film:** *Ratatouille* by Brad Bird. Nominations:

Persepolis by Vincent Paronnaud and Marjane Satrapi; *Surf's Up* by Ash Brannon and Chris Buck

>> **Best Animated Short Film**: *Peter & the Wolf* by Suzie Templeton and Hugh Welchman. Nominations: *Même les pigeons vont au paradis* by Samuel Tourneux and Vanesse Simon; *I Met the Walrus* by Josh Raskin; *Madame Tutli-Putli* by Chris Lavis and Maciek Szczerbowski; *Moya Lyubov* by Aleksandr Petrov

>> **Best Live Action Short Film**: *Le Mozart des pickpockets* by Philippe Pollet-Villard. Nominations: *Om natten* by Christian E Christiansen and Louise Vesth; *Supplente* by Andrea Jublin; *Tanghi argentini* by Guy Thys and Anja Daelemans; *The Tonto Woman* by Daniel Barber and Matthew Brown

>> **Best Documentary Feature**: *Taxi to the Dark Side* by Alex Gibney and Eva Orner. Nominations: *No End in Sight* by Charles Ferguson and Audrey Marrs; *Operation Homecoming: Writing the Wartime Experience* by Richard Robbins; *Sicko* by Michael Moore and Meghan O'Hara; *War Dance* by Andrea Nix and Sean Fine

>> **Best Documentary Short**: *Freeheld* by Cynthia Wade and Vanessa Roth. Nominations: *La Corona* by Amanda Micheli and Isabel Vega; *Salim Baba* by Tim Sternberg and Francisco Bello; *Sari's Mother* by James Longley

>> **Best Foreign Language Film**: *Die Fälscher* (Austria). Nominations: *Beaufort* (Israel); *Mongol* (Kazakhstan); *Katyn* (Poland); *12* (Russia)

>> **Honorary Award**: Robert Boyle

The 8th American Film Institute Awards: 16 December 2007

AFI Movies of the Year: Official Selections

▶ *Before the Devil Knows You're Dead*
▶ *Le Scaphandre et le papillon (The Diving Bell and the Butterfly)*
▶ *Into the Wild*
▶ *Juno*
▶ *Knocked Up*
▶ *Michael Clayton*
▶ *No Country For Old Men*
▶ *Ratatouille*
▶ *The Savages*
▶ *There Will Be Blood*

The 49th Australian Film Institute Awards: 6 December 2007

» Best Film: *Romulus, My Father*
» Best Actor: Eric Bana for *Romulus, My Father*
» Best Actress: Joan Chen for *The Home Song Stories*
» Best Supporting Actor: Marton Csokas for *Romulus, My Father*
» Best Supporting Actress: Emma Booth for *Clubland*
» Best Director: Tony Ayres for *The Home Song Stories*
» Best Screenplay: Tony Ayres for *The Home Song Stories*
» Best Production Design: Melinda Doring for *The Home Song Stories*
» Best Cinematography: *Nigel Bluck* for *The Home Song Stories*
» Best Sound: Emma Bortignon, Doron Kipen and Philippe Decrausaz for *Noise*
» Best Editing: Denise Haratzi for *The Home Song Stories*
» Best Visual Effects: Andrew Hellen, Dave Morley, Jason Bath and John Cox for *Rogue*
» Best Music: Anthony Partos for *The Home Song Stories*
» Best Costumes: *Cappi Ireland* for *The Home Song Stories*
» Best Documentary: Sally Regan and Anna Broinowski for *Forbidden Lie$*
» Best Direction in a Documentary: Bruce Petty for *Global Haywire*
» Best Short Fiction Film: Anthony Maras and Kent Smith for *Spike Up*
» Best Screenplay in a Short Fiction Film: David Michôd for *Crossbow*
» Best Cinematography in a Documentary: Malcolm Ludgate, Joel Peterson and Scott Carrithers for *Cuttlefish - The Brainy Bunch*
» Best Sound in a Documentary: Sam Petty for *Global Haywire*
» Best Editing in a Documentary: Vanessa Milton and Alison Croft for *Forbidden Lie$*
» Best Short Animation: Justine Kerrigan and Paul McDermott for *The Girl Who Swallowed Bees*
» Outstanding Achievement in a Short Film Screen Craft: Mark Lapwood for *Eclipse* (for the cinematography)
» AFI International Award for Best Actor: *Dominic Purcell* for *Prison Break*
» AFI International Award for Best Actress: Rose Byrne for *Damages*
» Raymond Longford Award

Awarded to: David Hannay
» Byron Kennedy Award Awarded to: Curtis Levy
» News Limited Readers' Choice Award: Eric Bana
» Excellence in Filmmaking: Jill Bilcock

The 58th Berlin International Film Festival: 17 February 2008

» Golden Bear for Best Film: *Tropa de elite/The Elite Squad* by José Padilha
» Silver Bear, Grand Jury Prize: *Standard Operating Procedure* by Errol Morris
» Silver Bear, Best Director: Paul Thomas Anderson for *There Will Be Blood*
» Silver Bear, Best Actor: Reza Najie in *Avaze Gonjeshk-ha* by Majid Majidi
» Silver Bear, Best Actress: Sally Hawkins for *Happy-Go-Lucky* by Mike Leigh
» Silver Bear for Best Music: Jonny Greenwood for *There Will Be Blood* by Paul Thomas Anderson
» Silver Bear for Best Script: Wang Xiaoshuai for *Zuo You/In Love We Trust*
» Alfred Bauer Prize: *Lake Tahoe* by Fernando Eimbcke

» The Best First Feature Award: *Asyl – Park and Love Hotel* by Kumasaka Izuruanaja
» Golden Bear for Best Short Film: *O zi buna de plaja* by Bogdan Mustata (Romania)
» Silver Bear for Best Short Film: *Udedh bun* by Siddharth Sinha (India)
» Prix UIP: *Frankie* by Darren Thornton (Ireland)
» DAAD Short Film Award: *B teme* by Olga Popova (Russian Federation)
» Short Film, Special Mentions: *Superfície* by Rui Xavier; *RGB XYZ* by David O'Reilly
❯ Prizes of the Generation Kplus Children's Jury:
    » Crystal Bear for Best Feature Film: *Buddha Collapsed Out Of Shame* by Hana Makhmalbaf
    » Special Mention: *The Ten Lives of Titanic the Cat* by Grethe Bøe
    » Crystal Bear for Best Short Film: *Nana* by Warwick Thornton
    » Special Mention: *New Boy* by Steph Green
❯ Prizes of the Generation 14plus Youth Jury:
    » Crystal Bear for Best Feature Film: *The Black Balloon* by Elissa Down
    » Special Mention: *Sita Sings the Blues* by Nina Paley

Tropa de Elite [*The Elite Squad*], winner of the Golden Bear for Best Film in Berlin.

Viggo Mortensen and Vincent Cassel in *Eastern Promises*. Awards for this film included numerous Genies and the Golden Globe for Best Motion Picture.

▶▶ **Crystal Bear for Best Short Film**: *Café com Leite* by Daniel Ribeiro
▶▶ **Special Mention**: *Take 3* by Roseanne Liang
▶ **Generation Kplus International Jury's Deutsche Kinderhilfswerk**:
▶▶ **Grand Prix for Best Feature Film**: *GO WEST! A Lucky Luke Adventure* by Olivier Jean-Marie
▶▶ **Special Mention**: *Mutum* by Sandra Kogut
▶ **Deutsches Kinderhilfswerk Special Prize**: *My Uncle Loved the Colour Yellow* by Mats Olof Olsson
▶▶ **Special Mention**: *POST!* by Christian Asmussen and Matthias Bruhn
▶ **Ecumenical Jury Prize**:
▶▶ **Forum**: *Il y a longtemps que je t'aime…| I've Loved You So Long…* by Philippe Claudel
▶▶ **Special Mention**: *Zuo You/ In Love We Trust* by Wang Xiaoshuai
▶▶ **Forum**: *Corridor #8* by Boris Despodov
▶▶ **Panorama**: *Boy A* by John Crowley
▶ **FIPRESCI Prizes**:
▶▶ **Competition**: *Lake Tahoe* by Fernando Eimbcke
▶▶ **Panorama**: *Rusalka (Mermaid)* by Anna Melikian
▶▶ **Forum**: *Shahida – Brides of Allah (Brides of Allah)* by von Natalie Assouline
▶▶ **German Arthouse Cinemas Guild**:

Restless by Amos Kollek
▶ **CICAE** (international confederation of art cinemas):
▶▶ **Panorama**: *Revanche* by Götz Spielmann
▶▶ **Forum**: *United Red Army* by Wakamatsu Koji
▶▶ **Label Europa Cinemas**: *Revanche* by Götz Spielmann
▶▶ **Gay Teddy Bear Award, Best Feature**: *Be Like Others* by Tanaz Eshaghian
▶▶ **Gay Teddy Bear Award, Best Documentary**: *Football Under Cover* by David Assmann and Ayat Najafi
▶▶ **Manfred Salzgeber Prize**: (to a film 'that broadens the boundaries of cinema today'): *Megane (Glasses)* by Naoko Ogigami
▶▶ **Special Mention**: *Improvvisamente l'inverno scorso/Suddenly, Last Winter* by Gustav Hofer and Luca Ragazzi
▶▶ **Peace Film Prize**: *Drifter* by Sebastian Heidinger
▶▶ **Special Mention**: *Lostage/Star-Crossed* by Bettina Eberhard
Panorama Audience Award:
▶▶ **The Berliner Morgenpost Readers' Jury Award**: (for a film in the Competition section): *Il y a longtemps que je t'aime…| I've Loved You So Long…* by Philippe Claudel
▶▶ **The Siegessäule Readers' Jury Award**: (for a film with gay content): *Be Like Others* by Tanaz Eshagian
▶▶ **The Tagesspiegel Readers' Jury**:

(for a film in the Forum): *God Man Dog* by Singing Chen
▶▶ **Honorary Golden Bear**: Francesco Rosi
▶▶ **International Competition Jury**: Costa-Gavras (president), Uli Hanisch, Diane Kruger, Walter Murch, Alexander Rodnyansky, Shu Qi

The 2008 British Academy of Film and Television Arts Awards ('BAFTAs'), Royal Opera House, Covent Garden, London, 10 February 2008

▶▶ **Best Film**: Tim Bevan, Eric Fellner and Paul Webster, for *Atonement*
▶▶ **David Lean Award for Direction**: Joel Coen and Ethan Coen for *No Country for Old Men*
▶▶ **Best Original Screenplay**: Diablo Cody for *Juno*
▶▶ **Best Adapted Screenplay**: Ronald Harwood for *Le Scaphandre et le papillon (The Diving Bell and the Butterfly)*
▶▶ **Best Actor**: Daniel Day-Lewis for *There Will Be Blood*
▶▶ **Best Actress**: Marion Cotillard for *La Vie en Rose*
▶▶ **Best Supporting Actor**: Javier Bardem for *No Country for Old Men*
▶▶ **Best Supporting Actress**: Tilda Swinton for *Michael Clayton*
▶▶ **Best Cinematography**: Roger Deakins for *No Country for Old Men*
▶▶ **Best Production Design**: Sarah Greenwood and Katie Spencer for *Atonement*
▶▶ **Best Editing**: Christopher Rouse for *The Bourne Ultimatum*
▶▶ **Anthony Asquith Award for Film Music**: Christopher Gunning for *La Vie en Rose*
▶▶ **Best Costumes**: Marit Allen for *La Vie en Rose*
▶▶ **Best Sound**: Kirk Francis, Scott Millan, David Parker, Karen Baker Landers and Per Hallberg for *The Bourne Ultimatum*
▶▶ **Best Special Visual Effects**: Michael Fink, Bill Westenhofer, Ben Morris and Trevor Wood for *The Golden Compass*
▶▶ **Best Make Up/Hair**: Jan Archibald and Didier Lavergne for *La Vie en Rose*
▶▶ **Alexander Korda Award for Best British Film**: Mark Herbert and Shane Meadows for *This is England*

▸▸ **Best Foreign Language Film:** Quirin Berg, Max Wiedemann and Florian Henckel von Donnersmarck for *The Lives of Others*

▸▸ **Best Short Film:** Diarmid Scrimshaw and Paddy Considine for *Dog Altogether*

▸▸ **Best Animated Feature:** Brad Bird for *Ratatouille*

▸▸ **Best Animated Short:** Jo Allen and Luis Cook for *The Pearce Sisters*

▸▸ **Carl Foreman Award for the Most Promising Newcomer:** Matt Greenhalgh (writer) for *Control*

▸▸ **Orange Rising Star Award:** Shia LaBeouf

▸▸ **Michael Balcon Award for Outstanding British Contribution to Cinema:** Barry Wilkinson

▸▸ **BAFTA Fellowship:** Anthony Hopkins

The 28th Canadian Film Awards ('Genies'), Toronto, 3 March 2008

▸▸ **Best Film:** *Away from Her,* by Daniel Iron, Simone Urdl and Jennifer Weiss

▸▸ **Best Director:** Sarah Polley for *Away from Her*

▸▸ **Best Actor:** Gordon Pinsent for *Away from Her*

▸▸ **Best Actress:** Julie Christie for *Away from Her*

▸▸ **Best Supporting Actor:** Armin Mueller-Stahl for *Eastern Promises*

▸▸ **Best Supporting Actress:** Kristen Thomson for *Away from Her*

▸▸ **Best Original Screenplay:** Steven Knight for *Eastern Promises*

▸▸ **Best Adapted Screenplay:** Sarah Polley for *Away from Her*

▸▸ **Best Cinematography:** Peter Suschitzky for *Eastern Promises*

▸▸ **Best Editing:** Ronald Sanders for *Eastern Promises*

▸▸ **Best Art Direction:** Rob Gray and James Willcock for *Fido*

▸▸ **Best Music (Original Score):** Howard Shore for *Eastern Promises*

▸▸ **Best Music (Original Song):** 'Kaya' by Valanga Khoza and David Hirschfelder from *Shake Hands with the Devil*

▸▸ **Best Costumes:** Carlo Poggioli and Kazuko Kurosawa for *Silk*

▸▸ **Best Sound Editing:** Wayne Griffin, Rob Bertola, Tony Currie, Goro Koyama and Michael O'Farrell for *Eastern Promises*

▸▸ **Best Overall Sound:** Stuart Wilson, Christian T. Cooke, Orest Sushko and Mark Zsifkovits, for *Eastern Promises*

▸▸ **Best Documentary:** Gary Burns, Jim Brown, Bonnie Thompson and Shirley Vercruysse for *Radiant City*

▸▸ **Best Live-Action Short:** Alexis Fortier Gauthier and Élaine Hébert for *Après tout*

▸▸ **Best Animated Short:** Maciek Szczerbowski, Chris Lavis and Marcy Page for *Madame Tutli-Putli*

▸▸ **Special Achievement Genie:** Stephan Dupuis, for *Eastern Promises*. For outstanding achievement in make-up design

▸▸ **Special Award:** Harry Gulkin

▸▸ **Claude Jutra Award:** Sarah Polley for *Away from Her*

▸▸ **Golden Reel Award:** Christian Larouche and Pierre Gendron for *Les 3 p'tits cochons*

The 61st Cannes Film Festival Awards, 14-25 May 2008

▸▸ **Palme d'Or for Best Film:** *Entre Les Murs (The Class)* by Laurent Cantet

▸▸ **Grand Prix du Jury:** *Gomorra (Gomorrah)* by Matteo Garrone

▸▸ **Best Actor:** Benicio del Toro for *Che*

▸▸ **Best Actress:** Sandra Corveloni for *Linha De Passe*

▸▸ **Best Director:** Nuri Bilge for *Üç Maymun (Three Monkeys)*

▸▸ **Best Screenplay:** Jean-Pierre Dardenne and Luc Dardenne for *Le Silence de Lorna (Lorna's Silence)*

▸▸ **Special 61st Anniversary Award:** Catherine Deneuve, Clint Eastwood

▸▸ **Palme d'Or for Best Short:** *Megatron* by Marian Crisan

❯ **Jury Prize:** *Jerrycan* by Julius Avery

  ▸▸ **Prix du Jury:**

  ▸▸ **Camera d'Or** (for first feature): *Hunger* by Steve McQueen

Tilda Swinton was awarded a BAFTA for her performance in *Michael Clayton*.

Toni Collette in *The Dead Girl*, a winner at the Deauville Festival of American Cinema.

>> **Special Distinction**: *Vse Umrut A Ja Ostanus (Everybody Dies But Me)* by Valeria Gai Guermanika

>> **Awards Cinéfondation**:
>> **First Prize**: *Himnon (Anthem)* by Elad Keidan
>> **Second Prize**: *Forbach* by Claire Burger
>> **Third Prize** (ex-aequo): *Stop* by Jae-Ok Park; *Kestomerkitsijat (Roadmarkers)* by Juho Kuosmanen

>> **Une Certain Regard**:
>> **Prix Un Certain Regard – Fondation Gan pour le Cinéma**: *Tulpan* by Sergey Dvortsevoy
>> **Une Certain Regard Special Jury Prize**: *Tokyo Sonata* by Kiyoshi Kurosawa
>> **Jury Coup de Cœur**: *Wolke 9 (Cloud 9)* by Andreas Dresen
>> **Knockout Prize**: *Tyson* by James Toback
>> **Prize of Hope**: *Johnny Mad Dog* by Jean-Stéphane Sauvaire

>> **FIPRESCI (International Film Critics)**
>> **Official Competition**: *Delta* by Kornél Mundruczó
>> **Un Certain Regard**: *Hunger* by Steve Mcqueen

>> **Critics' Week and Directors' Fortnight**: *Eldorado* by Bouli Lanners
>> **International Critics' Week Grand Prize**: *Snow* by Aida Begic
>> **SACD – French Society of** Dramatic Authors and Composers: *Moscow, Belgium* by Christophe Van Rompaey

>> **Canal + Grand Prize for the Best Short Film**: *Next Floor* by Denis Villeneuve
>> **Kodak Discovery Award for Best Short Film**: *Skhizein* by Jérémy Clapin

>> **Ecumenical Jury Prize**:
>> **Youth Prize**: *Blood Appears* by Pablo Fenderick
>> **French National Education Administration Prize**: *Tulpan*, by Sergey Dvortsevoy

Juries:
Official competition: **President**: Sean Penn; **Members of the Jury**: Jeanne Balibar, Rachid Bouchareb, Sergio Castellito, Alfonso Cuaron, Alexandra Maria Lara, Natalie Portman, Marjane Satrapi, Apichatpong Weeraseethakul
Cinéfondation and short films: **President**: Hsiao Hsien Hou; **Members of the Jury**: Olivier Assayas, Susanne Bier, Marina Hands, Laurence Kardish
Un Certain Regard: **President**: Fatih Akin; **Members of the Jury**: Anupama Chopra, Yasser Moheb, Catherine Mtsitouridze, José Maria Prado
Caméra d'or: **President**: Bruno Dumont; **Members of the Jury**: Isabelle Danel, Jean-Michel Frodon,

Monique Koudrine, Willy Kurant, Jean Henri Roger

52nd David Di Donatello Academy Awards ('The Davids'), Rome, 18 April 2008

>> **Best Film**: *La Ragazza del lago* produced by Nicola Giuliano and Francesca Cima, directed by Andrea Molaioli
>> **Best Film from the European Union**: *Irina Palm* by Sam Garbarski
>> **Best Foreign Film**: *No Country for Old Men* by Joel Coen and Ethan Coen
>> **Best Documentary Feature**: *Madri* by Barbara Cupisti
>> **Best Documentary Short**: *Uova* by Alessandro Celli
>> **Best Director**: Andrea Molaioli for *La ragazza del lago*
>> **Best New Director**: Andrea Molaioli for *La ragazza del lago*
>> **Best Screenplay**: Sandro Petraglia for *La ragazza del lago*
>> **Best Producer**: Nicola Giuliano for *La ragazza del lago*
>> **Best Actor**: Toni Servillo for *La ragazza del lago*
>> **Best Actress**: Margherita Buy for *Giorni e nuvole*
>> **Best Supporting Actor**: Alessandro Gassman for *Caos calmo*
>> **Best Supporting Actress**: Alba Rohrwacher for *Giorni e nuvole*
>> **Best Cinematography**: Ramiro Cinita for *La ragazza del lago*
>> **Best Music**: Paolo Buonvino for *Caos calmo*
>> **Best Original Song**: Ivano Fossati for 'L'amore Trasparente', from *Caos calmo*
>> **Best Production Design**: Francesco Frigeri for *I vicerè*
>> **Best Costume Design**: Milena Canonero for *I vicerè*
>> **Best Editing**: Giogiò Franchini for *La ragazza del lago*
>> **Best Sound**: Alessandro Zanon for *La ragazza del lago*
>> **Best Visual Effects**: Paola Trisoglio and Stefano Marinoni for *La ragazza del lago*
>> **Best Make-up**: Gino Tamagnini for *I vicerè*
>> **Best Hair Stylist**: Maria Teresa Corridoni for *I vicerè*
>> **Young David**: Silvio Muccino for *Parlami d'amore*
>> **Honorary Davids**: Carlo Verdone,

for his thirty-year career (1978-2008); Luigi Magni, for his 80th birthday; Gabriele Muccino, for his success as director/screenwriter in the United States

The 33rd Deauville Festival of American Cinema, 31 August – 9 September 2007

▸▸ **Grand Prix for Best Film**: *The Dead Girl* by Karen Moncrieff
▸▸ **Jury Prize**: *Never Forever* by Gina Kim
▸▸ **International Critic's Award**: *Grace is Gone* by James C Strouse

The 20th European Film Awards ('the Felixes'), Berlin, 1 December 2007

▸▸ **Best European Film**: *4 Months, 3 Weeks and 2 Days* by Cristian Mungiu
▸▸ **Best European Director**: Cristian Mungiu for *4 Months, 3 Weeks and 2 Days*
▸▸ **Best European Actor**: Sasson Gabai for *The Band's Visit*
▸▸ **Best European Actress**: Helen Mirren for *The Queen*
▸▸ **Best European Screenplay**: Fatih Akin for *The Edge of Heaven*
▸▸ **Best European Cinematographer**: Frank Griebe for *Perfume: The Story of a Murderer*
▸▸ **Best European Music**: Alexandre

Desplat for *The Queen*
▸▸ **Co-Producer Award**: Margaret Menegoz and Veit Heiduschka
▸▸ **European Film Academy Award for an Artistic Contribution**: Uli Hanisch for *Perfume: The Story of a Murderer* (Production Design)
▸▸ **European Film Academy Lifetime Achievement Award**: Jean-Luc Godard
▸▸ **Best Achievement in World Cinema**: Michael Ballhaus
▸▸ **Discovery of the Year (Fassbinder Award)**: *The Band's Visit* by Eran Kolirin
▸▸ **Critics Award, Prix Fipresci**: *Private Fears in Public Places* by Alain Resnais
▸▸ **Documentary, Prix Arte**: *Paper Cannot Wrap Up Embers* by Rithy Panh
▸▸ **Short Film, Prix UIP**: *Alumbramiento* by Eduardo Chapero-Jackson
▸▸ **The People's Choice Awards**: *La Sconosciuta (The Other Woman)* by Giuseppe Tornatore
▸▸ **Honorary Award**: Manoel de Oliveira

28th The Golden Raspberries ('The Razzies'): Santa Monica, 23 February 2008

▸▸ **Worst Picture**: *I Know Who Killed Me*
▸▸ **Worst Actor**: Eddie Murphy in *Norbit*
▸▸ **Worst Actress**: Lindsay Lohan as twin sisters Aubrey and Dakota in *I Know Who Killed Me*
▸▸ **Worst Supporting Actor**: Eddie Murphy in *Norbit*
▸▸ **Worst Supporting Actress**: Eddie Murphy in *Norbit*
▸▸ **Worst Director**: Chris Sivertson for *I Know Who Killed Me*
▸▸ **Worst Screenplay**: Jeffrey Hammond for *I Know Who Killed Me*
▸▸ **Worst Prequel or Sequel**: *Daddy Day Camp*
▸▸ **Worst Remake or Rip-Off**: *Daddy Day Camp*, based on several films
▸▸ **Worst Screen Couple**: Lohan & Lohan in *I Know Who Killed Me*
▸▸ **Worst Excuse for a Horror Movie (New Category)**: *I Know Who Killed Me*

The 65th Hollywood Foreign Press Association ('Golden Globes') Awards, 14 January 2008

▸▸ **Best Motion Picture – Drama**: *Eastern Promises*
▸▸ **Best Motion Picture – Musical or Comedy**: *Sweeney Todd*
▸▸ **Best Director**: Julian Schnabel for *Le Scaphandre et le papillon (The Diving Bell and the Butterfly)*
▸▸ **Best Performance by an Actor in a Motion Picture – Drama**: Daniel Day-Lewis for *There Will Be Blood*
▸▸ **Best Performance by an Actress in a Motion Picture – Drama**: Julie Christie for *Away from Her*

La Ragazza del lago, winner of a David for Best Film at the David Di Donatello Academy Awards in Rome.

>> **Best Performance by an Actor in a Motion Picture – Comedy/Musical:** Johnny Depp for *Sweeney Todd*

>> **Best Performance by an Actress in a Motion Picture – Comedy/Musical:** Marion Cotillard for *La Vie En Rose*

>> **Best Performance by an Actor in a Supporting Role:** Javier Bardem for *No Country for Old Men*

>> **Best Performance by an Actress in a Supporting Role:** Cate Blanchett for *I'm Not There*

>> **Best Screenplay:** Joel Coen and Ethan Coen for *No Country for Old Men*

>> **Best Original Score:** *Atonement*

>> **Best Original Song:** 'Guaranteed' from *Into the Wild*

The 28th London Film Critic's Circle Awards, Grosvenor House Hotel, London, 28th February 2008

>> **Best Film:** Joel and Ethan Coen for *No Country For Old Men*

>> **Best Actor:** Daniel Day-Lewis for *There Will Be Blood*

>> **Best Actress:** Marion Cotillard for *La Vie En Rose*

>> **Best Director:** Paul Thomas Anderson for *There Will Be Blood*

>> **Best Screenwriter:** Florian Henckel von Donnersmarck for *The Lives of Others*

>> **Best British Film (The Attenborough Award):** Anton Corbijn for *Control*

>> **Best British Director:** Paul Greengrass for *The Bourne Ultimatum*

>> **Best British Producer:** no award

>> **Best British Actor:** James McAvoy for *Atonement*

>> **Best British Actress:** Julie Christie for *Away From Her*

>> **Best British Supporting Actor:** Tom Wilkinson for *Michael Clayton*

>> **Best Supporting Actress:** Kelly Macdonald for *No Country For Old Men*

>> **Best British Newcomer:** Sam Riley for *Control* (acting)

>> **Best Foreign Language Film:** *The Lives of Others* by Florian Henckel von Donnersmarck

>> **Dilys Powell Award:** no award

The Los Angeles Film Critics' Association Awards, InterContinental Hotel, Los Angeles, California, USA, 5 January 2008

>> **Best Picture:** *There Will Be Blood*

>> **Best Actor:** Daniel Day-Lewis for *There Will Be Blood*

>> **Best Actress:** Marion Cotillard for *La Môme*

>> **Best Supporting Actor:** Vlad Ivanov for *4 luni, 3 saptamâni si 2 zile*

>> **Best Supporting Actress:** Amy Ryan for *Gone Baby Gone* and *Before the Devil Knows You're Dead*

>> **Best Director:** Paul Thomas Anderson for *There Will Be Blood*

>> **Best Screenplay:** Tamara Jenkins for *The Savages*

>> **Best Foreign Film:** *4 luni, 3 saptamâni si 2 zile*

>> **Best Documentary:** *No End in Sight*

>> **Best Cinematography:** Janusz Kaminski for *Le Scaphandre et le papillon (The Diving Bell and the Butterfly)*

>> **Independent Filmmakers' Award:** Pedro Costa for *Juventude Em Marcha*

>> **Best Production Design:** Jack Fisk for *There Will Be Blood*

>> **New Generation Award:** Sarah Polley for *Away from Her*

>> **Best Animation (ex aequo):** *Persepolis, Ratatouille*

>> **Career Achievement Award:** *Sidney Lumet*

>> **Special Citations:** Peter Sellars

The London Film Critics' Circle were among those who admired Daniel Day-Lewis's performance in *There Will Be Blood*.

A thoughtful Joe Wright directs Saoirse Ronan on the set of the BAFTA-winning *Atonement*.

(artistic director); Simon Field (producer); Keith Griffiths (producer)
▶▶ **Legacy of Cinema Award**: Outfest; UCLA Film & Television Archive; Dennis Doros and Amy Heller

The awards were dedicated to the memory of the late Robert Altman, Michelangelo Antonioni, Ingmar Bergman, Ousmane Sembene and Edward Yang.

MTV Movie Awards, Sony Pictures Studio, Culver City, California, 2 June 2008

▶▶ **Best Movie**: *Transformers* by Michael Bay
▶▶ **Best Female Performance**: Ellen Page *for Juno*
▶▶ **Best Male Performance**: Will Smith for *I Am Legend*
▶▶ **Best Comedic Performance**: Johnny Depp for *Pirates of the Caribbean: At World's End*
▶▶ **Best Breakthrough Performance**: Zac Efron for *Hairspray*
▶▶ **Best Villain**: Johnny Depp for *Sweeney Todd*
▶▶ **Best Fight**: Sean Faris versus Cam Gigandet in *Never Back Down*
▶▶ **Best Kiss**: Briana Evigan and Robert Hoffman in *Step Up 2 the Streets*
▶▶ **Best Movie Spoof**: *Juno*
▶▶ **MTV Generation Award**: Adam Sandler
▶▶ **Best Summer Movie So Far**: *Iron Man* by Jon Favreau

79th National Board of Review of Motion Picture Awards, New York, 5 December 2007

▶▶ **Best Film**: *No Country for Old Men*
▶▶ **Best Actor**: George Clooney for *Michael Clayton*
▶▶ **Best Actress**: Julie Christie for *Away from Her*
▶▶ **Best Supporting Actor**: Casey Affleck for *The Assassination of Jesse James by the Coward Robert Ford*
▶▶ **Best Supporting Actress**: Amy Ryan for *Gone Baby Gone*
▶▶ **Best Director**: Tim Burton for *Sweeney Todd: The Demon Barber of Fleet Street*
▶▶ **Best Adapted Screenplay**: *No Country for Old Men* by Ethan Coen and Joel Coen

▶▶ **Best Original Screenplay (ex aequo)**: Diablo Cody for *Juno;* Nancy Oliver for *Lars and the Real Girl*
▶▶ **Best Foreign Language Film**: *Le scaphandre et le papillon (The Diving Bell and the Butterfly)*
▶▶ **Best Animated Feature**: *Ratatouille*
▶▶ **Best Documentary**: *Body of War*
▶▶ **Best Ensemble Cast**: *No Country for Old Men*
▶▶ **Breakthrough Performances (Actor)**: Emile Hirsch *for Into the Wild*
▶▶ **Breakthrough Performances (Actress)**: Ellen Page for *Juno*
▶▶ **Best Directorial Debut**: Ben Affleck for *Gone Baby Gone*
▶▶ **William K Everson Award for Film History**: Robert Osborne
▶▶ **Career Award for Cinematography**: Roger Deakins
▶▶ **Special Recognition of Films that Reflect the Freedom of Expression (ex aequo)**: *The Great Debaters; Persepolis*
▶▶ **Special Mention for Excellence in Filmmaking (top ten films)**: *The Assassination of Jesse James by the Coward Robert Ford, Atonement, The Bourne Ultimatum, The Bucket List,*

Julie Christie's moving performance in *Away From Her* received a Golden Globe and recognition from the New York Film Critics' Circle, amongst others.

Into the Wild, Juno, The Kite Runner, Lars and the Real Girl, Michael Clayton, Sweeney Todd: The Demon Barber of Fleet Street
▶▶ **Top Five Foreign Films** (in alphabetical order): *4 Months, 3 Weeks and 2 Days, The Band's Visit, The Counterfeiters, La Vie En Rose, Lust, Caution*
▶▶ **Top Five Foreign Documentaries:** *Toots* (and, in alphabetical order) *Darfur Now, In the Shadow of the Moon, Nanking, Taxi to the Dark Side*
▶▶ **Top Independent Films** *Great World of Sound* (and in alphabetical order) *Away from Her, Honeydripper, In the Valley of Elah, A Mighty Heat, The Namesake, Once, The Savages, Starting Out in the Evening, Waitress*

The National Society of Film Critics' Awards, Sardi's Restaurant, New York, 5 January 2008

▶▶ **Best Film:** *There Will Be Blood*
▶▶ **Best Actor:** Daniel Day-Lewis for *There Will Be Blood*
▶▶ **Best Actress:** Julie Christie for *Away from Her*
▶▶ **Best Director:** Paul Thomas Anderson for *There Will Be Blood*
▶▶ **Best Supporting Actor:** Casey Affleck for *The Assassination of Jesse James by the Coward Robert Ford*
▶▶ **Best Supporting Actress:** Cate Blanchett for *I'm Not There*
▶▶ **Best Screenplay:** Tamara Jenkins for *The Savages*
▶▶ **Best Cinematography:** Robert

Elswit for *There Will Be Blood*
▶▶ **Best Foreign Film:** *4 luni, 3 saptamâni si 2 zile*
▶▶ **Best Non-Fiction Film:** *No End in Sight*
▶▶ **Best Experimental Film:** *Profit Motive and the Whispering Wind*
▶▶ **Special Citation:** Fox Home Video for the 21-disc box set *Ford at Fox*
▶▶ **Special Film Heritage Award:** Ross Lipman, UCLA Film and Television Archive

The 73rd New York Film Critics' Circle Awards, American Media Incorporated, New York City (announced 10 December 2007, awarded 6 January 2008)

▶▶ **Best Film:** *No Country for Old Men* by Joel Coen and Ethan Coen
▶▶ **Best Film (runners up):** *There Will Be Blood* by Paul Thomas Anderson, *I'm Not There* by Todd Haynes
▶▶ **Best Actor:** Daniel Day-Lewis for *There Will Be Blood*
▶▶ **Best Actor (runner up):** Viggo Mortensen for *Eastern Promises*
▶▶ **Best Actress:** Julie Christie for *Away from Her*
▶▶ **Best Actress (runner up):** Ellen Page for *Juno*
▶▶ **Best Supporting Actor:** Javier Bardem for *No Country for Old Men*
▶▶ **Best Supporting Actress:** Amy Ryan for *Gone Baby Gone*
▶▶ **Best Director:** Joel Coen and Ethan Coen for *No Country for Old Men*
▶▶ **Best Screenplay:** Joel and Ethan Coen for *No Country for Old Men*
▶▶ **Best Cinematographer:** Robert Elswit for *There Will Be Blood*
▶▶ **Best Foreign Film:** *The Lives of Others* by Florian Henckel von Donnersmarck
▶▶ **Best Animated Film:** *Persepolis* by Vincent Paronnaud and Marjane Satrapi
▶▶ **Best First Feature:** Sarah Polley for *Away from Her*
▶▶ **Special Critics Award:** Charles Burnett for *Killer of Sheep*

The 24th Sundance Film Festival, Park City, Utah, 17-27 January 2008

▶▶ **The Documentary Grand Jury Prize:** *Trouble the Water* by Tia Lessin and Carl Deal

≫ **The Dramatic Grand Jury Prize:** *Frozen River* by Courtney Hunt

≫ **Audience Award – Documentary:** *Fields of Fuel* by Josh Tickell.

≫ **Audience Award – Dramatic:** *The Wackness* by Jonathan Levine

≫ **Special Jury Prize – World Cinema Documentary:** *Man on Wire* by James Marsh

≫ **Special Jury Prize – Dramatic:** *King of Ping Pong (Ping Pongkingen)* by Jens Jonsson

≫ **Special Jury Prize – World Cinema Dramatic:** Ernesto Contreras for *Blue Eyelids (Parpados Azules)*

≫ **Special Jury Prize – Documentary:** Lisa F. Jackson for *Greatest Silence: Rape in the Congo*

≫ **Special Jury Prize – Dramatic ('The Spirit of Independence'):** Chusy Haney-Jardine for *Anywhere, USA*

≫ **Special Jury Prize – Dramatic ('Work by an Ensemble Cast'):** The cast of *Choke*

≫ **Audience Award – World Cinema Documentary:** *Man on Wire* by James Marsh

≫ **Audience Award – Dramatic:** *Captain Abu Raed* by director Amin Matalqa.

≫ **Directing Award – Documentary:** Nanette Burstein for *American Teen*

≫ **Directing Award – Dramatic:** Lance Hammer for *Ballast*

≫ **The World Cinema Directing Award – Documentary:** Nino Kirtadze for Durakovo: *Village of Fools (Durakovo: Le Village Des Fous)*

≫ **The World Cinema Directing Award – Dramatic:** Anna Melikyan for *Mermaid (Rusalka)*

≫ **Cinematography Award – Documentary:** Phillip Hunt and Steven Sebring for *Patti Smith: Dream of Life*

≫ **Cinematography Award – Dramatic:** Lol Crawley for *Ballast*

≫ **The World Cinema Cinematography Award – Documentary:** al Massad for *Recycle*

≫ **The World Cinema Cinematography Award – Dramatic:** Askild Vik Edvardsen for *King of Ping Pong (Ping Pongkingen)*

≫ **Waldo Salt Screenwriting Award:** Alex Rivera and David Riker for *Sleep Dealer*

≫ **The World Cinema Screenwriting Award:** Samuel Benchetrit for *I Always Wanted to be a Gangster (J'ai toujours rêvé d'être un gangster)*

≫ **Jury Prize in Short Filmmaking:** *My Olympic Summer* by Daniel Robin and *Sikumi (On the Ice)* by Andrew Okpeaha MacLean

≫ **International Jury Prize in International Short Filmmaking:** *Soft* by Simon Ellis.

≫ **Honorable Mention – Short Filmmaking:** *Aquarium* by Rob Meyer

≫ **Honorable Mention – Short Filmmaking:** *August 15th* by Xuan Jiang

≫ **Honorable Mention – Short Filmmaking:** *La Corona (The Crown)* by Amanda Micheli and Isabel Vega

≫ **Honorable Mention – Short Filmmaking:** *Oiran Lyrics* by Ryosuke Ogawa

≫ **Honorable Mention – Short Filmmaking:** *Spider* by Nash Edgerton

≫ **Honorable Mention – Short Filmmaking:** *Suspension* by Nicolas Provost

≫ **Honorable Mention – Short Filmmaking:** *W* by The Vikings.

≫ **Documentary Film Editing:** Joe Bini for *Roman Polanski: Wanted and Desired*

≫ **World Cinema Documentary Editing Award:** Irena Dol for *The Art Star and The Sudanese Twins*

≫ **Alfred P. Sloan Feature Film Prize:** *Sleep Dealer* by Alex Rivera

≫ **Sundance/NHK International Filmmakers Award Winners:** Alejandro Fernandez Almendras for *Huacho*, Braden King for *Here*, Aiko Nagatsu for *Apoptosis* and Radu Jude for *The Happiest Girl in the World*

The 2008 Sundance Film Festival Juries consisted of: Dramatic Competition: Marcia Gay Harden, Mary Harron, Diego Luna, Sandra Oh and Quentin Tarantino; **Documentary Competition:** Michelle Byrd, Heidi Ewing, Eugene Jarecki, Steven Okazaki and Annie Sundberg; **World Dramatic Competition:** Shunji Iwai (Japan), Lucrecia Martel (Argentina) and Jan Schütte (Germany); **World Documentary Competition:** Amir Bar-Lev (US), Leena Pasanen (Finland/Denmark) and Ilda Santiago (Brazil); **American and International Shorts:** Jon Bloom, Melonie Diaz and Jason Reitman; and **The Alfred P. Sloan Prize:** Alan Alda, Michael Polish, Evan Schwartz, Benedict Schwegler and John Underkoffler.

Trouble the Water won the Documentary Grand Jury Prize at Sundance.

In Memoriam

July 2007 – June 2008

by Jonathan Rigby

Given the hundreds of film personalities who died during the period under review, the following round-up of just 47 people must obviously remain a purely personal one. (Anyone wishing to argue with the choices made can take a look at the list appended at the end, in which virtually everyone included could just as easily have made it into the main entries.) The period was a notable one from the outset, because the penultimate day of July 2007 marked the deaths of two giants of European 'arthouse' cinema …

MICHELANGELO ANTONIONI

Born: 29 September 1912, Ferrara, Italy.
Died: 30 July 2007, Rome, Italy.
Starting as a part-time film critic and documentarist, Antonioni made his first feature, *Cronaca di un amore* (Love Story), in 1950. With the 1960-62 sequence of *L'avventura*, *La notte* and *L'eclisse*, he was hailed as a modernist master, a bleak, enigmatic chronicler of alienation and emotional paralysis. His first colour film, *Il deserto rosso* (1964), was followed two years later by a modish smash hit for MGM, *Blow-Up*, and by the less commercially successful but equally intriguing *Zabriskie Point* (1970) and *Professione: reporter* (The Passenger, 1974). His last major films were *Il mistero di Oberwald* (1982, originally for TV and reuniting him with longtime muse Monica Vitti) and *Identificazione di una donna* (1985). In 1996 he was awarded a Lifetime Achievement Oscar, and his last work was a contribution to the 2004 anthology film *Eros*.

INGMAR BERGMAN

Born: 14 July 1918, Uppsala, Sweden.
Died: 30 July 2007, Faro, Sweden.
Son of a Lutheran pastor, Bergman brought a uniquely sombre Scandinavian chill to his morally probing cinematic parables. His reign as a genuine colossus of arthouse cinema began with *Sommarnattens leende* (Smiles of a Summer Night, 1955) and encompassed *Det Sjunde inseglet* (The Seventh Seal, 1956;

reissued in the UK just ten days prior to his death), *Smultronstället* (Wild Strawberries, 1957), *Ansiktet* (The Face, 1958), *Jungfrukällan* (The Virgin Spring, 1960), *Såsom i en spegel* (Through a Glass Darkly, 1961), *Nattvardsgästerna* (Winter Light, 1962), *Tystnaden* (The Silence, 1963), *Persona* (1966) and *Vargtimmen* (Hour of the Wolf, 1967). Recipient of a special Oscar in 1971 – the same year in which he made *Viskningar och rop* (Cries and Whispers) – he foreswore further films after the latterday triumph of *Fanny och Alexander* (Fanny and Alexander, 1982), though he remained active in television into the 21st century. One final masterpiece, however, was accorded a cinema release; this was *Saraband* (2003).

CYD CHARISSE

Born: 8 March 1921, Amarillo, Texas, USA.
Died: 17 June 2008, Los Angeles, California, USA.
With legs insured by MGM for $5 million, Cyd

Opposite:
Ingmar Bergman

Right:
Michelangelo
Antonioni

Far right:
Cyd Charisse

Hazel Court

Jules Dassin

Charisse was a supremely elegant exemplar of the Hollywood musical at its post-war height. In addition to her oneiric dance sequence with Gene Kelly in *Singin' in the Rain* (1952), she also graced *The Band Wagon* (1953), *Brigadoon* (1954), *It's Always Fair Weather* (1955), *Meet Me in Las Vegas* (1956) and *Silk Stockings* (1957). Non-musical roles included *Two Weeks in Another Town* (1962), *Maroc 7* (1967) and *Warlords of the Deep* (1978).

ANN CHEGWIDDEN
Born: 27 April 1921, Hampstead, London, England.
Died: 6 September 2007, London, England.
Three times BAFTA-nominated for her television work, Ann Chegwidden edited such varied films as *Kill Me Tomorrow* (1957), *The Dock Brief* (1962), *Crooks in Cloisters* (1963), *Daleks' Invasion Earth 2150 A.D.* (1966), *The Last Grenade* (1969), *And Soon the Darkness* (1970), *Wuthering Heights* (1970) and *The Hiding Place* (1974). Her most famous credit, however, remains Roger Corman's lurid Poe picture *The Masque of the Red Death* (1963). She was awarded an OBE in 1989.

HAZEL COURT
Born: 10 February 1926, Sutton Coldfield, Warwickshire, England.
Died: 15 April 2008, Lake Tahoe, California, USA.
Titian-haired Hazel Court appeared in such Gainsborough titles as *Dear Murderer* and *Holiday Camp* (both 1947) – plus obscurities like *Ghost Ship* (1952) and *Devil Girl from Mars* (1954) – before becoming Britain's first 'scream queen' in Hammer's *The Curse of Frankenstein* (1956). She followed it with, among others, *The Man Who Could Cheat Death* (1958), *Doctor Blood's Coffin* (1960), and three for Roger Corman – *Premature Burial* (1961), *The Raven* (1962) and *The Masque of the Red Death* (1963).

EVA DAHLBECK
Born: 8 March 1920, Saltsjö-Duvnäs, Sweden.
Died: 8 February 2008, Hässelby, Stockholm, Sweden.
Cast in five of the director's 1950s films (and one other), Eva Dahlbeck exemplified the lighter side of Ingmar Bergman. Noted for her on-screen chemistry with Gunnar Björnstrand – and also as a playwright, screenwriter, poet and novelist – Dahlbeck's best-known role remains jaded actress Desiree Armfeldt in Bergman's *Sommarnattens leende* (Smiles of a Summer Night, 1955). Among numerous other credits, she played opposite William Holden in *The Counterfeit Traitor* (1962) and appeared in Mai Zetterling's debut film, *Älskande par* (Loving Couples, 1964).

JULES DASSIN
Born: 18 December 1911, Middletown, Connecticut, USA.
Died: 31 March 2008, Athens, Greece.
Being blacklisted as a Communist sympathiser turned out to be a blessing in disguise for Jules Dassin. Having directed such noir classics as *Brute Force* (1947) and *Night and the City* (1950), he made *Du Rififi chez les hommes* (1954) in France and *Pote tin Kyriaki* (Never on Sunday, 1960) in Greece, receiving two Oscar nominations for the latter and also starring in it opposite his future wife Melina Mercouri. He followed them with the hugely popular caper comedy *Topkapi* (1964) and only retired after *Circle of Two* in 1980.

JEAN DESAILLY
Born: 24 August 1920, Paris, France.
Died: 14 June 2008, Dourdan, France.
A graduate of the Comédie Française and the Compagnie Renaud-Barrault, Jean Desailly founded his own Compagnie Valère-Desailly with his wife Simone Valère and enjoyed a long career in French cinema, ranging from *Sylvie et le fantôme* (1946) and *Occupe-toi d'Amélie* (1949) through *The Assassination*

Julie Ege

Mel Ferrer

of Trotsky (1972) to *Le Radeau de la Meduse* (1994) and
La Dilettante (1999). In 1960 he was BAFTA-nominated
for 'Best Foreign Actor' in *Maigret tend un piège* (1958).

JULIE EGE

Born: 12 November 1943, Sandnes, Norway.
Died: 29 April 2008, Oslo, Norway.
Having been crowned Miss Norway of 1962, Julie
Ege appeared in the sixth James Bond film, *On Her
Majesty's Secret Service* (1969), and thereafter in an
engagingly dodgy run of British comedies and horrors:
Every Home Should Have One (1969), *Up Pompeii*
(1970), *Rentadick* (1971), *The Mutations* (1972), *Craze*
(1973), *The Amorous Milkman* (1974). She remains
best remembered for her Hammer films, though they
numbered only two: *Creatures the World Forgot* (1970)
and *The Legend of the 7 Golden Vampires* (1973).

CLIVE EXTON

Born: 11 April 1930, London, England.
Died: 16 August 2007, London, England.
Ace television playwright Clive Exton also notched
up a decent number of film credits, including *A Place
to Go* (1963), *Night Must Fall*, Antonioni's *I tre volti*
(both 1964), *Isadora* (1968), *Entertaining Mr Sloane*,
10 Rillington Place (both 1970), *Doomwatch* (1971),
Running Scared (1972), *The Awakening* (1980) and *Red
Sonja* (1985). With Terry Nation, he also co-wrote and
co-produced the charming Frankie Howerd vehicle
The House in Nightmare Park (1972).

MEL FERRER

Born: 25 August 1917, Elberon, New Jersey, USA.
Died: 2 June 2008, Santa Barbara, California, USA.
A long, lean and sometimes lugubrious leading man,
Ferrer had a string of notable roles in the 1950s,
from *Scaramouche* (1952) and *Lili* (1953) to *War and
Peace* (1956), *The Sun Also Rises* (1957) and *The World,*

the Flesh and the Devil (1959). Many of his latterday
assignments, however, were exploitation pictures made
in his adopted Europe. As director, he showcased his
then-wife Audrey Hepburn in *Green Mansions* (1959)
and, as producer, *Wait Until Dark* (1967).

RICHARD FRANKLIN

Born: 15 July 1948, Melbourne, Australia.
Died: 11 July 2007, Melbourne, Australia.
Having started with sex comedies like *Fantasm* (1976),
director Richard Franklin made his name with two
edgy Australian thrillers, *Patrick* (1978) and *Roadgames*
(1981). He then took on the unenviable task of
making *Psycho II* (1982) for Universal – and made a
commendably creepy job of it. His other films were
variable, including *Cloak & Dagger* (1984), *Link* (1985,
made in the UK), *F X 2* (1990) and, back in Australia,
Hotel Sorrento (1994), *Brilliant Lies* (1995) and *Visitors*
(2003).

CHARLES B GRIFFITH

Born: 23 September 1930, Chicago, Illinois, USA.
Died: 28 September 2007, San Diego, California, USA.
Through his association with Roger Corman, writer
Charles B Griffith bequeathed to posterity such
uniquely crazed divertissements as *The Undead* (1956),
Attack of the Crab Monsters (1957), *A Bucket of Blood*
(1959) and *The Little Shop of Horrors* (1960). Later
credits included *The Wild Angels* (1966), *Death Race
2000* (1975) and *Eat My Dust!* (1976), which he also
directed. Several of his scripts have been remade in
the past 20-odd years, one of them – *Not of This Earth*
(1957) – twice.

KARL HARDMAN

Born: 22 March 1927, Pittsburgh, Pennsylvania.
Died: 22 September 2007, Pittsburgh, Pennsylvania.
Karl Hardman had only one significant film credit,

Charlton Heston

Deborah Kerr

but what a credit. A radio celebrity in his native Pittsburgh, in 1967 he co-produced George A Romero's epoch-making *Night of the Living Dead*, also contributing make-up, electronic sound effects and, most memorably, an iconic performance as mean-minded patriarch Harry Cooper, who famously maintained that the cellar was the safest place ... and ended up eaten by his daughter – played by Hardman's own daughter, Kyra Schon.

CHARLTON HESTON

Born: 4 October 1923, Evanston, Illinois, USA.
Died: 5 April 2008, Beverly Hills, California, USA.
A truly epic figure in post-war Hollywood, Heston's monolithic image was defined by such massive hits as *The Ten Commandments* (1956, playing Moses) and as the title characters in *Ben-Hur* (1959, for which he won as Oscar) and *El Cid* (1961). Further heroic landmarks followed – *55 Days at Peking* (1963), *The Agony and the Ecstasy* (1965), *Khartoum* (1966) – together with a shift into speculative science fiction initiated by *Planet of the Apes* (1968). Other roles included *Touch of Evil* (1957), *Major Dundee* (1965), *Julius Caesar* (1969) and *Earthquake* (1974).

KON ICHIKAWA

Born: 20 November 1915, Mie, Japan.
Died: 13 February 2008, Tokyo, Japan.
Though little known in the West, director Kon Ichikawa crafted a highly influential series of visually striking films, among them *Biruma no tategoto* (The Burmese Harp, 1956), *Kagi* (The Key), *Nobi* (Fires on the Plain) (both 1959), *Yukinojo henge* (An Actor's Revenge), *Taiheiyo hitori-botchi* (Alone on the Pacific) (both 1963) and *Tôkyô orimpikku* (Tokyo Olympiad, 1965). His last picture, *Inugamike no ichizoku* (2006: a 30-years-later remake of one of his own films), was released a mere 14 months before his death.

DEBORAH KERR

Born: 30 September 1921, Helensburgh, Scotland.
Died: 16 October 2007, Botesdale, Suffolk, England.
A delicate beauty who was more than capable of subverting her genteel image when required, Deborah Kerr shone with special luminosity in the British cinema of the 1940s, notably in the Powell and Pressburger classics *The Life and Death of Colonel Blimp* (1943) and *Black Narcissus* (1947). She then decamped to Hollywood, scoring in *Edward, My Son* (1949), *From Here to Eternity* (1953), *The King and I* (1956) and *Separate Tables* (1958). She also triumphed as the haunted governess in *The Innocents* (1961) and in her last film, *The Assam Garden* (1985).

HARVEY KORMAN

Born: 15 February 1927, Chicago, Illinois, USA.
Died: 29 May 2008, Los Angeles, California, USA.
Lofty (6'3") and masterful comic actor Harvey Korman

Harvey Korman

Charles Lane

John Phillip Law

won four Emmys for his ten-year stint on TV's *The Carol Burnett Show* (1967-77) and on film became a conspicuous feature of the Mel Brooks repertory company, appearing in *Blazing Saddles* (1973), *High Anxiety* (1977), *History of the World: Part I* (1981) and *Dracula: Dead and Loving It* (1995). Other titles included *Huckleberry Finn* (1974), *Herbie Goes Bananas* (1981) and *Radioland Murders* (1994).

LASZLO KOVACS
Born: 14 May 1933, Cece, Hungary.
Died: 22 July 2007, Beverly Hills, California, USA.
Cinematographer Laszlo Kovacs fled the Hungarian uprising and made his US breakthrough with Peter Bogdanovich's debut picture *Targets* (1967). He then shot an impressive series of highly influential films, from *Psych-Out* (1968), *Easy Rider* (1969) and *Five Easy Pieces* (1970) to *The King of Marvin Gardens* (1972), *Paper Moon* (1973) and *F.I.S.T.* (1978). Later credits included *Frances* (1982), *Ghostbusters* (1984), *Copycat* (1995) and *Miss Congeniality* (2000).

CHARLES LANE
Born: 26 January 1905, San Francisco, California, USA.
Died: 2 July 2007, Brentwood, California, USA.
Charles Lane was arguably the most ubiquitous character actor of Hollywood's Golden Age. His gaunt, forbidding features graced such films as *42nd Street* (1933), *Twentieth Century* (1934), *Mr Deeds Goes to Town* (1936), *You Can't Take It With You* (1938), *Arsenic and Old Lace* (1941) and *It's a Wonderful Life* (1946). In the 1950s he became a staple of TV's *I Love Lucy* and at his death he was working on an aptly named documentary self-portrait called *You Know the Face*.

JOHN PHILLIP LAW
Born: 7 September 1937, Los Angeles, California, USA.
Died: 13 May 2008, Los Angeles, California, USA.

Another Sinbad (like Kerwin Mathews) to die in the period under review, Law found his most iconic roles in Italy, where he appeared in two pop-art fantasies, Mario Bava's *Diabolik* (1967) and Roger Vadim's *Barbarella* (1968), for producer Dino de Laurentiis. Other films included *The Red Baron* (1971), *The Golden Voyage of Sinbad* (1973), *Open Season* (1974), *The Cassandra Crossing* (1976) and *Tarzan, the Ape Man* (1981).

HEATH LEDGER
Born: 4 April 1979, Perth, Australia.
Died: 22 January 2008, Manhattan, New York City, USA.
Killed by an accidental drug overdose, Heath (short for Heathcliff) Ledger had come to prominence in the Australian film *Two Hands* (1999) prior to appearing in major Hollywood releases like *10 Things I Hate About You* (1999), *The Patriot* (2000), *A Knight's Tale*, *Monster's Ball* (both 2001) and *The Brothers Grimm* (2005). Having won an Oscar for his role in *Brokeback Mountain* (also 2005), his Joker in *The Dark Knight* (2008) won similar acclaim, albeit posthumously.

Heath Ledger

IRA LEVIN

Born: 27 August 1929, Manhattan, New York City, USA.
Died: 12 November 2007, Manhattan, New York City, USA.
Ira Levin could boast an impressive range of films based on his elaborately plotted works. His plays yielded *No Time for Sergeants* (1958), *Critic's Choice* (1962), *Deathtrap* (1982) and *Footsteps* (2003). His novels, likewise: *A Kiss Before Dying* (1955; remade 1991), *Rosemary's Baby* (1967), *The Stepford Wives* (1974; remade 2004), *The Boys from Brazil* (1978) and *Sliver* (1993). He also collaborated, uncredited, on the screenplay for *Bunny Lake is Missing* (1965).

DELBERT MANN

Born: 30 January 1920, Lawrence, Kansas, USA.
Died: 11 November 2007, Los Angeles, California, USA.
A distinguished graduate from live television, Mann broke through with the thoughtful sleeper smash *Marty* in 1955 and for over four decades remained the only director to win the Best Director Oscar with his debut film. Subsequent credits included two 1958 stage adaptations, *Desire Under the Elms* and *Separate Tables*, plus *The Dark at the Top of the Stairs* (1960), *That Touch of Mink* (1962), *Kidnapped* (1971), and a slew of latterday TV movies.

KERWIN MATHEWS

Born: 8 January 1926, Seattle, Washington, USA.
Died: 5 July 2007, San Francisco, California, USA.
Kerwin Mathews achieved immortality as a clean-cut adventure hero pitted against Ray Harryhausen monsters in *The 7th Voyage of Sinbad* (1958) and *The 3 Worlds of Gulliver* (1960). In similar vein, he played the title role in Nathan Juran's *Jack the Giant Killer* (1962). Other roles included *The Last Blitzkrieg* (1959), *The Devil at 4 O'Clock* (1961), two very different Hammer thrillers – *The Pirates of Blood River* (1961) and *Maniac* (1962), *Barquero* (1970) and *The Boy who Cried Werewolf* (1973).

LOIS MAXWELL

Born: 14 February 1927, Kitchener, Ontario, Canada.
Died: 29 September 2007, Fremantle, Australia.
Prior to being immortalised as Miss Moneypenny in

Lois Maxwell

Kieron Moore

the first 14 James Bond films (pining after, successively, Sean Connery, George Lazenby and Roger Moore), Lois Maxwell gained a 'Best Newcomer' Golden Globe for *That Hagen Girl* (1947). Mishandled by Hollywood, she opted instead for British films such as *Women of Twilight* (1952), *Time Without Pity* (1957), *Lolita* (1961), *The Haunting* (1963) and *Endless Night* (1971). She made her last film, *The Fourth Angel*, in 2000.

ANTHONY MINGHELLA

Born: 6 January 1954, Ryde, Isle of Wight, England.
Died: 18 March 2008, London, England.
A television dramatist and award-winning playwright prior to entering films, Anthony Minghella's first big cinema success was in fact a TV film, *Truly Madly Deeply* (1990). *Mr Wonderful* (1993) and *Breaking and Entering* (2006) were both misfires. But, in between, the sprawling canvas of *The English Patient* (1996) carried off nine Oscars while *The Talented Mr Ripley* (1999) was nominated for five. *Cold Mountain* (2003) maintained a similar standard, on a budget of $83 million. He was awarded a CBE in 2001.

KIERON MOORE

Born: 5 October 1924, Skibbereen, County Cork, Ireland.
Died: 15 July 2007, Charente-Maritime, France.
Coming out of the Abbey Theatre Dublin, Kieron Moore made an impression in *Mine Own Executioner* in 1947 and went to Hollywood for *Ten Tall Men* and *David and Bathsheba* (both 1951). Thereafter his somewhat deadpan style was mainly confined to British films such as *The Green Scarf* (1954), *The Blue Peter* (1955), *The League of Gentlemen* (1960), *The Day of the Triffids* (1962), *Crack in the World* (1964) and *Arabesque* (1966).

AKEMI NEGISHI

Born: 26 March 1934, Tokyo, Japan.
Died: 11 March 2008, Kawasaki, Kanagawa, Japan.

Suzanne Pleshette

Sydney Pollack

Discovered performing in a Japanese cabaret by Josef von Sternberg, Negishi was given top billing in his final film, *Anatahan* (1953). She projected a frank sensuality unusual in Japanese cinema of the period, and among her numerous films are four by Akira Kurosawa: *Ikimono no kiroku* (I Live in Fear, 1955), *Donzoko* (The Lower Depths, 1957), *Akahige* (Red Beard, 1965) and *Dodes'ka-den* (1970). She also appeared in *Shurayukihime* (Lady Snowblood, 1973), the inspiration for *Kill Bill*.

MAILA NURMI
(aka VAMPIRA)
Born: 11 December 1921, Petsamo, Finland.
Died: 10 January 2008, Los Angeles, California, USA.
Groomed for movie stardom by Howard Hawks, Maila Nurmi actually attained immortality (despite no copies of the show surviving) via her creation of television's first 'horror host' in KABC-TV's *The Vampira Show* (1954-5). Though she was nominated for an Emmy, Vampira's subsequent films never rose above the level of Poverty Row potboilers like Ed Wood's notorious *Plan 9 from Outer Space*, *The Beat Generation* (both 1959) and *Sex Kittens Go to College* (1960).

SUZANNE PLESHETTE
Born: 31 January 1937, New York City, USA.
Died: 19 January 2008, Los Angeles, California, USA.
Memorable as the second female lead in Alfred Hitchcock's *The Birds* (1963), Suzanne Pleshette was best known on TV for her continuing role in *The Bob Newhart Show* (1972-8). Having made her film debut in the 1958 Jerry Lewis comedy *The Geisha Boy*, she went on to appear in such titles as *Fate is the Hunter* (1964), *Nevada Smith* (1966), *The Power* (1968), *Support Your Local Gunfighter* (1971) and *Oh, God! Book II* (1980).

SYDNEY POLLACK
Born: 1 July 1934, Lafayette, Indiana, USA.
Died: 26 May 2008, Pacific Palisades, California, USA.
With Burt Lancaster for a mentor, actor-director Sydney Pollack's early feature films included the Lancaster vehicles *The Scalphunters*, *The Swimmer* (both 1968)

Maila Nurmi

Roy Scheider

Paul Scofield

and *Castle Keep* (1969). He then proved himself one of Hollywood's most polished journeyman directors with *The Way We Were* (1974), *The Electric Horseman* (1979), *Absence of Malice* (1981), *Out of Africa* (1985, for which he received an Oscar) and *The Firm* (1993). His best films, however, remain *They Shoot Horses, Don't They?* (1969) and the much lighter *Tootsie* (1982). As an actor, he was especially notable in later years for Kubrick's *Eyes Wide Shut* (1999).

BRAD RENFRO
Born: 25 July 1982, Knoxville, Tennessee, USA.
Died: 15 January 2008, Los Angeles, California, USA.
Brad Renfro died of an accidental heroin overdose a mere week prior to the similarly untimely death of Heath Ledger. Making a splash as an 11-year-old in *The Client* (1994), he showed a precocious talent in such films as *Tom and Huck* (1995), *Apt Pupil* (1998), *Ghost World*, *Bully*, which he also co-produced (both 2001), *The Jacket* (2005) and, his last film, *The Informers* (2008).

ALAIN ROBBE-GRILLET
Born: 18 August 1922, Brest, Finistère, France.
Died: 18 February 2008, Caen, Calvados, France.
As a novelist, Robbe-Grillet was a controversial exponent of the 'nouveau roman'; as a filmmaker, he made his debut at the forefront of the 'nouvelle vague'. His script for Alain Resnais' *L'année dernière à Marienbad* (1961) led to his both writing and directing such provocative puzzles as *L'Immortelle* (1963), *Trans-Europ Express* (1966), *L'Homme qui ment* (1968), *Glissements successifs de plaisir* (1974), *La Belle captive* (1983), *Un Bruit qui rend fou* (1995) and *C'est Gradiva qui vous appelle* (2006). He was a recipient of France's Légion d'honneur and, aptly, is also credited with the invention of a hybrid form, the 'ciné-roman'.

ELEONORA ROSSI DRAGO
Born: 23 December 1925, Genoa, Italy.
Died: 2 December 2007, Palermo, Italy.
Directed on film by Antonioni, Rossellini, Comencini and others (and on stage by Visconti), Rossi Drago transcended her Italian sex-bomb origins to become the award-winning star of *Estate violenta* (Violent Summer, 1959). Other notable credits: *Sensualità* (1952), Antonioni's *Le Amiche* (1955), *Kean* (1956), *La Strada lungo un anno* (1958), the German krimi *Der Teppich des Grauens* (1962) and – the Europudding potboiler that prompted her retirement – *Das Bildnis des Dorian Gray* (1970).

ROY SCHEIDER
Born: 10 November 1932, Orange, New Jersey, USA.
Died: 10 February 2008, Little Rock, Arkansas, USA.
Roy Scheider will be forever remembered for his role as Police Chief Martin Brody in *Jaws* (1975 ... and its sequel *Jaws 2* three years later), but had scored a hat-trick of ace early 1970s parts before this, in *Klute*, *The French Connection* (both 1971) and *The Seven-Ups* (1973). Other appearances included *Marathon Man* (1976), *Sorcerer* (1978), *All That Jazz* (both 1979), *Blue Thunder* (1983), *2010* (1984) and *The Russia House* (1990).

PAUL SCOFIELD
Born: 21 January 1922, Hurstpierpoint, Sussex, England.
Died: 19 March 2008, Brighton, East Sussex, England.
A giant of the theatre, Scofield won an Oscar and a BAFTA for the film version of his stage triumph as Thomas More in *A Man for All Seasons* (1966), but was extremely sparing in his choice of other film roles. They included *That Lady* (his BAFTA-winning debut, 1954), *Carve Her Name with Pride* (1958), *The Train* (1964), *King Lear* (1970), *Scorpio* (1973), *Henry V* (1989), *Hamlet* (1990), *Quiz Show* (1994) and *The Crucible* (another BAFTA, 1996).

Michel Serrault

Ned Sherrin

PETER GRAHAM SCOTT

Born: 27 October 1923, East Sheen, Surrey, England.
Died: 5 August 2008, Windlesham, Surrey, England.
A major figure in British television – with credits ranging from *Danger Man* through *The Avengers* and *The Onedin Line* to *Children of the Stones* – Scott made his debut as a film director with *Panic at Madame Tussaud's* in 1948. Other titles included *The Big Day* (1960), *Father Came Too!*, *The Cracksman* (both 1963), *Mister Ten Per Cent* (1967) and his most fondly remembered film, the spooky Hammer swashbuckler *Captain Clegg* (1961).

MICHEL SERRAULT

Born: 24 January 1928, Brunoy, Essonne, France.
Died: 29 July 2007, Honfleur, Calvados, France.
Schooled in cabaret, the Comédie Française and *Les Diaboliques* (1954), Michel Serrault won three Césars for Best Actor, for *La Cage aux folles* (1978), *Garde à vue* (1981) and *Nelly & Monsieur Arnaud* (1995). He enjoyed a long on-screen association with Jean Poiret (author of *La Cage*), stretching from *Cette sacrée gamine* (1956) to *Liberté, egalité, choucroute* (1984), and also scored a latterday triumph as WWII serial killer *Docteur Petiot* (1990).

NED SHERRIN

Born: 18 February 1931, High Ham, Somerset, England.
Died: 1 October 2007, Chelsea, London, England.
Something of a Renaissance man in the UK media, Ned Sherrin gained fame as the force behind such 1960s TV hits as *That Was the Week That Was* and *BBC-3*. He later made a string of British comedies with production partner Terry Glinwood, including *Every Home Should Have One* (1969), *Up Pompeii* (1970), *Girl Stroke Boy* (1971), *Rentadick* (1971), *The Alf Garnett Saga* (1972) and *The National Health* (1973). He also acted in *Orlando* (1992).

TONY TENSER

Born: 10 August 1920, London, England.
Died: 5 December 2007, Southport, Lancashire, England.
A legendary figure in British exploitation, Tony Tenser began as a distributor and coined the term 'sex kitten' (vis-à-vis Brigitte Bardot). Later, through his companies Compton-Cameo and Tigon, he sponsored young directors Roman Polanski (*Repulsion*, 1964) and Michael Reeves (*Witchfinder General*, 1967). He also produced sex extravaganzas like *London in the Raw* (1964), *Secrets of a Windmill Girl* (1966) and *Zeta One* (1969) alongside latterday horror classics such as *Blood on Satan's Claw* (1970), *The Creeping Flesh* (1972) and *Frightmare* (1974).

MIYOSHI UMEKI

Born: 8 May 1929, Otaru, Hokkaido, Japan.
Died: 28 August 2007, Licking, Missouri, USA.
The first Asian performer to win an Oscar, the diminutive Miyoshi Umeki was recognised in the Best Supporting Actress category for *Sayonara* (1957), in which she played opposite Red Buttons as a racially mixed couple who commit suicide together. *Flower Drum Song*, *Cry for Happy* (both 1961), *The Horizontal Lieutenant* (1962) and *A Girl Named Tamiko* (1963) followed. After that she had a recurring role in the TV sitcom *The Courtship of Eddie's Father* (1969-72) prior to retiring.

DAVID WATKIN

Born: 23 March 1925, Margate, Kent, England.
Died: 19 February 2008, Brighton, East Sussex, England.
Innovative lighting cameraman David Watkin won an Oscar for the luscious vistas of *Out of Africa* (1985). His other credits form a digest of some of the most striking films of the last five decades, including *The Knack, Help!* (both 1965), *The Charge of the Light Brigade* (1968), *The Devils, The Boyfriend* (both 1971), *The Three Musketeers* (1973), *Chariots of Fire* (1981), *Moonstruck* (1987), *Jane Eyre* and *Night Falls on Manhattan* (both 1996).

Richard Widmark

Jane Wyman

RICHARD WIDMARK

Born: 26 December 1914, Sunrise, Minnesota, USA.
Died: 24 March 2008, Roxbury, Connecticut, USA.
Schooled in radio, Richard Widmark shot to stardom
with his Oscar-nominated giggling psychopath,
Tommy Udo, in *Kiss of Death* (1947). Further edgy
noir thrillers, from *Panic in the Streets* and *Night and
the City* (both 1950) to *Pickup on South Street* (1953),
were supplemented by such disparate titles as *Don't
Bother to Knock* (1952), *The Alamo* (1960), *Judgment
at Nuremberg* (1961), *Cheyenne Autumn* (1964),
The Bedford Incident (1965) and *Madigan* (1968).
Increasingly impatient with the vagaries of filmmaking, he made his last film, *True Colors*, in 1990.

STAN WINSTON

Born: 7 April 1946, Richmond, Virginia, USA.
Died: 15 June 2008, Malibu, California, USA.
A master magician of both make-up and visual effects,
as well as so-called 'monster mogul', Stan Winston's
credits read like a roll-call of the most significant
fantasy films of the past 30 years, from *The Thing*
(1982), *Aliens* (1986) and *Predator* (1987) to *Edward
Scissorhands* (1990), *Terminator 2: Judgment Day* (1991)
and *Jurassic Park* (1993). Ten times Oscar-nominated
and four times a winner, he also directed the grisly
potboiler *Pumpkinhead* (1988).

JANE WYMAN

Born: 4 January 1914, St Joseph, Missouri, USA.
Died: 10 September 2007, Rancho Mirage, California, USA.
A Warner Bros contractee in the 1930s, Jane Wyman
made a big impact in *The Lost Weekend* (1945), *The
Yearling* (1946) and *Johnny Belinda* (1948); she was
Oscar-nominated for the second and won Best Actress
for the third. Further Oscar nominations followed for
The Blue Veil (1951) and *Magnificent Obsession* (1954),
with other notable roles in *Stage Fright* (1950), *Just for*

You (1952), *All That Heaven Allows* (1955) and *Miracle
in the Rain* (1956).

AIDA YOUNG

Born: 14 August 1920, Stepney, London, England.
Died: 12 August 2007, London, England.
Producer Aida Young began as an assistant director in
the late 1940s, worked on TV series like *William Tell*
and *Danger Man*, and then produced such evergreen
Hammer titles as *She* (1964), *One Million Years B.C.*
(1966), *Dracula Has Risen from the Grave* (1968), *When
Dinosaurs Ruled the Earth* (1970) and *Hands of the
Ripper* (1971). Her other films included *Steptoe and Son*
(1971), *The Thief of Baghdad* (1978), *The Country Girls*
(1983) and *To Be the Best* (1990).

Aida Young

The following people also died during the period under review ...

July 2007 – critic and screenwriter George Melly; composer Robert G McBride; director Jorg Kalt; screenwriters Mark Behm and George Tabori; actors Ivor Emmanuel, Eleanor Stewart, Subhendu Chatterjee, Jerry Ito, Ruth Kettlewell, Mike Reid and John Normington.

August 2007 – writer-director Mel Shavelson; producer-director Anthony Carras; directors Franz Antel and Richard T Heffron; actor-director Richard Compton; actor-writer José Luis de Villalonga; actors Ernesto Alonso, Eduardo Noriega, Terri Jean Messina, Hansjorg Felmy, Ann Hovey and Roef Ragas.

September 2007 – writer-producer-director Robert Enders; sfx artist Emilio Ruiz del Rio; mime artist Marcel Marceau; child star Marcia Mae Jones; actors Vijayan, Alice Ghostley and Loretta King.

October 2007 – composer Ronnie Hazlehurst; director Rauni Mollberg; writer-director Antoni Ribas; actors George Grizzard, Jirina Steimarová, Marion Michael, Raymond Pellegrin, Barbara Sheldon, Don Fellows, Moira Lister and Robert Goulet.

November 2007 – novelist and director Norman Mailer; editor Peter Ziner; writer-directors Ferdinando Baldi and Pierre Granier-Deferre; writer-director-actor Fernando Fernán Gómez; screenwriter Peter Viertel; sound recordist Peter Handford; child star Sonny Bupp; actors Clarice Sherry, Hilda Braid, Laraine Day, Reg Park, Jeanne Bates, Al Mancini and Michael Blodgett.

December 2007 – composer András Szöllösy; producer Franka Capra Jr; director Jerzy Kawalerowicz; cinematographer John McPhearson; screenwriter James Costigan; actors Anton Rodgers, Ken Parry, Pat Kirkwood, Mary Hughes, Floyd 'Red Crow' Weserman and Jeanne Carmen.

Marcel Marceau

January 2008 – novelist and screenwriter George Macdonald Fraser; art director Edward Richardson; composer Sergio Guerrero; cinematographer Edward Klosinski; screenwriter Ugo Pirro; director Claude Whatham; editor Russell Lloyd; actors Aleksandr Abdulov, Lois Nettleton, Kevin Stoney, Jane Easton and Manuel Padilla Jr.

February 2008 – cinematographer and sfx artist Bryan Langley; screenwriters Emilio Carballido and Oscar Brodney; producer Sidney Beckerman; director Carlos Aured; cinematographers Larry Pizer and Gayne Rescher; art director Trevor Williams; actors Barry Morse, Ben Chapman, Augusta Dabney, Tamara Desni and Perry Lopez.

March 2008 – producers George Justin, Bill Hayward and Paul Raymond; novelist and screenwriter Arthur C Clarke; screenwriters Marvin Wald, Abby Mann and Rafael Azcona; composer Leonard Rosenman; actors Brian Wilde, Sofiko Chiaureli and Claude Farrell (aka Monika Burg).

April 2008 – editors Maury Winetrobe and Genevieve Winding; composers Bebe Barron and Tristram Cary; director Alex Grasshoff; producer Jack Roe; animator Ollie Johnson; actors Jacques Berthier, Lloyd Lamble, Willoughby Goddard, Jacqueline Voltaire, Dieter Eppler, June Travis, Joy Page and Kay Linaker.

May 2008 – director Joseph Pevney; art director Harry Lange; screenwriter-directors Fred Haines and Luigi Malerba; composer Earle Hagen; producer Sandy Howard; actors Bernard Archard, Robert Russell, Terry Duggan, Wong Yue, Claudio Undari (aka Robert Hundar), Jill Adams and John Forbes-Robertson.

June 2008 – couturier Yves Saint Laurent; writer-directors Dino Risi and Jean Delannoy; writer-director-actor Stig Olin; producers Bill Vince and Howard Brandy; comedian George Carlin; child star Robert J Anderson; actors Gene Persson, Henry Beckman, John Furlong, Pinkas Braun, Tony Melody and Don S Davis.

Moira Lister

Title Index

All Kinds of Plants

by Anita Ganeri

CAMBRIDGE
UNIVERSITY PRESS

UCL
Institute of Education

All kinds of plants

There are all kinds of plants.

Some plants are big.

Some plants are small.

Some plants have leaves.
Some plants have **spikes**.

Some animals eat plants.
Giant pandas eat plants
called **bamboo**.

3

Flowering Plants

Some plants have flowers.

Flowers have colourful **petals**.

The biggest flower grows in the **rainforest**.

Trees

Trees are plants. They have a woody **stem** called a **trunk**.

Some trees are very tall.

The tallest tree in the world is a giant redwood.

A giant redwood
can grow taller
than 10 houses.

7

Cacti

Cacti grow in the **desert**.

It is very dry in the desert. Cacti keep water in their stems to drink.

Cacti have spikes to stop animals eating them.

8

a giant cactus

9

Trapped!

This plant is a Venus Flytrap.

It eats flies and spiders.

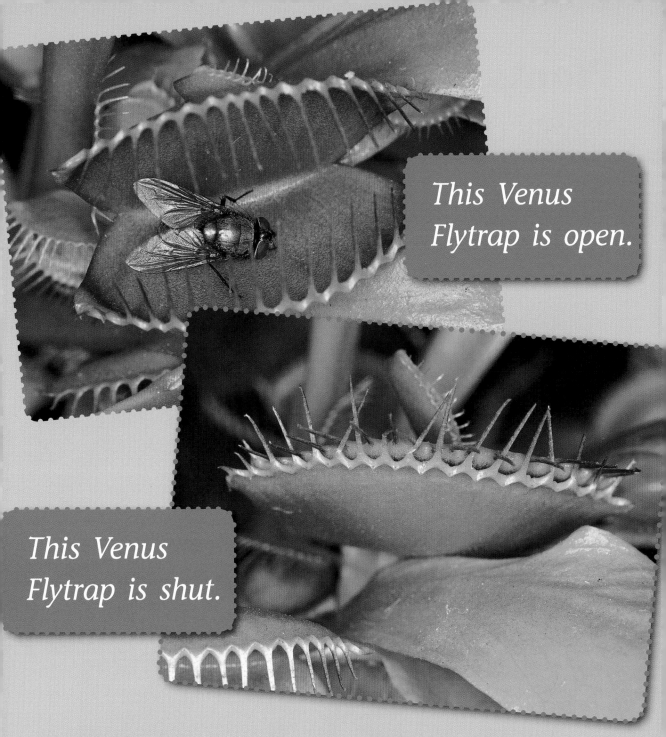

This Venus Flytrap is open.

This Venus Flytrap is shut.

A fly lands on the leaves.
The leaves snap shut.
The fly is trapped inside.

Plants for food

People can eat many kinds of plants.

Some plants grow fruit.

Some fruit grows on trees.

Strawberries grow
close to the ground.

Rice comes from plants that grow in fields.

Rice needs a lot of water to grow.

Glossary

bamboo	plant with long stems
desert	hot, dry place
petals	colourful parts of a plant
rainforest	hot, wet forest
spikes	long, thin, sharp parts
stem	long part of a plant
trunk	thick stem of a tree

Index

All Kinds of Plants ✸ Anita Ganeri

Teaching notes written by Sue Bodman and Glen Franklin

Using this book

Developing reading comprehension

This non-chronological report explores different types of plants from all around the world. A range of non-fiction features support the text: labels and captions provide supplementary information, and the book includes a contents page, an index and a glossary. The book will provide a useful starting point for science work on growth and living things. It could link with 'Water' (Pink A band of the Cambridge Reading Adventures) and 'Where Do They Grow?' (Pink B band).

Grammar and sentence structure

- Grammatical features of non-chronological reports are used: continuous present tense, an impersonal sentence structure and a focus on generic participants.
- Captions are fully punctuated whilst labels are not.
- Sentence lengths are sometimes shorter to make the point more clearly: 'A fly lands on the leaves. The leaves snap shut.'

Word meaning and spelling

- Technical vocabulary and unfamiliar words are defined in the glossary.
- Two and three syllable words ('redwood', 'flytrap', 'rainforest') can be read in chunks, looking for known parts within the words.

Curriculum links

Science – Link to the plants that grow in your region: for example, children could visit a rice field or an orchard to study plants growing. Plants that grow very tall very quickly (such as sunflowers) can be measured and planting conditions compared.

Literacy – Children could use a traditional tale such as 'The Enormous Turnip' as a framework to innovate on a story about one of the plants in this text: 'The Gigantic Cactus' for example.

Learning Outcomes

Children can:

- reread to clarify precise meaning after problem-solving of novel or less well-known words
- understand the features of non-chronological reports
- attend to changes in sentence structure, considering authorial impact.

A guided reading lesson

Book Introduction

First talk with the children about their experiences of growing things, as a class topic perhaps, or of helping parents or grandparents. Read the title and the blurb with the children. Ask: *What type of book is this? How do you know?* Note some of the non-fiction features, and remind the children of the purpose of non-fiction texts to find information. The title is very generic: *What plants do you think we might find in this book?* Use the front and back cover to predict.

Orientation

Give a brief overview of the book, using sentence structures appropriate for the report genre: *This book tells some interesting facts about many different kinds of plants.* Point to the Venus Flytrap on the front cover: *I'm interested to find out about this one! Does anyone know what it's called? Yes, it's a Venus Flytrap. Shall we go to that page first? How will I find it?*

Note: non-chronological reports are not generally read from beginning to end. Rather, children decide on what information they want to find, and use the location devices (contents and index) to retrieve information.

Preparation

Draw the children's attention to the fact there is no contents page in this text. Demonstrate skimming through the book to locate the section on the Venus Flytrap (pages 10 and 11). Practise separating the component parts of *'flytrap'* using framing fingers. Note the short sentences on page 11, discussing why the author has written like this – it's a bit like the Flytrap snapping shut!